CONTEMPORARY
JEWELRY A Studio Handbook

CONTEMPORARY JEWELRY A Studio Handbook

PHILIP MORTON

HOLT, RINEHART AND WINSTON, INC. New York Chicago
San Francisco Atlanta Dallas Montreal Toronto London Sydney

Design: Marlene Rothkin Vine

PREFACE

My purpose in writing *Contemporary Jewelry* has been to bring together in one comprehensive source—for artists, students, and generally interested readers—the ideas, history, esthetic principles, design concepts, standards of craftsmanship, and technical information relating to an art that has found brilliant expression in the 20th century. This is not a formula book, for in twenty years of teaching and designing contemporary jewelry, I have found that only by abandoning tradition and precedent can the artist and the student find the freedom necessary to achieve in their work those qualities of invention and originality that make art genuinely contemporary with its time. Because I have endeavored sedulously to avoid formulas in my own work, I have not meant here to propose them to others. Thus, this is not intended to be a "how-to-do-it" textbook, but a compendium of full and accurate information that I have organized topically and flexibly in the hope of making it accessible to the user according to his individual needs at any level of his artistic development.

The major portion of the book consists of chapters on the fundamental processes of working with materials. But since, in art, procedures and materials are significant only insofar as they can serve to create expressive form, I have prepared as a general introduction to the functional aspects of working in contemporary jewelry a section on the history of jewelry and on the elements and principles of design. The two historical chapters are no more than a mere sketch of what is a remarkably rich tradition, but they can perhaps suggest something of the multicultural dimensions of the art of metal and gemstone adornment. The historical pieces have been selected and reproduced to enrich the reader's awareness of certain forms and expressions, but they are not offered as prescriptions for new work, although the individual craftsman may well wish to find ideas and inspiration in them. In the second of the two historical chapters I have wanted to establish, if only briefly and incompletely, the record of the work produced by those innovating artists who developed in this century what we understand as "contemporary jewelry." In Appendix A, at the end of the book, there is further documentation for this chapter. The design chapters are concerned with problems in both esthetics and function. Prior to dealing with procedures, I have thought it important to indicate in the design chapters that the most expressive forms derive fundamentally from the processes demanded by the physical substances the artist works with.

The major processes for creating contemporary jewelry are presented in the series of chapters that make up Part II. Here, I have attempted to provide complete, detailed, accurate subject matter, and my principal device for doing this has been to assemble a series of "sequences," in which procedures for achieving a desired form or effect — such as reticulation — are described and illustrated step by step, from raw material to finished work. Since one process is often dependent on another and processes can in the artistic endeavor enhance each other, the subject matter throughout the book is interrelated by a network of detailed cross-references. It is a system in which section numbers in boldface refer the reader to related sequential concepts, techniques, or technical data. In this way the beginning student or the artist attempting something new is never left to search blindly in the maze of procedures for the completion and expansion that supplementary information can provide. The advantage of this kind of organization is that each reader is free to adapt the handbook to his own program of activity. Many of the demonstrational sequences presented in the book, particularly two — for the link bracelet and the tie clip in Chapter 6 — are entirely within the range of the beginning jeweler.

There are also chapters on gems and semiprecious stones, on tools and their construction, and, for more advanced students and mature artists, on marketing and production. Two additional appendixes treat tools, findings, and supplies, and certain useful technical data not covered in the body of the text. The appendixes offer the kind of valuable minutia that promised to be difficult to assimilate within the narrative exposition of the chapters. The appendix on tools lists all the tools illustrated and discussed in the text and refers to them by figure and section numbers. Appendix B, therefore, is a quick and comprehensive source on tools.

The handbook is illustrated by more than 450 procedural diagrams and photographs of contemporary and historical examples of the metalsmith's art. Sixteen of these are reproduced in full color. In color also are a plate containing more than 50 different gemstones and a chart of the color progression exhibited by carbon steel when it is being tempered with heat. The illustrations and text are integral to each other, and no essential material or process is discussed without reference to the visual evidence that only a line drawing or a halftone can provide.

Once the quantity and character of the illustrations have been cited, I must immediately begin to identify the people to whom I owe acknowledgment for their generous and willing contributions to this book. Such a comprehensive handbook as Contemporary Jewelry cannot be the exclusive work of one individual. It must be seen as the cumulative result of the skills and insights of many artists, technicians, and historians, combined with the stimulation provided by the students and colleagues that I have associated with during my teaching career. The legends accompanying the figures throughout the book reveal the debt I owe American and European jewelers for the ideas and illustrations they have contributed. Their response to my appeal for information and illustrations and their interest in and enthusiasm for this project have been not only helpful but genuinely inspirational. Among these there are several that I must thank in particular. Mrs. Hazel Olson Brown of the Boston Museum School of Fine Arts, Professor Eleanor Caldwell of Northern Illinois University, and Professor Winifred Clark Shaw of the University of New Hampshire offered assistance to me and to the publisher at an early state in the preparation of the manuscript. When the manuscript was complete, Professor Shaw went through the entire work, as did Professors L. Brent Kington of Southern Illinois University and Stanley Lechtzin of the Tyler School of Art in Philadelphia, and both I and the book's readers are the beneficiaries of their refined and knowledgeable scrutiny of every line of the unpublished manuscript. In addition, I want to acknowledge the help that I received from Fred Fenster, Michael Jerry, Ronald Pearson, Christian Schmidt, and Olaf Skoogfors, all master jewelers and teachers.

I should also like to thank the many museums and art centers that gave assistance in gathering illustrations and records for the historical chapters. In this regard, I am glad to cite in a special way Martin Friedman, Ruth Sussman, and Don Borrman of the Walker Art Center in Minneapolis, Malcolm Lein and Miriam Lein of the St. Paul Art Center, and Margery Smith of the American Craftsmen's Council in New York.

I am grateful to Robert Kohlhammer, editor of *Gold + Silber, Uhren + Schmuck*, the journal published in Stuttgart for the professional jeweler, to Graham Hughes, author of two splendid historical books on jewelry and director of Goldsmith's Hall in London, and to Gerda Flöckinger, outstanding contemporary jeweler in London, for enabling me to communicate with a number of important European jewelers.

At Holt, Rinehart and Winston it is a pleasure for me to acknowledge the help of Dan Wheeler and his staff responsible for the art books—Karen Dubno, Rita Gilbert, and Marlene Rothkin Vine—whose counsel, interest, skill, and conviction really conjured this book into actual existence. And I must make a special citation of Theresa Brakeley for her sensitive and masterful editing of what developed into a very complex manuscript.

At last, but certainly the most, I want to thank my wife, Beatrice, who carefully and faithfully perused the proof and provided encouragement during the long and arduous preparation of the manuscript.

Jackson Hole, Wyoming   P. M.
May 1969

CONTENTS

Preface   **V**

Part I   HISTORY AND DESIGN

Chapter 1   INTRODUCTION   **3**

Chapter 2   AN APPROACH TO CONTEMPORARY JEWELRY DESIGN   **11**

2-1. Associative Values   2-2. Magical Values   2-3. Symbolic Values   2-4. Commemorative Values   2-5. Relation of Associative Values to Jewelry   2-6. Expressive Values   2-7. Subjective Aspect

Chapter 3   THE JEWELRY OF THE PAST   **15**

3-1. Contemporary Jewelry and the Past   3-2. Primitive Jewelry   3-3. Pre-Columbian Jewelry   3-4. North American Indian Jewelry   3-5. Jewelry of the Ancient World   3-6. Medieval Jewelry   3-7. Renaissance Jewelry   3-8. Baroque, Rococo, and 18th-century Jewelry   3-9. The 19th Century

Chapter 4   THE HISTORY OF CONTEMPORARY JEWELRY   **33**

4-1. The Ethics of Contemporary Design   4-2. The Rational Expressive Mode   4-3. The Nonrational Mode   4-4. The Emergence of Contemporary Jewelry in America   4-5. Pioneers in Contemporary Jewelry in America   4-6. Recent Directions in Contemporary Jewelry   4-7. Contemporary Jewelry Abroad

Chapter 5   PRINCIPLES OF CONTEMPORARY JEWELRY DESIGN   **57**

5-1. The Elements of Design   5-2. Principles of Designing with Visual Elements

5-3. Design Ideas   5-4. Line-Space Relationships   5-5. Graphic Design   5-6. Attributes of Line   5-7. The Study of Line   5-8. Differentiation between Organic and Technological Line Movements   5-9. Linear Organizations   5-10. Definition of Shape   5-11. Graphic Study of Shape   5-12. Attributes of Shape   5-13. Analysis of Shape   5-14. Analysis of Organic Shapes   5-15. Area Distribution in Shape   5-16. Shapes in Material   5-17. The Effect of Scale Variation   5-18. Scale in Jewelry   5-19. Graphic Studies of Texture   5-20. Differentiation of Areas with Texture   5-21. External Design Relationships of Jewelry   5-22. Internal Design Relationships of Jewelry   5-23. Design within a Field   5-24. Equilibrium   5-25. The Focal Point in Jewelry   5-26. The Development of Complex Jewelry Forms   5-27. Shapes in Relationship   5-28. The Integration of Shapes   5-29. Summary

Chapter 6   ADVANCED DESIGN: The Means of Achieving
Expressive Form   **79**

6-1. Classification of Means   6-2. Fused Forms, Esthetics   6-3. Fused-form Design and Construction   6-4. Electroforms   6-5. Linear Forms, Esthetics   6-6. Linear Wire Forms, Design and Construction   6-7. Linear Strip Forms, Design and Construction   6-8. Linear Forms, Chasing   6-9. Linear Forms, Piercing   6-10. Plate Shapes   6-11. Complex Plate-shape Forms   6-12. Strip-plate Forms, Esthetics   6-13. Strip-plate Forms, Design   6-14. Strip-plate Forms, Construction   6-15. Constructed Forms   6-16. Carved Forms   6-17. Forged Forms   6-18. Repoussé Forms   6-19. Cast Forms   6-20. Cast-form Design, Charcoal and Other Carved Molds   6-21. Cast-form Design, Patterns for Sand Casting   6-22. Cast-form Design, Patterns for Rubber Molds   6-23. Enamel Forms

Chapter 7   FUNCTIONAL DESIGN   **111**

7-1. The Functional Aspects of Jewelry   7-2. The Wedding Band   7-3. The Engagement Ring   7-4. The Dinner or Cocktail Ring, the "Conversation Piece"   7-5. The Man's Ring   7-6. The Earring, Dangle Type   7-7. The Earring, Button Type   7-8. The Earring, Pierced-ear Type   7-9. The Bracelet   7-10. The Necklace   7-11. The Pendant   7-12. The Brooch   7-13. The Cuff Link   7-14. The Tie Clip   7-15. The Tie Tack   7-16. The Barrette   7-17. The Comb   7-18. The Buckle

Part II   FUNDAMENTAL PROCESSES
AND PRACTICAL PROCEDURES

Chapter 8   INTRODUCTION TO PROCESSES: Fusing and Soldering   **127**

8-1. Classification of Processes   8-2. The Structure of Metal   8-3. Work Hardening and Annealing of Metal   8-4. Torch Equipment   8-5. The Use of Torches   8-6. Fusing Beads on a Wire   8-7. Fusing Granules and Beads   8-8. Granulation   8-9. Torch Textures   8-10. Reticulation   8-11. Melting Metal   8-12. Casting Ingots   8-13. Picklings   8-14. Firecoat   8-15. Hard Solders   8-16. Fluxing   8-17. Soft Solders   8-18. Special Soft-soldering Problems   8-19. Paillon Method of Applying Hard Solder   8-20. The Strip or Wire Method of Applying Hard Solder   8-21. The Pick Method of Applying Hard Solder   8-22. Sweating Surfaces Together, Sweat Soldering   8-23. Solder Filings   8-24. Solder Powder   8-25. Rules for Soldering   8-26. Methods of Holding Work for

Soldering   8-27. Holding Work Together with **Binding** Wire or Steel Pins
8-28. Holding Work in Position with Plaster of Paris   8-29. Preparation for
Soldering Joints and Catches   8-30. Soldering Joints and Catches   8-31. Fastening the Pin Tong to the Joint   8-32. Soldering Jump Rings, Rings, and Ring
Shanks

Chapter 9 FORMING   **149**

9-1. Preparing Wire for Drawing   9-2. Drawing Wire   9-3. Drawing Tubing
9-4. Rolling Ingots into Sheet Metal   9-5. Rolling Wire   9-6. The Mechanics
of Bending   9-7. General Bending Techniques   9-8. Bending a Wide Strip of
Sheet Metal   9-9. Bending a Strip to Any Circular Radius, Sizing the Ring Band
9-10. Rolling a Wire Ring   9-11. Bending Oval Strip Rings of Wire Rings
9-12. Bending a Rectangular Box from Sheet   9-13. Bending a Corner for a
Solder Joint in Strip Shape   9-14. Bending up Jump Rings   9-15. Repoussé
9-16. Sandbag Forming   9-17. Block Forming   9-18. Embossing and Dapping
9-19. Electroforming   9-20. Hardening Wire by Twisting   9-21. Twisted
Wires   9-22. Making Chain   9-23. Filigree

Chapter 10 ELEMENTARY LAYOUT FOR JEWELRY   **173**

10-1. Basic Geometric Constructions   10-2. General Layout Rules   10-3. Circle Division: The Circle Template   10-4. Ellipse Division and Construction
10-5. Layout of Ring-band Lengths   10-6. Layout of Necklace Arrays.

Chapter 11 CUTTING   **178**

11-1. Shearing, Clipping, and Chisel Cutting   11-2. Stringing the Saw Frame
11-3. Position for Sawing   11-4. Form for Sawing   11-5. Sawing an Inside
Hole in Sheet Metal   11-6. Piercing   11-7. Form for Drilling   11-8. Carving
with Scorpers   11-9. Scraping   11-10. Form for Engraving   11-11. Adjusting
and Sharpening Gravers

Chapter 12 HAMMERING   **187**

12-1. Form for Hammering   12-2. Striking   12-3. Punching   12-4. Forging
12-5. Planishing   12-6. Stakes and Anvils   12-7. Exploration of Metal Tool
Marks   12-8. Chasing Tools and Punches   12-9. Form for Chasing   12-10.
Form for Texturing   12-11. Stamping Sheet and Gallery Wire

Chapter 13 FASTENINGS   **193**

13-1. Flanges   13-2. Clips   13-3. Rivets   13-4. Flush Rivet   13-5. Tube
Rivet   13-6. Integral Rivet   13-7. The Rivet Set   13-8. Interlocking Joints
13-9. Catches   13-10. Fastening Wire   13-11. Simple Hinges   13-12. The
Joint Tool   13-13. Procedure for Soldering Hinge Joints   13-14. The Full
Hinge   13-15. The Silversmith Hinge   13-16. Cementing   13-17. Riveting
Metal to Soft Materials

Chapter 14 CASTING   **203**

14-1. Equipment and Methods   14-2. General Casting Principles   14-3.
Steatite-mold Casting   14-4. Cuttlebone-mold Casting   14-5. Plaster-mold
Casting   14-6. Charcoal-mold Casting   14-7. Sand-mold Casting   14-8.
Making Patterns for Casting   14-9. The Rubber Mold   14-10. Wax Patterns,
Direct Modeling   14-11. Wax Patterns Modeled with Heated Tool   14-12.

Wax Patterns, File-Wax Carving   14-13. Wax Patterns Cast in the Rubber Mold
14-14. Setting up Wax Patterns   14-15. Investing Wax Patterns   14-16. Investment Burnout   14-17. Centrifugal Casting   14-18. Vacuum Casting
14-19. Pressure Casting

Chapter 15   FINISHING METAL   **223**

15-1. Files   15-2. Position for Filing   15-3. Form for Filing   15-4. Flexible Shaft for Grinding, Emerying, and Polishing   15-5. Emery Paper   15-6. Emery Sticks   15-7. Emery Shells for Ring Sticks   15-8. Cutting and Polishing on the Buffing Wheel   15-9. Buffing Practice   15-10. Burnishing   15-11. Finishing with Powdered Pumice   15-12. Coloring Metal   15-13. Electroplating
15-14. Cleaning Jewelry

Chapter 16   GEMS AND SEMIPRECIOUS STONES   **233**

16-1. The Forms of Gemstones   16-2. Selecting Gemstones for Contemporary Jewelry   16-3. Designing Gemstone Forms   16-4. Designing Jewelry for Stones

Chapter 17   STONE SETTING AND SETTINGS   **239**

17-1. Closed Setting (Bezel Setting)   17-2. Claw Setting and Flange Setting
17-3. Paved Setting and Gypsy Setting   17-4. Bead Setting   17-5. Channel Setting   17-6. Crown Setting

Chapter 18   TOOLMAKING   **248**

18-1. Forging Carbon-steel Drill Rod   18-2. Grinding Tool Steel   18-3. Tool Steels   18-4. Characteristics of Steel   18-5. Hardening Steel   18-6. Tempering Steel by the Color Method   18-7. Making Repoussé Tools   18-8. Making Chasing Tools   18-9. Making Punches   18-10. Hardening Tools   18-11. Tempering Tools   18-12. Final Finishing and Polishing of Tools

Chapter 19   MARKETING AND PRODUCTION   **255**

19-1. Marketing   19-2. The Exhibition as a Marketing Aid   19-3 Production Design   19-4. The Production Record and Job Card   19-5. Production Methods and Problems

APPENDIXES

Appendix A   LISTS OF HISTORICAL EXHIBITORS OF CONTEMPORARY JEWELRY   **271**

Appendix B   TOOLS, FINDINGS, AND SUPPLIES   **284**

Appendix C   TECHNICAL DATA   **290**

Appendix D   GEMSTONES AND OTHER MATERIALS FOR SETTING   **296**

Bibliography   **300**

Index   **303**

1

HISTORY
AND DESIGN

1

INTRODUCTION

For the purposes of this book the term "contemporary jewelry" is applied to jewelry that reflects the ideas, forms, and relationships of the world we live in today (Fig. 1). Its artistic roots lie in the tradition of modern art (Pl. 1), and its character is based upon the creative observation of the art images of our times, as well as upon a mastery of techniques that can express those images in jewelry. Such jewelry often demonstrates a nonobjective sculptural means of expression (Figs. 2, 3).

Fig. 1. Eero Saarinen. Trans World Flight Center, interior, Kennedy International Airport, New York.

Abstraction has always been an important aspect of jewelry. Contemporary jewelry appears unusual to many people, not because it is abstract but because its shapes and forms differ from those of the jewelry they have commonly seen and worn. These shapes and forms derive from the modern world, just as those of traditional jewelry derive from the world of the past.

Jewelry design is a special application of universal design principles. The design of all objects, whether functional or not, involves important visual aspects. The chair and the suspension bridge (Figs. 4, 5), which perform special functions, have very important and different visual appearances. These visual appearances may all be reduced to basic *visual elements:* line, shape, surface texture, mass, color, value, and scale. The organization of visual elements into specific relationships gives rise to visual *forms* that can be recognized and distinguished from one another. Beyond the mere differentiation of object forms, however, design is concerned with the organization of materials and visual elements into forms that are meaningful and fulfill some human need.

In addition to functional needs, human beings also feel the need to organize materials into relationships that are esthetically satisfactory, dramatic, expressively meaningful, and visually comprehensible. A chair need consist only of a seat, a back, and three or four legs in order to be functionally complete, but the esthetic relationships of these parts are also extremely important. The *scale* of the chair (its size in relation to the human figure and to the surrounding environment, Fig. 6); the proportion of the parts to one another; the

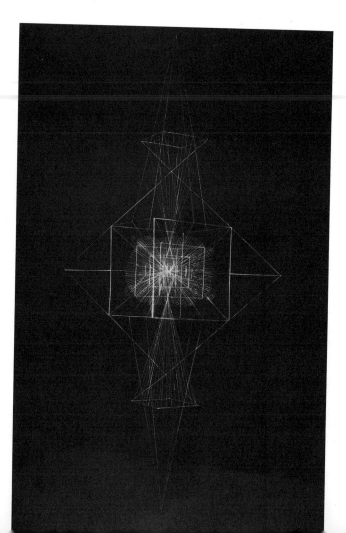

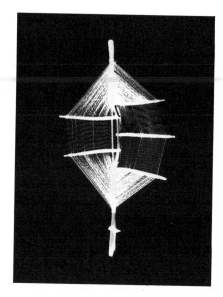

left: Fig. 2. Richard Lippold.
Variation Number 7: Full Moon. 1949–1950.
Brass rods, nickel-chromium,
and stainless steel wire, 10'.
Museum of Modern Art, New York,
Mrs. Simon Guggenheim Fund.
above: Fig. 3. Harry Bertoia. Brooch. 1945.
Sterling silver and nylon thread.

Plate 1. Jackson Pollock. *Full Fathom Five*. 1947.
Canvas, with nails, tacks, buttons, keys, coins, cigarettes, matches, and so on, 50⅞ × 30⅛".
Museum of Modern Art, New York (gift of Peggy Guggenheim).

Plate 2. Friedrich Becker. Ring. 1967. Constructed white gold.

Plate 3. Svetozar Radakovich. Pendant. 1964. 18-kt. yellow gold,
cast and forged by the lost-wax technique. Collection Mrs. Helen Robinson, Winnetka, Ill.

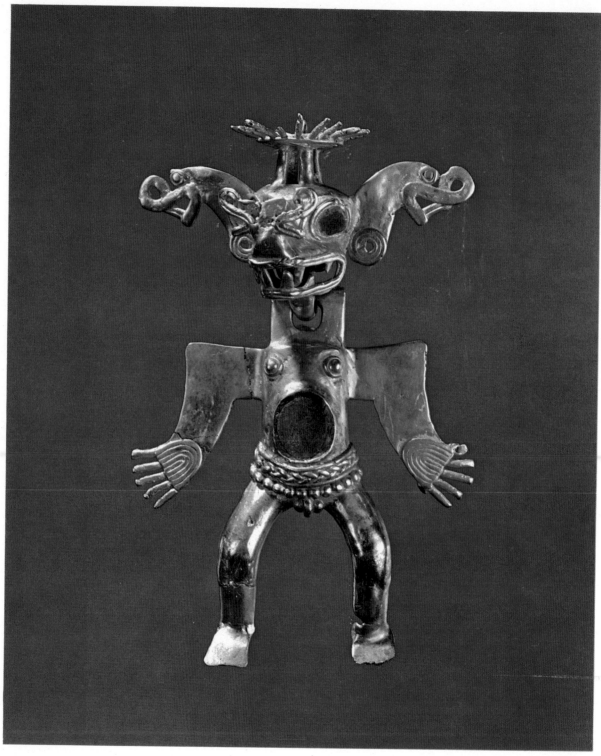

Plate 4. Alligator deity pendant, Costa Rica. Pre-Columbian.
Cast gold, with pyrite inlay, ht. 6″. Museum of Primitive Art, New York.

above left: Fig. 4. Shaker chair. 1830–1850.
Hancock Shaker Community, near Pittsfield,
Massachusetts. Height 26".
Henry Francis du Pont Winterthur Museum,
Winterthur, Delaware.
above right: Fig. 5. Ammann & Whitney.
Verrazano-Narrows Bridge, New York.
left: Fig. 6. René Magritte. *Personal Values*.
1952. Oil on canvas, 31⅝ × 39½".
Collection Jan-Albert Goris, Brussels.

top: Fig. 7. Plant pod.
above: Fig. 8. Duncan Phyfe.
Empire-style chair. 1805–1815.
Metropolitan Museum of Art, New York
(gift of Mrs. Bayard Verplanck, 1940).

selection of *materials, colors, textures,* and *mass;* the *shapes* and *lines* of the parts—all these elements are relevant. These elements and their relationships together create the totality or *form* of the chair.

In jewelry the importance of function is at a minimum, and the esthetic problem of formal relationships is paramount. Rings, of course, must be designed functionally to be worn comfortably upon the finger, earrings upon the ear, and bracelets upon the arm, but within such limitations the main problem is the esthetic and effective design of the formal visual elements. Because jewelry is so small in scale, the form must always be dramatic and every visual element must work with maximum effectiveness. Fulfilling these requirements involves not only the organization of dramatic relationships but also a selection of shapes, lines, and textures. When we make a study of jewelry design, the question immediately arises: What kind of shapes, lines, and textures?

Even if we assume that all shapes are derived from nature, or from the world of reality, we are faced with a profusion of material. Everywhere we look we can find shapes of rich and varied character: the roots of trees, rock formations, ripples on a pond, clouds, insects, animals, leaves, fruits, flowers, and the infinite variations of the human form (Fig. 7). But man lives not only in a world of nature; he lives in a world of culture, too. Culture consists of customs, habits, institutions, language, and literature; it consists of architecture, artifacts, and art objects; and it consists of *technology,* the systematic knowledge of the arts and sciences. Therefore the selection of shapes and forms for jewelry is complicated by the fact that, while we live in the present, we inherit all historical culture. Each generation builds upon its cultural inheritance from the preceding generations. We possess vast treasures of art and design from almost every age and place in the world, and it is natural that our ideas of design should be greatly influenced by this heritage, which is to be found not only in museums, but also in most of our homes.

Most furniture and accessories manufactured today are still designed to imitate historical art forms (Fig. 8). This tendency, too, is perfectly normal, and some confusion may arise in the minds of people who grow up surrounded by all this traditional design and continue to accept it as art appropriate to the present. In earlier times tradition continued to have validity for long periods, because living conditions changed very slowly. China and India are good examples of this fact. Today, however, a great deal of our traditional Western culture is obsolete, because our conditions of living have greatly changed with the development of industry, science, and technology, and with the thrust of many peoples toward freedom and security.

In the design of the past the chief source of all forms and shapes has been nature, and it would be a grave mistake to believe that nature, as the ground of all man's historical experience, is any less important today. However, man, out of his technology, has created other forms and shapes not necessarily found in nature. The forms of the automobile and airplane are examples, even though the jet and the duck have aerodynamically similar shapes.

In ancient times, when man began to conceive of abstract principles concerning the relationships existing in the physical world, he gave them graphic expression in geometric forms (Fig. 9). These forms were abstract in the sense that they represented intangibles or ideals, rather than natural organic or inorganic forms. The square, the circle, and the triangle are examples of such geometric abstractions. These, with variations, were very early used in designs and decorations. Their existence indicates the need of man to see, by means of visual images, abstract relationships that are physical, intellectual, emotional, or spiritual.

This need is perhaps a basis for the visual arts. A shape is an abstract idea existing apart from its manifestation in materials. A shape drawn with a pencil defines a pure abstraction existing apart from natural forms. Its reality consists in its visual image in our minds, made tangible by a smear of carbon on a piece of paper. This fact, perhaps, goes to the root of the reality of contemporary painting. The process of formalizing, or conventionalizing, natural forms, such as leaves, flowers, or animals (Fig. 10), began early in the history of man and is a product of the application of abstract, technological, graphic ideas to natural forms in accordance with design principles. Abstraction may thus be interpreted as a spiritualizing kind of expression.

The economy of primitive and folk societies was hunting and gathering, pastoral, or agricultural. It is not surprising to find that the importance of nature to these societies led artists to utilize natural forms in design. They also utilized religious, magical, and nontechnological, as well as abstract images, in conjunction with natural forms.

below left: Fig. 9. Athenian Geometric amphora with encircling bands of geometric patterns interrupted by rows of grazing deer, recumbent goats, and geese. c. 750 B.C. Height 16⅛″. Staatliche Antikensammlungen, Munich.
Fig. 10. *below top:* Acanthus *(Acanthus longifolius).*
below bottom: Corinthian capital. Epidaurus, Tholos. Height 49½″.

a

b

Fig. 11. Stanley Tigerman.
City Shape/21.
Plan for central core of city
built over water on pontoons.
Reynolds Metals Company.

In the advanced civilizations throughout history up until the Industrial Revolution, design continued to be similarly linked with the world of nature. The Industrial Revolution applied scientific technology so rapidly and extensively that a new environment came into existence (Fig. 11) and man's fundamental ideas about the world of reality changed. The world of nature, though still important, ultimately came to occupy a role of secondary importance in society. Traditional institutions, laws, customs, and modes of living became obsolete, along with old patterns of human relationship. New relationships demanded new standards of conduct and new esthetic and philosophical values.

The movement of modern art arose when artists intuitively realized the artistic implications of the great changes in the Western world, and the art of the present is now established upon the characteristics and conditions of a modern industrial society.

Technology has not only changed living conditions; it has also brought into view realms of the natural world that formerly were invisible to the normal senses of man and therefore unknown. The 200-in. telescope at Mount Palomar, California, enormously enlarges man's view of the universe (Fig. 12), and the radio telescope even more. The electron microscope reveals minute details of the structure and relationship of particles (Fig. 13). Indeed, the ordinary microscope revealed a world of cellular structures and single-celled organisms never before dreamed of. The airplane provided a panorama of the world far broader than that seen from mountaintops. Rockets shot into outer space expanded it thousands of miles farther. The movie camera has given to the masses of the public images of the entire world of reality, and the cinema promises to become one of the great integrative art media of all times.

The significance of technology in relation to art has always been important: technological ideas have been expressed graphically throughout the history of mankind, and these abstract expressions have been utilized in art forms. The answer to the question of what kind of shapes and lines and forms are utilized in contemporary jewelry should be obvious. There is now an entire new world which must be given esthetic expression. "Op" and "pop" art are only more recent efforts in this direction. Contemporary jewelry utilizes those shapes, lines, textures, relationships, and forms which reflect this vast new world.

It is true that many people still prefer the traditional and representational treatment of natural forms that corresponds to the normal realm of human vision and human experience, perhaps because these people cling to old familiar things in the face of the new and sometimes terrifying environment. Also, many people have come to view art as something set apart from daily life. "Art" consists of the paintings, sculptures, and architecture to be seen in picture

right: Fig. 12.
Messier 101. Spiral nebula
in the constellation Ursa Major.
Mount Wilson & Palomar Observatories,
Pasadena, California.
below: Fig. 13. A minute sea creature
(Trypanosphaera transformata),
one of the Radiolaria. Model by
Herman Mueller, glassblower.
The American Museum of Natural History,
New York.

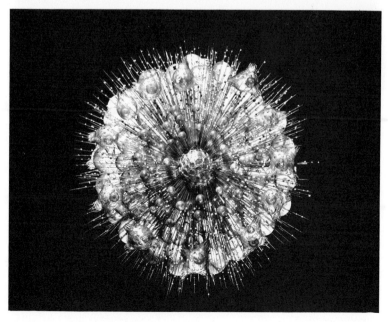

books, encyclopedias, and museums (Fig. 14). All else, therefore, appears to be "nonart," and people fail to recognize the esthetic qualities existing in their own ordinary world. Current movements in sculpture and painting that tend toward the creation of "environments," rather than "art objects," may indicate a fundamental transfer of esthetic values out of the museum and picture book into the everyday world.

The designer of today feels obliged to reject the popular traditional artistic taste and to draw his design ideas from his own time (Pl. 2). While he must always depend upon his own experience and observation for esthetic ideas, he is not dependent upon these alone. He can draw upon the tradition of modern art that has been developing over the past century and more. A study and understanding of this tradition is essential to the successful design of contemporary jewelry. This is why jewelry can no longer be taught or learned as a traditional craft, isolated from the study of art.

Contemporary jewelry is another means of giving artistic expression to the world of today. The jeweler's success in doing this is a measure of his powers of observation and esthetic insight, as well as of his skill in mastering his techniques. Yet when all the analytical and explanatory ideas about art and design have been written, there is still a dimension of creativity which is untouched. One may learn all the rules of design and become a competent craftsman. This will not of itself lead to expressive art. The free play of the imagination is essential to art, and this must come from the student. The teacher can only offer encouragement, guidance, and inspiration. This book is written as an introductory guide for those who wear and admire contemporary jewelry and are interested in 20th-century art, as well as for those who are interested in making contemporary jewelry. It offers an approach to the problems of organizing design elements and translating them into expressive jewelry forms. Perhaps it can play a small part in helping the young artist to realize his task of interpreting "reality" to contemporary society.

left: Fig. 14. Michelangelo. *David.* 1501–1504. Marble, height 14′ 3″. Accademia, Florence.

2

AN APPROACH
TO CONTEMPORARY
JEWELRY DESIGN

Jewelry is an art form designed to be worn. All the visual arts are concerned with the expression of form by means of visual elements, which, regardless of function, are an inseparable aspect of materials. Properly designed jewelry achieves esthetic forms that are complete and independent of external surroundings (Pl. 3).

2–1 Associative Values   Historically, the expressive character of jewelry has been obscured by an accumulation of secondary associations. All ideas about the origin of jewelry are rather conjectural. Perhaps the first piece of jewelry appeared when some early human being first found an object that was fascinating in color, pattern, or shape and that he enjoyed looking at and thinking about. In primitive societies animal claws, shells, and other organic materials are worn (Fig. 15). With more advanced techniques, gold, silver, and gems in time became the dominant materials of jewelry. However, in addition to intrinsic esthetic aspects many other values have been attached to jewelry.

2–2 Magical Values   Primitive man's outlook is magical. He believes that all processes of the natural world are the result of mysterious spiritual powers. Magical powers are ascribed to many objects: animal hair, claws, or teeth are thought to endow the possessor with the strength, ferocity, cunning, or fleetness of the vanquished animal. Certain forms of wood or stone become amulets, able to ward off evil spirits, disease, death, or the malign spells of an enemy (Fig. 16).

Certain forms have evolved into idols made in the image of anthropomorphic or thermiomorphic creatures. Many of these magical or religious objects have been worn as pendants, necklaces, or rings (Pl. 4). The Egyptian scarab and the Christian cross are examples (Fig. 17). A belief in the magical properties of stones and gems, originating in the primitive world, has operated throughout history. For example, the Assyrians developed a highly complex system of

above left: Fig. 15. Tlingit necklace from Alaska.
Bone, with fibers, length of longest pendant 7½".
Museum of Primitive Art, New York (gift
of Mr. and Mrs. Robert W. Campbell).
above right: Fig. 16. Egyptian turtle amulet. Carnelian,
Metropolitan Museum of Art, New York
(gift of Helen Miller Gould).
left: Fig. 17. Devotional cross, folk carving from
the Valtellina, northern Italy. Painted wood, ht. 13½".
Collection Mamie Harmon, New York.

astrology in which stars and precious stones were grouped in accordance with their occult influence upon human affairs.

Today we no longer acknowledge the influence of magical powers, but surprisingly fetishistic images are still with us. The attraction of primitive art may not be completely esthetic.

2-3 Symbolic Values As historical culture developed, certain visual images assumed symbolic roles. The scribed, painted, or modeled image came to symbolize a real experience, whether inner or outer. These symbolic values became closely associated with jewelry forms (Fig. 18). In ancient times the seal or talisman was worn around the neck or on the finger. The seal symbolized authority, and its impression on clay or wax authenticated a given message. The ring itself assumed importance as a symbol of rank and authority. All sorts of jewelry forms are used as symbols of institutional relationships. Fraternity, lodge, and club emblems are worn as pins and rings. Engagement rings and wedding rings symbolize the personal and institutional relationship of man and woman. Such symbolic values have a wide currency in present-day commercial jewelry.

2-4 Commemorative Values Not least in importance is the use of jewelry for gifts which commemorate special relationships, occasions, or deeds. Egyptian Pharaohs gave their generals and heroes gifts of jewelry as rewards for victory in battle. The same practice is followed today by many social and civic institutions. Jewelry gifts commemorate birthdays, graduations, retirements, and many types of anniversaries.

2-5 Relation of Associative Values to Jewelry It is important to realize that the associative values have almost obscured the most significant aspect of jewelry—its esthetic value. Today most all jewelry is still purchased for the purpose of investment or as a method of displaying wealth or social rank. The major demand made upon the trade jewelry of today is that it be different but not too different, expensive or apparently expensive, and suitable as a gift for a particular associative value.

Fig. 18. Baule animal mask pendant from the Ivory Coast. Gold, ht. 3⅜". Museum of Primitive Art, New York.

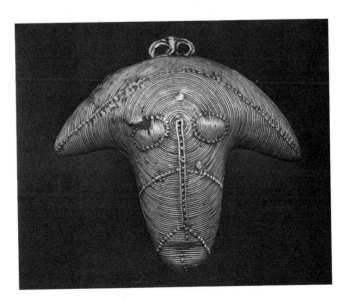

None of these associative values is an intrinsic part of jewelry. These values are in the *mind,* not in the jewelry, yet they are often so dominant that the jewelry form and its esthetic aspect are obscured. In this regard contemporary jewelry has had an increasingly stimulating and challenging impact upon the public, for it affirms the primary value of esthetic expression and demands a reexamination of conventional attitudes toward jewelry and therefore toward the current world of reality.

2–6 Expressive Values   The intellectual disillusionment that has taken place during the 20th century over the failure of science to solve the world's problems is expressed today in almost every cultural field. Existentialism, Dadaism, the Theatre of the Absurd, John Cage's "silent" music—all these reflect the artist's growing mistrust of reason as the dominant approach to human living. If Western man, in the post-Renaissance period, has tended to exaggerate the value and power of intellect because it brought about so many fantastic technological advances, the artist has persistently clung to his faith in intuition and feeling as guides to the nature of reality. The expressive power of art stems from a deep and sensitive regard for the total depths of human existence. The present-day focus on material and technological products is a manifestation of the extent to which people have been severed from their emotional and spiritual roots in reality as an integral part of the natural world. The split, of course, cannot be remedied by an abandonment of science and a return to nature. The answer lies in humanizing our technological environment so that it is reciprocal and not antagonistic to the human organism. This is one function of contemporary art. The visual arts, like music, convey an expression of reality that cannot be made verbally, and this expressive function is shared by contemporary jewelry.

2–7 Subjective Aspect   The esthetic value of jewelry is inherent in its form. Subjectively all art is an expression of an artist's insight into life. The artist's own feeling and thought, his experience and inner compulsions, and his intuitions all determine the means he employs to achieve his esthetic forms. The forms are a product of his reactions to existence—both positive and negative. Thus his jewelry forms will always satisfy his own personal needs. To achieve successful jewelry each artist must find his own characteristic *means* of expression (Chap. 6). This is the subjective aspect of jewelry.

Insofar as an artist's esthetic forms are meaningful to others, an objective aspect of his art comes into being, and his art is studied, understood, and appreciated. At this point there also arises a subjective aspect on the part of the observer and the purchaser. Everything we buy, own, wear, and use is to some extent an expression of our own personality. Jewelry is an extremely personal form of art. Personality operates in the selection of the type, kind, and form. The person who wears a Navajo ring may have picked it up merely to commemorate a vacation in the Southwest. This is a minor expression of personality. The person who, from this modest beginning, makes a study of Indian jewelry and collects genuine pieces to enjoy and wear, manifests a definite expression of personality. When jewelry is selected and worn in relation to the knowledge, interests, and temperament as well as appearance of a person, it becomes an integral expression of that personality.

THE JEWELRY
OF THE PAST

3–1 Contemporary Jewelry and the Past   Contemporary jewelry, in its origin and development, did not follow the earlier jewelry traditions of Western culture. Like contemporary architecture, it sprang from more particularly scientific and technological sources, as well as from the movements of modern art, rather than from bygone tradition. For this reason the contemporary jeweler looks back at the past with a somewhat different perspective than might otherwise prevail. His roots are in the comparatively recent past and in the current scene.

Modern art, of which contemporary jewelry is a part, represents a major break with the immediately preceding 19th-century tradition of art, for the post-Renaissance centuries, which brought the scientific-industrial society into existence, created an environmental reality that the esthetic traditions of the past were unable to encompass. Siegfried Giedeon, in *Space, Time and Architecture*, emphasized the incompetence of the traditional esthetic value system to deal with the esthetic problems of the industrial world, illustrating his point with an early steam engine designed with a housing composed of Greek columns in cast iron. The irrelevancy of historical artistic styles to the problems of design in the modern world was equally obvious in other fields of application.

The early 19th century had inherited an enthusiasm for antiquity that burgeoned into neoclassicism. There followed a series of romantic revivals of Gothic, Romanesque, and Byzantine styles. These in turn were augmented by Rousseau's back-to-nature movement and a preoccupation with Oriental philosophy and artistic styles. All these revival movements, described by William Fleming in his book *Arts and Ideas* as "flights from reality," reflected the anguished inability of 19th-century society to face up to the reality of industrialization. The real break in artistic tradition came when modern artists devised realism and impressionism as stylistic means of dealing with the contemporary world. These styles were undoubtedly empiricist in essence, reflecting the same preoccupation with direct experience and the material world that characterized science.

In this sense, contemporary jewelry, too, was empiricist in its origins, rather than traditional. The contemporary jeweler, like the constructivist of the early 20th century and the more recent "minimal" artist, wants to work with the basic processes and fundamental materials and forms. He wants to experience his own realization of the beauties and capacities of metal, rather than to see these qualities through the eyes of second-hand tradition.

What all the new perceptions of the 20th century will be like has certainly not yet been established. But in the search for new values, modern artists look with fresh eyes upon every detail of the environment, whether good, bad, beautiful, ugly, trivial, or vital in terms of the esthetics of tradition. It was with this fresh look that modern artists discovered, or rediscovered, the vitality of primitive art. Today, the contemporary jeweler has established the foundations of a contemporary style of jewelry and feels free to admire the intricacies of the design and craftsmanship of jewelry from every age and culture without feeling the slightest need to imitate past historical styles.

3–2 Primitive Jewelry   The modern artist constantly marvels at the skill and sensitivity manifested in primitive works of art. No matter where primitive man has lived or what kind of raw materials have been available to him, he has never failed to exhibit his dexterity at making and using tools and creating expressive images (Figs. 19 – 23).

right: Fig. 20. African Baule pendant mask from the Ivory Coast. Gold, ht. 3½". Museum of Primitive Art, New York. This pendant illustrates the universality of basic metal techniques. *far right:* Fig. 21. Ahmed ould Moilid. Central plaque of a Boutilimet anklet, from Mauritania. Collected 1951. Hammered and chiseled silver, 2 × 3¼". Museé d'Ethnographie, Neuchâtel, Switzerland (Collection J. Gabus). The chiseled pattern in this piece is clearly African in style. The technique probably derived from the old Ghana empire and the Ashanti metalworkers.

left: Fig. 19. Melanesian pectoral ornament (*kapkap*) from the Admiralty Islands. Tridacna and turtle shell, ht. 4⅞". Ubersee Museum, Bremen. Melanesian art is distinguished by its dynamic and rich figural form and pattern, deriving from magical and religious inspiration. This piece is exquisitely carved, the dark appliqué of turtle shell over the Tridacna disk providing strong but delicate contrast.

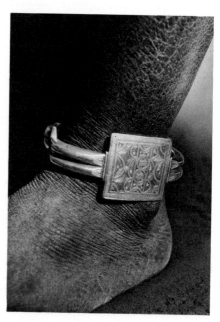

above: Fig. 22. Kabyle ornament from northern Algeria. Silver with coral and enamel, l. c. 12". Pitt Rivers Museum, Oxford. This type of assembled ornament, consisting of small shapes and beads, appears consistently throughout the history of jewelry and is reappearing in contemporary jewelry. *right:* Fig. 23. Ornaments of the Man Pan Gni and Man Lan Tien, from northern Vietnam. Silver. Musée de l'Homme, Paris. These stylized sun symbols are engraved and chased with extremely complex designs.

Most of the fundamental processes of jewelry making were known and used in early times: carving, engraving, chasing, chiseling, repoussé, hammering, drawing wire, finishing, polishing, and casting. It was the straightforward expressiveness and symbolic imagery of primitive art, however, that provided the modern artists with a new point of departure in the development of a modern esthetic, so that the symbolic and spiritual significance of the image in art regained its precedence over mere representation of the object (Fig. 24).

Fig. 24. Constantin Brancusi. *Fish.* 1930. Gray marble, 21 × 17". Museum of Modern Art, New York. (Lillie P. Bliss Bequest). This sculpture illustrates the contemporary search for expressive form in the rational mode, with purity of form preferred to description or decoration.

above left: Fig. 25. Ornament in spider form from Costa Rica. Gold, l. 3¾". Brooklyn Museum.

above right: Fig. 26. Sinu pendant from Colombia. Gold, l. 7". Museum of the American Indian, Heye Foundation, New York. This is a fine example of the abstraction of the human figure. The head is formed of soldered wire, and the legs rise as simple shapes from an engraved pedestal.

right: Fig. 27. Pendant in frog form from Panama. Gold, ht. 1¾". Museum of Primitive Art, New York. The frog is made of fused spiral wires.

3–3 Pre-Columbian Jewelry   In South America, Colombia, and Peru were the ancient centers of goldsmithing, though it cannot be said exactly where this art began. The Chibcha tribes on the eastern slopes of the Andes, the Quimbayas, the Sinus, the Darians, the Mochicans, the Chavins, the Chimus, and others all participated in the development and production of gold jewelry over a period from at least the 2d to the 16th century (Figs. 25–27).

Goldsmithing did not appear in Mexico until the 11th century. The Mayan world worked gold and copper during the Second Empire; bronze was unknown. The vast amount of goldwork that was ultimately carried off to Europe by treasure seekers is beyond belief. It is said that Mayan gold financed European capitalism—a strange outcome to the fateful convulsions of the earth's crust which, in the Tertiary period, filled the vast structure of the Andes Mountains with veins of gold and silver.

Out of the rivers the Indians took almost pure gold nuggets, and it was the Mochicans of Peru who led in the smithing of gold in the 4th century. They mastered the techniques of welding, hammering, smelting, repoussé, gilding, enameling, and the lost-wax method of casting.

18   *History and Design*

3–4 North American Indian Jewelry For America, a history of jewelry would not be complete without some mention of the work of native American Indians, or at least those tribes of the Southwest who work in metal. There are three significant facts about the Indian jewelry of the Southwest. First, jewelry making was not an ancient art with the Navajo or Zuni Indians. It was learned from Mexican silversmiths sometime during the decade of the 1860s. The stamping of Navajo jewelry is in imitation of Mexican leather work. Some of the so-called Indian motifs, such as the Thunderbird, are actually derived from sources outside their own culture.

Second, the great esthetic qualities of the genuine Indian jewelry derive from the direct techniques and simplicity of tools and processes that have been found to be so characteristic of all so-called primitive peoples. Genuine Indian jewelry can be defined as that which the Indians made for their own use. In the production of such jewelry time and effort were not spared to achieve the technical limits of perfection.

Third, the quality of the jewelry and, indeed, the incentive of the Indians to engage in jewelry making has decreased year by year as a result of the corrupting influence of commercial tourism and the traditional practices of exploitation visited upon the Indians. Today tourist shops are filled with inferior, cheap Indian jewelry which lacks the vitality and powerful esthetic qualities of the genuine. Some shops carry elaborate and expensive pieces, which, although sold as Indian jewelry and perhaps even made by Indians, have little design relationship to genuine Indian jewelry.

It is interesting that the jewelry of the Navajo and Zuni Indians took distinctive lines of development. The Navajo jeweler was much more concerned with the process of working with metal and used stones only to enrich the process of the worked metal surfaces (Fig. 28). The Zuni jeweler became fascinated with turquoise stones, and almost all Zuni jewelry is characterized by the massing of stones in patterns, beneath which the metal is little more than a supporting frame (Fig. 29).

 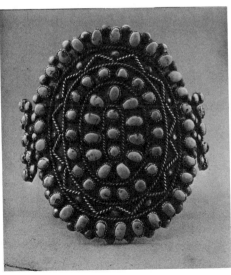

left: Fig. 28. Navajo squash-blossom
necklace. c. 1890.
Coin silver and turquoise.
Collection of the author.
right: Fig. 29. Zuni bracelet. c. 1910
Silver and turquoise, $2^1/_5 \times 2^2/_5$".
Collection of the author.

Fig. 30. Egyptian necklace and pectoral with the name of Senusret (Sesostris) II, from the Lahun Treasure. 12th dynasty, c. 1900 B.C. Drop beads of gold, carnelian, lapis lazuli, and green feldspar; enamel on pectoral. Metropolitan Museum of Art, New York (Henry Walters and Rogers Fund, 1916).

3–5 Jewelry of the Ancient World The cultural continuity of the ancient world is marked by the interrelationships to be found in much jewelry from the Mediterranean area and the Near East (Pl. 5).

Egyptian jewelry was symbolic of the religious life of the people. The scarab, a beetle-shaped emblem of Khempera, the rising sun; the symbolic eye; Horus, the falcon-headed sun god; the uraeus, or sacred asp, emblem of sovereignty—these and many more images and life symbols were worn as ornaments for their magical protection and religious meanings. Going back to at least 3000 B.C., Egyptian jewelry reached a peak of accomplishment by about 1600 B.C., almost 2000 years before the Indians of Peru began to work in gold, and though the tools used were crude, the work was exquisite (Fig. 30).

Repoussé, a technique that seems to have occurred naturally to all metal-working peoples, is found in Egyptian jewelry. Enameling, stone setting, engraving, and embossing, too, are found. The last-named technique was used to form hollow halves that could be soldered together for beads and volume figures. Granulation appeared in jewelry of the Middle Kingdom, about 1991–1650 B.C. This technique is the massing of infinitesimal grains of metal on the surface and fusing them in place.

Of the wealth of jewelry production from the ancient Near East two examples may give a slight idea (Figs. 31, 32).

below left: Fig. 31. Babylonian or Kassite necklace, earring, and seal caps. 18th–16th cents. B.C. Gold, l. 15¾". Metropolitan Museum of Art, New York (Fletcher Fund, 1947).
The necklace beads were made by burnishing thin gold sheets into stone molds to make hollow halves, which were then soldered together.
below right: Fig. 32. Bracelet from Zawiyeh, Iran. c. 7th cent. B.C. Gold. Metropolitan Museum of Art, New York (lent by the Gasnol Collection).
This bracelet exemplifies the skill of ancient craftsmen in repoussé.

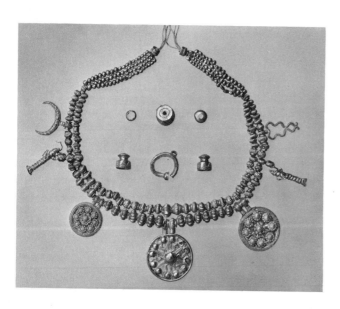

Plate 5. Headpiece, earrings, and necklace of "Queen" Shubad, from Ur, in Sumer. c. 2600 B.C.
Gold, lapis lazuli, and carnelian. University Museum, Philadelphia.

Plate 6. René Lalique. Pin *(left)* and pendant *(right)*. 1899, 1900.
Gold and enamel, ht. 3¼, 4″. Musée des Arts Decoratifs, Paris.

left: Fig. 33. Greek fibula
of spectacle type. Geometric period,
10th–8th cent. B.C. Bronze.
Metropolitan Museum of Art, New York
(Harris Brisbane Dick Fund, 1937).
right: Fig. 34. Bracelet from Græsted,
Denmark. Nordic Bronze Age,
11th–8th cent. B.C. Gold, diam. 2⁷/₈″.
Danish National Museum, Copenhagen.

    The early Greek style of jewelry known as Mycenaean goes back to the 16th century B.C. It consists generally of simple gold sheet shapes, embossed or raised by repoussé into simple abstractions of insect and animal life. Much of this jewelry utilizes the spiral motif, so basic a process for dealing with metal in wire or rod form, and found in so many cultures, including that of the Bronze and Iron Age Celts of the first millennium B.C. and that of the Nordic tribesmen of about the same era (Fig. 33).

    Other techniques found in ancient Greek jewelry include chasing, filigree, granulation, gold cloisonné with insets of stones, used in rings, pendants, earrings, headbands, and so on. The design motifs range from geometric (Fig. 34) to floral, animal, and human forms. However, jewelry was not a major art contribution of the Greeks, for during much of their history lavish personal adornment was contrary to custom.

    Etruscan jewelry utilized all the basic techniques common to the ancient Mediterranean world, particularly those of the Greeks, but, whereas Greek jewelers came to prefer filigree to granulation, the Etruscans developed the art of granulation to a level of skill unsurpassed in any period. Each grain in their work seems to stand free except at the point of contact (Fig. 35).

    Roman jewelry of the Republic was not particularly outstanding or original. Ostentation was frowned upon, as it had been in the Athens of the Golden Age. Some forms of Greek work were carried on, as may be seen in the bracelets and rings with engraved or carved stones recovered from the ruins of Pompeii. The most common item was the fibula, a pin similar in construction to our safety pin, which served to hold the toga in position.

    Hellenistic Roman jewelry, on the other hand, became large and elaborate, with interest in the metalwork subordinated to an enthusiastic use of cameos and other carved gemstones with portraits or mythological subjects.

3–6 Medieval Jewelry The designs of medieval jewelry were derived from many sources. The Byzantine world, which filtered Eastern influences toward western Europe when the Roman empire split into two spheres of power, produced little personal jewelry during the early Christian period, but its skills in

below: Fig. 35. Etruscan fibula
decorated with animals in filigree.
7th cent. B.C. Gold.
Metropolitan Museum of Art, New York
(purchased by subscription, 1896).
Notice the perfect proportion and
decorative restraint of this piece.
The granulation technique
seems to be completely mastered.

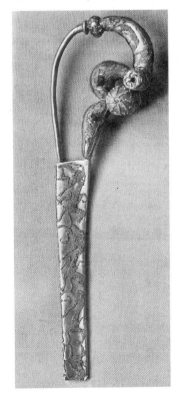

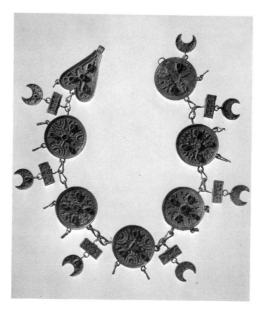

left: Fig. 36. Necklace from Zalesie, USSR. 6th cent. Gilded silver with glass, l. 20⅜". Kunsthistorisches Museum, Vienna. *right:* Fig. 37. Celtic penannular brooch. Early 10th cent. Silver. National Museum of Ireland, Dublin. This simple, functional structure has a strong contemporary appeal.

cloisonné enamels, filigree work, mounting of cabochon stones, engraving, and niello were broadly carried over into much medieval European jewelry. The barbarian tribes that poured westward as the Roman empire disintegrated brought with them a style of interlace, animal decoration, inlaid stones, and pierced metalwork (Fig. 36). Celtic designs retained the primitive vigor of the early simple gold and bronze work even as late as the 10th century of our era, well into the medieval period (Fig. 37).

Anglo-Saxon jewelry almost begins and ends with its impressive cloisonné enamels. The fondness for glass beads and enameling must have reflected the existence of a well-developed glass-making industry.

In the Carolingian period, from the 8th to the 10th century, an attempt was made to renew the Roman empire, and there appeared more classical designs combined with Christian images and symbols. Enameling, inclusion of antique gems, and embossing were characteristic techniques applied to items chiefly for royal or religious use.

The brooch was a necessary item for the dress of medieval times, and examples have come down to us in circular, oval, cruciform, and other shapes (Figs. 38, 39). The Roman pin was more or less discarded, and the ring brooch, with pin hinged on one side of the ring and resting on top of it on the other side, became dominant. Another popular item of jewelry was the devotional pendant, chased or enameled with religious subjects. Animal motifs were also much used.

Although we may look upon the Middle Ages as a somewhat static period, the jewelry reflects many strong historical influences. The growth and expansion of the Catholic church provided a great impetus for increased artistic activity. The building of new churches demanded every kind of art and craft, and artist-monks, working in monastery workshops, produced all sorts of craft products. One such artist-monk named Theophilus compiled an encyclopedia of crafts, which describes the processes of goldsmithing.

left: Fig. 38. Eagle brooch. c. 1025.
Gold with chasing and cloisonné enamel, 3³/₄ × 3⁵/₈″.
Mittelrheinisches Landesmuseum, Mainz.
This piece reveals the strong interest
of medieval jewelers in animal forms.
above: Fig. 39. Ring brooch. Gold with rubies and sapphires.
British Museum, London. This form is still popular today.

Gothic jewelry shows the application of typical architectural forms of the period to the goldsmith's repertory, but, more important, the Gothic spirit influenced jewelry design by emphasizing a plastic, three-dimensional quality, which had been lacking in the Romanesque work of the preceding centuries, and by turning again to the mastery of metal processes. Filigree, incrustation of precious stones, enameling, and niello were utilized widely (Fig. 40). The ring was perhaps the most popular item of jewelry, even beyond the bracelet.

During this period craft guilds were being formed for the purpose of determining standards and practices and for training apprentices. The French goldsmiths formed a guild in the 13th century. The demand for jewelry increased to such a point that craftsmen specialized in such activities as brooch making, girdle making, and jet working. Jewelry was becoming an industrial art in the towns.

The Crusades brought into Europe immense quantities of gems and pagan cameos, thus contributing to the habit of utilizing gems with jewelry.

Fig. 40. Hinged collar from Ålleberg, Sweden.
6th cent. Gold with repoussé and granulation,
diam. 8¹/₄″. Statens Historiska Museum, Stockholm.

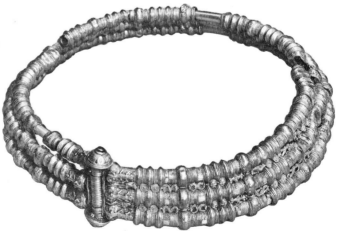

3–7 Renaissance Jewelry By the time of the Renaissance, jewelry was becoming a part of the regular costume of the times. The Renaissance brought three revolutionary changes to the character of jewelry and to the attitude toward it. During the Middle Ages gold and silver plate, as well as gems and jewelry, had become a kind of portable wealth, easily hidden or carried about in strong boxes. During the Renaissance elaborate forms of jewelry, enameled and richly set with colorful gems (Fig. 41), became a form of investment and a symbol of status, and clergyman and layman alike loaded their persons with jewels. The aspect of jewelry as investment and as pretentious display has survived to the present.

The second revolutionary change in jewelry was the emergence of the goldsmithing craft as a basic training for all the arts, an emphasis that is re-emerging in the contemporary scene in American art programs. Botticelli (1445–1510), for example, was trained as a goldsmith. The ideal of the artist as the universal man appeared, as it was to appear briefly in Art Nouveau at the beginning of the 20th century, and as it seems to be reappearing today. In consequence, work in precious metals became increasingly sculptural and colorful.

The third revolutionary change in jewelry during the Renaissance was the development of facet-cut diamonds, credited to Louis van Berquem of Antwerp, in 1476. Faceted gems finally displaced stones *en cabochon* and became dominant in jewelry until the emergence of Art Nouveau and the later appearance of contemporary jewelry as a distinct style in the 1940s.

Fig. 41. Eagle and dragon pendant and necklace. Late 16th or 17th cent. Gold, enamel, and jewels. Metropolitan Museum of Art, New York (gift of George Blumenthal, 1941).

During the Renaissance the brooch or pendant-brooch was the most popular single item of jewelry, though the other items continued their popularity from the Middle Ages. Classical subjects and engraved gems of classical type were in demand. Little enameled pictures were also used. Designs incorporated brilliant color with stones, as well as enamels, and large, irregularly shaped pearls were used as the basis for figural forms in pendants.

In time, as designs became standardized throughout Europe by the distribution of engravings, forms tended to become less three-dimensional (Fig. 42).

Probably the most renowned goldsmith of the late Renaissance was Benvenuto Cellini, whose jewelry style was widely imitated for centuries to come, though few pieces survive that can be positively authenticated today (Figs. 43, 44).

left: Fig. 42. Hans Holbein the Younger.
Design for a pendant. British Museum, London.
below: Fig. 43. Style of Benvenuto Cellini.
Necklace with pendant representing a sphinx. 16th cent.
Gold with enamel, pearls, and gemstones, 5 × 20½".
National Gallery of Art, Washington, D.C.
right: Fig. 44. Italian pendant representing a triton.
16th cent. Gold with enamel, pearls, and gemstones, l. 5½".
National Gallery of Art, Washington, D.C.
(Widener Collection).

Fig. 45. French or Italian brooch.
Early 18th cent. Gold with gemstones.
Metropolitan Museum of Art, New York
(gift of Mrs. Antonia Draper Dixon
and Mrs. Annie Dixon McCline, 1915).

The reformation and the classical revival largely put an end to medieval religious symbolism, except in Spain and Italy. There was, however, renewed interest in mythological and natural forms. Gem carving was revived, and chains became extremely important in jewelry.

3–8 Baroque, Rococo, and 18th-century Jewelry

In the 17th century a wave of sensualist thought and an increased emotionalism, beginning in Italy, led to the baroque nonrational mode of expressive forms. Jewelry of the period became more colorful and glittering. The invention of the brilliant cut was an important event for the development of baroque jewelry, which helped to confirm the dominant position held by faceted stones in traditional jewelry to this day.

The baroque emotionalism led eventually to sentimentalism and to capricious and exotic ornamentation in the 18th century (Fig. 45), when the appearance of a strong middle class led to a demand for imitations of precious gems.

The rococo style, which began in France in the early 18th century and spread all over Europe, takes its name from the *rocaille*, or shell-shaped, decoration (Fig. 46). Rococo jewelry was expressive of the pomp of the nobility and the social aspirations of the wealthy bourgeoisie. As its popularity increased, especially in Germany and Eastern Europe, the middle-class demand was met by inexpensive multiple production of pieces simulating richness (Fig. 47).

France led the parade of fashions in art, and each political change brought about a corresponding change in styles. The archeological discovery of Pompeii in 1755 stimulated a wide interest in antiquity, which under the Directory

culminated in a fad for antique jewelry. Women appeared on the streets of Paris in sandals and classical costumes with jewelry on their toes. By the third quarter of the 18th century the last-remaining baroque fondness for color, form, and movement had been displaced by the rational sobriety of neoclassicism.

With the style of the First Empire the imitation of classical antiquity became a principle of design. Cameos, mosaics, and engraved gems were all treated in the classical manner. Jewelry in the style of this period was still quite popular in America until the turn of the 20th century.

3–9 The 19th Century Artistically, the 19th century was a period of confused cultural values, brought about by the conflict between the economic and industrial changes that were taking place and the carry-over of esthetic tastes from the past. The interests and activities of the expanding middle class and the business community led to more serious and sober ways of life, but the admiration for the more sumptuous products of earlier times persisted. Levels of both taste and craftsmanship declined with the development of machine production and the transfer from hand skills to machine operation.

The metalwork of this period was frequently inferior. A great deal of the jewelry was made of thin, low-karat gold or of a zinc-copper alloy called pinchbeck or ormolu (**C-2**). Antique motifs were pierced, chased, or stamped, and granulation and mat textures were much used. With production machinery came the first cheap stamped jewelry made of paper-thin gold.

The Gothic revival, beginning about 1820, ushered in a romantic style of jewelry, but Gothic designs were used in a debased manner, as so frequently happens in the adaptation of a historical mode.

left: Fig. 46. Matthias Lock. *Rocaille.* 1764.
right: Fig. 47. French necklace and earrings. Late 18th cent. Silver, set with pastes. Victoria and Albert Museum, London (bequeathed by Mrs. A. E. Stuart).

The Jewelry of the Past   27

At the mid-point of the 19th century another second-hand tradition displaced the Gothic revival. This was a return to Louis XVI style—a "neorococo" fashion in which the metalwork was concealed under a massed overlay of gems.

The Second Empire period, during the second half of the century, was the last great era for jewelry associated with the luxury of the French nobility and court. Its influence was strongly felt in American fashions.

At the same time, the artists' revolt against stereotyped and outworn modes of seeing and of creating images of reality was in the making. Before the last quarter of the 19th century the painters spear-headed the attack. The innovations of Courbet, Monet, Pissarro, and others, and the early showings of works by Manet, Renoir, Cézanne, Degas, and their contemporaries, had set off the movements that were to turn the art world upside down. The other arts, however, were slow to follow, and jewelry reflected none of the turmoil of the new vision. The fabulous trinkets created at the turn of the century for the Russian czars by Carl Fabergé, one of the most technically accomplished jewelers of all times, were costly, intricate, and meticulously and ingeniously crafted, but, for any hint of the artistic ferment of the period, they might as well have been produced during the Renaissance.

Only the final phase of 19th-century jewelry comes close to providing a style that the contemporary jeweler can regard with feelings of sympathy. This was Art Nouveau, which flashed meteorlike across the dividing line of the 19th and 20th centuries and then disappeared from view for almost half a century. In the words of Robert Schmutzler, "Art Nouveau was an intentionally created style that claimed very seriously to be a 'new art' (Art Nouveau) and a 'modern style.' It was indeed a protest against the repetition of old styles. . . ."[1]

Art Nouveau was antagonistic to the historicism of the 19th century, with its imitation and mixture of historical styles. The new style emerged out of a strong revulsion on the part of artists and craftsmen toward historical forms no longer possessing expressive power.

Following Schmutzler, the characteristics of Art Nouveau might be listed as follows, in opposition to those of historicism:

Art Nouveau	Historicism
Closed form	Open form
Surface form	Sculptural form
Delicate relief	Strong relief
Consonant forms	Conflicting forms
Slender forms	Thick forms
Light, cool colors	Dark, warm colors
Unity of form	Multiplicity of form
Dynamic form	Static form
Structures ornamental in themselves	Structures hidden by surface ornament
Biomorphic forms	Traditional forms
Asymmetry	Symmetry

---

[1] *Art Nouveau*, Harry N. Abrams, Inc., New York, 1962, p. 29.

Fig. 48. William Blake. *Paolo and Francesca in the Whirlwind of Lovers in the Circle of the Lustful,* illustration for Dante's *Divine Comedy.* 1824–1827. City Museum and Art Gallery, Birmingham, England.

The essence of Art Nouveau lies in its use of the sinuous line, expressive of the "life force," Bergson's *élan vital*. This line derives from William Blake's response to the rhythmic, dynamic life force, so characteristic of his graphic work and his poetry (Fig. 48). The roots of his style might be found in figures of *rocaille* and certainly can be traced back to the Gothic. "Grecian is Mathematic Form; Gothic is Living Form," was Blake's succinct summary.

The aim of Art Nouveau was decorative: to integrate subject and background compositionally, so that, to achieve unity, the emphasis is upon formal elements, rather than upon subject. At a time when society was in the throes of industrial upheaval, it seemed natural and inevitable to find artists groping for some means of simplifying and integrating diversity and confusion. The principle of "formalization" led to a remarkable synthesis of the arts, quite similar to the fusion of painting, sculpture, and architecture which appears to be taking place today. The artist becomes the universal man, capable of dealing with multiple media and crossing the dividing lines of the arts.

The material of Art Nouveau consisted of formalized natural shapes, as well as formalized mythical hybrids such as mermaids and the metamorphosis

left: Fig. 49. Aubrey Beardsley. *J'ai baise ta bouche, Iokanaan*
(Salome with the head of John the Baptist). 1893.
India ink with green water-color wash, 10¹⁵/₁₆ × 5¹³/₁₆″.
Princeton University Library, Princeton, N.J.
below: Fig. 50. Alphonse Marie Mucha. *XXme Exposition du Salon
des Cent.* 1896. Lithograph, 25¼ × 17″.
Museum of Modern Art, New York
(Gift of Ludwig Charell).

of nonliving forms into living forms. In Art Nouveau jewelry all these aspects can be seen: the formalization of natural forms, with emphasis upon linear composition; essentially flat, even graphic design; a structure that is, in itself, ornamental and delicate; and, finally, a unity of organization incorporating every element into a totality (Figs. 49–51, Pl. 6).

One result of the Art Nouveau movement was to revive enameling. Another was to broaden the use of semiprecious stones as a reaction to the baroque overemphasis upon an overlay of brilliant-cut diamonds. In England the Art Nouveau influence upon jewelry was essentially as a craft movement. The traditional preoccupation of major European jewelry houses with historicism was hardly disturbed.

Since our American culture is derived largely from Europe, we are the inheritors of traditions that come from as long ago as the early 17th century, only a few short years after the death of Queen Elizabeth I of England and William Shakespeare, and as recently as the early 20th century, when the Armory Show of 1913 shook the American art establishment to its founda-

Fig. 51. René Lalique. "Hazelnut" necklace. c. 1900. Gold, enamel, diamonds, and gemstones, 4¾ × 5". Museé des Arts Decoratits, Paris.

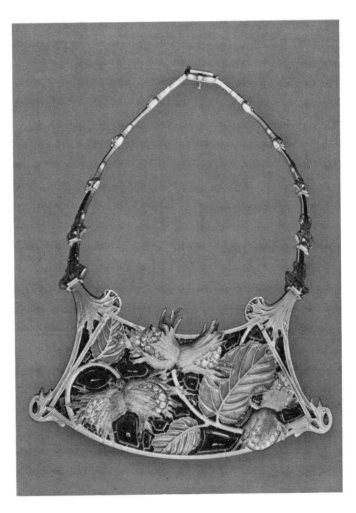

tions. The 19th century, in particular, became a sort of time funnel through which the styles of jewelry from many ages and many cultures poured in upon America. The fact that the contemporary jeweler, along with the modern artists in many fields, has rejected many aspects of earlier European tradition, particularly historicism, does not prevent his responding with appreciation to the sensitivity and skill exhibited by craftsmen working within that tradition, nor his utilization of the processes passed on to him by skilled artisans from time immemorial.

4

THE HISTORY OF CONTEMPORARY JEWELRY

4–1 The Ethics of Contemporary Design   A recognition and exploitation of the intrinsic characteristics of materials is fundamental to the ethics of contemporary design. This view rejects the arbitrary imposition of form upon any material and requires fresh exploration of the possibilities and capacities of materials and tools. This approach, coupled with the rejection of traditional design conventions, placed contemporary jewelry in America upon a primitive level of craftsmanship at its historical beginning. In traditional jewelry, techniques are almost inseparable from traditional design concepts. Technique is important to the contemporary jeweler, but craftsmanship is secondary to expressive integrity. Honest treatment of materials is more important than refinement of craftsmanship; thus the contemporary jeweler learned to work within the limitations of his own skill while searching for expressive form.

4–2 The Rational Expressive Mode   Simplicity is a direct corollary to honest use of materials and tools. Historically, contemporary jewelry utilized simple forms. But simplicity is not merely a quality of primitive or unskilled craftsmanship. It is a quality of one of the two dominant modes of esthetic expression, the *rational mode*. Simplicity is expressive of the nature of a rationalized milieu which always seeks the simplest, most direct, most effective, and most economical forms. Rational design eliminates all nonfunctional elements (Fig. 52). Today there is a demand for clean form and pure structure. No doubt this demand is related to the nature of scientific technology, the machine, and modern industrial processes, all of which avoid the rationally superfluous.

In the rational expressive mode tool textures and the natural textures of materials have generally displaced almost all surface decoration. At one period in its history, modern art, as expressed in architecture and industrial design, followed a severe simplicity stripped of emotional overtones. The term for this type of design was ''modernistic,'' and the style died in the thirties. Afterward the term ''modern'' was considered less desirable to use in relation to current

Fig. 52. Alexander Calder. Hammered wire necklace. Shown at Museum of Modern Art, New York, 1946.

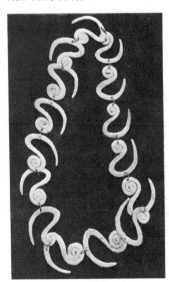

developments in art, and the term "contemporary" was adopted to refer to the design characteristics of the postwar crafts. It is in this sense that we speak of contemporary jewelry as a unique historical style in America.

Contemporary jewelers, working in the rational mode, strive to achieve the most direct expression of form arising from simple processes and depend upon the qualities of the materials themselves.

4–3 The Nonrational Mode   The *nonrational mode* of esthetic expression is an antinomy to the scientific age, with its reliance upon a purely intellectual appraisal of the human condition and its compulsive insistence upon pure objectivity. Disillusionment with science calls forth the affirmation of the unconscious aspects of existence, the affirmation of the nonrational by life itself.

In art the nonrational mode takes the forms we know as surrealism and Dadaism and is reflected in the recently awakened interest in the esthetic qualities dominant in Art Nouveau. In contemporary jewelry, as in sculpture, particular forms celebrate the natural, the chance happening, the organic, with its strange alloy of patterned structure and unique occurrence, as seen in the crystal, which never departs from its own molecular pattern yet always appears in individual variations. Surrealism and Dadaism celebrate, not the aspects of existence which stand forth in the illuminating light of the mind, but those subterranean relationships which have their movement behind the bright face of nature, in the half-light and shadow of uneasy mystery and uncertain meaning. The burden of the nonrational mode of expression is wholeness, not perfection; symbol, not concept; myth, not description. Not evil, not good; but good and evil taken together to make up the wholeness of existence. Thus surrealism and Dadaism, as expressions of esthetic compensation, tend to stress the aspects of existence which are ignored, rejected, and repressed by our scientific

Fig. 53. Marcel Duchamp. Installation photograph of Marcel Duchamp Retrospective Exhibition, 1963, Pasadena Art Museum. Dadaist use of the product image to attack the 19th-century concept of esthetic beauty.

Fig. 54. Robert Mallary.
La Marseillaise. 1961. Plywood,
billboard tearings, polyester,
and welded steel, ht. 7' 6".
Collection Mr. and Mrs. Maremont,
Chicago. Dadaist use of junk materials
to organize a picture space,
challenging the historical concept
of what is beautiful.

culture—evil, ugliness, the useless, the nonutilitarian, the unknown, the chance, the turbid, the playful, the terrifying, the incomprehensible—in other words, the spontaneous creative randomness of nature.

However, surrealism and Dadaism celebrate the nonrational in quite different ways. They appear to be the positive and negative sides of the question. Surrealism makes a direct affirmation of the nonrational in terms of the historical and mythical images of the unconscious. The work of Hieronymus Bosch, Max Ernst, and Germaine Richier comes to mind (Figs. 135, 136). Dadaism, on the other hand, affirms the nonrational by utilizing images derived from the rational, objective, scientific, industrial world of the present. It points out the negative, ridiculous, useless, contradictory, or ugly aspects of modern civilization, including the narrowly restrictive ethical, moral, and esthetic principles of the past. It does so by means of the product images of civilization, and for this reason its expression appears as an inversion of values (Figs. 53, 54).

The reappearance of those esthetic principles underlying the Art Nouveau movement of the late 19th century may be viewed as a possibly significant new turn in the development of artistic sensibility today. If the rational mode of expression, utilizing technological forms for the most part, was a product of an overemphasis upon an intellectual approach to reality, and the non-

The History of Contemporary Jewelry　35

Fig. 55. Aubrey Beardsley.
The Peacock Skirt, from *Salome.* 1907.
Drawing, $8^7/_8'' \times 6^1/_4''$.
Fogg Art Museum, Harvard University,
Cambridge, Mass. (Grenville L.
Winthrop Bequest).

rational mode of expression was an equally exaggerated celebration of the unconscious forces of life, as a compensatory reaction, the reappearance of the esthetics of Art Nouveau may signal a coming into balance of both of these expressions. For Art Nouveau expresses the *élan vital,* but in a controlled form (Fig. 55).

The long, sinuous line found in nature and pertaining to natural patterns of growth speaks of a renewed interest in the life force within all nature. At any rate, both the rational and the nonrational modes of expression are found in the historical beginnings of contemporary jewelry, and both of these modes continue in the current scene.

4–4 The Emergence of Contemporary Jewelry in America   To the best of my knowledge, contemporary jewelry made its appearance in America no earlier than 1936, with Sam Kramer's work. Officially, contemporary jewelry in America began with the first national exhibition, put together by the Museum of Modern Art in 1946. In that show 135 pieces of jewelry by 26 artists were exhibited. These early artists were not all professional working jewelers, but they all participated in an important historical event.

Almost all the jewelry reflected the influence of modern art. It was about equally divided as to expressive modes: rational and nonrational. Among the professional jewelers appearing in this show, Fred Farr, Paul A. Lobel, and Ward Bennett exhibited plate-shape forms. Linear forms of jewelry were exhibited by Alexander Calder and Julio de Diego. Fannie Hillsmith and Adda Husted-Andersen showed constructed forms. Strip-plate forms were exhibited by Margaret De Patta and Hurst & Kingsbury. Harry Bertoia, in this show, employed fused forms. (See Appendix A for illustrations.)

The second national exhibition of contemporary jewelry was held by the Walker Art Center, of Minneapolis, in the spring of 1948. This show was sponsored by the Everyday Art Gallery, directed by Hilde Reiss. It was packaged as a traveling exhibit by Bill Friedman, Assistant Director of the Walker Art Center, and toured for two years, stimulating interest in contemporary jewelry throughout the country.

This exhibit included 282 pieces of jewelry by 30 artists. It is interesting that only seven of these artists were represented in the Museum of Modern Art Exhibition of 1946. They were Ward Bennett, Harry Bertoia, Margaret De Patta, Hurst & Kingsbury, Fred Farr, Adda Husted-Andersen, and Paul A. Lobel. Of the 30 exhibitors, 16 were then working in the nonrational mode of expression and 14 in the rational mode of expression. Except for electroforms, every one of the means of expression (see Chap. 6) was represented. Only four jewelers exhibited cast jewelry; eleven jewelers exhibited plate-shape forms; nine exhibited constructed forms; three exhibited enamels; two exhibited fused forms; two exhibited strip-plate forms; two exhibited forged forms; one exhibited repoussé forms; and two exhibited plastic forms.

The Walker Art Center followed up its first show with another national exhibition of contemporary jewelry in 1955. This show was sponsored by the newly organized *Design Quarterly*, edited by Meg Torbert, and featured the work of five artists: Harry Bertoia, Margaret De Patta, Sam Kramer, Philip Morton, and Bob Winston. It also exhibited 115 pieces of jewelry by 84 artists. Much of this jewelry was derivative of the work of the pioneers, even though all of it was well executed. Work which appeared outstanding in terms of freshness of concept and expressive effectiveness deserves mention.

The niello cuff links of Philip Fike transcended the ordinary conception of this type; also, the utilization of the traditional technique of niello in a contemporary manner encouraged experimentation.

The open-ended ring by Jerome Gates represented an important new direction that was to be increasingly explored.

The pure simplicity and unity of form and construction of Mary Kretsinger's pin is another example of creative design.

The dramatic impact of Lawrence McKinin's combination of simple shapes to form a pendant, and the effect of the subdued surface texture, testify to the value of simplicity inherent in the rational mode of expression.

The enamel pendant of B. M. Reid went beyond the usual level of enameled jewelry in complexity of design and subtlety of color.

The silver pin of George K. Salo established a direction of sculptural forming and finishing to be much followed in later contemporary jewelry.

The inlaid bracelet of Christian F. Schmidt established a high level of disciplined craftsmanship.

The work of the five pioneers in contemporary jewelry reveals independent direction and maturity of execution. (See Appendix A for illustrations.)

By the time of the third Walker Art Center Exhibition (the fourth national exhibition of contemporary jewelry), held in 1959, a new roster of names had appeared. Eighty-eight artists exhibited 155 pieces of jewelry. Only two of these artists had exhibited in the Museum of Modern Art: Margaret De Patta and Adda Husted-Andersen. Only seven of them had shown in the first Walker Art Center Exhibition. Forty-four of them had exhibited in the Walker Art Center Exhibition of 1955. These figures reveal the increasing interest in contemporary jewelry and give some indication of the number of young people newly at work in the field.

This show was extremely important, because it forecast many tendencies that were to become dominant in the sixties. The general level of originality of design and craftsmanship was high, and the major expressive means were clearly illustrated. Thirty-two of the 88 artists utilized the nonrational mode of expression, and it seemed that, with one or two exceptions, the rational mode was becoming less fruitful as an area of exploration and less interesting to experimental artists.

Only three jewelers showed an interest in primitivity: Howard Brown utilized a piece of polished bone; Philip Morton used a found quartz pebble, polished on one side and left natural on the other side; and Jan Smith exhibited a charcoal-cast sterling pendant which in form preserved the qualities of the process. This primitivity was also to appear in the work of certain European jewelers in the sixties.

The open-ended ring reappeared with Irena Brynner's stone-set entry. The rings of Juanita Brown and Shirley Lege Carpenter were outstanding in conception. Indeed, with this show the ring became a form of dominant interest in contemporary jewelry. Russell E. Day transcended the conventional concept of the ring. John Dickerhoff, with his ring, discovered a relationship for tubing which Christian Schmidt was to adapt later to exceptionally interesting fusing projects. Gudmund Jon Elvestand, a visiting jeweler from Norway, David Hatch, Wiltz Harrison, Michael Jerry, Ruth Pennington, and Richard G. Thiel all exhibited work that was to set a pattern for contemporary design in the sixties. For example, the interlocking wedding-ring set, which has become so popular in the sixties, was first exhibited in this show by Robert Engstrom.

In other areas work of originality and refinement was exhibited by Robert Dhaemers, William George Haendel, Ronald Hayes Pearson, Ruth and Svetozar Radakovich, and Donald B. Wright. The forms shown by these artists were all sculptural, extremely refined and finished. For the first time in a national exhibition the rediscovered art of granulation was represented by the entry of John Paul Miller (8–8).

The exhibition revealed the immense popularity of the process of casting, which was almost to dominate the field both in America and Europe. Of 88 exhibitors 27 utilized cast forms. Fused forms were of interest to only three jewelers. Linear forms were exhibited by 21 jewelers. Only nine jewelers utilized plate-shape forms. Twenty-eight jewelers exhibited constructed forms. Strip-plate forms were utilized by only five jewelers. Three items of jewelry were forged; one item was carved. There was no repoussé exhibited.

A brooch by Irena Brynner anticipated the design quality attained in some of the current work being done in Europe today. Also, some intimations of Art Nouveau appeared in the ring of Gudmund Jon Elvestand, the seed pods of Christian Schmidt, and the lyrical movement of the pendant by Robert von Neumann.

This final exhibition of the Walker Art Center was of great significance in revealing the heights of contemporary jewelry in 1959 and in forecasting the potentials that would be developed in the following decade.

A notable national exhibition of contemporary crafts was organized in this period. The St. Paul Gallery initiated its biennial exhibition "Fiber, Clay, and Metal" in 1951. Up to this time there had been no sustained support for the contemporary crafts movement on the part of regional communities outside of the eastern seaboard. The early historical exhibitions of contemporary jewelry must be seen as a national rather than a regional affirmation of the importance of contemporary jewelry as a historical style. The St. Paul Gallery commited itself to a sustained program for the encouragement and support of independent craftsmen working in the contemporary idiom. Through the important decade of the fifties this program set high standards and attracted outstanding craftsmen from all sections of the country. Through purchase awards the St. Paul Gallery acquired an outstanding collection of contemporary crafts (Figs. 56-58).

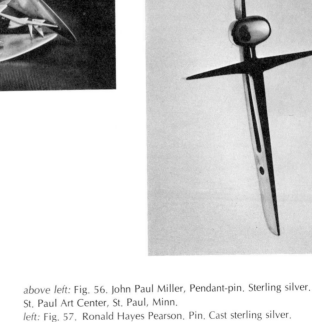

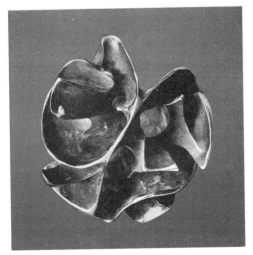

above left: Fig. 56. John Paul Miller, Pendant-pin. Sterling silver. St. Paul Art Center, St. Paul, Minn.
left: Fig. 57. Ronald Hayes Pearson. Pin. Cast sterling silver. St. Paul Art Center, St. Paul, Minn.
above right: Fig. 58. Svetozar Radakovich. Cross with stone. St. Paul Art Center, St. Paul, Minn.

By 1964 the exhibition had attracted nearly 4000 entries. Only 101 pieces were chosen by the jury for exhibit. This exhibition marked a change in the character of the contemporary movement in the crafts and confirmed that the contemporary practice of crafts is, indeed, an expressive art. In the foreword to the catalogue of this show Malcolm E. Lein, the director, wrote:

> Pieces which are primarily functional in character made up only a small part of the total. In a broad sense the work submitted is a radical departure from that seen in previous exhibitions. At the same time it further erases the once hard line between crafts and fine art.

Only eight jewelers were included in the 1964 St. Paul Gallery show, and none had shown in the exhibit of ten years earlier.

The entry under the name of Abraham marks the entrance of "pop" jewelry into the contemporary field (Fig. 59). Actually it was submitted by Christian Schmidt, one of the jurors, as a satirical protest against the lack of a consistent criterion for the evaluation of the merit of the entries in the various crafts. To the consternation of Schmidt the piece was enthusiastically accepted, but its presence in the exhibition leads the craftsman to reflect carefully upon the meaning of Dadaism to contemporary life (Fig. 60).

In 1946 the Wichita Art Association of Wichita, Kansas, had organized an annual exhibition entitled "Decorative Arts and Ceramics Exhibition." By

left: Fig. 59. Abraham (Christian Schmidt). "Pop" pendant, *Medal of Honor.* 1964. Assorted gems, wire, and found pieces. St. Paul Art Center, St. Paul, Minn. *right:* Fig. 60. J. Fred Woell. Pin-pendant, *Patriotism Medal.* 1967. Copper, silver, brass, and tin.

1954 such jewelers as Imogene Bailey, Margaret De Patta, Charles Piper, and Byron Wilson were exhibiting annually in this show.

Meanwhile, another sustaining influence for the development of the contemporary craft movement had been germinating in the East. The American Craftsmen's Council, growing originally out of a number of long-established local 19th-century crafts groups and the American Craftsmen's Cooperative, was established in 1943, under the inspiration and leadership of Mrs. Vanderbilt-Webb. Mrs. Vanderbilt-Webb had a vision of organizing a program to sustain and strengthen the crafts, which were threatened with extinction by the natural economic forces operating in America.

The depression of the thirties had almost destroyed the market for handcrafts. The war in the forties, however, created a new interest and activity in the crafts by drying up foreign imports. At the close of the war a new demand for handcrafts appeared, and Mrs. Vanderbilt-Webb was already at work with her crafts revival. The factors on her side were the vacuum in the postwar luxury market and the vitality of the contemporary esthetics being brought into the old craft tradition by young artists steeped in the developments of modern art.

Mrs. Vanderbilt-Webb had already been interested in the problems of the craftsman as early as 1930, when she started a small group called Putnam County Products in her own Hudson River community. By 1939 her activities had aroused enough interest to bring about the Vermont conference which organized the American Craftsmen's Council. This group, in 1940, opened America House on 53d St., in New York City, for the purpose of marketing the work of council members. From the beginning America House set high standards of craftsmanship and on that basis justified the higher costs of hand production. America House is now strongly established and nationally known, with branches in Birmingham, Michigan; Sun Valley, Idaho; and San Francisco, California.

In 1941 the Cooperative Council founded *Craft Horizons* as a newsletter for its America House craftsmen. This publication has since become an extensive organ for the exchange of information about the activities of American craftsmen and is a source of stimulation to craftsmen throughout the world.

In 1943 the present American Craftsmen's Council was chartered by the State of New York as a nonprofit organization which continued the development of a national crafts program. In 1944 the Council established the School for American Craftsmen at Alfred, New York. At this school young apprentices in pottery, weaving, metalwork, jewelry, and woodworking carried out an eight-hour-day, five-day-week learning and working program. In 1951 the school was moved to Rochester, New York, where it became a division of the Rochester Institute of Technology.

The crowning result of Mrs. Vanderbilt-Webb's vision was the establishment, in 1955, of the Museum of Contemporary Crafts in New York City. This museum has become a craft center for the nation.

In 1960 the American Craftsmen's Council initiated a program to organize regional centers throughout the country, and today there are regional craftsmen-trustees heading six regional councils. The regional councils sponsor workshops, seminars, exhibitions, fairs, and conferences and form institutional centers for regional craftsmen.

Finally, the American Craftsmen's Council formed under grant, in 1960, a department of research and education. This department carries out a number of important functions of benefit to artists, designers, craftsmen, and their patrons. It has a library of folios and slides on American craftsmen. It conducts an architectural and interior-design service for all those requiring access to sources of custom arts and crafts. Educational films, film strips, and slide kits are provided for class or group presentation. Directories of craftsmen, craft courses available, and crafts shops in America are currently published.

The most recent activity of the American Craftsmen's Council has been sponsorship of the First World Congress of Craftsmen, during which a World Crafts Council was formed, in 1964. If craftsmen themselves are brought into positions of leadership and participation, this organization can be of great value in reinforcing standards of craftsmanship and design and in bringing about a close exchange of ideas and work among world craftsmen.

4–5 Pioneers in Contemporary Jewelry in America   It is difficult to submit a list of pioneers of contemporary jewelry in America without risking error or incompleteness. The following list is offered subject to future corrections where error or omission has occurred. It includes only artists who began to work professionally as contemporary jewelers before 1950.

David Aaron   Aaron was among the exhibitors in the 1948 show at the Walker Art Center. As a sculptor and designer he was trained at the Institute of Design in Chicago. Later he headed the Design Workshop at the King-Smith School in Washington, D.C.

Franz Bergmann   A graduate of the National Academy of Fine Arts in Vienna, Bergmann began his career as a painter. About 1940 he began to concentrate on ceramics and jewelry, and thereafter his major work was in those crafts. His jewelry was shown in the Walker Art Center show of 1948.

Harry Bertoia   Bertoia came to America from Italy. After graduating from Cranbrook Academy of Art, he moved to California. His contribution lay in exploration of the expressive means of fusing combined with forging. From the beginning he was also interested in devising fastenings suitable to the form. His forms belong to the nonrational mode of expression (Fig. 61). Since 1950 Bertoia has concentrated on sculpture. Nevertheless, it is doubtful whether his sculpture transcends the sensitivity and sheer creative vigor of his jewelry.

Ward Bennett   Ward Bennett was Art Director for Hattie Carnegie for several years. He exhibited in the Museum of Modern Art in 1946 and in the Walker Art Exhibition of 1948. He worked in plate-shape forms, achieving very sensitive shape-configurations in the nonrational mode of expression.

Alexander Calder   Alexander Calder was one of the first modern artists to utilize jewelry as a means of contemporary art expression in America. Many of Calder's forms are similar to those of primitive jewelry; but it cannot be assumed that they were copied. Wire is a form of material that suggests its own

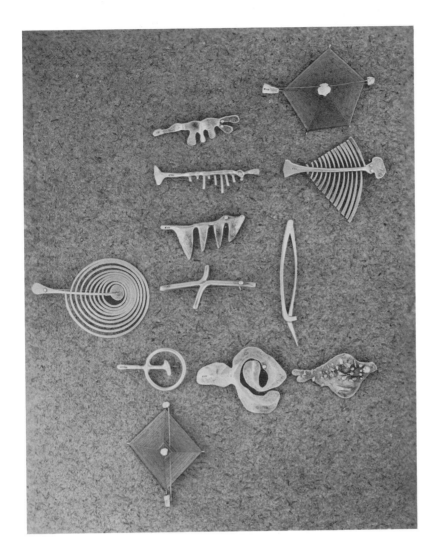

possible relationships. Any artist who naïvely explores the form capacities of wire will independently arrive at identical forms.

Calder's contribution has been his recognition of the esthetic principle inherent in a fresh and untrammeled treatment of his materials (Fig. 62). He pioneered wire-linear forms, having had his first exhibition of wire jewelry at the Willard Gallery in New York, in 1940.

Margaret De Patta   Born in Tacoma, Washington, Margaret De Patta studied at the San Diego Academy of Fine Arts, the California School of Fine arts in San Francisco, and the Art Students League in New York, where she was twice winner of national scholarships.

She began making jewelry in the shop of an Armenian jeweler in 1930. Her contemporary work began after study with Moholy-Nagy and Eugene Bielawski at the Chicago Institute of Design, in 1941. She established a studio in the Bay area, where she remained throughout her life.

Fig. 63. Margaret De Patta. Pendant.
c. 1960. White gold and faceted crystal.

Her contribution to contemporary jewelry lay in her development of strip-plate forms and her exploration of faceted stones (Fig. 63). Rejecting the traditional forms of faceting because of their narrow formal limitations, she carried out a study of reflection, refraction, magnification, and distortion, designing facet forms to exploit these qualities. The integration of the setting with the total form was also an important creative problem for her.

Her work was included in the Museum of Modern Art Exhibition of 1946, all three of the Walker Art Center Exhibitions, and many other important shows. She was one of the American jewelers to be included in Aloi's *Esempi di Decorazione Moderna di Tutto il Mondo,* published by Hoepli in Milan in 1954, and was also included in the "First International Exhibition of Modern Jewellery, 1890–1961," held in London in 1961 at the Victoria and Albert Museum.

Fred Farr   Fred Farr studied at the University of Oregon, the Portland Art Museum, and the American Artists School. A painter, muralist, sculptor, and designer, he exhibited widely. His work was included in the Museum of Modern Art Exhibition of 1946 and in the Walker Art Center Exhibition of 1948. He worked with plate shapes and constructed forms.

Doris Hall   Having studied at the Cleveland School of Art, Doris Hall concentrated on enameling, producing for retail outlets throughout the country.
Her work was included in the Walker Art Center Exhibition of 1948.

Fannie Hillsmith   Well-known as a painter, Fannie Hillsmith studied at the
Boston Museum of Fine Arts and at the Art Students League in New York. Her
work was included in the Museum of Modern Art Exhibition of 1946 and the
Walker Art Center Exhibition of 1948. She was one of the American jewelers
to be included in Aloi's *Esempi di Decorazione Moderna di Tutto il Mondo,*
published by Hoepli of Milan in 1954. (See Fig. 64.)

Adda Husted-Andersen   Adda Husted-Andersen was born in Denmark and
studied in Copenhagen. She was president of the New York Society of Craftsmen for several years and maintained her own shop in New York. An active
exhibitor, she displayed her work in the Museum of Modern Art Exhibition of
1946 and in all three of the Walker Art Center Exhibitions, as well as many
other national shows. She was included in Aloi's *Esempi di Decorazione Moderna di Tutto il Mondo,* published by Hoepli in Milan in 1954. Her work is
essentially in plate-shape and constructed forms and is somewhat more influenced by European tradition than most American contemporary jewelers
(Fig. 65).

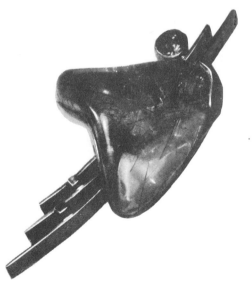

left: Fig. 64. Fannie Hillsmith. Belt pendant. 1966.
Silver and composition stone.
below: Fig. 65. Adda Husted-Andersen. Pin. c. 1959.
Yellow gold with rutilated quartz and tourmaline.

Fig. 66. Sam Kramer. Cross. 1956.
Fused silver with cabochon settings.

Sam Kramer   After making "surrealist" jewelry on the West Coast in 1936, Sam Kramer moved to New York in 1939 and established a shop in Greenwich Village, where he worked until his death in 1964. He was well known for his humorous and far-out promotional flyers and his consistently sincere and expressive surrealist jewelry. His studio is now operated by his widow, Carol Kramer, a gifted jeweler in her own right, who shared the success of the studio with Sam.

The forms of Kramer's jewelry are a combination of fused forms and forged forms made of sheets of heavy-gauge metal (Fig. 66). He exhibited widely, being included in all three Walker Art Center Exhibitions and many other important shows.

Paul A. Lobel   Paul A. Lobel came from Rumania to the United States as an infant. He studied at the Art Students League in New York, becoming a designer, sculptor, silversmith, and craftsman in many materials. In 1925, in a one-man show in Paris, he exhibited drawing, painting, etching, and metalwork.

During the late thirties and early forties he designed a line of decorative objects in bent glass, called Benduro, for which he won two awards in the 1937 Exposition of Decorative Arts in Paris. During World War II he opened a jewelry shop on West 4th Street in Greenwich Village, which he operated until 1964. During this period he exhibited widely in national and regional exhibitions, including the 1946 contemporary jewelry exhibition at the Museum of Modern Art in New York and in the Walker Art Center Exhibition of 1948. In 1949 the Museum of Natural History showed a collection of his handwrought jewelry and silver sculpture under the title of "Shining Birds and Silver Beasts."

Lobel's jewelry reflects an imaginative skill in designing three-dimensional forms from flat sheet metal (Fig. 67). These forms were often lyrical formalizations of such natural images as flowers and fish, and they always expressed a respect for the integrity of the material.

In recent years Lobel's imagination has found a significant outlet in the creation of exciting mobile paper sculptures.

Keith Monroe   Having graduated from the University of California in painting and sculpture, Keith Monroe began making jewelry in 1946, expressing interest in the "found" object primarily. He exhibited in the Walker Art Center Exhibition of 1948.

Ronald Hayes Pearson   Ronald Pearson attended the School for American Craftsmen at Alfred, New York, in 1947. In 1948 he opened his own workshop at Alfred, where for the next five years he produced spun-bronze hollow ware. He moved to Rochester in 1952, where with three other craftsmen he organized Shop One, an outstanding retail craft shop.

During the fifties he participated in many exhibitions, winning awards and commissions. From 1959 to 1962 he taught at the School for American Craftsmen at Rochester, and currently he operates a large workshop with several assistants, producing for a select group of retail shops throughout the country.

Fig. 67. Paul A. Lobel. Pin. Sterling silver.

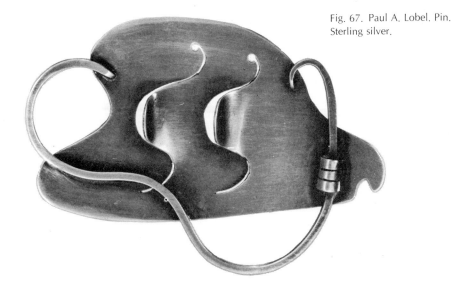

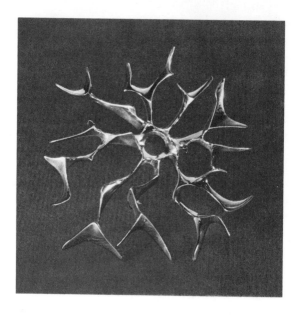

Fig. 68. Ronald Hayes Pearson.
Pin. 1966. Cast 14-kt. gold.

Pearson has concentrated on forged and cast forms (Fig. 68). His forged forms demonstrate the ultimate refinement to which a process can be taken by a master craftsman. With Shop One he demonstrated that a high-quality crafts shop can survive and prosper in modern society.

Caroline G. Rosene   Caroline Rosene studied at Washington University and at Radcliffe College. She has been a director of the City Art Museum at St. Louis and of the Art Center at Fitchburg, Massachusetts, and has produced jewelry in her own shop for many years. She has participated in many exhibitions, including the first two Walker Art Center Exhibitions. Her work is essentially of plate-shape and constructed forms.

Pearl S. Schecter   Pearl S. Schecter received her A.B. and M.F.A. from Columbia University and thereafter studied at the Hans Hoffman School and the Chicago Bauhaus School of Moholy-Nagy. When she became interested in jewelry, she studied enameling and metal with Adda Husted-Andersen in New York.

She has maintained a studio in New York City for many years and has been a lecturer and instructor at the New York University and art director at the Little Red Schoolhouse High School in New York City.

Her jewelry is concerned with the elements of space, line, tension, and negative-positive relationships.

Bob Winston   Bob Winston received an M.A. from the University of California and for many years taught jewelry and design at the California College of Arts and Crafts in Oakland, California. He exhibited in all three Walker Art Center Exhibitions as well as in many important national and local shows.

His work tends toward the surrealistic, the pagan, or primitive and exotic, utilizing constructed and assembled forms as well as cast forms in the non-rational mode of expression.

4–6 Recent Directions in Contemporary Jewelry Contemporary jewelry has now moved beyond the level of primitive craftsmanship, in the sense that mature contemporary jewelers who have been practicing their art for twenty years or more have mastered their techniques and achieved a sophistication impossible at the inception of the trend. The younger jewelers have been able to participate in well-developed instruction programs of contemporary jewelry, which exist in all parts of the country. Much of the jewelry in the sixties is vigorous in design and skillful in execution, though a few artists approach a kind of generalized form and polished surface more typical of trade jewelry.

The 1964 St. Paul Gallery Exhibition raised the question of whether contemporary jewelry has reached a plateau of expression. The jury of that show found the majority of entries "repetitive or imitative, or contrived with the obvious effort to be different." We are perhaps confronted here with two inevitabilities in the growth and maturation of contemporary jewelry. First, it seems unavoidable that creative pioneers will lay out the lines of development in their own exploratory programs and that there must be ultimate limits to the range of expression characteristic of any social milieu. Chapter 6 outlines various means of expression which have emerged in esthetic response to our contemporary culture. This is not to say that creative artists will not extend the range of expression. Indeed they have done and are doing so. But as increasing numbers of people move into a new country it is bound to become less unexplored. Second, it seems inevitable that as increasing numbers of people become involved in any art activity the level of quality may become lowered. Nevertheless, current explorations are moving both forward into new forms and backward toward a reexamination of some traditional forms.

Since the historical exhibitions of the fifties, a great many exhibitions have appeared throughout the country, featuring the crafts and, specifically, contemporary jewelry. In these shows, too, appear the trends foreshadowed by the earlier exhibitions. Of major significance has been the program of shows held by the Museum of Contemporary Crafts in New York City. Such shows as "Emergence: Student Craftsmen," held in 1963; "The American Craftsman," 1964; "The Art of Personal Adornment," 1965; and "Acquisition," 1967, have been consistently encouraging to the practicing contemporary jeweler.

Also important have been the regional craft exhibitions sponsored by the regional councils of the American Craftsmen's Council. These exhibitions produce catalogues which include exhibiting craftsmen in every area.

There have also been a large number of significant museum or university craft exhibitions. Some of these are the "Kansas Designer-Craftsman Exhibition," held annually since 1953 at the University of Kansas in Lawrence, Kansas; the "American Crafts 1963, New Talent Exhibition," held at the University of Illinois at Urbana; the Purdue University "Invitational Jewelry Exhibition" at Lafayette, Indiana; the "American Jewelry Today" exhibition held by the Everhart Museum at Scranton, Pennsylvania, in 1963, 1965, and 1967; the "First Survey of Contemporary American Crafts," held at the University of Texas Art Museum in Austin, in 1967; and the "Jewelry International Exhibition," held at State University of New York in Plattsburg each year since 1963. These and many other exhibitions held in various parts of the country have clearly defined the current trends prevailing in contemporary jewelry during the sixties.

Among the influential young contemporary jewelers in America today are the following:

Haakon Bakken, Port Credit, Ontario (Fig. 69)
Fred Fenster, Madison, Wisc. (Fig. 70)
Philip Fike, Detroit, Mich. (Pl. 11)
Michael Jerry, Menomenie, Wisc. (Pl. 13)
Brent Kington, Carterville, Ill. (Fig. 71)
Earl Krentzin, Detroit, Mich.
Stanley Lechtzin, Philadelphia, Penna. (Fig. 72, Pl. 9)
Paul Mergen, Kalamazoo, Mich. (Fig. 73)
Frank Patania, Tucson, Ariz.
Alvin Pine, Long Beach, Calif. (Fig. 74)
Victor Ries, Mill Valley, Calif.
Heikki Seppa, St. Louis, Mo. (Fig. 75)
Olaf Skoogfors, Philadelphia, Penna. (Pl. 7)

A study of the jewelry of this group reveals the major tendencies in the current period. Gold and precious stones are being used to a much greater extent than formerly. The increased utilization of more precious metals and precious gems is no doubt inevitable. Contemporary jewelry can probably enter into the larger jewelry market only in terms of the preciousness of materials demanded by the public. While the use on the part of early contemporary jewelers of silver and even of valueless materials was a necessary part of the affirmation of expressive form over extrinsic values, there seems to be little tendency among contemporary jewelers to sacrifice expressive means to extrinsic values.

below left: Fig. 69. Haakon Bakken. Pin. 1968. Cast sterling silver with coral.
bottom left: Fig. 70. Fred Fenster. Ring. 1966. 14-kt. gold with diamond.
below right: Fig. 71. Brent Kington. Pendant, *Trapeze.* 1965. Cast 14-kt. gold.

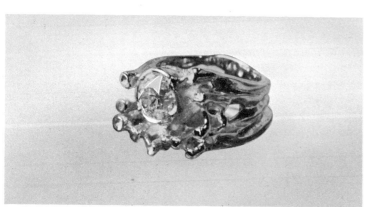

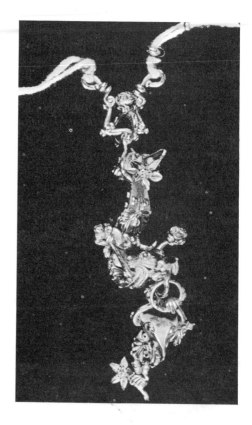

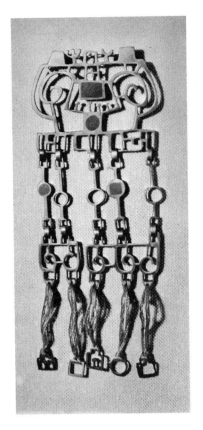

far left: Fig. 72. Stanley Lechtzin. Pin. 1967. Electroformed gilt sterling silver with amethyst.
left: Fig. 73. Paul Mergen. Pendant-pin. 1966. Bronze with copper inlay.

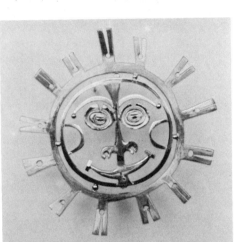

left: Fig. 74. Alvin Pine. Pin, *Sun Face.* 1966. 14-kt. gold, cast and constructed.
right: Fig. 75. Heikki Seppa. Pin. 1967. Reticulated gold.

One of the important achievements of contemporary design was to cast off associative values which had come to obscure expressive values in jewelry. Current design trends appear to treat gold with a primitivism that is a reflection of the processes used. Some of these forms are seen almost as pieces torn out of nature's fabric rather than as formalized creations.

The tendency to use traditional faceted gem forms is possibly a temporary phase that will lead more and more jewelers to follow the explorations begun by Margaret De Patta. Several American and European jewelers are experimenting with form in the gem as well as in the metalwork. The increased use of natural found forms and natural crystal forms, as well as a continuation of the use of cabochon forms for transparent gems, suggests an awareness of this question. This last tendency also appears to be another manifestation of the primitivism mentioned above. Where such primitivism is found, there is nevertheless a careful organization of the visual elements of design.

The History of Contemporary Jewelry   51

In current tendencies, both in America and Europe, there is a movement away from technological forms, as though the artist had now assimilated the Industrial Revolution, become surfeited with the humanized geometric form, and hungered for a new *rapprochement* with nature. This can be interpreted as a positive move toward the nonrational mode of expression, also.

Another characteristic of current tendencies is the relative flatness of many designs. This seems to reflect the reappearance of some aspects of the early 20th-century Art Nouveau (Fig. 76). We must be careful to note that the Art Nouveau style does not reappear as though some artist had accidentally run across an old book of Art Nouveau designs and impulsively picked them up. Style is always a matter of inner feeling on the part of the artist. Among the tendencies that call Art Nouveau to mind is the effort to treat metal as metal in all its qualities of color, ductility, fusibility, and malleability. In some cases even the sinuous line reappears. In place of the application of the forms of nature at the normal or human level of perception, we find the forms of nature at the macro- or microscopic levels of existence. This latter aspect, however, is in direct contradiction to the Art Nouveau insistence upon the formal quality of decorative design. Art Nouveau was and is the fundamental effort of the artist to preserve a style independent of historicism, free from pretension, and genuinely expressive. Such tendencies are even an aspect of "pop" jewelry, although the most thoroughgoing craftsmen will probably not be able to respond very completely to an esthetic limited, almost exclusively, to symbolic, preformed images.

There are also to be found among the current tendencies in Europe and America not only a strong dominance of casting as an expressive means but also, more recently, a reaching out toward other means than casting. This may possibly have come about because wax modeling for casting does not demand the involvement in metal that many jewelers find most exciting. Not only is there interest in such newer means as electroforming, which Stanley Lechtzin has been exploring, and the process of etching, but also in a reexamination of such traditional means as granulation, repoussé, and chasing and in assembled

Fig. 76. René Lalique. *Dragon Fly.* c. 1900. Gulbenkian Foundation, Lisbon.

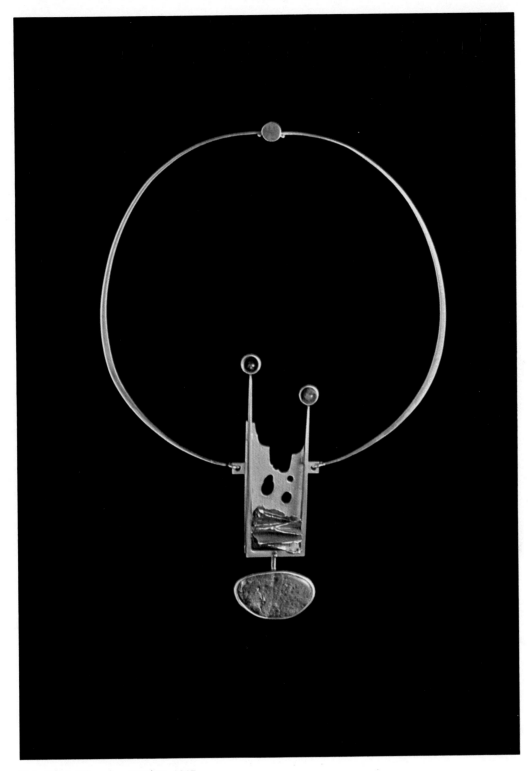

Plate 7. Olaf Skoogfors. Pendant. 1967.
Gold-plated silver, cast and constructed, with tourmaline, amethyst, and sodalite.

Plate 8. Reinhold Reiling. Brooch. 1967. Gold, reticulated, with moonstone, yellow sapphire, green and blue sapphire, diamond, quartz, and pearls.

constructions such as are being done by Skoogfors in America and the Pomodoro brothers in Italy. Nonetheless, casting as an expressive means has been well explored and mastered by contemporary jewelers, and as a production means for duplication of designs it is an important instrument for the penetration of the major jewelry market. It remains for the contemporary jeweler, now, to begin the exploration of other production and design means, such as the drop hammer with dies and the kick press for duplicating assembled or multiple parts from cutting and forming dies (Chap. 19). Perseverance with the ethics of contemporary design combined with a characteristically independent and creative approach to production methods should lead contemporary jewelry to a dominant position in modern society.

At present an important new development is the contact and communication now taking place between American and European jewelers. It becomes essential to include a discussion of the work being done abroad. It is not surprising that, for the most part, the tendencies are similar.

4–7 Contemporary Jewelry Abroad   We have rather extensively defined the meaning of contemporary jewelry as that esthetic in jewelry which is non-objective and is concerned with the expression of objective images corresponding to the inner states of the human soul produced by the contemporary social milieu. Although the history of modern art began in Europe, the expression of this movement in jewelry appears to have begun first or at least more strongly in America in the thirties. To my knowledge no official recognition of contemporary jewelry occurred prior to Robert Aloi's world encyclopedia of design entitled *Esempi di Decorazione Moderna di Tutto il Mondo*, published by Ulrico Hoepli at Milan in 1954. This publication included a survey of world jewelry of the current period. Forty-three jewelers were represented. Of these, seven were American: Adda Husted-Andersen, Hilda Krause, Margaret De Patta, Philip Morton, Pearl S. Schecter, Harry Bertoia, and Fannie Hillsmith. Of the 36 European jewelers only six can be regarded as contemporary: Henning Koppel, Ebbe Weiss, Max Fröhlich, Max Bill, Thom Hannan, and Sigurd Persson. The expressive means of these European jewelers included strip-plate forms, cast forms, carved forms, and plate-shape forms. Much of this jewelry was strongly inventive and well executed.

The "First International Exhibition of Modern Jewellery," held in London in 1961, makes no particular mention of the movement of contemporary jewelry as a historical phenomenon. Of the period in which this movement made its initial development in America, the catalogue carries this statement:

> The third period is 1945 onwards. Designers have discovered the beauty of uncut stones carefully selected and mounted to show their crystal structure, often sharper and more interesting than formal cuts can be, and always showing impurities which the carefully cut stones sometimes hide. Machine production of chains has evolved into a refined art so that a bracelet may be more beautiful than what it holds. But the big revolution has been in casting.

This statement certainly reflects an awareness of important tendencies of what we define as contemporary jewelry, even though the style is not distinguished from other historical styles. This might be accounted for by the fact that the European is to a greater extent immersed in his own rich tradition.

This tradition includes not only esthetic styles but also habits of craftsmanship and the domination of long-established jewelry firms catering to a conservative market. On the other hand modern art may have found a more responsive reaction on the part of American jewelers just because America has had no indigenous tradition of its own in jewelry.

The First International Exhibition, covering a period from 1890 to 1961, includes a fine representation of Art Nouveau jewelry. Designs deriving from earlier traditions are numerous. The French "ribbon" school, as well as the cubist designs of the twenties, are included.

In Europe a large number of exhibitions have given support to the contemporary jeweler: in England at Goldsmiths' Hall, directed by Graham Hughes; at the Institute of Contemporary Arts at Oxford, and at the Victoria and Albert Museum in London; in Italy at Vicenza, Milan, and Venice; in Germany at Munich, Pforzheim, Stuttgart, Berlin, Düsseldorf, Hamburg, and Hannover; and in the Scandinavian countries in Stockholm, Copenhagen, and Helsinki. Some of the fine magazines which support the crafts in Europe are *Form*, published in Stockholm; *European Jeweler*, published in Stuttgart; *Gold + Silber Uhren + Schmuck* published in Stuttgart; and *Kunst + Handwerk*, published in Hamburg.

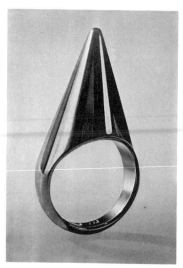 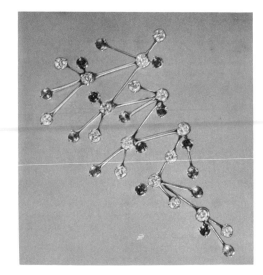

right: Fig. 77. Friedrich Becker. Ring. 1966. Gold.
far right: Fig. 78. Friedrich Becker. Kinetic brooch. 1967. White gold with diamonds. Eight small, adjustable levers bear on hinge points to allow variation of shape in the brooch.

 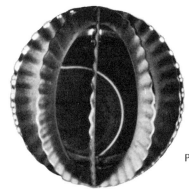

far left: Fig. 79. Gunter Wyss. Pin with warped surfaces. 1966. Gold.
left: Fig. 80. Manuel Capdevila. Pin. 1967. Gold with malachite.

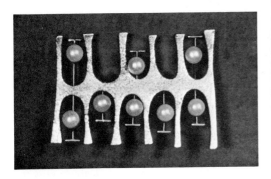

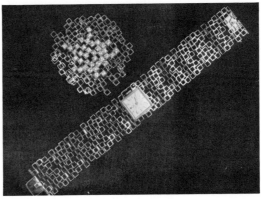

above left: Fig. 81. Joaquin Capdevila. Brooch. 1967. Gold with pearls.
above right: Fig. 82. John Donald. Watch bracelet and matching pin. 1967. Gold, with diamonds in pin.
left: Fig. 83. Gerda Flöckinger. Necklace. 1967. Silver with tourmaline, turquoise, moonstone, and pearls.
below: Fig. 84. Andrew Grima. Necklace and matching ring. 1967. 18-kt. gold with green aventurine and diamond darts.
right: Fig. 85. Hanna Ruth Gratch-Levy. Necklace and earrings. 1967. Silver.

A number of interesting tendencies have appeared in European contemporary jewelry. Friedrich Becker has explored gem forms (Fig. 361) and metal forms (Fig. 77, Pl. 2), and has also experimented with kinetics resulting in variable forms (Fig. 78). Gunter Wyss displays a lyrical mastery of sheet-metal forms (Fig. 79). Max Bill has produced strongly structural innovations in stone settings. The Capdevilas, in Spain, employ very primitive but commanding and delicate forms (Figs. 80, 81). John Donald reveals the beauties of crystalline natural forms (Fig. 82). Gerda Flöckinger brings a very desirable feminine sensitivity to jewelry that is sometimes lacking in more purely technical execution (Fig. 83). Andrew Grima utilizes rich textural effects with strong, simple forms and thus escapes being overwhelmed by sheer costliness of materials (Fig. 84). Hanna Ruth Gratch-Levy, in Israel, reminds us how rich effects can still be produced with simple assemblies (Fig. 85). Henning Koppel has moved

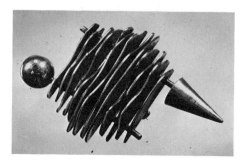

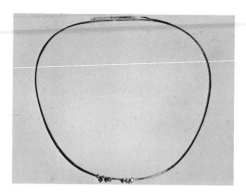

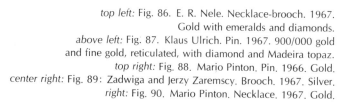

top left: Fig. 86. E. R. Nele. Necklace-brooch. 1967.
Gold with emeralds and diamonds.
above left: Fig. 87. Klaus Ulrich. Pin. 1967. 900/000 gold
and fine gold, reticulated, with diamond and Madeira topaz.
top right: Fig. 88. Mario Pinton. Pin. 1966. Gold.
center right: Fig. 89: Zadwiga and Jerzy Zaremscy. Brooch. 1967. Silver.
right: Fig. 90. Mario Pinton. Necklace. 1967. Gold.

from the folk tradition into powerfully carved organic forms. E. R. Nele (Fig. 86), Reinhold Reiling (Pl. 8), von Skal, Klaus Ulrich (Fig. 87), Mario Pinton (Fig. 88), and the Pomodoros all celebrate a kind of Zen reverence for chanced-upon aspects of form. Textural richness, as found in the subtle art of reticulation, is an important means to many European jewelers. The Zaremscys (Fig. 89), as well as Cepka and Pinton (Fig. 90), reaffirm simplicity, and Sigurd Persson illustrates imaginative richness in original forms.

It is apparent from a study of European contemporary jewelry that non-rational modes of expression are dominant abroad as they are in America, and no doubt for the same reasons. Contemporary jewelers everywhere seem to be in a common search for esthetic values appropriate to the modern milieu.

5

PRINCIPLES
OF CONTEMPORARY
JEWELRY DESIGN

Design is the organization of materials into forms that fulfill human needs. Many ideas and terms are required to explain the process of design. Since the field is extensive, you will find it desirable to enlarge your background by studying books that deal thoroughly with design problems. The material presented here will provide a description and an application of the ideas and terms referring particularly to jewelry design.

5–1   The Elements of Design   The definition at the opening of this chapter presents four basic concepts: *organization, materials, form,* and *need.* Human needs, the great moving forces in human behavior, are biological, psychological, social, and spiritual. All of them play a part in the process of design.

Function is the role that a given form plays in the fulfillment of human need. The function of a house is to provide an enclosure of privacy and shelter from the external environment, in which the occupants may carry out personal and social living activities in security, comfort, and happiness. The function of a house is therefore extremely complex, and the form of the house reflects that complexity.

Form may be defined as the "totality" resulting from an effective organization of design elements. These elements are *materials, tools, technology,* and *function.* Form is not only a reflection of function but also a reflection of the character of materials, the character of the tools used upon the materials, and the technology, or the way in which the tools and materials are manipulated in relation to the function. All the elements of design are so interdependent in a given form that it is possible to separate them only by a process of theoretical abstraction.

Since a given form is a product of the unified relationship of all the design elements, it follows that the *visual images,* or *visual elements*—the shapes, lines, spaces, and textures of the form—are dependent upon the character of the design elements. For this reason jewelry design requires both a study of graphic drawing and work with tools and materials.

5–2   Principles of Designing with Visual Elements   Design concepts are usually presented as "design principles," but design principles are really *relationships* of the visual elements. The reason that some relationships are "good," or effective, and others are not arises out of the capacities and limitations of our own physical and psychological equipment for seeing and understanding what we see. For those interested in pursuing this aspect of design further, a study of the psychology of perception, particularly Gestalt psychology, will be helpful. The following discussion, however, will be limited to the relationships of visual elements as a means of achieving effective jewelry design.

5–3   Design Ideas   The first step in jewelry design is the development of design ideas. Each person brings to his design problems a cultural heritage of traditional ideas unconsciously and casually acquired in the process of growing up. The average person has not had an opportunity to make a study of historical jewelry, and therefore even his traditional ideas may be generalized and vague. His first efforts at original design may result in inaccurately remembered images of what he has seen in the past. It is important to replace this approach with a conscious study of images based on fresh, careful observation of the immediate environment and of contemporary art.

Design ideas sketched freely serve as a starting point for the design process. The sketches must be examined first in the light of the esthetic responses they evoke: Which ones evoke dramatic graphic qualities; which ones seem dead or uninteresting; which ones are trite or stereotyped? This evaluation is perhaps the most difficult for the beginner. Unfortunately, there are no rules or formulas for making esthetic judgments, but consistent study of paintings and sculptures develops understanding of formal relationships and provides a basis for esthetic judgments. The study of art and books on art, artists, and craftsmen should accompany your work in jewelry, especially if you are unable to take studio courses and must work alone at home.

5–4   Line–Space Relationships   The single most important emotional factor in life, and therefore in art, is *dramatic conflict*. We are accustomed to think of dramatic conflict in terms of the great forces of nature and the physical struggles of mankind. Yet it may appear in the subtlest processes of doing, thinking, and feeling.

In jewelry design dramatic conflict is manifested visually in terms of line and line movement. The polar opposite of movement is inactivity, or death, as manifested by empty space. Inanimate space surrounds each self-sufficient or independent form. Where space is organized or included within such a form, it becomes a *shape*—a specially articulated space. Whereas empty space is devoid of movement, properly designed shapes possess varying degrees of movement **(5–12).** One problem of design is to achieve an appropriate relationship between line activity, or movement, and inactivity, or space. The *field* of a design **(5–23)** is the space that line movements occupy or activate.

5–5   Graphic Design   Drawing is a legitimate expressive means in itself, as well as a method of recording and organizing design ideas. The traditional method of rendering is a graphic means used as an aid to seeing ideas three-dimensionally. Rendering of a simple sort is useful in the designing process, but it should not be mistaken for design. Drawing is a more or less required skill for the designer, even though many jewelers eventually come to design directly in terms of materials.

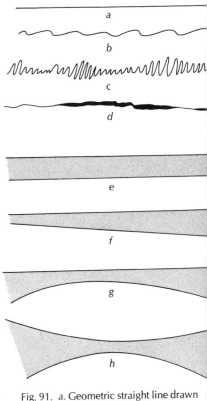

Fig. 91. a. Geometric straight line drawn with a straightedge. b. Moving line drawn freehand. c. Rhythmically flowing freehand line. d. Line of varying width. e. Parallel geometric straight lines. f. Diverging geometric straight lines. g. Curved line working against geometric straight line. h. Two curved lines opposing each other. Implied areas are shaded.

LINE

5–6 Attributes of Line   The attributes of line are *direction, width,* and *implied area,* as well as *intensity,* or *value.* This definition, like all definitions pertaining to art and design, can serve only as a sort of clue, which may guide you in the right direction until you begin to develop your own feeling for esthetic qualities. You can give these attributes specific attention, but they are only partial ideas of what line really is. A line may have an independent life and vitality of its own, but this can be felt only as you experience line for yourself.

A line is significant or interesting to the extent that it demands continued visual inspection in order to be comprehended (Fig. 91). A geometrically straight line is usually lacking in emotional quality and devoid of interest in itself, because it can be comprehended instantly in all its relations. A straight line (Fig. 91a) may be compared to a single musical tone sounded continuously —and monotonously. A moving line (Fig. 91b) is more interesting. A line that is variable in its movement (Fig. 91c) is still more interesting. A line that varies in width (Fig. 91d) is also more interesting. It should be noted that while some of these lines vary in movement, all of them have the same direction as the straight line.

Parallel straight lines (Fig. 91e) create a relationship that is static because the direction of the lines is identical. In addition, they create an implied area (indicated by shading) that is also static, because the relationship of the boundary lines is constant and unchanging.

Straight lines that diverge in direction (Fig. 91f) create dramatic conflict and, therefore, offer more visual interest because of the opposition of line direction. The implied area is also more interesting, because the relationships of the area are constantly changing. This visual activity can be called *area transition* or *area modulation;* it imparts movement to shape.

A moving, or curved, line works more dramatically against a straight line (Fig. 91g) or against another moving line in opposition (Fig. 91h) because of the opposition of direction and because of the area transition that takes place.

A single moving line creates implied areas by itself, and such areas may need to be dealt with as design problems **(5–11, 5–23).**

5–7 The Study of Line   A line is a sort of track that records the movement made by the arm and hand. In order to draw different line movements, you must think of different ways of moving your hand. In jewelry silver wire is a linear form of material. Chasing and engraving are techniques for achieving line. The edge of a metal sheet is a line. Lines may be sawed into a sheet of metal. All these lines, like the pencil line, depend for their movement upon the movements you make with your hands.

Your first design problem is to explore with a pencil all movements your hand and arm can make. Use a soft, sharply pointed pencil and a large sketchbook (18 × 24 in.).

Fig. 92. Freehand line variations.

You should search every part of your environment for line movements, not only in the world of nature but also in industrial plants, grain elevators, machines and industrial equipment, and scientific laboratories. Your observations should be translated first into graphic line movements. Then you should begin to try out these line movements with actual materials, utilizing the techniques mentioned above.

Example *a* (Fig. 92) is a zigzag line resulting from the vibration of the hand. The second example, *b,* is a wider wiggly line, in which the arm swings from the elbow. The third example, *c,* is the same, but the hand swings from the wrist. Even though the configuration is identical in these examples, each line possesses its own unique graphic quality.

How many ways can you find to express this and other ideas? Explore variations of every graphic idea you can discover. This should be a daily exercise.

One reason for working your line drawings over one another in the sketchbook is that it will strengthen your graphic sensitivity. You will find many beautiful relationships of line, value, contrast, and shape. The pressure of the pencil should be varied in order to achieve variations of line width and intensity. Many of these graphic line relationships will serve as a point of departure for jewelry ideas.

5–8 Differentiation between Organic and Technological Line Movements

Since the pencil line drawn freely with the hand is a record of the subtle organic tensions and movements of the hand and arm, it may be considered to be an *organic movement*. Its sensitivity and variation arise from the delicately balanced functioning of muscles and nerves, and thus it is completely different in visual quality from a line drawn along a straight edge (Fig. 91a).

This difference is important because the two lines evoke different feelings and esthetic responses, and art and design are concerned with expressing emotional qualities by means of graphic symbols. In general the geometric line has an impersonal quality that is powerful in direction but lacking in expressive sensitivity, and the response to a geometric line is more intellectual than emotional.

A cold and insensitive character is commonly ascribed to geometrical forms as compared with organic forms. For example, the square, with its geometric, hard lines and static line and space relationships, is probably one of the earliest of abstract shapes (Fig. 93a). The equilateral triangle (Fig. 93b), though different in shape, is similar in feeling quality.

The arc of constant radius (Fig. 93c) is another early technological abstract line movement, also strong, static, and insensitive. The characteristic line movements of modern technology retain the precision and strength of earlier geometric lines, but they are sometimes more subtle, as may be illustrated by the curve of simple harmonic motion, the sine curve (Fig. 93d).

For centuries designers have utilized the triangle in many ways. It represents graphically an understanding of plane geometric dimensions. The sum of the squares of the two sides was known to equal the square of the hypotenuse: $x^2 + y^2 = z^2$. These dimensions involve simple, direct, two-dimensional space relationships.

The development of technology led eventually to concepts enabling men to deal mathematically with space and time. The sine curve is a graphic symbol expressing such technology. The first step was the discovery of relations between the angles of a right-angled triangle and the sides (Fig. 94). This is trigonometry. When the hypotenuse is equal to 1, the size of the angle and the length of sides x and y vary directly. When the angle is 40°, x is always 0.164.

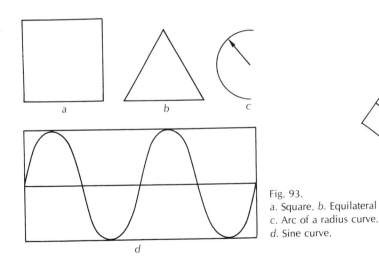

Fig. 93.
a. Square. b. Equilateral triangle.
c. Arc of a radius curve.
d. Sine curve.

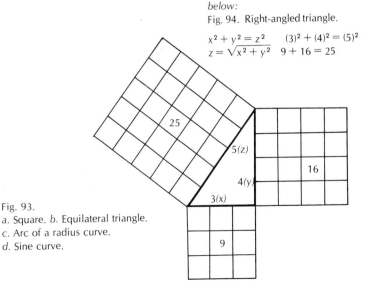

below:
Fig. 94. Right-angled triangle.

$$x^2 + y^2 = z^2 \qquad (3)^2 + (4)^2 = (5)^2$$
$$z = \sqrt{x^2 + y^2} \qquad 9 + 16 = 25$$

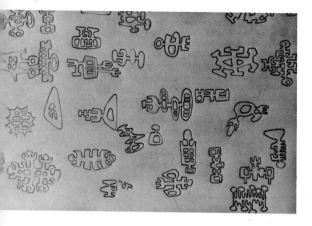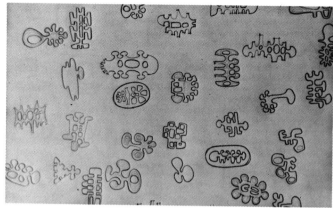

Fig. 95. Student sketches of linear organizations.

This number is called the sine of 40°. As the angle increases from 0° to 90°, the sine varies from 0 to 1. As the angle increases from 90° to 180°, the sine decreases from 1 to 0. If these sine values are plotted on a coordinate system in relation to the increasing size of the angle, we obtain a graphic line movement that reflects the changed relationships. The sine curve is typical of the technological graphic lines that symbolize wave motion.

Examine carefully the visual characteristic of this sine curve (Fig. 93d). The line is strong, yet more sensitive than elementary geometric lines. It stands somewhere midway in sensitivity between purely geometric and purely organic line movements. The line curvature is constantly varying, and the transition is smooth. The line is no longer static or two-dimensional but moves through time and space. It is dynamic and complex, though predictable.

An understanding of the characteristics of modern technological lines will come with a study of industrial forms and mathematical curves based upon trigonometry, analytical geometry, and calculus, for the forms of industry are based upon mathematical engineering calculations as well as upon the character of materials. Such graphic lines are widely used in modern art.

5–9 Linear Organizations The drawing of closed linear organizations is an essential exercise in the development of jewelry design ideas (Fig. 95). These drawings should be done freely and rapidly, without too much regard for control until you begin to understand the design relationships involved. Try to preserve a free and flowing quality of line, even as you attempt to guide the line in terms of the design principles discussed above (**5–6**). Some of the freely drawn sketch ideas illustrated (Fig. 96) will be analyzed in terms of design relationships. All these sketches are organic in line quality; some of them may be modified or conventionalized by applying contemporary technological line movements to them.

These sketches are not, of course, presented as dogmatic or absolute design solutions. The purpose of the illustrations is merely to indicate how the questions of space division and space relationships can be dealt with in order to increase unity and dramatic impact.

Example 1 Figure 97a is redrawn freely, rather than copied or traced from the first sketch (Fig. 96). There is nothing sacred about a free line drawing. The

Example 1  Example 2  Example 3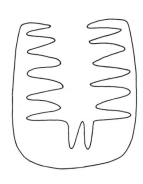

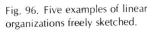
Fig. 96. Five examples of linear organizations freely sketched.

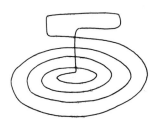

Example 4

Example 5

idea, or *configuration,* consists of the basic relationships that have been established. A final design organization will consist of the best possible placement of the elements that make up the configuration.

One of the first things to be observed about a linear organization is that, although it consists of pure line, it inevitably involves two-dimensional space or area. In this sketch there is both actual area and implied area. The implied area is indicated by shading and is just as important as the enclosed area. With the actual area, it constitutes the field **(5–23).**

Lines 1 and 2 are two verticals that work with maximum dramatic contrast against 7, which is the entire zigzag movement. Line 6 works with maximum contrast against 1; 4 and 5, though parallel, work against 1, 2, and 3. Line 3 also works against 7, restating the direction of 1 and 2. The general line relationships work fairly well. However, the area relationships are poor. The area between 1 and 2 is too small in relation to the area between 2 and 3. The area between 8 and 2 is too far from line 3, and in the area between 2 and 3 there is a feeling of emptiness. How can these weak relationships be strengthened?

One way of studying modifications of your designs is to lay tracing paper over the original sketch and on it make changes in the unsatisfactory relationships, while retracing those lines which are good. By using tracing paper over successive sketches you can gradually bring the design into complete control without losing anything good. However, this process will almost always give rise to a tightness of line unless you consciously strive for freedom.

In Figure 97*b* the large area between 2 and 3 has been reduced. However, the lower end is now too narrow in relation to the top. The organization is out of balance, because too much of the space in the implied area is excluded

Fig. 97. Modifications of linear organization of Example 1, Fig. 96.

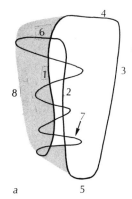

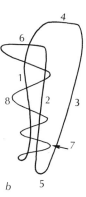

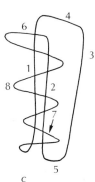

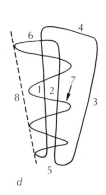

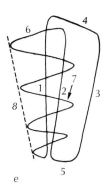

a   b   c   d   e

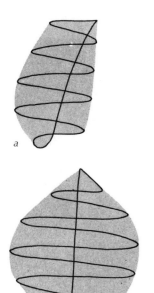

a

b

Fig. 98. Modifications of linear organization of Example 2, Fig. 96.

by the design. The loop of the zigzag line at 7 comes too close to 3 and pinches off the area between 2 and 3. At the bottom, 1 and 2 come too close together, thus pinching the space there too tightly.

In the next sketch (Fig. 97c) a correction of the mistakes noted has been attempted. Space at the bottom has been increased. The direction of 4 has been altered to avoid duplicating the direction of 6. Now, however, 4 is not long enough to provide a sufficient space at the top between 2 and 3. These lines are parallel. Finally, 7 is not smooth enough rhythmically.

In Figure 97d many of the errors have been corrected, but the loops of 7 do not come across 2 far enough to make significant areas. These loops must be lengthened.

Figure 97e is a final solution to the design problem. Compare it with the original sketch. It has been transformed into a technological line organization. The spaces between 8 and 1, between 1 and 2, and between 2 and 3 all vary interestingly in width. Maximum line opposition has been developed. The area distributions are well balanced and the design "works." Notice how the terminations of loops of the zigzag create implied space divisions as indicated by dotted lines.

Example 2   The idea in Example 2 of Figure 96 consists of a zigzag line set against a straight line. The relationships are so simple that successful design depends upon scale relationship and rhythmic area modulation. Observe the over-all shape created by the implied area of this sketch (Fig. 98a). The element of shape will be dealt with extensively later in this chapter, but it is clear in the illustration that this shape is irregular and does not flow smoothly in its outline. Also, the boundary lines at each side do not work against each other dramatically. The method of solving this problem is to vary the over-all shape and create a smooth transition of the frequency of the zigzag.

With the shape in Figure 98b the loops of the zigzag line flow smoothly in frequency and amplitude. Frequency refers to the number and therefore to the size of the waves. Amplitude refers to the length of the waves. This is a technological line movement.

Example 3   Example 3 of Figure 96 differs in an important way from preceding sketches. Here none of the lines cross or intersect. When you work with strips of silver as a linear material, you will find that design ideas without intersections work more successfully than designs with strips crossing one another. Wire linear designs should likewise be planned to avoid crossing movement unless they are conceived three-dimensionally. If wires are to be applied to flat plates, they probably should not cross over.

Figure 99a has two weaknesses: first, the emptiness at 1, and second, the uninteresting repetition of the line and area relationship at 2 and 3.

The first weakness can be solved as illustrated in Figure 99b or c. In either case more care must be given to the balancing of the areas, as illustrated in b. Shape 1 is rather stronger than 5. Both are weak with respect to 2 and 4.

Sketch 99d is an attempt to introduce a variation between 1 and 2, and 3 and 4, but the outside lines are parallel, and thus the outside shape is static.

In Figure 99e a certain control has been imposed on the design. The moving zigzag lines have been adjusted to create an interesting variation in the im-

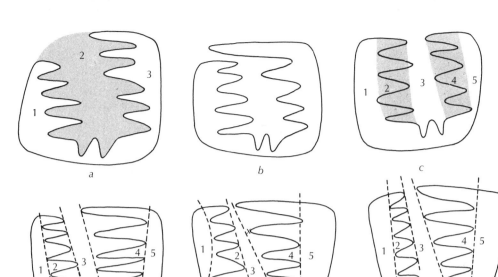

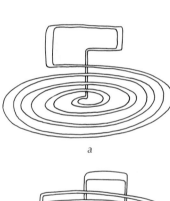

Fig. 99. Modifications of linear organization of Example 3, Fig. 96.

plied space divisions, as indicated by the dashed lines. But the areas at 1 and 2 are not in scale with areas 3 and 4. Also, one loop of the zigzag line does not meet the space-dividing line at x. The outside shape has been improved.

Figure 99f offers a final solution. The implied areas are in better relationship. There is a nice variation of widths, and the dashed lines work nicely against each other, creating additional opposition or visual movement. In this design, too, you can see the influence of modern technology upon its conventionalized movements.

Example 4 The line attribute of width can be introduced in Example 4 (Fig. 96). The design problems so far have been treated on a graphic basis, without reference to metal processes. However, in jewelry design it is impossible to think of the variation of linear width apart from the method of achieving it in metal. If you have experimented with the process of hammering wire and have developed some control in bending, shaping, and widening it, you will understand that when you increase the width of a wire line, the surrounding space must also be increased.

Figure 100a indicates a possible manner of utilizing width variation in a linear-wire design idea.

When you reach the stage of design at which it is necessary to reproduce the volume of a wire line, as in this sketch, do not spend too much time in rendering your graphic idea, because it must ultimately be worked out in terms of what tools and materials can do. Therefore, go right to work with silver wire. Never give a thought to the amount of material you are spoiling in unsuccessful experiments. You will acquire freedom and courage by working directly and experimentally. Eventually your design ideas should emerge in the form of expressive sketches which you will work out in detail in the material. You will find that many a design idea will improve as its construction in material suggests modifications or new possible relationships.

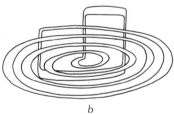

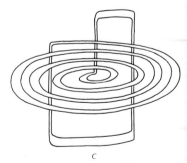

Fig. 100. Modifications of linear organization of Example 4, Fig. 96.

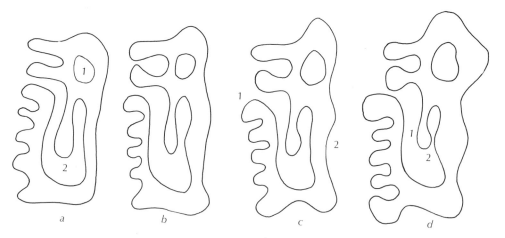

Fig. 101. Modifications of linear
organization of Example 5, Fig. 96.

If you were working directly in materials with this design idea, it might occur to you to fold the rectangle at the top of the spiral directly underneath, as
in Figure 100b. Such an idea might never occur while you were working
graphically, except as you recall other experiences of working with wire.

This suggestion raises the question of a technique for exploration of ideas.
The technique is always to try out every possible relationship that occurs to
you in terms of opposite possibilities. If the direction is up, try it down. If it is
moving left, try it moving right. If it is forward, try it backward.

If you were to try folding the rectangle directly underneath, you would find
that the scale of the rectangle needed changing in order to work well against
the spiral, as in Figure 100c. You would also find that this wire design idea
cannot be completely bent to shape and then hammered. It must be bent and
hammered step by step. Rather extensive experiment and planning is necessary to execute this type of design, but you have to start at the beginning,
anyway.

Example 5   This sketch (Fig. 96, Example 5) is similar to Example 3, in that
nowhere do the lines cross. Since all previous examples have been designed
as technological line organizations, this one will be preserved as an organic
idea. It might well be left as is, since the area distribution and the line relationships are fairly good. Some of the relationships can be strengthened, nevertheless.

The lines at 1 pinch too closely together and have the effect of weakening
this portion visually as well as physically. In a plate shape such as this, care
must be taken to make any extended part thick enough to hold its position
physically. The excluded area 2 is not particularly interesting in shape. The
lines at 3 also pinch the area at that point.

The sketches in Figure 101 show four successive steps in an attempt to develop the organic quality of the design and to strengthen some of the weaknesses noted.

The shape (Fig. 101a) is made more interesting. A perforation of the area
has been added at 1, to fill that empty space. More organic variation has been
introduced in Figure 101b, which is fairly well designed as is. In Figure 101c
the form is changed somewhat, to allow the area at 1 to extend outward beyond

the general outline of the original area. This adds visual interest, but the tapered shape at 2 is rather weak. Figure 101d is fairly satisfactory. It is a bit tight at 2 and somewhat wide at 1, but these failings can be easily corrected.

Area transitions between lines are crucial in organic shapes, which must be dealt with in a more intuitive manner than technological shapes. Design becomes more expressive and dramatic as it becomes more intuitive. When you begin to design in terms of line relationships, you must *feel* the emptiness, the tightness, the rightness. After you carry out your own graphic studies of linear organization, try out the most successful ones in strip and wire.

THE SEARCH FOR SHAPE

5-10 Definition of Shape   A shape is nothing more than an area with a boundary line around it. For convenience, shapes, like line, can be classified as technological or organic, though naturally all sorts of variations are possible. Figure 102 illustrates some distinct types.

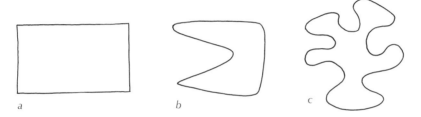

Fig. 102. Types of technological and organic shapes.

5-11 Graphic Study of Shape   For the purposes of design a shape does not exist until it has been drawn. Every shape you draw increases your stock of ideas for design use. Your knowledge of shapes should come from five sources: direct experience in working with tools and materials, study and observation of contemporary environment, knowledge of modern art, knowledge of technology, and graphic experiments in drawing. All these sources offer a rich supply of shapes with which to work. Do not expect to rely upon your casually acquired memory of shapes. You must make a special search for them.

One method of exploring shape is to begin with a simple one and develop it into a family of related shapes by applying one or more *deviations* (Fig. 103).

Fig. 103. Simple shape developed into a family of shapes by one or more deviations.

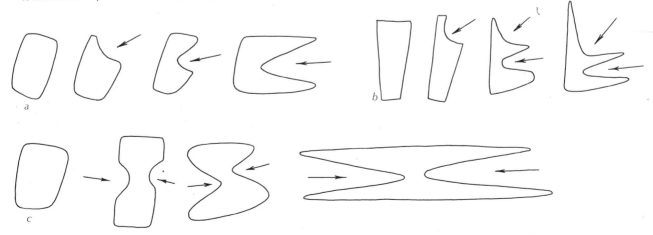

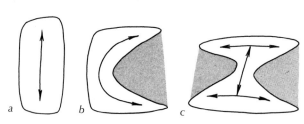

Fig. 104. Three attributes of shape: direction, or thrust;
area; and boundary line.

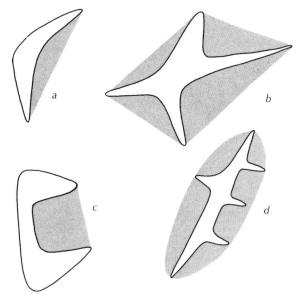

Fig. 105. The area and the field
of a shape do not always coincide.

5–12 Attributes of Shape

Three attributes of shape are *direction,* or *thrust, area,* and *boundary line.* Both the thrust and the disposition of the area are determined by the configuration of the boundary line (Fig. 104). The thrust of a shape may be considered to be a line that can be set in opposition to other lines or movements in the design organization.

The area of a shape and the field do not always exactly coincide, as the illustrations show (Fig. 105). The *excluded space* will give a clue to the family of shapes to which a given shape belongs. These families are, in general, the circle, the oval, the rectangle, the ellipse, and the triangle. This fact is not so important in itself, since we are not particularly interested in a system of classifying shapes, but the concept of the field is extremely useful in evaluating shapes and the space within which equilibrium must be achieved **(5–23, 5–24).**

5–13 Analysis of Shape

The usefulness of these ideas will become clear in the following analysis of several shapes (Fig. 106).

Is shape *a* effective? Notice first the relationship of lines. They work in opposition to each other, thus creating an interesting transition of area. The thrust of the shape is clean and definite and is itself a moving line that can be set in

Fig. 106. Examples of
effective shapes: modified triangle,
rectangles, and oval.

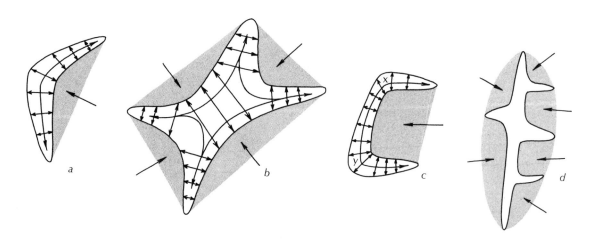

opposition to other lines which might be added. The area flows smoothly from its central disposition in each direction. The shape is slightly asymmetrical, and this in itself creates more visual interest. The shape is basically a triangle with a strong deviation that excludes considerable space at the right side. To organize this shape, the *implied area* will also require organization.

Shape *b* in Figure 106 is a modified rectangle, as the shading indicates. The rectangle is visually interesting because its lines work in opposition. Deviations occur on all four sides. The simple thrust of the rectangle (field) has been transformed into four strong thrusts. There is a clean transition of area moving from its central disposition along each thrust. The lines of the shape work in opposition. The spaces excluded from the shape are well distributed in scale (see below) and are effective shapes in themselves.

Shape *c* (Fig. 106) is also a modified rectangle, with the corners rounded or softened and with one strong deviation from the right. The excluded space of the field is greater than the area of the shape itself. In using this shape, it would be necessary to organize the excluded space, rather than the area of the shape. The area is distributed into two separate locations *x* and *y* but makes a flowing transition from one to the other and to the ends of the thrust. The thrust is clean and strong, and additional line movements could be set across the thrust effectively.

Figure 106*d* shows a modified oval with six deviations. Here also the excluded space is greater than the area of the shape. The figure is also similar to the preceding shape in that it could be dealt with almost as a wide line movement, and again the excluded space of the field, rather than the area of the shape, would require organizing. The area is distributed in smooth transitions.

5–14 Analysis of Organic Shapes   Organic shapes are more or less amorphous or undefined, but they are always characterized by a nongeometric flowing movement of line. Area transitions may or may not be smooth. Area disposition is usually centralized, and the thrust is usually absorbed in the central area disposition. For this reason additional line elements cannot ordinarily work across the thrust successfully but must work within the shape itself.

The shape in Figure 107*a* is a modified rectangle. The *boundary line variation* does not materially alter the character of the longitudinal thrust. Another way of saying this is that the size of the excluded spaces is not significant in relation to the main shape. Therefore the line variations do not accomplish a significant distribution of area. The line variation at 1 is so local that its effect in modifying the total shape is no more than the dashed line indicates. It is obvious that any deviation or change of direction of a boundary line, to be effective, should significantly alter the area disposition. If it fails to do so, it must be considered to be merely a local line variation. In this sense a line variation may be considered to be a *line texture.*

The space that perforates the shape in the lower center is ineffective because it does no more than repeat in line the movement of the boundary line, setting up static parallel line relationships. It is useful sometimes to lighten the broad area of a shape by perforating it and allowing space to flow through, but the perforated shape must work dramatically against the lines of the whole.

The shape in Figure 107*b* is basically a circle with one central deviation and a number of minor deviations that do little to modify the major thrust. They

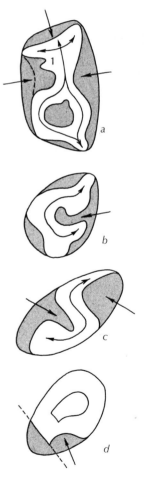

Fig. 107. Examples of shapes: *a,* organic; *b,* circular; *c,* modified oval; *d,* truncated circle.

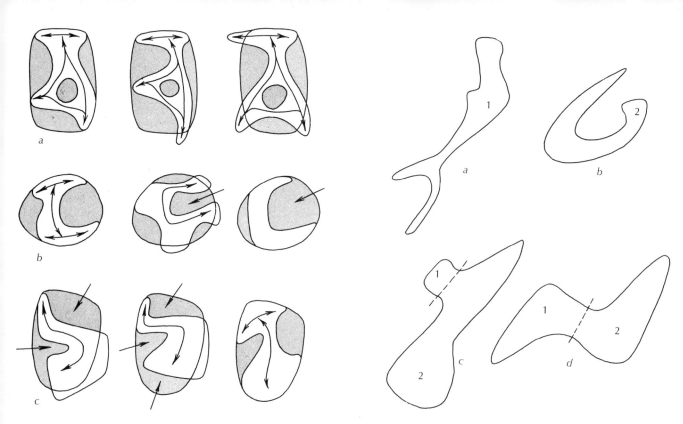

left: Fig. 108.
Modification of organic shapes
to technological shapes.
right: Fig. 109.
Examples of area distribution
in shape.

do, however, suggest something of the esthetic quality of an organic shape. The size of the central excluded space is small, and for this reason it would be difficult to work an additional line element across the thrust of the shape, except perhaps vertically across the movement of the deviation thrust (indicated by arrow).

Figure 107c is a modified oval shape with two strong deviations that change the area distribution significantly. The shape is weak because there is little line opposition or variation of the area distribution. The lines move around in almost parallel relationships, and the shape is almost sluglike. The excluded shapes are effective, and there is a strong organic quality in the whole.

The next shape (Fig. 107d) is basically a circle, but it has been truncated, as indicated by the dashed lines. Such truncated shapes should be avoided unless there is a definite design purpose. The central perforation is weak because the line repeats the movement of the main shape. Generally, organic shapes cannot be utilized for strip-plate construction (6–12) and must be treated as fused, cast, or carved forms (6–2, 6–19, 6–16), or they may be redesigned as technological shapes and then utilized in strip-plate construction. Figure 108 illustrates the modification of organic shapes to technological shapes.

5–15 Area Distribution in Shape   Area distribution involves scale, because it is related to the location and size of one part of the area of a shape as compared with the location and size of another part. Figure 109 shows some shapes that illustrate area distribution:

The area in a is concentrated somewhat at 1, and this concentration balances the extensions at the lower end.

In 109*b* the area is concentrated at 1 and slightly at 2.

In *c* the area is out of balance; 2 outweighs 1.

In Figure 109*d* areas 1 and 2 are in too static a balance.

The search for shape is never ended. You should carry out daily graphic studies in modifying and balancing the shapes you find.

5–16 Shapes in Material   The principles of shape design that have been discussed will be put into practice in the early stages of experimentation. Shapes can be sawed out of 18-gauge brass, bronze, or copper sheet. There is a wide range of design possibility in the shape—from classically simple to extremely complex. The pierced designs of Paul Mergen are good examples of the simple shape carried to a high point of development (Fig. 110).

Fig. 110. Paul S. Mergen. Pin. 1957. Pierced bronze with copper inlay.

SCALE

Scale has to do with the relation of one dimension to another. This simple relationship, however, has important physical, emotional, and esthetic implications. Man, as an organic form of limited size, is a criterion for all scale relationships. All his psychological responses to the world are conditioned not only by his scale relationship to the rest of the world but also by the breadth of his imagination and the intensity of his emotions. Esthetically, power is associated with size, and, according to the demands, sculpture ranges in physical and esthetic scale from the gigantic to the infinitely small and subtle. More technically, in design, scale involves the correct relationship of lines, areas, and volumes to one another and the relative dimensions of the elements utilized.

5–17 The Effect of Scale Variation   The effect of variations in scale relationship of width to length is clearly illustrated in Figure 111*a*. The terms used to describe these three shapes indicate how differently we respond to them visually and esthetically. The first shape is long and thin, or slender. The second is short and thick, even though it is of the same length as the first. The third shape is a wide rectangular area, seemingly without relationship to the first, except that we know it is the result of varying the width in proportion to a constant length.

Another way of illustrating the dramatic importance of scale is indicated in Figure 111*b*. The heavy line movement is set in relation to shapes of two different sizes. This movement works effectively in modifying the area disposition of the first shape but becomes a local line variation in the second (**5–13**).

Fig. 111*a*. Effects of scale variation on shape.

Fig. 111*b*. Line movement in relation to scale.

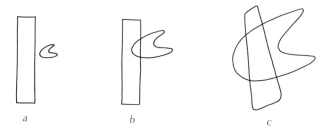

The scale relationship of the two shapes in Figure 112 is similar in effect. In the first sketch the size of the organic shape is insignificant in relation to the geometric shape. In the second sketch the organic shape is still overwhelmed by the geometric shape. In the third an appropriate scale relationship is established.

The variation of shape arising out of scale variation (Fig. 113) may appear to be an obvious development, but it is important to the understanding of proportion. This variation of shape has sometimes been called distortion, but in contemporary design there is no such thing as distortion—all is variation.

5–18 Scale in Jewelry Jewelry falls within the sculptural range of the small and subtle, and personality exercises an individual choice in scale, both physical and esthetic. Scale in jewelry is also determined by the functional requirements of neck, arm, finger, and so forth. Appropriate scale relationship of the shapes chosen for jewelry is extremely important.

TEXTURE

Texture is one of the fundamental elements of design. It is the visual result of massing detailed elements closely enough together over an area to create an appearance that differs from the appearance of a single visual element. Texture is equivalent to tone or color value and may be used in the same way to

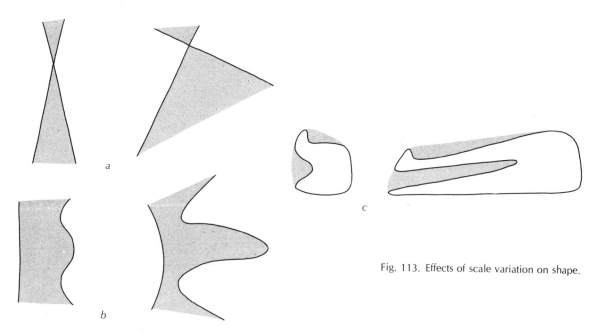

Fig. 113. Effects of scale variation on shape.

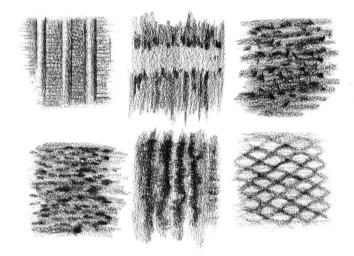

Fig. 114. Textures from rubbings.

differentiate areas by contrast and to achieve an emphasis of space in the third dimension. Natural textures proliferate from the surface appearance of the structure of materials. These textures have always been recognized and used in design, but they are of especial importance in contemporary jewelry.

5–19 Graphic Studies of Texture   One direct method of understanding the infinite variety and subtlety of texture is to make pencil rubbings of materials. This is done by taking a sheet of thin paper, laying it against the material, and then rubbing a light or dark value on the paper with the side of a pencil or a conté crayon. The variety of graphic textures you acquire will depend upon your initiative in finding materials of varying surfaces. The rubbings in Figure 114 come from materials around the workshop.

Explore with a pencil the textural variations you can devise (Fig. 115) for later reproduction with chasing tools (Fig. 291).

Fig. 115. Pencil textures for chasing.

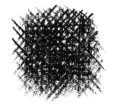 

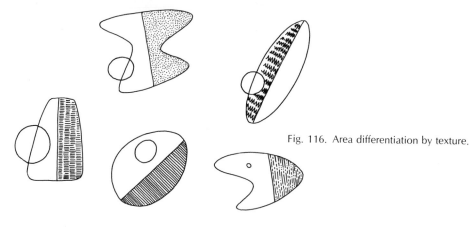

Fig. 116. Area differentiation by texture.

Fig. 117. John Paul Miller.
Fiddler Crab, pendant brooch. 1959.
Gold and silver with texture
variation in granulation.

5–20 Differentiation of Areas with Texture   In designing two-dimensional jewelry, the jeweler may differentiate areas by texture, as in Figure 116. Such differentiation is also useful in any jewelry design for creating a changing visual pattern across an area. It should be used, however, as a means of achieving contrast with highly polished areas, as, for example, John Paul Miller utilizes it with his granulations (Fig. 117).

ORGANIZATION OF VISUAL ELEMENTS FOR JEWELRY

Design problems become more difficult to solve as the number of visual elements is increased. This is true because the number of relationships increases and because each additional element tends to limit the design possibilities of the form. Though esthetic form becomes more complex and visually interesting as the number of elements is increased, the change in expressive quality is one of kind, not of degree. That is, extremely simple elements may be organized to evoke a powerful esthetic feeling. A single shape in metal may become powerful because of its internal or external relationships.

5–21 External Design Relationships of Jewelry   Jewelry that is worn always becomes an integral part of the visual appearance of the wearer; it is seen as a part of the person and as a dimension of the personality. As a part of the person, jewelry may become a focal point, a visual accent in the design of personal appearance or in the organization of costume, a visual movement at the neck or on the ear, an *element* of design emphasis and contrast. The definition of jewelry as purely "decorative" fails to clarify this specific demand to serve as a design element for the whole person. The simplest shapes or forms may fulfill this demand. Color and quality in jewelry materials are of primary importance, for they create harmony or contrast with the visual appearance and the personality of the wearer.

5–22 Internal Design Relationships of Jewelry   At a closer level of visual inspection the internal design relationships of jewelry become important. The spatial field becomes limited to that immediately in and around the jewelry, and other relationships are temporarily excluded from observation.

Simple forms of jewelry now serve primarily to dramatize the color and textural qualities of the jewelry materials and to invite a close examination and appreciation of these esthetic qualities. The form becomes significant in relation to the personality and to the cultural values in the process of forming. Upon the internal design relationships depends the quality of expressive form (Chap. 6), which relates the wearer's inner values to the external scene.

5–23 Design within a Field   Visual elements activate a field of space. When we use a shape as the starting point in design, the shape automatically indicates the field. The significance of the field is that once it has been established by one or more visual elements, an *equilibrium* of those elements must be achieved within the field.

5–24 Equilibrium   Equilibrium, or balance, refers to the relationship of visual elements in terms of *visual weight*, the directions, or thrusts, and the position of the elements in the field. Visual weight is determined by the size of a visual area or element and by its value in terms of color and texture. *Area transition* refers to the disposition of the area of a shape in terms of visual weight. It can be seen, therefore, that equilibrium can be achieved by redistributing the area of any given shape.

   Most of our experience with the idea of "balance" refers to our physical relationship to the force of gravity and hence to the center of the earth as an external point of reference. In design, however, equilibrium refers to the internal relationships of a designed form. The traditional term "occult balance" is an old-fashioned reference to asymmetrical equilibrium. Symmetrical equilibrium is a result of equal visual weights or movements placed or operating at equal distances or with equal force across a center of equilibrium. Asymmetrical equilibrium is the result of unequal visual weights or movements placed or operating at proportionately unequal distances across the center of equilibrium in the field. Certain typical cases may prove a basis for understanding the implications of equilibrium in jewelry design.

   The implied area of a line (Fig. 118a) is the approximate field of that line (5–6). The center of equilibrium is the approximate center of this field.

   An additional shape can organize the empty space of the field by establishing equal weight or movement across the center of equilibrium (Fig. 118b). The added shape works against the line movement in this case.

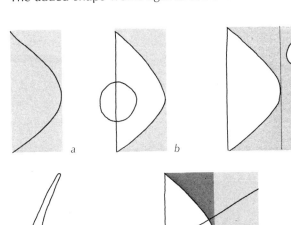

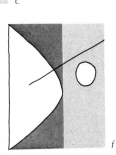

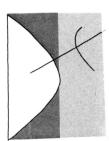

Fig. 118. Equilibrium and the field.
a. Implied area of a line as the field.
b. Achieving equilibrium by adding a shape.
c. Enlargement of the field.
d. Balancing shapes across the center of equilibrium.
e. A line generates a field.
f. Achieving equilibrium by adding a shape.
g. Achieving equilibrium by adding a line.

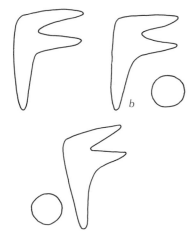

above: Fig. 119. Balancing
a linear organization by adding
a shape or by modifying
the shape to increase visual weight.

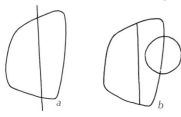

above: Fig. 120. Focal point
used to organize empty space.

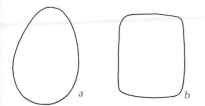

above: Fig. 121. Simple shapes.
below: Fig. 122. Shape with
active configuration.

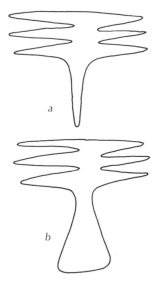

The field is enlarged by placement of another shape outside the existing field (Fig. 118c). The two elements establish equilibrium across the center of the field.

A small shape is set at a proportionately farther distance from the center and establishes equilibrium with the large shape in the field (Fig 118d). This is an example of asymmetrical equilibrium. A stone of color or a metal shape with color and texture may be much heavier, visually, than this empty space shape.

In Figure 118e the lines generate a field indicated as a rectangle. The lines work strongly in opposition, but there is not sufficient visual weight on the right side. Equilibrium can be achieved by adding another shape. A linear organization or shape like this one may be placed in equilibrium in two ways:

Placing an additional shape in the empty space balances the visual elements across the center of equilibrium (Fig. 118f).

Another curved line may be placed in opposition to the first curved line, thus organizing the field (Fig. 118g).

A linear organization or shape like the one in Figure 119a may be brought into equilibrium in two ways:

Placing an additional shape in a position that extends the field may also achieve equilibrium across a new center (Figs. 119b and c).

The shape which incompletely establishes equilibrium in a field may be modified to increase its visual weight at the crucial location.

5–25   The Focal Point in Jewelry   In design a center of interest, or *focal point*, is often necessary, as may be demonstrated on the basis of visual observation. Which of the two shapes in Figure 120 seems to be more nearly complete?

The *focal point* serves as a point of entry into a design. It also serves as a point of rest or of final attention for the eye. An empty or unorganized area of a design may be activated by the correct placement of a focal point. The focal point provides the jeweler with an opportunity to achieve maximum contrast of materials and color through the use of stones, bone, wood, or special colored or textured metal shapes or forms. The focal point may be used at the beginning and/or end of a line movement. Try adding a circular shape as focal point to some of your shapes. Translate the best ones into material.

5–26   The Development of Complex Jewelry Forms   Since the complexity and, therefore, the visual interest generally increases with the number of visual elements, the process of design may be illustrated by beginning with a single element and successively adding more elements. In actual practice such a procedure might or might not be followed, since many design ideas occur in a more or less complete state. Nevertheless, it will serve as the method of revealing the process of design.

The first step beyond the use of a single, simple shape (Fig. 121) is the use of a shape with more active configuration (Fig. 122a). In this case, added visual interest is achieved by making the boundary line work in dramatic opposition to itself (Fig. 122b). The resulting form, consisting of surface aspects of the area as well as shape configuration, may evoke significant emotional and symbolic associations.

a

b

a

b

The addition of a focal point, as you have seen, renders a shape more complete as well as providing contrast of materials.

The addition of a line movement to a shape begins to create further complexity, because additional shapes arise from the space divisions created by the line or lines (Fig. 123). If we assume that a single shape is a single visual element, then a single line establishes three visual elements: three shapes plus the line itself.

If the two adjacent areas are differentiated by means of texture, another visual element is added (Fig. 124). If a focal point is added, a total of five visual elements will be at work creating seven relationships. This rather mechanical analysis is not particularly desirable from the standpoint of design, but it is given to suggest the complexity arising from the addition of elements (Fig. 125). Each increase in the number of design elements tends to limit the further possibilities of relationship, so that there is a point of diminishing returns to complexity.

5–27 Shapes in Relationship A further step in the development of complexity is the use of two or more shapes set up in space in relationship to one another. The key to successful solutions to this type of problem lies in the concepts of *field* and *excluded space*. For example, the shape in Figure 124 would be difficult to use with any additional shape, since the field is already completely activated by the shape and its thrusts. Additional elements could only be added within the shape. The thrusts of the shape are in equilibrium and there is no resultant thrust against which an additional shape or movement might work.

left: Fig. 123.
Addition of line movement
to shape increases complexity.
right: Fig. 124. Adjacent areas
differentiated by texture.

Fig. 125. Shapes drawn by students.

a

b

c

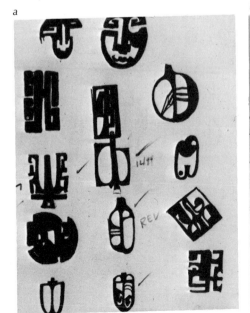

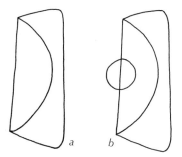

Fig. 126. Organization of the excluded space of a field.

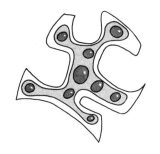

Fig. 127. Complex shape does not accommodate space-dividing line.

On the other hand, in the shape in Figure 126 the excluded space of the field is not organized and there is opportunity for the organization of additional shapes.

5-28 The Integration of Shapes The achievement of greater complexity demands an integration of two or more shapes in a single design organization. There are no rules for successful solutions, beyond the proper regard for the achievement of equilibrium within the field that is established and the principles of contrast and opposition of line movements and of textured areas or color areas.

A shape that is complex in its boundary-line configuration (Fig. 127) will not lend itself readily to the addition of space-dividing lines. The area of the shape is already organized sufficiently, and additional elements can be added only to the inner shape.

Space-dividing lines, texture differentiation, and a focal point can be added only to a simple shape (Fig. 128). Otherwise, the problem becomes one of establishing a composition within a defined field (Fig. 129).

5-29 Summary This chapter has provided a point of view toward jewelry and an analysis of the graphic problems of designing jewelry forms. Ultimately the jeweler will work directly in materials with hardly more than a note or two to guide his design concept. Even so, he will be working mentally with the visual elements and the relationships that have been discussed and illustrated.

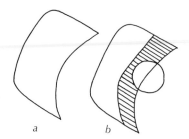

above: Fig. 128. Simple shape can accommodate dividing line, texture, and focal point.
right: Fig. 129. Examples of shape composition within a simple field shape.

6

ADVANCED DESIGN
The Means of Achieving
Expressive Form

As the jeweler acquires experience, he gradually comes to realize that the esthetic quality of a piece of jewelry is determined completely by the forms of the raw material he uses, the tools he employs, and his own interaction with them. These factors together constitute the means by which the jeweler achieves expressive form.

The characteristics of the material determine the entire range of procedures by which it can be worked. Inversely, the processes are an operational description of the material.

Metal, for instance, can be softened by heat, melted to a liquid state, hardened by compression, or bent by various operations. It can be ionized in certain solutions and deposited electrolytically. It can be powdered and pressed into molds or sprayed in molten form. The tool, the metal, and the craftsman complement one another. Metal must be struck by a hammer or melted by fire. The sole function of the hammer is to strike. And it is the result of the striking or melting—the natural effect of the tool upon the material—that is the concern of the designer. It is by means of the effects, the tool marks, that the artist achieves expressive form in the metal. Varying the effects has the power of varying the form.

Expressive form is, on the one hand, the product of the particular effects of specific tools and materials; this is its *objective* aspect. On the other hand, expressive form is the manifestation of an inner pattern of human responses; this is its *subjective* aspect. The inner patterns of human response arise in relation to the cultural milieu of a given historical epoch. When that milieu changes, as it changed in the 19th century and is changing today, new inner patterns come into being. Man preserves his unity with the external world by harmonizing the subjective and objective aspects of form. It is the task of the artist to create, through works of art, those aspects of expressive form which are truly in harmony with the patterns of human response produced by the changing conditions of existence.

Many people are unaware of how out of phase man is with his contemporary computer culture.

We are no longer confronted by the machine-age milieu—that structure of reality which Cézanne and Picasso and Duchamp labored to express. It ended in the forties, with World War II, even before the masses of the people had assimilated the subjective forms characteristic of it. Now we have moved into an electronic age, in which speed is instantaneous. Some idea of the impact of this new age can be derived from the tremendous energy of art tendencies in the 1960s—"op," "pop," "kinetic," and "minimal."

Since the turn of the century the artist, the philosopher, and the scientist have been restructuring reality. Einstein's theory of relativity and Picasso's cubism make analogous statements of the same phase of reality as applied to their respective fields. This phase is relativity—every point of view being regarded as relative to a given context. Levin's field theory can be seen to express the same reality concept. There are no more absolutes, apparently.

The abandonment of Newton's world-centered physics corresponds to the rejection on the part of artists of the principles of Renaissance perspective as a theory of indeterminacy reintroduces to the contemporary world the view that some important aspects of reality cannot be grasped by reasoning. Wittgenstein's rejection of traditional philosophical disciplines reflects a new structural vision of a universe too complex to be summed up in neat conceptual patterns of thought. The artist's departure from representation corresponds to the collapse of Cartesian dualism, which first divided the world into two separate realities, one of which many scientists assume to be nonexistant.

The newer views of reality require new images to express them visually, and it is the artist's role to provide images appropriate to the present-day milieu—expressive forms by which modern man can relate himself through intuitive and sensory means to his environment.

Traditional categories of artistic expression such as painting and sculpture are merging and being transformed into environmental settings and situations (Figs. 130–132). This transformation may be a sign that art is moving into the

Fig. 130. David Novros. *6:32*. 1966 Vinyl lacquer on canvas, 7' ¼" × 14' 6½". Collection Charles Cowler

Fig. 131. Ronald Bladen.
Untitled sculpture. 1963–1965.
Painted wood and metal.
9′ × 17′ 2″ × 10′.
Fischbach Gallery, New York.

arena of everyday life. Indeed, if we look around, we see that art is everywhere and in everything. Contemporary jewelry, as one of the most personal types of expressive form, is playing a useful part in helping people to harmonize the objective and subjective aspects of contemporary existence.

Thus it is valuable for each artist to become aware of his own responses to the present milieu by exploring every means of achieving forms corresponding to those responses. Eventually each artist will find that a particular means has an unusually strong esthetic appeal for him, which will in time establish his own unique style. Therefore the rest of this chapter consists of a careful examination of the means of achieving expressive form.

Fig. 132. Edward Kienholz. *The Beanery.* c. 1966. Mixed media,
7 × 6 × 22′. Los Angeles County Museum of Art (lent by the Kleiner Foundation).

Advanced Design: The Means of Achieving Expressive Form   81

left: Fig. 133. Christian Schmidt. Pendant. 1967. Sterling silver.
Example of fused form.
right: Fig. 134. Mary Kretsinger. Brooch. 1965. Silver with brass.
Example of fused form.

6–1 Classification of Means   In the author's experience these means may
be classified in 11 categories, though others may analyze them somewhat
differently. These 11 categories are discussed below in the following order:
fused forms, electroforms, linear forms, plate-shape forms, strip-plate forms,
constructed forms, carved forms, forged forms, repoussé forms, cast forms, and
enamel forms.

6–2 Fused Forms · *Esthetics*   Fused forms belong to the nonrational mode
of expression (see Chap. 4) and emerge as a natural result of heating metal with
a hot flame **(8–5)** until it melts. When the flame is applied to such metals as
silver, brass, copper, and gold, the surface usually bubbles, oxidizes, and becomes darkly textured in patterns that are characteristic but variable from one
time to another **(8–9, 8–10)**. The molecular forces within the molten metal
pull it together into round forms, which are dependent partly upon the original
shape and partly upon the accidental operation of the natural forces involved. It
is from this operation that the unique esthetic quality of the fused form emerges
(Figs. 133, 134).

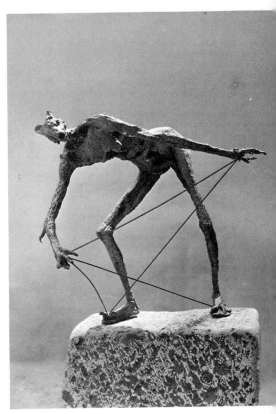

left: Fig. 135. Hieronymus Bosch. *The Garden of Delights,* central panel. c. 1505–1510. Oil on Canvas, 86⅝ × 38¼". Prado, Madrid.
right: Fig. 136. Germaine Richier. *The Devil with Claws (Le Griffu).* 1952. Bronze, ht. 34½". Museum of Modern Art, New York (Wildenstein Foundation Fund).

Automatism in painting is an attempt to achieve the same kind of non-rational or unconscious result. Fused forms possess characteristics similar to those of organic forms of life produced by the cumulative impact of natural forces. The paintings of Hieronymus Bosch have a similar quality, as do the sculptures of Germaine Richier (Figs. 135, 136).

Surrealism seems to approach the mystical depths of the very beginnings of mankind, so distant from the surface level of conscious rationality as to create a strong sense of emotional estrangement and awe and at the same time to call up forgotten primordial memories. The appearance of surrealism may have been a call to modern, overintellectualizing man to return to his emotional roots. Indeed, a major tendency to reject the intellect in contemporary art is not an isolated manifestation. Modern writers such as Robbe-Grillet, following Proust and Joyce, have rejected the logically tight chronological plot line of the 19th-century novel in their attempt to present life in the chaotic fullness of the immediate moment. Nineteenth-century scientific philosophies, such as dogmatic realism and positivism, have been seriously challenged by the creative thinking of Heisenberg and Schrödinger. Playwrights such as

Ionesco and Beckett are suspicious of literary elaboration of language, believing that it serves the intellectual function too exclusively to express the living experience.

All these attitudes arise from the intuitive realization that earlier intellectual models of life have in various ways betrayed life itself in favor of an abstracted system. The "happening" would seem to be rooted in this kind of realization. If so, the position of its exponents is far from being nihilistic; it is, rather, an expression of high human values. What appears as nihilism is a judgment of the past that could be adequately expressed only by an extreme inversion of values (the nonesthetic held up as esthetic). Like a teeter-totter, the value of one side goes up only as the value of the opposing side goes down. To celebrate the spontaneous spirit—the nonrational aspect of life—is to attack the philosophies of the amoral and rationalizing intellect. To celebrate the ugly as a true part of all existence is to attack the decadent theory of beauty that is carefully blind to ugliness, suffering, and destruction of war.

Such compensatory reaction corresponds to the ancient Greek concept of *enantiodromia:* that exaggeration automatically transforms its subject into its opposite. Marshall McLuhan discusses the principle of *enantiodromia* with reference to points of departure, or "break-boundaries," which mark such reversals as the shift from mechanical to organic concerns in modern society.

This kind of shift is pertinent to the use of fused forms, for they, too, are organic in quality. The contemporary artist, whose temperament responds to the broad range of esthetic values in fused forms, may be involved in the vast compensatory spiritual reaction against the emphasis upon machines and upon abstract mathematical and physical theory at the expense of humanity. A great

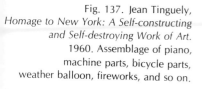

Fig. 137. Jean Tinguely, *Homage to New York: A Self-constructing and Self-destroying Work of Art.* 1960. Assemblage of piano, machine parts, bicycle parts, weather balloon, fireworks, and so on.

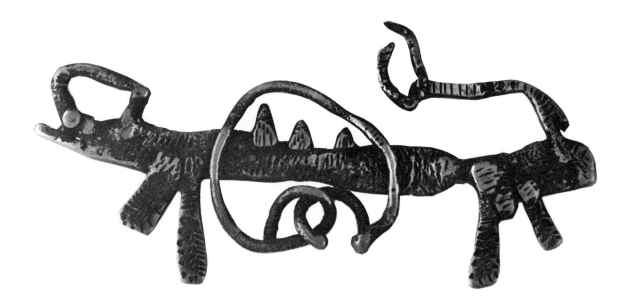

deal of the art produced since World War II seems to affirm those negative values which challenge the esthetic philosophy of the past (Fig. 137).

The contemporary jeweler is involved in a common artistic effort to create an appropriate setting in harmony with the dynamic forces of modern society. Although such forces may appear to the objective mind in the guise of technology, they can also be seen as spiritual forces standing above technology.

6–3 Fused-form Design and Construction   The design of fused forms may follow the usual procedure of either direct experiment or preliminary sketches. The beginning student should start with direct experiment in order to acquire a basis for thinking about design in terms of the process and his experience with it. It is desirable to have a good supply of silver scraps on hand, so that new silver need not be wasted (Fig. 138).

The design of fused forms begins with a study of what happens to silver when it is heated by the torch (**8–5**). Fused metal produces organic and accidental qualities, as well as rich textural effects. An interesting variety of effects is easy to get, but a specific result is hard to control. At a certain temperature point the fused metal will roll up into a molten ball. Experiment is needed partly to establish judgment about this limitation. Practice in fusing develops an understanding of the capacities and limits of molten metal.

Pieces of scrap silver of various sizes and gauges can be assembled into simple compositions and fused together. Combinations of means such as fusing with forging offer infinite design possibilities. The design of fused forms is generally freer and more subject to chance effects than that of other forms. Emotional fullness and visual richness may replace intellectual precision. This does not mean, however, that design falls by the wayside; it does mean that design becomes a product less of the mind than of the spirit.

On the other hand, powerful forms can be developed through fusing techniques that retain a degree of free and unexpected quality. For best results in fusing, the metal should be pickled once or twice and handled with copper tongs so that oil or grease will not interfere with the free flowing of the metal.

Fig. 138. Felt Lair. Brooch. 1952. Sterling silver scrap pieces organized and fused.

Flux need not be used with this process if the metal is clean, unless it is desired to interfere with the natural movement of molten metal. Yellow ocher, and possibly other materials, may be applied if the designer wishes to interfere with the free flow of metal. Pieces of sheet, wire, or tubing may be wired together in complex relationships and fused together, after which shaping by filing or grinding can be carried out.

6–4 Electroforms Electroforming (**9–19**) is a mode of electrodeposition. No matter what the material, the process creates an esthetic quality that is unique (Figs. 139, 140). It requires the equipment necessary for electroplating (**15–13**). Electroforms are similar to cast forms in that they are dependent upon the organization of a pattern to be duplicated in the metal. The pattern may be made of any kind of material capable of accepting a coating of metallic lacquer and of being removed after electrodeposition. Such removal can be made by firing in a kiln, by melting in hot water, or by dissolving in an appropriate solvent, such as lacquer thinner. The pattern may be made of wax, expanded polystyrene, wood, certain plastics, and possibly other materials, subject to experimentation.

The esthetic qualities of electroforms depend somewhat upon the matrix material used. Expended polystyrene gives a characteristic rough or rippled surface that can be duplicated exactly, regardless of the particular form of the pattern.

One of the important characteristics of electroforming is that the forms can be made hollow directly, thus opening up many possibilities not available in other techniques. For example, a wax pattern can be melted out of the electroform very readily, leaving the form hollow, thin, and relatively light in weight.

Exploratory work does not, naturally, follow procedures readily adaptable to other techniques. An attractive possibility of electroforming is that stones and other materials may be directly embedded in the matrix (pattern), so that

left: Fig. 139. Stanley Lechtzin. Electroformed brooch. 1967. Silver-gilt with amethyst.
right: Fig. 140. Stanley Lechtzin. Electroformed brooch. 1967. Silver-gilt with agate.

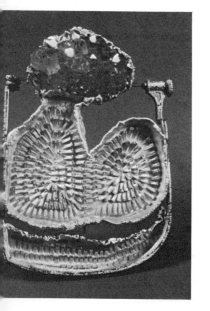

electrodeposition produces an automatic "setting" which just fits the stone. Such "settings" must be designed in a manner appropriate to the technique, of course. Porous materials to be set in metal by this method should be sealed to prevent the plating solution from soaking into them. If hollow forms are designed with the intention of removing the pattern material after electrodeposition, some hole must be provided in an inconspicuous place for the fumes, ashes, or the actual matrix to escape.

Hollow forms may be sawed apart, if necessary, for the installation of concealed hinges or fasteners. Furthermore, there is no limit to the possibilities of executing very light, hollow forms and delicate traceries achieved by painting interrelated lines of metallic lacquer over the surface of a wax volume.

June Schwarcz of Sausalito, California, was an early experimentor in this period in the United States, with electroforming bowls for enameling, but Stanley Lechtzin, of Philadelphia, probably has carried out the most extensive and successful explorations of the techniques for electroformed jewelry.

This technique requires elaborate facilities and considerable technical knowledge of electrolysis. Probably it should be attempted only by the mature craftsman whose disciplines have been tried in a number of techniques.

Like casting, the electroform belongs to the nonrational mode of expression, and although it may move in almost any direction, the forms are likely to be organic, rather than geometric, and to have a greater affinity with natural or found gem forms than with traditionally finished mechanical or geometrical faceted gems.

6–5 Linear Forms *Esthetics* Metal in wire form evokes unique and consistent esthetic responses in the designer and in the observer (Figs. 141, 142). Linear organizations are a reflection of basic capacities and limitations of the human mind. The exact esthetic effects of line may be described in terms of clarity, sharpness, and precision. There is an old saying that there are no lines

left: Fig. 141. Philip Morton. Pin. 1946. Sterling silver wire. Example of linear organization. *right:* Fig. 142. Haakon R. Bakken. Ring. 1966. 14-kt. yellow gold wire with pearls.

Fig. 143. Pablo Picasso.
Girl with Necklace. 1944.
Pen drawing. Private Collection.

in nature. If this is true, line is an intellectual construct, an abstraction by means of which man clarifies borders or directions in his perception of reality.

The emotions generated by line seem to be related to the delicacy and sensitivity of a pure relationship between spaces and borders or edges. Abstractions from life, rather than life itself, seem to be portrayed by line. The linear work of Pablo Picasso is a good example of this quality (Fig. 143).

Delicacy, not depth, is achieved by line. Bear in mind that line, not lines, is being discussed. When lines are massed, we begin to get value, which is quite a different visual element.

It is significant that contemporary jewelers have returned to an honest reappraisal of the expressive qualities inherent in such a basic material form as wire. Calder, of course, was the first American artist to make this investigation of linear wire forms. By rejecting earlier European jewelry traditions, the contemporary jeweler can escape the limitations of conventional attitudes of design. This escape allows him to explore for himself all those forms, both simple and complex, which speak of the unity of man with his tools and materials—with his world. In just this spontaneous approach lies the true excitement of discovery.

6–6 Linear Wire Forms *Design and Construction*   For serious research of linear wire forms, the student will need coils of 24-, 20-, 18-, 16-, 14-, and 12-gauge sterling wire. It is true that 12-gauge wire can be drawn down to the finer gauges, if a drawplate and drawtongs are at hand **(9–2).** However, 24-gauge is somewhat difficult for the beginner to draw out. The drawplate for square, triangular, and half-round wire should be available, and each of these forms of wire explored. Such exploration will come under the following headings, and these sections can be reviewed: fusing (pp. 131–139), planishing **(12–5),** bending **(9–6),** twisting **(9–21),** forging **(12–4),** stamping **(12–11).**

Exploration of wire must start with improvisation. Begin with any tool. Take a pair of roundnose pliers, for example, and try out the patterns of bending that can be achieved. Remember that it is the way you use your tools that leads to variations of form. The exploratory attitude can be described simply: In my right hand a hammer, in my left hand a piece of wire, before me an anvil, in my mind no preconceived image! What will happen?

In every case the creative task is to search out your own responses to this type of situation. Only when you repeatedly place yourself in this situation do you give intuition an opportunity to bring forth the possibilities inherent in it. This attitude will not come easily to the student who believes that he must always know in advance what he is doing before he can do it. In general, however, the artist has often experienced the presence of ideas and images clearly independent of conscious recollection or volition. In describing how he composed music, Stravinsky once spoke of being the agent of an inner entity who really carried out the entire process of composition. The artist senses the operation of his unconscious psyche when he is creating, and he seldom has precise ideas of what he is doing until after the work is finished. The student's slogan might well be: Act in haste and reflect at leisure.

The beginning of experimentation requires a special attitude toward materials and tools. They should be tried out in every way and position—backward, forward, upside down, down-side up, inside out, outside in. In no case

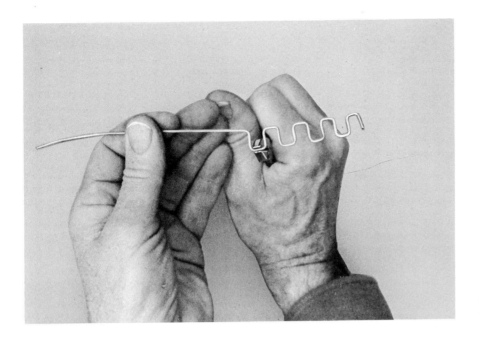

Fig. 144. Bending up zigzag
wire for bracelet.

can the student be stingy with materials. A reluctance to use up materials in experimenting because of cost will lead to an immediate tightness. This should be avoided, since the beginner is usually already inclined to be tight in his approach to design.

Often students expect each trial to lead to a finished work. Actually, each trial must be seen as a preliminary step to the final form. Several trials may be necessary in order to arrive at correct relationships or dimensions. For example, if short lengths of 20-gauge wire are being prepared to join links of a bracelet, the space between the links must be neither too small nor too great. How long should the wire be cut? On the first trial two lengths are cut. One length is tried. If it is found to be too long, the second is trimmed and then used to measure out lengths for the entire bracelet. This dimension should then be noted down in the student's *Production Record* (**19–4**), as a reference for the next time. If the length turns out to be just right, the second length is ready to be used as a pattern for the rest of the units.

Fig. 145. Philip Morton.
Bracelet. 1956.
Sterling silver wire.

The seeking artist must spend his time, his energy, and his materials lavishly in order to advance his own creative development. There is no other way. Carrying out direct experiments in material is the best way of discovering what is possible. Designs should emerge from the process.

A line motif made with two pairs of pliers of different jaw widths is shown in Figure 144. One set of bends was made around the jaws of the wider pair of pliers, and the other set around the jaws of the narrower pair of pliers. The problem of this type of line movement is to keep the zigzag elements uniform, and the use of pliers to establish the intervals between the bends reveals an important principle of designing in terms of the tools. After the necessary length of this zigzag line was bent up, the horizontal flanges were hammered flat. This created a variation of line width. This particular line motif lent itself to use both as bracelet (Fig. 145) and as necklace.

Advanced Design: The Means of Achieving Expressive Form   89

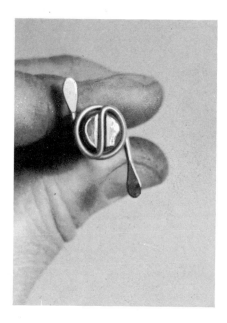 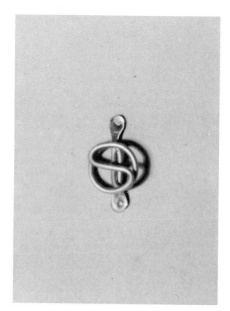

left: Fig. 146. One link of round-link bracelet being bent on slotted drill-rod jig. *right:* Fig. 147. Completed round link.

Another bracelet emerged from the foregoing experiment. It was a simple step to see that, by sawing a slot in the end of a piece of ½-in. carbon-steel drill rod with a hack saw, one could make a uniform duplication of units for a bracelet (Fig. 146). All that was necessary was to determine the proper length of the wire and to hammer the ends flat so that holes could be drilled. Then, with the drill rod in a vise, the wire was centered in the slot and the ends twisted around the rod. The ends of the wire were then bent under the ring and evened up (Fig. 147). These links were fastened together with 20-gauge wire, the ends of which were fused into beads.

After this bracelet was made, another design was tried, using square drill rod with the slot sawed diagonally. It worked equally well, while giving a somewhat different form (Fig. 148).

The discovery of the possibility of hammering facets on a length of wire emerges rather quickly from a little experimentation with the hammer. This motif can be applied to a variety of designs. A spiral bracelet and a loop neck-lace are obvious but effective designs. The ends of the bracelet can be finished off by fusing.

Nothing seems simpler than hammering the end of a wire flat. Yet the result may all depend upon how the hammered section relates to other relationships. Bracelets of varying design may be made by taking short lengths of wire and hammering each end flat, drilling holes, and joining the links with short wires with beaded ends. The gauge size of the wire is important in determining the esthetic effects in each case.

Twisted wire might be called a form of textured wire. Experimentation with twisting wires of different sizes together will lead to interesting possibilities, although results must be carefully evaluated to avoid triteness. Another form of texture in wire can be achieved by stamping with punches and chasing tools (12–11). Rich surfaces for rings or structural members can be made in this way. Again, experiment is the only approach to the possibilities.

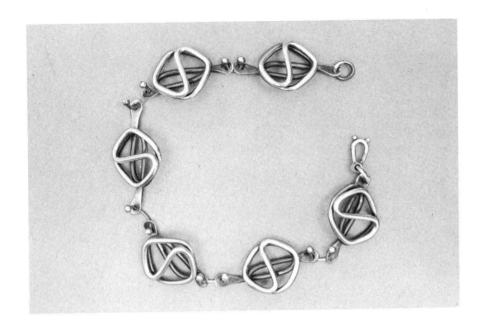

Fig. 148. Philip Morton. Bracelet with square links. Sterling silver wire.

6–7 Linear Strip Forms *Design and Construction*   A strip design must be kept in a single plane. Metal strip that is cut with hand shears or with squaring shears will invariably be curved and twisted if it is of narrow dimension. Therefore it is necessary to straighten out all twists in a strip before doing any bending for shape. Straightening can be done by taking each end of the strip in a pair of squarenose pliers and twisting the ends in the opposite direction while pulling on the strip. When bending to the desired shape with the pliers, be sure bends are perpendicular to the length of the strip as each bend is made. After each bend, check to see that the strip is still in a single plane, and adjust the bend if necessary.

Strip forms are seldom successful if the ends do not come together to form a closed line. Leaving the ends wild is not satisfactory for the simple reason that a visual line always leads the eye to its ending. If there is no significant focal point at the end, the line is better closed on itself to form a continuous movement.

When designing such a closed strip form, start with one end at a point on the outside of the organization, rather than at a point within it, so that soldering can be done on the periphery of the form (9–13). Avoid placing solder joints on a flat section. Always put the solder joint in the center of a sharp bend.

After a strip form has been soldered and trued up, it may be placed on a flat anvil and tapped lightly along the top edge to ensure that the piece lies in a single plane. To finish such a form, take a large, flat hand file and file across the top and bottom surfaces until the edges of the strip are of uniform width and lying in a single plane. In order to avoid filing slots in the surface, always slide the file across the piece, sideways, as you file forward and back. Rotate the pieces every few strokes to ensure that an even surface is attained (15–1).

If the strip has been correctly bent up, there should be no kinks in the sides that require filing. The jewel-like quality of every form will depend upon the perfection of the surfaces, unless the design requires a rough finish.

left: Fig. 149. Felt Lair. Pendant. 1952. Brass strip.
above: Fig. 150. Philip Morton. Buckle. 1965. Chased 14-kt. gold.

Figure 149 shows a simple strip form done by a student. It was soldered to a back plate, which really takes it into the category of strip-plate construction. The linear strip form can be utilized for a wide range of jewelry, including pendants, brooches, buckles, cuff links, and ear clips.

6–8 Linear Forms *Chasing* Everything that has been said about the visual aspects of line holds true for any means of achieving line, though the technical processes vary and each one must be mastered. Nevertheless, the expressive form of chasing does differ from that of wire, for the chased line must be carried on a metal surface (Fig. 150). The design problem is that of relating an inner linear organization within a shape to the boundary line of that shape **(5–9)**. If the inner linear design is complex, the outer shape is best kept fairly simple. The designer should avoid letting such simplicity lead to dullness and making the outer shape too large in scale. A review of contemporary jewelry shows that chasing is a neglected technique. While it is restrained in form, being relatively two-dimensional, it deserves somewhat more attention in both jewelry and metalwork.

6–9 Linear Forms *Piercing* Piercing, which is the technique of sawing lines and other openings in metal sheet according to designed pattern, is another technique that deserves more attention from the contemporary jeweler. Designs of extreme delicacy can be achieved. Small holes are drilled at the beginning and end of the line movement before sawing, and the line is designed so that the metal is not cut apart entirely from the support of adjacent metal. Piercing requires a relaxed and quiet approach on the part of the jeweler. Results can be quite exciting (Fig. 110).

6–10 Plate Shapes Simple shapes cut from sheet metal are the easiest form to achieve and can be the most banal of jewelry forms. It is just for this reason that an especially careful study of shape is necessary if meaningful,

Fig. 151. Sam Kramer Studio. Pendant. 1952. Sterling silver with chrysocolla, labradorite, and ruby eye.

contemporary, expressive shapes are to be achieved. When sensitively designed, the simple shape can be almost as dramatic as the most complex piece. In dealing with simple shapes, every stereotype that comes to mind must be rejected, and come to mind they will. This is why the constant drawing of shapes is necessary for the contemporary jeweler. Every acquired image must be explored so that the designer will have a range of possibilities, while at the same time every dull image must be discarded. Amoebic shapes, once new and exciting, are monotonous from overuse, just as words, when overused, become lusterless and no longer contribute insight into the contemporary milieu. The search for unique configurations of meaning can follow a systematic procedure, once the given expressive area has been selected. Shapes fall within almost every category of esthetic feeling, even though as flat planes they tend to retain an elemental and symbolic rather than a strong, emotional quality and therefore usually belong to the rational mode of expression. Compare the shapes adopted by David Aaron with those of Lawrence McKinnin (see Appendix A).

Plate shapes preserve a certain degree of intellectual delicacy and symbolic purity comparable to line, unless some kind of modulation of the edges or surface is applied. Thinness or thickness of the metal also modifies the feeling quality from delicacy to massiveness. A shape cut from heavy gauge can be transformed esthetically if the edges are fused or rounded and the surface curved (Fig. 151).

With the exception of certain geometric shapes, such as the perfect circle, square, or rectangle, it is almost a rule that the boundary-line configuration of simple plate shapes must be sufficiently active in its movements and in its area disposition to achieve dramatic interest (5–4, 5–10). Other exceptions to this rule might be simple shapes that are given interest by textural treatment of the surface. Even so simple a texture as that resulting from forging or planishing can be effective, especially if the hammering modulates the thickness of the sheet.

Fig. 152. Paper cutouts for designing shapes.

The design of shapes may be studied quite effectively by making scissors cutouts of stiff paper or thin cardboard (Fig. 152). If the paper shapes are of differing colors or values, the visual impact is more stimulating. Two or more colors assist the study of combined shapes.

Ordinarily the edges of the top surface of a shape should not be rounded by filing if the sheet is as thin as 16-gauge. With 14-gauge or heavier, a sculptural effect can be achieved by rounding the top edge. Otherwise, a clean, crisp boundary line is more effective.

6–11 Complex Plate-shape Forms   As soon as other visual elements are added to a simple shape, the complexity is increased and the form moves out of the category of the simple plate-shape form. However, these categories are merely abstractions which permit a systematic presentation of the material; they should not be regarded as absolute, dogmatic divisions of form.

The addition of a single line to make a space division of a single shape can be effected in two ways. One is to solder a wire or strip across the shape. When this is done, it is practical to lay the wire across the plate with the ends projecting beyond the edges of the plate. Binding wire may be used to hold the wire in position (**8–27**). After the wire has been soldered, the projecting ends are sawed off flush with the edges of the shape and filed smooth. It bears repetition that, whenever possible, it is wise to leave extra material to be trimmed away after soldering. This is much easier than attempting to fit two exact lengths together before soldering.

The other usual way of creating a space division of a simple shape is by utilizing the boundary line of another plate, which is soldered on top of the first plate shape. In effect this is a partial lamination of two plates (Fig. 153). The simplest way to carry out this step is by sweat soldering (8–22). It is easier to get an exact fit if the additional plate is rough-cut to extend over the boundary line of the simple shape. After soldering, it may be sawed to the edge of the simple shape and filed and finished.

A line creating a space division offers the opportunity to differentiate each area by means of texture. In every case the texture should be applied before any other part is soldered to the surface. The final edge of the plate should be prepared only *after* the texturing, because stamping the edge with punches will smash it down. After texturing the final boundary line can be sawed, filed, and finished.

Unlike the pure plate shape, which may function as an image complete in itself, a shape to which a line and texture have been added seems incomplete, usually, until some kind of focal point is added (5–25). This focal point may be a bead or disk of silver, a wire ring, a strip ring, a round stone set in a bezel, or even a hole drilled or sawed through the plate. The only requirement is that it be of appropriate scale in relation to the area of the main shape (5–17, 5–18).

There is hardly a limit to the manner in which additional elements can be used on a simple shape.

Though most contemporary jewelry is nonobjective and deals structurally or sculpturally with the formal elements of design, each artist must make his own choice as to the content of his work. If natural forms are used as a point of departure, the problem of avoiding trite shapes becomes crucial. Those wishing to utilize natural forms must carry out an exacting observation of the details of natural forms and an intensive study of how they may be formalized uniquely and expressively.

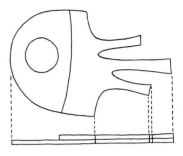

Fig. 153. Simple plate shape with dividing line formed by the edge of another plate.

6–12 Strip-plate Forms *Esthetics*   Complex plate forms ultimately lead from the two-dimensional surface to three-dimensional forms, which are designated as strip-plate constructions. When we add a line through a simple shape as a space division, we have created, in addition to the textural possibilities discussed above, another possible dimension. That is, we may displace one part of the shape from the plane into the third dimension along the space-dividing line (Fig. 154). The only limit to the complexity which displacement can achieve is that imposed by the need to maintain clarity. Dramatic impact does not depend on complexity alone. More important is the unity arising from the complete functioning and perfect relationship of each element in the design. Nevertheless, three-dimensional forms are generally of more potential interest than flat, two-dimensional forms.

The esthetic quality of strip-plate construction derives from the intellectual delight of pure and simple relationships of planes and space that are essentially geometric. In such designs every relationship must be ordered and precise. Such forms therefore belong to the rational mode of expression. Unruly emotions, more characteristic of the nonrational mode of expression, are out of place here. The possible effect of bareness, if unwanted, may be reduced by carefully proportioned space divisions and by the addition of rich textures and of focal points.

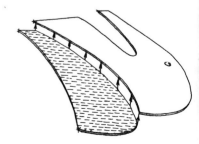

Fig. 154. Shape displaced along a space-division line.

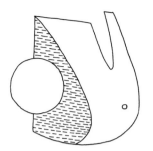

Fig. 155. Strip-plate design sketch.

The beginning designer may wish to start with the simple formula described in **5–26.** This formula is offered only as a point of departure to involve the student directly in three-dimensional design. The following section describes the procedure for designing such a formula.

6–13 Strip-plate Forms *Design* As rendered, the design in Figure 155 can be seen three-dimensionally as a forward, highly polished, silver surface plane and a textured and oxidized **(5–12)** back plane, upon which a gemstone cabochon is set as a focal point. The relationship of forward polished plane and back textured plane, from which the setting rises, is part of the formula for two reasons. First, the forward plane is polished because the buffing wheel can readily reach the forward parts of a piece of jewelry. Second, the back plane is textured and colored black because it is normally impossible, or at least difficult, to polish a back plane. While it would be possible, with effort, to reverse this relationship of contrast, the contemporary jeweler follows the "law of parsimony" and deals with his materials in the simplest and most logical manner. When we encounter natural limitations as a part of a design problem, we usually adapt our design ideas to take these limitations into account.

When we begin designing for the strip-plate formula, we begin with a simple shape. All simple shapes can be made to work, but some are more successful than others. Examine the illustrated collection of simple shapes (Fig. 156), to each of which has been added a line as space divider and a focal point.

Compare the results of adding the line in Shapes 1 and 2. A space-division line should always go through the entire space of the primary shape in order to achieve the maximum possible active relationship to the boundary line of the primary shape as well as to work through the area. In Shape 1, the space-dividing line works ineffectively *across* the main axis of the shape; only a small portion of the area is affected, and hardly any significant space relationship is established with the boundary line. In Shape 2 the space-dividing line works through the entire space of the shape and against its two boundary lines.

The placement of the line must also create two spaces within the primary shape which are in appropriate scale relationship. Shape 3 shows a line placement that creates an ineffective scale relationship. The space on the right is much too small, and the space on the left much too large to be organized by the focal point. Shape 4 shows a more effective line placement, putting all three shapes in scale relationship.

Care must be taken that the back, textured plane is always kept a bit smaller than the forward plane. Shape 3 shows why. A darkened and textured area is

Fig. 156. Twelve simple shapes with space divider and focal point.

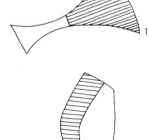

1

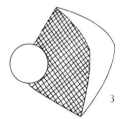

2

3

4

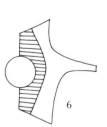

5

6

stronger, visually, than a smooth, polished area. To achieve visual balance, therefore, always keep the textured area smaller. The back plane must be seen as a field across which the forward plane and the focal point work in relationship.

You must also become immediately aware of the scale relationship between the primary shape and the focal point. The setting in a piece of jewelry should, first of all, be regarded as a simple shape to be related in scale to the primary shape. Traditional jewelry has often utilized small cabochons, of about 10 mm. in size, without regard for the scale of the primary shape. Such settings do not function as focal points, but rather as accents. Shapes 5 and 6 illustrate the difference in visual effect. The focal point should be a shape large enough to work effectively in the primary shape.

The focal point can be placed in one of two positions with respect to the primary shape: It can be placed entirely *within* the back plane, so that it is surrounded by a textured field, or it can be placed exactly *across* the outside boundary line of the primary shape. In some cases placing the focal point within the textured back plane works very well, but often this placement requires such an enlargement of the back plane that it becomes too large in relation to the forward plane. Shape 7 illustrates this point, whereas Shape 4 shows how placement of the focal point across the boundary line of the shape allows the designer to reduce the area of the back plane to a scale that is appropriate.

A round focal point permits a simpler design solution than any other shape, because the circle is nondirectional. An oval stone must usually be set in opposition to the thrust of the primary shape, since setting it parallel overemphasizes the thrust. Shape 8 shows this.

The placement of the focal point depends upon the available area along the boundary line of the primary shape. A designer would not put a grand piano in a coat closet nor a large stone in a cramped space. A certain amount of shoulder room is required, not only visually but for the practical operation of burnishing down the bezel of a close setting (17–1). Generally speaking, the boundary line of the focal point should never pinch off the space by being placed too close to the boundary line of the primary shape. When the focal point is placed across the boundary line of the primary shape, as shown in Shape 4, it should be placed squarely across and over a relatively straight section of the line, rather than over a sharply curving section. The boundary line should continue moving away from the focal point a short distance before curving. Otherwise the design will appear cramped.

11

7

8

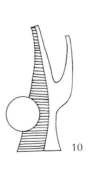

9

10

12

97

There is another aspect to the question of scale relationship between the focal point, as a secondary shape, and the primary shape. This question has to do with equilibrium and the focal point as the center of equilibrium. Shape 9 illustrates the weakness of moving the ends of the primary shape too far beyond its logical field. The size of the field cannot be dogmatically fixed, but once you become aware of this problem, you will intuitively exercise appropriate judgment. Shape 9 certainly extends beyond its logical or reasonable field in relation to the size of the focal point, whereas Shape 10 seems more satisfactory.

Finally, the unity of the design will be strengthened if the primary shape moves *around*, rather than *away* from, the focal point. Shapes 11 and 12 illustrate this point.

Having considered all the subtle relationships of a primary shape, its line space-divider, and its focal point, we are ready to consider texture. Two factors must be considered in selecting a texture. First, the scale of the unit of texture (the tool mark) must be related to the size of the area. Too large a tool mark will not usually be effective in a small area. Second, if there is a direction to the texture, as with rows of tool marks, this directional movement must be set against the major thrust of the primary shape, rather than parallel to it; or it must be set in opposition to the dominant direction of the design. Shape 2 illustrates an effective directional application of texture. Shape 1 shows an ineffective directional use of texture. It will be useful to detail the textures carefully in your design drawings.

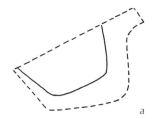

Since we are designing a three-dimensional piece of jewelry, we observe that the strip that is to separate the forward plane from the back plane must run along the boundary line between these planes (Fig. 157a). It may also run around the outside boundary of the forward plane (Fig. 157b), or it may run around the entire boundary of the forward plane (Fig. 157c).

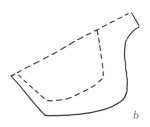

6–14 Strip-plate Forms *Construction*   The width of the strip used in a piece of jewelry usually depends upon the height of the cabochon being used. Sometimes a low or flat cabochon can be lifted up on a high bezel. In this case the strip should be appropriately high, just as if a high cabochon were being used (**16–1**). Ordinarily, for a low cabochon, a strip about 1/8 in. wide is suitable, but unusual effects can be achieved by making a deep three-dimensional space. The strip should be at least 18-gauge in thickness (**C-10**). In fact, the sheet shapes themselves can usually be of this gauge.

If a texture is desired on the strip, the texturing must be done first, so that the strip may be straightened if distortion results from the stamping.

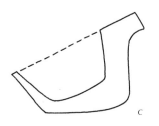

The strip is then bent with the fingers and with half-round or round pliers to fit the space-dividing line (Fig. 158a). If the boundary of the primary shape is also to be made of strip, then that piece must be cut and its ends beveled to exactly fit into the other strip (Fig. 158b). The ends of the outer strip are usually left *wild* until after the line strip is soldered, after which the ends are cut and filed smooth. In this latter case the strip shape exactly duplicates the forward plane (Fig. 158c).

Fig. 157. a. Strip bent along boundary line of displaced plane. b. Strip around forward plane. c. Strip around entire form.

Now, with a large hand file, the top and bottom edges of the strip shape are smoothed. When filing such a shape, always slide the file from left to right while moving back and forth, to avoid making slots with the edge of the file.

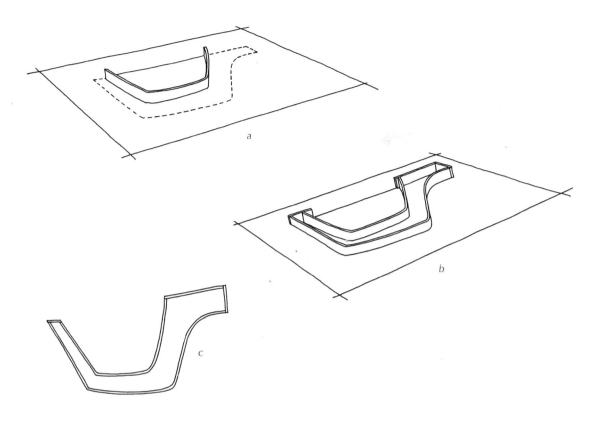

Fig. 158. a. Strip bent to fit line of sketch design.
b. Space-division strip and boundary-line strip fitted together.
Note wild ends of boundary-line strip. c. Finished strip shape.

After the strip shape is smooth, it is placed upside down on a sheet of 18-gauge sterling sheet cut just slightly larger than the actual strip shape. Never try to fit a strip shape to a sheet that has been cut to the same size. It is simpler to trim the sheet shape directly to the strip shape after soldering. This is done by sawing the excess away along the strip and then filing the side of the strip shape until all traces of the seam have disappeared. The side of the strip shape is then smoothed with an emery stick and finally polished on the tripoli wheel **(15–8)**.

The next step is to cut the shape of the back plane from a piece of 18-gauge sheet, leaving extra material all around. The back plane sheet is then textured all over with the selected punch marks or graver marks. The outside boundary, across which the focal point is to be placed, can now be trimmed and finished to exact size. However, the straight edge that is to go under the forward plane should have extra material, so that the bottom edge of the strip may be soldered to the back plane (Fig. 159). When soldering these two together, be sure to place a small piece of 18-gauge sheet under the back side of the forward plane to hold it horizontal when it is sitting on top of the back plane sheet. After soldering, the extra material at the two ends of the soldered joint are filed smooth and finished.

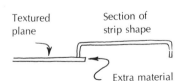

Textured plane   Section of strip shape

Extra material

Fig. 159. Section view of strip shape, showing extra material on bottom plane.

Fig. 160. Student. Brooch. 1953. Sterling silver with jade. Example of strip-plate construction.

At this point the beginning student may be tempted to oxidize the piece in order to see the effect, but it will save time to wait until all soldering has been completed before doing the final coloring and finishing.

A bezel is now made for the gemstone (17–1) and soldered in place across the outside edge of the back plane. After the joint and catch are soldered in place (8–30), the piece is oxidized (15–12), and the stone is set. The piece is finally polished on the tripoli wheel and then cleaned. A finished strip-plate pin is shown in Figure 160.

Each step of strip-plate construction has now been described in detail. With increased experience the student will wish to depart from the formula here presented.

6–15 Constructed Forms   This category includes forms assembled from various materials by methods that are not applicable to other forms. Esthetically such constructions may belong to either the rational or the nonrational expressive mode.

The pendant made of ivory and sterling (Fig. 161) is a good example of a constructed form. The stamped gallery wire is pinned into holes in the ivory by small functional rivets.

Composition problems are basic to every type of expressive form. Little need be said here about construction, for each design problem may be unique and require individual solutions. However, the jeweler should search for interesting and direct methods of fastening that can be incorporated as part of the design (Chap. 13). Direct fasteners are particularly good for use with softer materials such as wood or ivory. When nonmetallic materials are used, they must be fastened after all soldering or other heating is done, and ingenuity is required to design effective fasteners. There is a tendency on the part of amateurs to resort to glue for fastening materials, even stones. The best standards of craftsmanship require direct methods of fastening stones, because such fastenings are more permanent and because it is often necessary to disassemble the piece of jewelry for repairs.

Constructed forms also include complex pieces made by assembling multiple units for brooches, bracelets, necklaces, and other items of jewelry. The units themselves may be constructed or, perhaps, cast (Fig. 162). Such constructions usually require flexible fasteners, such as hinges.

6–16 Carved Forms   Carved forms tend to be sculptural or structural constructed by carving, grinding, filing, or casting. Esthetically, carved forms may be in either the rational or the nonrational expressive mode. The category includes all simple shapes that are too thick to be classed as simple plate shapes and must be shaped by working on all sides and edges. In other words, they are three-dimensional forms. A cuff link made of 8-gauge sheet would be better treated as a carved form than as a simple shape. Thick shapes of ivory or ebony would probably be treated as volumes to be carved.

6–17 Forged Forms   The design of the forged form must be based upon experience in the process of forging and upon experiment, for shape cannot be arbitrarily imposed upon a material. The shape must be drawn out of the metal by the action of the forging hammer in displacing the metal, blow by blow.

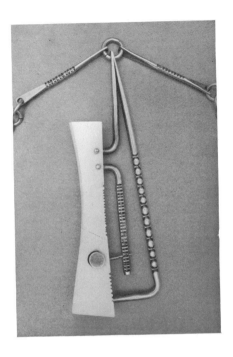

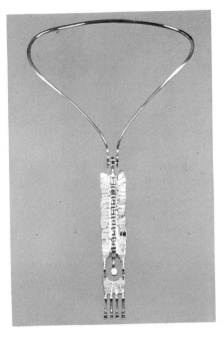

left: Fig. 161. Philip Morton.
Pendant. 1956. Ivory with sterling
silver stamped with punches.
Example of constructed form.
right: Fig. 162. Stanley Lechtzin.
Pendant. 1967. Cast and assembled
elements with citrine and tourmaline.

Forging is discussed in connection with hammering wire (12–4). It is a good idea to begin forging experiments with a short length of 6- or 8-gauge wire and see just how much variation in width you can make in the center of the piece and at one end. In forging a tapered movement from thick to thin along a bar of metal, one soon learns to adjust the weight of the blows to the tapered thickness of the material. Ronald Pearson has carried out the simple technique of forging into exquisite bracelets and necklaces (Fig. 163).

Fig. 163. Ronald Hayes
Pearson. Necklace. 1965.
Forged sterling silver.

The sequence of steps Pearson follows in forging such pieces is shown in Fig. 164, Steps 1–9, as follows:

1. Cut lengths of 6-gauge, square sterling wire.
2. Work on a clean, dent-free anvil with a cross-peen sledge of about 2 lb. Both ends of the sledge should be reshaped, with the flat face slightly rounded, or crowned, and the edges rounded, and the cross-peen end also slightly crowned and rounded at the edges. Set the anvil in a stump at a comfortable height; if the stool is 30 in. high, for example, the anvil surface should be about 40 in. high.
3. Forge the ends of the necklace first. Notice that they are forged vertically. The illustration shows how the cross peen of the forging hammer is worked across the length of the wire to stretch it and to thin the ends.
4. Use the flat face of the hammer to planish out the forging marks made by the cross peen. Taper the ends by striking harder toward the outside and lightening the blows toward the center.
5. The exact center of the wire is bent with a rawhide mallet and then forged wider. Do this by holding the cross peen parallel to the wire and working from the center outward in both directions. Avoid striking the very edge of the wire. Taper the wire from thicker on the inside to thinner on the outside. When the shape has been achieved, planish out the forging marks and smooth the surface with the flat end of the hammer.
6. Shape and true up the necklace, as shown, with a wooden mallet on a hollow in the stump.
7. If forging has been done carefully and symmetrically, only a little filing should be required to smooth the edges. Use a No. 2-cut file first and finish with a No. 6-cut file.
8. Polish on a 6-in.-diameter muslin buff with tripoli. Begin by holding the piece at right angles to the plane of the wheel and move it from one end to the other, bearing down hard. Then rotate the piece 180° to come at it from the opposite side. Finally polish lengthwise, as shown. Then wipe off excess tripoli and stamp name and quality underneath. Polish again with a 6-in. loose muslin buff. Use clean, white cotton gloves to hold the piece for this final polish.
9. Finished piece.

Step 1

Step 2

Step 3

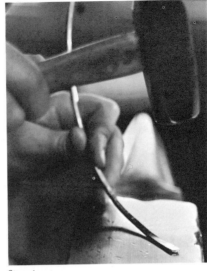

Step 4

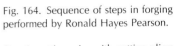
Fig. 164. Sequence of steps in forging
performed by Ronald Hayes Pearson.

Step 1, cutting wire with cutting pliers.
Step 2, cross-peen sledge
and wire on anvil.
Step 3, forging across
length of wire.
Step 4, tapering ends of wire.
Step 5, shaping center of wire.
Step 6, shaping and truing
with wooden mallet.
Step 7, filing edges.
Step 8, polishing.
Step 9, the finished piece.

Step 5

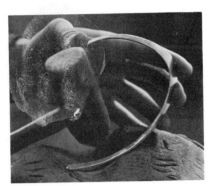

Step 6

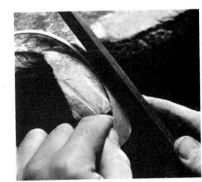

Step 7

Step 8

Step 9

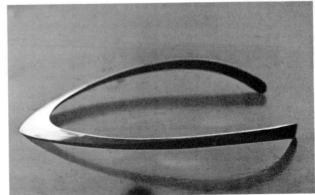

Advanced Design: The Means of Achieving Expressive Form   103

Free experiment with materials will lead to interesting design ideas.

Hot forging is the forging of heated metal. Usually a kiln is set at a temperature that will keep a metal blank at a very low red heat. Sometimes a small metal canopy, open at the front end, is set over a gas burner. The forging blanks are set on an iron screen over the burner and heated to a very low heat. The blank is seized by a pair of squarenose tongs (a variety of blacksmith tongs is best), and the forging is done on a suitable anvil. Hot forging is usually used for handcrafted flatware, because the pieces require a wide variation of thickness as well as width. Blanks heated to a low red heat are easily "upset" for the purpose of increasing the thickness and reducing the width. The term "upsetting" means forging a width thicker by hammering on the edge of the metal.

A tie clip may be made by forging a piece of 8-gauge sterling wire. A piece of wire about 2½ in. long is flattened down at one end (Fig. 165). The unhammered length is bent over the edge of the T-stake and flattened by planishing. The entire piece is then shaped and made symmetrical by filing, and then it is finished. A double bend is then made with the roundnose pliers. The back is stamped with the sterling stamp and the jeweler's hallmark and then cut to length and polished (Fig. 166). The final shaping is made with the roundnose pliers, and the final spring given to the clip (Fig. 167). A large number of variations may be made with this shape of clip.

6–18 Repoussé Forms Repoussé forms are actually sculptural relief forms pressed out from the back of a sheet of metal. They may range from natural to geometric, technological, or abstract images (Fig. 168). Because of the nature of the process, the forms most naturally emerge as organic forms and therefore are most likely to belong to the nonrational expressive mode. Regardless of the image, it should be remembered that repoussé relief is most effective when restricted to a moderate depth. Shallow relief can be well controlled, and many problems are avoided if the forms are not too deep. In ancient jewelry it can be seen that repoussé forms made by soldering together two hollow halves of

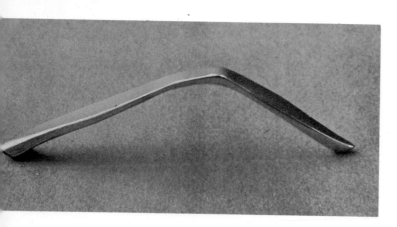

left: Fig. 165. Tie clip of 8-gauge sterling wire, 2½ in. long, being hammered to shape on T-stake.
below left: Fig. 166. Entire wire hammered to shape, polished, and stamped.
below right: Fig. 167. Completed tie clip.

sheet metal can be very effective. Embossing into a stone mold is another method of producing repoussé. Contemporary jewelers have yet to take full advantage of the possibilities of repoussé. Fred Fenster is one who has become interested in the process.

Although almost any image can be imposed upon sheet metal in relief, the image must be composed very carefully to avoid the problems of foreshortening, which cannot be effectively handled in relief on the scale of jewelry. Therefore, figures derived from natural forms must be composed in a plane parallel to the plane of the sheet-metal surface, and not perpendicular to it.

The technical process of repoussé is discussed in Chapter 9 (9–15). There can be no substitute for struggling out a first attempt. The process must be carried out freehand. The design is drawn in reverse on the back of the sheet, and the front surface is put against the pitch in a pitch pan or bowl, which supports the metal and permits forming the pattern with tools from the back. Only a generalized form can be pushed into the metal at the first stage. The design cannot be raised tightly or precisely from the back; deep and narrow forms must be pushed down quite broadly at first. When the sheet is turned over, the image can be somewhat more precisely defined as the general rounded areas are pushed back along boundary lines. This is a plastic process, and the design must be formed in the process. It is not a question of duplicating, accurately, a predesigned form. It is a question of bringing the form into precise existence in the metal through successive stages. This is the key to successful repoussé.

Fig. 168. Michael Jerry. Pendant. 1967. Sterling silver repoussé with moonstone.

6–19 Cast Forms   Cast forms are not necessarily sculptural, in the sense that almost any form can be cast—even a simple, flat shape that could better be sawed out of sheet. But casting is the means by which sculptural forms can be fully realized. There are two distinct and legitimate uses for casting. One is for the duplication of production pieces. The other is for realization of forms that can be achieved in no other way than by casting. The process is extremely complex—perhaps the most complex of all—and involves a great deal of equipment, especially if emphasis is placed upon controlled production. Yet in many ways it requires less skill to develop cast forms by modeling in wax than through the use of other jewelry means, such as chasing, repoussé, forging, or construction. It is for this reason that casting is often reserved for a second course in jewelry making. Even though casting is a most appealing means for jewelry production, every jeweler needs to master the direct, basic processes of working with metal. Waxmodeling, in itself, is not the most important of goldsmithing processes.

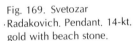

Fig. 169. Svetozar Radakovich. Pendant. 14-kt. gold with beach stone.

Cast forms depend for their dramatic impact not only on the movement of the elements through three-dimensional space but also very much upon the modulation of the elements themselves. The sculptural form *must,* itself, always show a transition from thin to thick, from narrow to wide, and back again (5–13). Sections should, in general, be more oval than round and move from oval to flat or vice versa, thus creating moving planes. These planes should rotate from place to place, so that everywhere movement of form is attained. Since jewelry forms are small, this means that the maximum sense of movement must be achieved if dramatic impact is to be high (Fig. 169). Cast forms normally belong to the nonrational expressive mode, although almost any kind of form can be imposed upon a plastic material.

above left: Fig. 170. Two charcoal blocks open, showing carved pattern, sprue, and channel.
above right: Fig. 171. Pouring molten silver into charcoal mold.
right: Fig. 172. Open charcoal mold with cast pattern in block.

Fig. 173. Completed pendant.

6–20 Cast-form Design *Charcoal Molds and Other Carved Molds* The direct carving of a pattern into a mold requires considerable freedom; the results will improve with practice. Charcoal is so soft that there are really no technical difficulties, except that it may chip out along the grain of the wood. Deep, narrow sections give more dramatic forms than shallow sections, although a combination of the two is effective. When a particularly striking form is developed, it may be used as a pattern for a rubber-mold duplication.

It is important that the two charcoal blocks used to make the mold (Fig. 170) be filed flat and smooth, so that they fit together tightly when wired together for casting. As shown, the sprue at the top, the channel to the pattern, and the pattern are all carved into one block only. The pattern is carved into the lower half of the block so that the sprue and channel will be as long as possible. The other block is flat and has only a matching sprue half at its top.

If a full-round form is desired, the carved half may be pressed onto a flat layer of talc until the surface is smoothly covered, leaving the carved form cleanly black. This half must be keyed with metal posts to the upper half and pressed against the upper half so as to make a talc imprint, which will locate the carved pattern and the channel on the uncarved block. This may then be carved in relation to the other block. Keys may be made of round sterling beads about 1/8 in. in diameter or of 6-gauge silver posts, which are set in the block by drilling.

After the pattern is completed, the blocks are wired together and the pour is made from a hand crucible (Fig. 171). When the metal has cooled somewhat, the mold is opened (Fig. 172) and the casting extracted. After pickling and finishing, the piece is complete (Fig. 173). The addition of gemstones (Fig. 174) to cast pieces may be made as instructed in Chapter 17.

6–21 Cast-form Design *Patterns for Sand Casting* The first rule for patterns for sand casting is **no undercuts**. Normally half the pattern must be embedded in each half of the mold. From the parting line, which lies between the two halves of the mold, the forms of the pattern must taper inward, not outward (Fig. 175). It is true that with larger patterns undercuts are sometimes possible, because "drawbacks" of sand may be used. This is not feasible with small jewelry pieces, although experimentation should not be ruled out.

Fig. 174. Charcoal-cast pendant with pearl.

Fig. 175. Casting flask setup for casting.

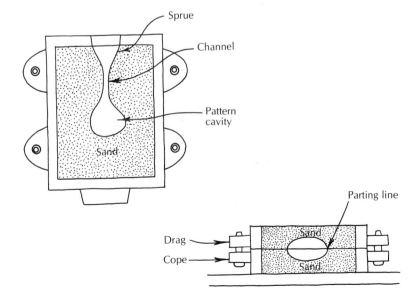

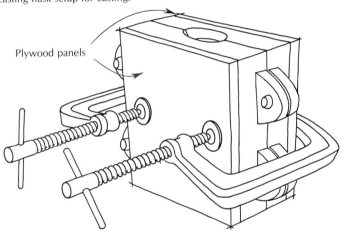

The second rule for sand-casting patterns is **smooth and polished surfaces,** so that the pattern may be drawn from the sand easily.

Wood patterns are not normally used for jewelry. If, for any reason, a wood pattern must be used, the wood must be very smooth, shellacked with two or three coats, and then steel-wooled down.

Patterns should be about 10 percent or more larger than the desired casting. If they are made to final size they produce castings with sections that are too thin. This is particularly true of ring shanks and bezel prongs (**14–8, 17–2).**

For a quick casting, even wax may be used for a sand-mold pattern. The wax should be hard, on the order of File-Wax (**14–12).** Sometimes a metal pattern for casting can be made more rapidly by sandcasting the metal pattern from a wax pattern. This usually involves considerable filing, but it still may be faster than fabricating the metal pattern.

The great advantage of sand casting, as compared to lost-wax casting, is its directness. The only workshop requirement for efficient sand casting is an adequate work space, such as a smooth, flat counter. A sand-casting outfit (**14–7)** does not take up a great deal of room. The sand should be kept clean, collected carefully after each casting, and kept tightly closed in its container.

6–22 Cast-form Design *Patterns for Rubber Molds*   Patterns for rubber molds are made of metal (**14–8, 14–9).** They may be constructed directly of metal or derived from modeled wax patterns that have been cast and finished. Undercuts are no problem with the rubber mold, which may be cut in such a way as to hinge out in order to release deeply undercut parts (Fig. 176).

The pattern for a rubber mold must be finished as perfectly as possible for the final casting. Every unwanted mark will be reproduced, so that the pattern must be free from flaws, scratches, and file marks.

If it is desired to cast forms in which stones are to be set, the setting must be made somewhat larger than the stone in order to allow for shrinkage of the wax pattern and the casting. When the pattern is first modeled in wax, it should be modeled right around the stone. If closed settings are to be used, these are better made directly in metal. If the piece is to be duplicated, a supply of stones must be available in standard sizes, and the bezel must be made to fit the standard millimeter size.

A hard wax is used when the patterns are to be of a geometric form. A softer wax is better when the forms are to be modeled into organic forms.

6–23 Enamel Forms   The art of enameling is much too important and complex to be dealt with in summary fashion. It deserves full treatment in a separate work. With this reservation in mind, the beginning jeweler may still find it useful to have here a brief outline of the process and some of the esthetic and design problems.

Successful enameling requires a good color sense and a good knowledge of color composition. Therefore it should not be approached purely as a technique. Enameling for serious purposes requires a complete set of facilities and especially a space that can be kept very clean, so that the enamels will not become dirty. Properly used, enamels can heighten the dramatic impact of jewelry, and the contemporary jeweler might well investigate the possibilities more fully. Historical examples are shown in Figures 38, 41, and 44.

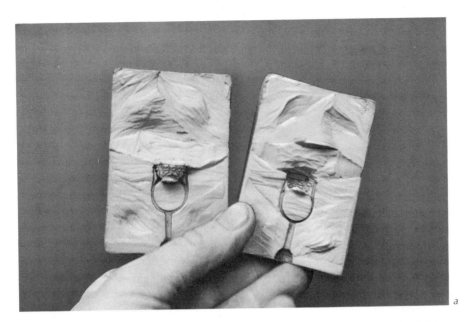

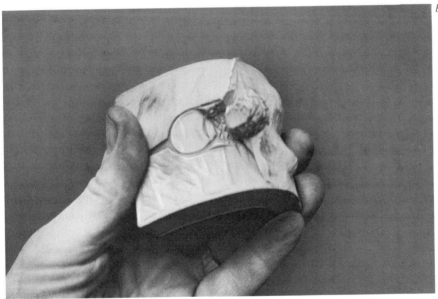

Fig. 176. Opened rubber mold, *(a)* showing slits *(b)* that release wax pattern from undercuts.

Enamels are made of colored glass (usually lead compounds), either opaque or transparent. The glass is ground up with a pestle and mortar to a fine powder of 60 to 80 mesh. After powdering, the enamels are washed several times in water to remove impurities and to render the colors clearer and brighter. The dry enamel powder may be sifted onto a metal surface that has been moistened with a gum tragacanth solution. While the enamels are sifted, a face mask or respirator must be worn, since inhalation of the powder will cause lead poisoning. The enamel powder may be applied with a spatula or a small sable brush. When applied with a sable brush, the enamels are usually placed in small containers with water and applied wet. Water may be added or removed from the

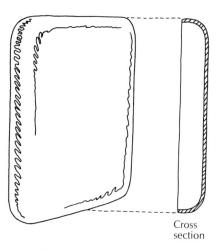

Cross
section

Fig. 177. Dapped panel for enameling.

applied enamels by means of the brush. The brush is squeezed dry with a paper towel and then touched to the wet, applied enamel to remove excess water.

Enamels are not placed upon perfectly flat panels of metal, since these have no resistance to bending, and bending tends to crack off the applied enamel. The metal forms must be three-dimensional or warped in two planes, so that they resist bending. Small rectangular or round panels may be dapped up, but rather flatly, in order to stiffen them (Fig. 177).

The metal surfaces are cleaned thoroughly to remove grease and then polished with steel wool to open the surface. If pieces to be enameled are soldered, only a high-fire solder, called I. T. solder, should be used. The back of a panel should be enameled first, by sifting. Transparent enamels should always be placed over an opaque white ground that has first been sifted on and fired.

After the enamels have been applied to the piece, it should be allowed to air-dry. Then it is placed carefully on a small iron sheet or stainless steel tray and set in a kiln, preheated to about 1400° F.

In the kiln the powdered glass fuses smoothly over the surface. The process of fusing takes only a minute or two, depending upon the temperature of the kiln and the size of the piece. Therefore the stage of fusing must be checked by visual inspection. When the piece has turned a glossy red, it should be removed quickly and placed on a metal cooling counter. Usually two or more applications of enamel must be made to cover the piece of work smoothly. Special designs may require many firings. After firing is complete, the edges, if any, are stoned down with a fine stone to smooth the enamel where it terminates.

Small enameled panels may be treated as settings and set in fine silver bezels. Enameled spheres or hollow volumes may be treated as stones.

The student seriously interested in this process should study a number of good texts on the subject.

7

FUNCTIONAL DESIGN

One of the major distinctions that has been made in the past between the fine arts and the crafts is that of function, according to which the fine arts have been classified as nonfunctional and the crafts functional. Today we are aware that function extends to intangible psychological and spiritual aspects of existence. For example, a broader recognition of the influence of space and scale upon the psychological well-being of man, long familiar to artists and architects, has recently been formally affirmed through the inauguration of a new field, architectural psychology. This new discipline is concerned with the design of space in buildings for mental patients and with the acceptance of space as psychological, as well as physical.

Art can no longer be regarded as nonfunctional, in the light of its role as an integrative process in human personality, bringing together thought, feeling, intuition, and sensation. Craft activities have long been thought of as therapy devices, but the application has been somewhat narrow in concept and practice. More recent opinion tends to view esthetic expression as a natural and inevitable aspect of every human activity.

7–1 The Functional Aspects of Jewelry From a practical point of view function in jewelry must be considered in relation to the special adaptations of jewelry forms to meet the demands of wearability. Each type of jewelry presents certain limitations and requirements. The ring must be designed to fit comfortably on the finger. The bracelet must fit comfortably on the arm and must be designed so that it can readily be put on or taken off.

The jeweler can learn a great deal about a client's design preferences by studying the dress, appearance, and behavior of the client. A somewhat reserved and reticent person who dresses modestly or quietly is not likely to be interested in a large, flamboyant design. A young woman wearing *avant-garde* fashions or strong color combinations and having an open and extrovert personality will not be likely to favor a severe or classic type of design.

111

Fig. 178. Alvin Pine. Wedding band. 1967. 14-kt. gold, constructed.

Without getting involved in the question of a specific design, the jeweler can orient himself by asking some very simple questions. "Do you like classic, or geometric, or organic forms? Do you enjoy simplicity or complexity in a design? Do you like the rational or the nonrational mode of expressive form?" A brief discussion along these lines will reveal the client's esthetic preferences, within which the jeweler should be able to create an acceptable design. There are certain pitfalls in custom designing that apply to all jewelry forms and might as well be discussed at this point. The creative designer-jeweler is not usually interested in producing the jewelry design of a lay client. In the author's experience, such designs are usually very trite. Furthermore, it is precisely the function of the designing jeweler to create the piece of jewelry to meet the client's personal expressive mode. But occasionally the client will come with a particular design in mind. Therefore, the jeweler will be well advised to formulate a policy on this question in advance. The simplest solution is to inform the client in a most friendly but firm manner that a designing jeweler produces only his own designs. Sometimes a client is offended, but at the loss of such a client the jeweler has preserved his reputation for creative design, particularly among his peers. The alternative to this policy is not particularly attractive in the eyes of the author, since it leads into many complications and still most often results in a design not at all satisfactory to the jeweler.

Another pitfall to custom designing concerns the presentation drawing. Many clients will ask for a rendered drawing so that they can see what they are getting. In this case a fee should be charged; it can be applied to the price of the finished piece if the design is accepted. For the skilled renderer, this request will present no problems, but quite often the creative designing jeweler finds his ideas only as he begins the actual process of designing in materials. For such jewelers the preferred policy is to inform the client that, having learned the esthetic preferences of the client, he will undertake to execute a design which will be to the client's satisfaction. However, lest the jeweler be-

Fig. 179. Typical wedding bands by students. 1966.

Fig. 180. Ring-size set.

come involved in having to produce several additional solutions before the client is satisfied, he must advise his client that he will work out a single design on a take-it-or-leave-it basis. If the client is not satisfied, the commission is to be terminated at no cost to the client. This may seem a somewhat rigorous policy, but the jeweler must take into consideration that a great many clients do not know exactly what they want. If the designing jeweler has been conscientious in ascertaining the esthetic preferences and in evaluating the personality of the client, he should seldom fail to come up with an appropriate design. Also, a very few clients will be impossible to satisfy. Each jeweler, as he becomes experienced, will form his own judgment on these policy questions.

Specific functional requirements for the various jewelry forms follow.

7–2　The Wedding Band　　The ring is perhaps the most common and popular item of jewelry. The functional parts of the ring are the ring band and the table, or setting, if any. One contemporary tendency is to merge these two parts into a single form (Figs. 178, 179). The design of a ring always raises, first, the question of size and width. It is obvious that the band must be of the right size to fit the finger. The ring must also be designed so that it fits into the position of adjacent fingers without being cumbersome or uncomfortable.

In taking an order for a wedding ring or wedding ring set, the jeweler uses the ring-size set (Fig. 180) to find out the required sizes, but the size also depends upon the desired width. A 1/2 in.-wide ring band has to be made about a half size larger than the measurement, if it is to fit comfortably. In determining the width of the band, the jeweler will examine the hand of the client. It is seldom that a person can comfortably wear a band that is much wider than 1/2 in. This width would normally be for the man's ring. The woman's wide band would not usually extend beyond 3/8 in. If the ring size is 7 or under, the band should probably be somewhat less than 3/8 in. wide. These functional limitations have seemed to be the most practical in the author's experience, though each jeweler will eventually form his own judgment (Fig. 181). At the same time, these limitations may sometimes be overruled by the client. The designer, however, is reluctant to produce a ring which will not be comfortable to wear, presumably over a lifetime.

top: Fig. 181. Gerda Flöckinger. Ring band. 1967. Fused silver and gold. *above*: Fig. 182. Philip Morton. Ring band with stamped texture. 1968. Sterling silver.

Aside from size and width, the jeweler will be interested in the kind of design expression that the client desires. As a part of this question the size and width of the client's hands will be discussed, as well as the expressive style.

From a functional point of view it is probably unwise to make a wedding band any thinner than 14-gauge for the woman's ring and 12-gauge for the man's ring. In the author's view, 16-gauge is too thin for long-term wear, as well as too slight visually; it should be used only for very small sizes or for children's rings. Here, again, ring size is correlated with thickness as well as width. For a size 5 ring 12-gauge might well be too heavy. For a size 12 ring 10-gauge might be suitable.

The thickness of a ring band is also determined by the kind of processing that is to be done. Bands that are to be stamped with a punch (Fig. 182) require a thick gauge—perhaps not less than 14—in order to take a sufficiently deep impression (**12–11**).

Fig. 183. Ring bender (*left*) and ring enlarger.

Fig. 184. Typical diamond engagement ring.

After the wedding band has been properly sized, it is important to remove the sharp edge on the inside of the band. This can be done with a half-round file, although production operations would call for the use of a cone on the spindle of a lathe or flexible shaft so that the rounding could be done more rapidly than by hand filing. When this rounding must be done by hand, it is best accomplished by taking a counted number of strokes at one position and then rotating the ring band and repeating the same number of strokes. This ensures an even rounding all around. Care must be taken, also, that the rounded bevel maintains the same width on the edge evenly all around. Depending upon the ring, the inner edge can be filed to a fairly wide roll (even up to the top edge of the ring in some designs) or merely to eliminate the sharp edge. In either case the edge must be emeried and then polished with tripoli to remove the file marks.

When a ring, already soldered at the seam, must be made smaller or larger, it is well to make the saw cut right at the solder seam in order to avoid having two soldered ring sections in the band. If stamped or other patterns are to be put into the ring band, the seam must come between units of the stamp pattern. A calculation must be made in advance to be sure that the adjustment where the seam is made is sufficient to allow the ring to roll up to the exact size required, or slightly under that size, in which case a ring enlarger (Fig. 183) can be used to bring the band to size.

7–3   The Engagement Ring   For contemporary jewelers the traditional concept of the engagement ring has undergone considerable modification. Conventional and traditional conditioning has led to the general acceptance of the diamond set in platinum or gold as the appropriate symbolic form of the engagement ring (Fig. 184). People who reject this conventional form become the clients of the contemporary jeweler, who is himself usually less interested in the restrictions of the conventional form than in the opportunity to exercise his creativity in designing an engagement ring within a relatively unrestricted range of possibilities. Even though the diamond or other conventionally faceted gems may be used, the contemporary jeweler will try to create an expressive form consistent with the client's esthetic orientation but interesting in form and color. It will become a "conversation piece," though on a somewhat more restrained level than the so-called "dinner ring" (see below). The design of mated or fitted wedding and engagement rings is becoming more popular (Pl. 9).

7–4   The Dinner or Cocktail Ring, the "Conversation Piece"   The ring as a conversation piece gives an opportunity to employ the full range of design resources. Combinations of stones and unique direct methods of setting stones are a part of the contemporary design trend (Figs. 185, 186). Rings of this type can be large, so long as they are designed functionally for comfortable wearing. Many women collect rings for wear on special occasions, and while they may prefer a ring of modest size for everyday wear, because, perhaps, they must wear gloves, they do not object to a larger size for the occasionally worn conversation piece.

In the past large rings have often been in fashion, and the tendency of contemporary jewelry toward larger rings has found a good response among clients.

If you happen to be wearing a ring, you will notice that the ring band fits into the crease between the palm and the inner finger joint. This crease usually determines the width of the ring band at that location. If the band is too wide there, the ring is likely to be uncomfortable to wear. If it is made quite narrow, however, it must be made with a thick gauge (up to 14-gauge for silver) in order to provide sufficient material for strength.

You will probably find from your own experiments that if the band is narrow at the bottom, it will be visually more satisfactory to taper the band wider toward the top than to have a band of uniform width. The width of the band where it joins the table, or setting, should be wide if the setting is long. If, for

far left: Fig. 185. Friedrich Becker.
Ring. 1966.
White gold with brilliants.
left: Fig. 186. Margaret De Patta.
Dinner ring. 1954.
White gold with rutilated quartz.

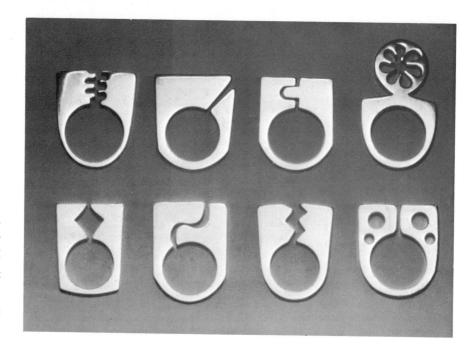

right: Fig. 187. Sigurd Persson.
Rings. 1966. Sterling silver.
below: Fig. 188. Alvin Pine.
Dinner ring, or "conversation piece."
1967. 14-kt. gold with amethyst
and moonstone.
bottom: Fig. 189. Philip Morton.
Wedding ring. 1967. 14-kt. gold
with scarab and oxblood coral.

example, you were using an oval cabochon 3 in. long and ³/₈ in. wide, it would
be wise to widen the band at the top to about 1 in. in order to hold the setting
along the finger. A narrow band would allow the long stone to twist sideways
on the finger. Ideally a ring should pass over the knuckle but not twist or turn
when being worn. Two solutions to this problem are a nonround ring shape
and an open, spring shape. Usually if a narrow ring band is used with a large,
heavy setting, the ring will be constantly sliding to one side.

Obviously, the corners and edges of a large ring must be smoothed to avoid
discomfort to the wearer. In designing a ring, too, sharp projections must be
avoided that will be a danger to the wearer's hand or clothing or to others.

7–5   The Man's Ring   The functional design of the man's ring does not involve many aspects not already discussed in relation to other rings. Because
the man's hand is larger than the woman's, the ring is usually designed more
massively (Figs. 187, 188). Delicacy is not normally a design quality of the
man's ring. Simplicity rather than extravagance will dominate. The ring will
be set in a more rugged manner, calculated to withstand the more vigorous
movements of the man and the knocks and bumping more likely to occur because of his greater physical activity (Fig. 189). Stones or gems should definitely
be of harder composition (not less than 6 or 7 on Mohs' scale, **16–4**) and softer
stones might well be set with protective elements around them (Pl. 10).

7–6   The Earring, Dangle Type   Probably weight and comfort are the two
most important functional factors to be considered in the design of the earring.
As with all forms of jewelry, the personality of the client is the point of departure for esthetic design. She will tell the jeweler whether she likes large, small,

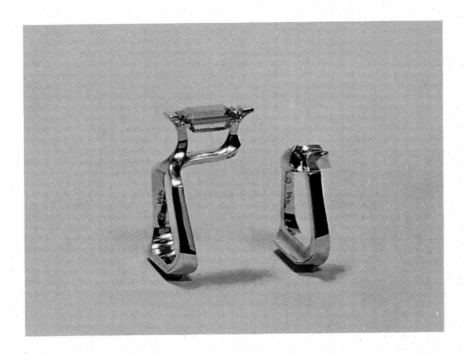

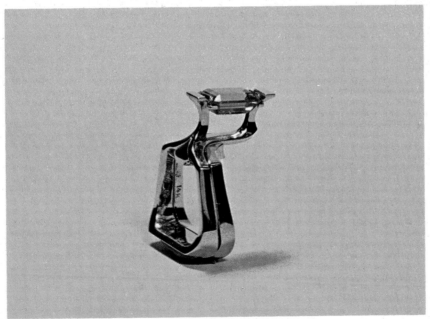

Plate 9. Stanley Lechtzin. Interlocking wedding ring set (*top*, separated; *bottom*, interlocked). 1967. Cast 14-kt gold with peridot.

Plate 10. Klaus Ulrich. Man's ring. 1966. Reticulated gold with black opal and Oriental pearls.

heavy, light, simple, or ornate design. If, on being asked, she does not know, the jeweler will have to make a careful evaluation. Regardless of size, excessive weight must be avoided, as in Figures 190 and 191.

The problem of weight and comfort are bound up with the type of ear back. The screw type (Fig. 429) is less comfortable than the spring-clip type (Fig. 430). This is because the area of the clip is larger than the area of the disk on the screw type. For many women it is possible to use the wing-back type that fits into the ear instead of on the lobe (Fig. 432). This ear back looks weird but fits perfectly and causes no pinching discomfort. Since it is unusual, many clients may need persuasion to be sold this type.

In general, a clip with a large area is more comfortable to wear and less likely to fall off than the typical screw back. Whenever possible, it is desirable for the contemporary jeweler to design his own clips as an integral part of the form of the earring (Fig. 192).

The dangle type requires an ear back with a small ring on which to hang the dangle, and usually this type of ear back must have a button above the ring to cover the screw disk. Many jewelers incorporate this feature into the design (Fig. 193). The length of the dangle will be determined by the client, but the jeweler must also relate his design to the length of the client's neck. A woman with a long neck can wear a long dangle effectively.

below left: Fig. 190. Heikki Seppa.
Pendant earrings. 1967.
14-kt. gold with pearls.
below right: Fig. 191. Brent Kington.
Bird pendant earrings. 1965.
14-kt. gold, cast.
bottom left: Fig. 192. Philip Morton.
Cage clip earrings. Sterling silver.
bottom right: Fig. 193. E. R. Nele.
Earrings and brooch. 1967.
Gold with tourmaline.

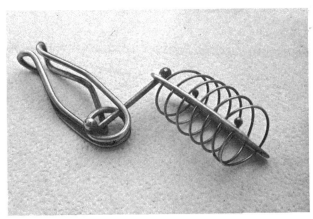

Fig. 194. Philip Morton.
Button earrings with clip, front (a)
and back (b) views. 1946. Enamel.

a   b

7–7 The Earring, Button Type   One of the functional problems of the button type of earring is to design it so that it does not tip over on the lobe of the
ear (Fig. 194). This means that it must not be topheavy, and the ear back must
be placed somewhere above the center, unless the button is quite small or
quite light. The button type may be made for pierced ears by using the post-
and-screw ear back. Otherwise a clip or screw back is necessary.

7–8 The Earring, Pierced-ear Type   The pierced ear is now in fashion, and
the pierced-ear wire can easily be made by the contemporary jeweler. If made
of silver wire, it should be hard-drawn, by beginning with at least 12-gauge
wire and drawing it down to 22- to 24-gauge without annealing. This will
stiffen the wire by work-hardening (**8–3**).
    Aside from considerations of weight and the type of ear back, questions of
size and shape are without restriction. However, observation of the client will
reveal how long and large the earring can be. A dangle hung on a small wire
through the ear lobe cannot be very heavy.

7–9 The Bracelet   The limitations of the bracelet are determined by the
preferences of the client. There are three types: link, open slip-on, and closed.
    The link type of bracelet (Fig. 195) must be sized to fit the wrist comfortably,
but it must not be so large as to slip over the hand. This type of bracelet can be
fastened with a sister hook (Fig. 435), a spring ring, or a ring and hook devised
by the jeweler.

Fig. 195. Philip Morton.
Link bracelet. 1951.
Cast sterling silver.

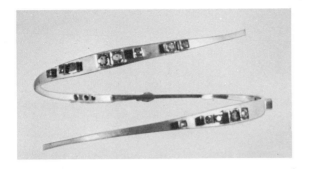

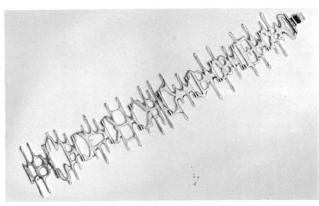

Fig. 196. Mario Pinton. Bracelet. 1966. Gold with rubies.
Fig. 197. Heikki Seppa. Bracelet. 1967. 14-kt. yellow gold.

The open, slip-on bracelet (Fig. 196) must be made so that the gap at the lower side will go over the side of the wrist, which is quite narrow. The metal of this type of bracelet must be work-hardened for stiffness, unless it is quite heavy, because a certain amount of spring is necessary. Even with a massive bracelet, it is desirable for the metal to have some spring tension.

The closed type of bracelet requires a hinge and locking catch (Figs. 197, 198) and offers the jeweler an opportunity to devise a concealed hinge and a special catch (13–9), which might be an integral part of the form of the bracelet.

Like the ring, the bracelet is likely to be bumped against hard objects. Stones used in the bracelet should be at least of 5 or 6 hardness on Mohs' scale (16–4).

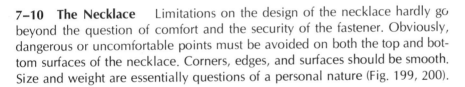

Fig. 198. Reinhold Reiling.
Bracelet. 1967.
Reticulated gold with cabochons.

7–10 The Necklace   Limitations on the design of the necklace hardly go beyond the question of comfort and the security of the fastener. Obviously, dangerous or uncomfortable points must be avoided on both the top and bottom surfaces of the necklace. Corners, edges, and surfaces should be smooth. Size and weight are essentially questions of a personal nature (Fig. 199, 200).

Fig. 199. Stanley Lechtzin.
Electroformed choker. 1967.
Silver-gilt, pearls, and moonstone.

left: Fig. 200. Alvin Pine. Necklace. 1967. 14-kt. gold, forged and fused.
right: Fig. 201. Michael Jerry. Necklace. 1967. Sterling silver,
forged and constructed, with pearl.

The choker made by forging heavy wire or rod must be carefully fitted to the individual neck (Fig. 201). Pendant necklaces that hang on a chain or cord must not extend too far onto the shoulders. As a rule of thumb, a limit of 90° is practical as a point of departure. Pendant forms tend to fall straight down from the chain, rather than fan out. They therefore assume a parallel relationship unless some special kind of spacing arrangement is devised to hold a fan position.

As a fastener, an ordinary wire hook through a jump ring may often fall open. One solution to this problem is to give the wire hook a spring tension by flattening it slightly and setting it so that a small pressure is necessary to slide it over the ring. The conventional spring-ring fastener is efficient and can always be used, but it is certainly less interesting to the creative jeweler than an interlocking device of his own design.

7–11 The Pendant There are practically no functional limitations to the design of the pendant. Within reason, weight and size can generally be designed to suit the limitations of the client, rather than those of function (Fig. 202). Comfort and security are the considerations here. Beyond these, one might follow the rule that the heavier the pendant, the larger the diameter of the cord or chain. Rayon or silk cord of ⅛ to ¼ in. diameter is universally popular. Both the necklace and the pendant offer an opportunity for unlimited expressive design. The contemporary jeweler generally designs a forged and modeled metal strap to carry a pendant or necklace array, and this strap may be open at the back, springing apart for putting on or removing.

Often the pendant is hung upon a swivel device so that it may be worn in all positions as a three-dimensional form in the round.

7–12 The Brooch   Beyond the functional limits of comfort and security, the weight of a brooch (Fig. 203) must be related to the type of dress material it is to be worn on. The client will give this information. The pin to be worn on a firm wool suit lapel can be heavy, if the client is willing. However, the pin to be worn on a thin blouse must not drag heavily on a weave of delicate material.

Once the weight problem is solved, there remains to be determined the position in which the pin will hang, so that the joint and catch location can be planned. In most cases the pin tong must be placed above the center of gravity of the pin so that it does not tip forward to expose only its upper edge. Sometimes a three-dimensional projection at the back of the lower edge will help maintain the pin in a vertical position. Otherwise the pin must be designed for its natural wearing position.

There has not been a great effort to find alternate solutions for fastening the brooch, beyond the pin, the joint, and the catch. As a substitute for the pin, the author has tried spring claws, which worked well on loosely woven materials, and has also attempted various substitutes for the commercial catch. Considerable opportunity awaits the experimenter in the direction of integral catches and, perhaps, more successful alternatives to the pin tong.

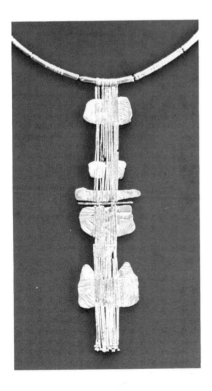

left: Fig. 202. Klaus Ulrich. Pendant. 1966. 900/000 yellow gold, reticulated.
below: Fig. 203. Klaus Ulrich. Brooch. 1967. 900/000 yellow gold, reticulated, with tourmaline.

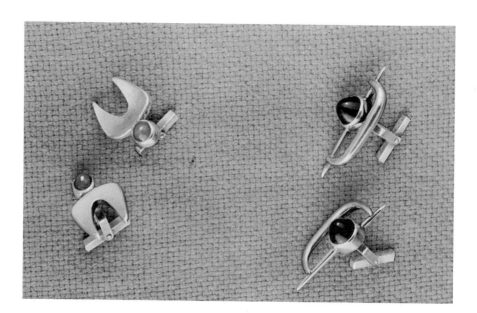

Fig. 204. Philip Morton. Cuff links. Cast sterling silver.

7–13 The Cuff Link   The functional problem of the cuff link is to design a back that can be readily attached or removed and yet not fall off. A nice compromise must be made as to size and shape of the cuff back. A double cuff link, each side of which fastens to a side of the cuff and then snaps and unsnaps, is an extremely attractive idea that has not, to the author's knowledge, been tried by the contemporary jeweler. Attractive to all designers is the idea of a cuff back that is an integral, if not equal, part of the design.

The typical commercial cuff backs are relatively unattractive in design. They are strictly functional (Fig. 433); and with the hinged bar that swings out, they are easy to attach and remove. The type that bends off at an angle is perhaps more functional in its fit than the straight type. (See Fig. 204.)

The chain link between a cuff-link front and the smaller back has a certain attractiveness. The back may then become an esthetic factor of design also. In designing this type, be sure to allow at least 5/8 in. between the front and the back, or the user will have difficulty in fastening them to the cuff. It is convenient to use a circular jump ring on each of the two parts of the cuff link and three oval jump rings, all soldered, between the rings.

Limitations of size and weight for the cuff link should be set by the client.

7–14 The Tie Clip   Comfort and security are basic limitations for the tie clip, but two additional requirements must be fulfilled. The space at the hinge or spring side must be wide enough to accommodate about 1/4 in. thickness of material, usually two thicknesses of tie—which may be wool and quite thick—and one thickness of shirt. The jaws of the clip must be designed in such a way as to grasp the material without causing snags or holes in it. The commercial tie-clip backs satisfy both of these requirements (Fig. 437).

If the clip back is to be custom designed, it must be work-hardened sufficiently to provide a durable spring tension. The double curve in the tie clip illustrated in Chapter 6 (Fig. 167) is necessary to provide both space and length

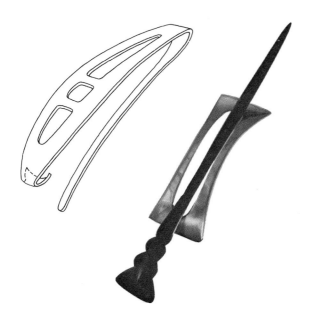
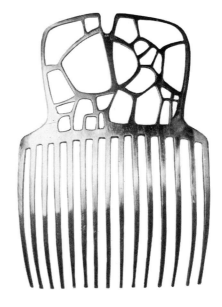

for sufficient spring tension. In finishing off the custom clip, all parts must be smoothed, so that no snags will occur. Also, in finishing, all grease and dirt must be removed, so that the clip will not soil the tie or shirt materials.

7–15   The Tie Tack   The main problems of the tie tack (Fig. 438) are to use a pin that is strong and stiff enough to resist bending without being much thicker than 18-gauge and to devise a simple spring clip that can be applied or removed by squeezing. Silver wire for this purpose can be stiffened somewhat by twisting (**9–20**). The use of nickel-silver wire is probably desirable, if the tie tack is in sterling. Gold wire, of course, possesses adequate stiffness.

7–16   The Barrette   The function of the barrette is to hold the hair in a pony tail. This usually calls for a slotted clip that extends about halfway around a circle 2 in. in diameter and a pin of metal, wood, or other material, which is placed through the hair in the slot (Fig. 205). An older style of barrette is flatter and utilizes a double spring clip and double pin hinged opposite the clip.

   Regardless of the form of the barrette, it must hold the hair and be held firmly by the hair. A great deal of design freedom is possible with this item of jewelry (Fig. 206).

7–17   The Comb   There has always been a small amount of interest in the comb, and particularly more when long hair is popular. The decorative comb may have a number of teeth, ranging from two on up, and is usually curved transversely to fit the shape of the head (Fig. 207). The teeth should not be less than 3 in. long and may need to be at least 4 in. long for increased security in fastening to the hair. The teeth, or pins, may be sawed into plate or assembled and soldered. They may be given a parallel or opposing movement to increase the visual pattern and supply an increased fastening security.

left: Fig. 205. Barrette with slotted clip.
center: Fig. 206. Philip Morton. Barrette. 1949. Ebony and sterling silver.
right: Fig. 207. Paul Mergen. Comb. 1967. Pierced brass.

Functional Design   123

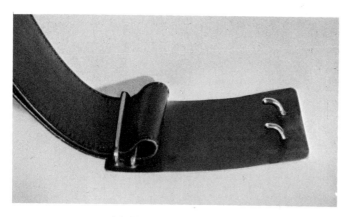

left: Fig. 208. Fastening device on belt buckle.
right: Fig. 209. Hinged loop on back of man's buckle.

7–18 The Buckle   The function of the buckle is to hold fast a cloth or leather belt. The woman's belt buckle may be fairly light in construction, but the man's buckle will be subject to more strain and should be constructed strongly, if not massively. Many interesting variations have been made in the devise that locks the belt in place (Fig. 208). The most common is a small pin or hook that penetrates a hole centered in the belt. Interesting functional solutions that are an integral part of the design are possible. In sterling, the loop that holds the belt end should be made of at least 10-gauge wire for the man's buckle. The pin should also be about 10-gauge wire. Otherwise the strain on the belt will cause these parts to bend out of shape. It is desirable to hinge the belt loop through a piece of tubing in order to allow this loop to swing flat against the belt rather than stand out from the back of the buckle (Fig. 209).

II

FUNDAMENTAL PROCESSES AND PRACTICAL PROCEDURES

8

INTRODUCTION
TO PROCESSES
Fusing and Soldering

Since legitimate design ideas can emerge only out of personal experience with tools and materials, it becomes necessary for the designer to think in terms of processes when designing jewelry.

INTRODUCTION

8–1 Classification of Processes   The fundamental processes are as follows: fusing and soldering, forming, layout, cutting, hammering, fastening, casting, finishing, stone setting, toolmaking.

The present chapter discusses the first of these fundamental processes. The following chapters describe the others, one by one. Bear in mind that the above classification is purely an abstraction designed to aid the presentation of processes in a systematic way. Any other system or order of classification may be equally valid.

8–2 The Structure of Metal   All metals consist of aggregates composed of large numbers of crystalline grains (Fig. 210). Though the internal structure of a grain consists of an orderly arrangement of atoms in a definite pattern, depending upon the particular metal, its external shape is determined by the manner and number of contacts with other grains. Therefore the crystalline planes of the grains run haphazardly in all directions.

8–3 Work Hardening and Annealing of Metal   When nonferrous metals are subjected to some form of work at normal temperatures (bending, hammering, twisting, drawing), the external force causes a distortion of the crystals along slip planes. This plastic deformation of the metal produces a condition of strain hardening, which varies with the amount of deformation. It is known as *work hardening*.

Fig. 210. Photomicrograph showing the structure of sterling silver. X1000.

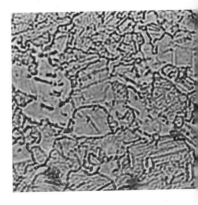

127

If work-hardened metal is heated to an appropriate temperature (a low red color in the case of silver, gold, and other nonferrous metals), the grains will assume their normal relationships and the strain will be eliminated. This is known as softening, or *annealing*. The jeweler quite often needs to anneal metal he has been rolling or hammering or drawing, in order to prevent it from cracking. Repoussé, in particular, work-hardens the metal and therefore requires systematic annealing. A large, soft reducing flame (8–11) is usually best for annealing metal, and the metal should not be heated past a low red color, since overheating increases the firecoat (8–14) that forms on the surface of alloys, particularly silver. The low red color will hardly be visible in a brightly illuminated room, and silversmiths usually prefer to work in an annealing booth, which has sides around to protect the work from being cooled by air drafts and to shield the work from the room light. Annealing can best be done in a small annealing pan (Fig. 372) filled with pumice stone. Immediately after annealing, the metal is dropped into a pickle solution, which cleans off all oxides (8–13).

FUSING AND SOLDERING

In ancient times work for fusing and soldering was heated in a small open-hearth furnace built of firebrick. A charcoal fire was built up and the work placed inside. A hollow reed, covered with clay to prevent its burning, was used to blow up the heat for soldering. This method was generally practiced by the metalsmiths of ancient cultures. There was little advancement in the means of heating and soldering metal until fairly recent times, and many of the older methods are still in use. Variations of these methods were employed until the discovery of illuminating gas.

8–4 Torch Equipment   There are many kinds of soldering torches available on the market and in use in jewelry and metal workshops. The kind of work you will be able to do depends upon the kind of torch equipment you have. An alcohol lamp or gas was used with a small mouth blowpipe (Fig. 211) in Europe and America up to the end of the 19th century, and this equipment is still found in many old workshops. Foot bellows (Fig. 212) often replaced lung power in the use of the blowpipe. Though these old methods may seem clumsy in relation to modern equipment, extremely delicate soldering operations have been done with them. The use of the mouth blowpipe is still a superior method for soldering pewter. If other equipment is lacking, work may be placed upon a heating frame (Fig. 213) over a gas plate and heated to a low red color. The final soldering is then done with a mouth blowpipe and the flame of a bunsen burner. Soldering with the blowpipe and bunsen burner is often more perfectly accomplished than when the modern torch is clumsily used.

The alcohol torch, the blowpipe, the prestone tank, and the propane or butane tank limit the range of work that can be done, because higher temperatures cannot be reached. More often provided in the modern workshop are the air-gas torch, utilizing natural gas or propane gas and air from a compressor, and the oxygen-gas torch.

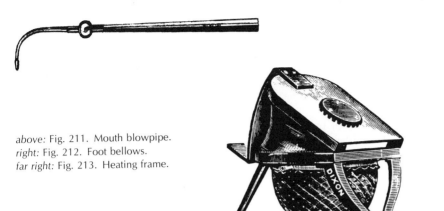

above: Fig. 211. Mouth blowpipe.
right: Fig. 212. Foot bellows.
far right: Fig. 213. Heating frame.

Compressed air-gas torches are preferred for general nonferrous metalwork and silversmithing, because the flame is softer but still hot enough for annealing and soldering. These torches are provided with various tips. Small hand torches with fine-pointed tips may be used for delicate work. Large hand torches with large flame tips provide a flame that is large and soft, and ideal for annealing or soldering large work. Air-gas torches are usually installed in an annealing booth. Most jewelry shops, however, use an oxygen-gas torch that gives a flame with a wide range of temperatures. Such torches are necessary for gold and platinum work and can be used to heat or fuse nonferrous metals readily. The oxygen-gas torch requires an oxygen tank, a tank regulator to adjust the pressure of the oxygen, and a torch with hoses. For melting metals for casting, a torch can be used with a hand crucible (Figs. 171, 220) or a graphite crucible (Fig. 214) in a gas-air barrel furnace (Fig. 215).

left: Fig. 214. Graphite crucible.
below: Fig. 215. Gas-air melting furnace.

Introduction to Processes: Fusing and Soldering 129

8–5 The Use of Torches   You can learn more from actually experimenting with the torch than can be usefully written. Nevertheless, there are a number of ideas that will help you to carry out your initial experiments.

- A large flame should be used to heat a large piece of metal.
- The size of the flame can be varied by increasing or decreasing the amount of gas.
- The intensity of heat of the flame will then be varied by increasing or decreasing the amount of oxygen or air you mix with the gas.
- The hottest part of the flame is at the tip of the blue cone of gas inside the flame where it leaves the tip (Fig. 216).
- Light an oxygen-gas or air-gas torch by first igniting the gas and then turning on the other valve. Turn off the torch by first turning off the oxygen and then the gas.
- If the oxygen-gas torch pops and goes out, it is because the oxygen is blowing the flame off the torch tip. If the gas will not light, it is probably because too much gas has been turned on. In order to avoid a possible burn, **be careful to turn on only a small amount of gas** when lighting the torch.
- To solder a special local place on your work, heat up the entire work to a point just below the melting point of the solder, using a medium-hot flame. Then apply a small but hotter flame to the local area to be soldered.
- Always keep your flame aimed directly at the work and always **keep your flame moving** around and around over the work. If the flame remains in one place, the metal may melt.
- To fuse pieces of metal together without solder, first flux the pieces at the joint **(8–16).**
- When soldering a piece of work that has already been soldered elsewhere, flux all the solder seams or paint them over with yellow ocher **(C–8).**
- To protect the surfaces of the metal from firecoat **(8–14)** the work may be painted with Prip's Flux **(C–9)** or with yellow ocher. Yellow ocher must be kept away from seams you are about to solder. In painting your work, therefore, leave a margin around such seams, or flux your seams first and dry the flux with a clean flame. After painting yellow ocher on a piece of work, allow it to air-dry before heating, or it will crack off.
- When annealing metal, use a large, bushy but clean flame. To anneal wire, coil it up in order to increase the volume of metal; otherwise it may melt.
- After heating metal up for annealing, fusing, or soldering, always pickle it before it cools, if possible. Otherwise it will have to be soaked for 15 or 20 minutes or boiled in a pickle pan.

Most oxygen-gas torches are designed for low-pressure gas. In most cities low-pressure city gas (LPCG) is maintained at a pressure of about 8 lb. If you use such a torch with propane or butane, you will need a regulator to reduce the tank pressure. There are two kinds: the automatic regulator, which is preset for appropriate pressure, and the adjustable regulator. If you have the adjustable regulator, it should be set at from 7 to 10 lb. The oxygen tank will always require a regulator, and this should be set to about 15 lb. pressure unless you are forging or hardening tool steel, in which case it might be set up

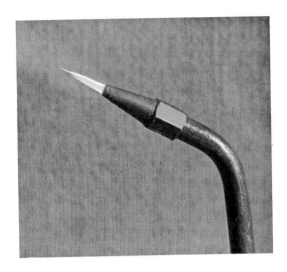

Fig. 216. Torch flame, showing the cone of concentrated heat.

to 25 lb. Tank valves should always be turned off at the end of the working period. The line valves, too, should be closed, and the torch valves opened to relieve the pressure on the regulator diaphragms.

The prestone tank was almost the only available torch for the small workshop until the development of the small hand propane or butane torches. Oxygen-gas, equipment is expensive, though necessary for the professional craftsman. The prestone tank is small, containing acetylene gas and having a single hose and a single valve at the torch. At the tank there is a tank valve and an air regulator that may be opened or closed to adjust the flame. The air regulator should be turned so that enough air flows through the torch to burn up the carbon of the gas completely. A reddish-colored flame indicates insufficient air; the air should be increased until the flame burns clean and bright.

The small portable propane or butane torch which has a replaceable tank is handy for the amateur or the beginner. The air adjustment on these torches is set at the factory. The torch is lighted by simply turning on the valve slightly and igniting the gas. A striker, or sparker, is usually used to ignite a torch in preference to matches.

FUSING

Nonferrous metals may be readily fused with the torches described above. When carrying out experiments in fused metal, be sure to use a level charcoal block or asbestos block, since fused metal may roll off an inclined surface. Study carefully the color changes and other transformations that take place as the metal becomes molten. It requires little skill to fuse silver into a ball. If pieces of metal are cleaned thoroughly and pickled several times, they will fuse together cleanly. The use of flux will also ensure good fused joints (8–16). It will take some practice to control the fusing within desired limits. Practice is the answer.

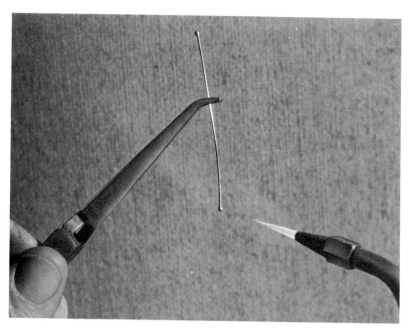

Fig. 217. Fused bead on end
of silver wire, held
by soldering tweezers,
with proper size of flame.

8–6 Fusing Beads on Wire   Small beads may be fused on the ends of wire very easily. Hold the wire with the end down, and hit this end quickly with a tight, hot flame. When the end begins to fuse, it will draw up into a bead (Fig. 217). Flux the end of the wire for a smoother flow. These molten beads will drop off after attaining a certain maximum size. Large beads can be made by supporting the end of the wire on an asbestos block and fusing to the desired size.

8–7 Fusing Granules and Beads   Granules or beads of silver or gold are made from wire cut into equal lengths. To get exactly matched granules, make a coil of jump rings of the desired size and cut them off with the saw (**9–14**). These rings can be mixed with powdered charcoal in a crucible and heated in a furnace to melting temperature. Afterward the contents are emptied into a pan of water and the charcoal washed away. The beads are then pickled. The jump rings may be fused one at a time on the asbestos block if there are only a few to be made.

Beads of large size may be made separately on a charcoal block by the following method. A small hole of appropriate size is drilled a little way into the block. Then a *dapping punch* of the right size is pressed and rotated into this hole until a perfect hemispherical hollow is formed. A small scrap of silver of proper size is placed carefully over this depression and melted with the torch. The lower half of the molten metal is supported as a perfect sphere. The upper half is pulled into spherical shape by molecular attraction of the molten metal. If this bead is to be finished perfectly and polished, it is best to solder it to a wire. The wire may then be placed in a pin vise (Fig. 235) and the bead can be filed, finished, and polished quite readily everywhere except at the point of attachment. Afterward, the wire is sawed away from the bead.

8–8 Granulation The appearance of granulation from early times has been mentioned in Chapter 3. How the Etruscans were able to organize the extremely fine beads (as small as $\frac{1}{200}$ in.) into patterns and then fasten them so neatly and cleanly to the background metal surface remained a mystery for a long, long time. Up to very recent times it was believed that these granules were soldered, each on its own pedestal, to the background metal. Yet no one was able to achieve this feat. A German metallurgist named Rosenberg thought that if some carbon could be absorbed to the granules, it would lower the melting point at the surface and allow them to become fused to the background metal. John Heins carried on some experimentation with fusing and found that gold could be heated to a point at which just the surface melted. Using pure gold, he was able to fuse small granules to a background in this manner.

In modern times the first successful granulations were accomplished by an Englishman named H. A. P. Littledale. His process is covered by British Patent 415, 181, accepted August 23, 1934. He uses metallic salts of the metals rather than solder alloys of those metals.

> When metallic oxides are heated in the presence of carbon, they are reduced to the metallic state. When properly compounded, the metals thus obtained fuse together and form an alloy and at this stage become a metallic solder, and the fusing takes place at a temperature below that of the fusing point of the individual metals.[1]

For gold granulation Littledale proposed using 1 part gold oxide, 1 part copper hydrate, and 2 parts dried glue. These materials are mixed with water and applied to the work. The glue furnishes excess carbon to the process and serves to hold the granules in place. The work is then heated in a reducing atmosphere. Littledale, by his process, reproduced some of the finest granulation of antiquity and also did original work in fine gold.

In recent times, John Paul Miller, one of the outstanding contemporary jewelers, has achieved marvelous success with granulation, even granulating with 14-karat gold. Miller uses a gold alloyed with copper for the granules and, by his own secret process, is able to utilize the copper within the granule in forming the fused attachment. He does not follow the Littledale process of applying metallic salts. The essence of Miller's principle is that gold in juxtaposition with copper has the effect of lowering their melting point. Miller believes that any serious research of granulation by the contemporary jeweler will probably lead to a successful solution, and that is one reason why he keeps his own process a secret. He has been proved correct in his belief.

In 1950 Patrick F. Maher and Donald Tompkins, two students of Ronald Pearson, set to work on the problem of granulation. After working through the available literature, briefly described above, they finally arrived at the following procedure:

1. Use two grades of metal, for example, fine silver for the parent metal and sterling (925 silver, 75 copper) for the granules.
2. Prepare the parent metal as to shape and finish.
3. Prepare the granules in an iron box with charcoal.

---

[1] Lines 53 to 61 of the patent.

4. Heat the box in the kiln to above 1640° F.
5. Remove and wash granules.
6. Adhere granules to parent metal with Elmer's Glue or gum tragacanth.
7. After the glue has thoroughly dried, fire the work in a carefully controlled reducing flame. This is the critical point in the process, since there are only a few degrees between fusing of the granules and melting the piece.
8. Finish the work by pickling and then pumicing, buffing, or scratch brush. But finish the work gently so that the granules are not scraped off.

In a gas furnace a reducing atmosphere is created by providing a slight excess of gas over oxygen. In an electric kiln the addition of small blocks of wood or the introduction of nitrogen gas into the furnace will create a reducing atmosphere.

At Cranbrook Academy in 1962, Stanley Lechtzin did his master's thesis on granulation: *Granulation: Methods for Granulating Karat Golds*.

In 1961 William Haendel wrote a beautifully clear and accurate technical paper on the process of attaching granules to jewelry forms. He called this process "eutectic soldering" because a eutectic solder is formed in the process. The term "eutectic" refers to an alloy having a melting point lower than any of its constituent metals. In the process he describes, granules are coated with copper by immersing in an iron pan containing a sulphuric acid pickle solution (about 1 part acid to 10 parts water) to which copper carbonate has been added.

8–9 Torch Textures   Some experimentation with the torch, fusing scraps of metal, will lead directly to the discovery of torch textures and to John Heins's discovery that the surface of a sheet of metal can be brought to a molten state while preserving the shape of the sheet. The texture for the pin in Figure 218 was accomplished by putting the disk on a cold asbestos block, hitting the surface with a very hot flame, and removing the flame quickly once the surface wrinkled up. The natural oxidized color was left on the disk. The fish design was chased on and the joint and catch soldered on the back. Sterling silver was used. Filings and small chips and beads may be fused to a surface to create rich textures also (Fig. 219).

8–10 Reticulation   Reticulation is the term for a type of torch texture that involves a more complex procedure. The process is based upon the fact that a coating of oxides, free metal, or, perhaps, loam or yellow ocher will help to hold a surface in place when a sheet of silver or gold is heated to the molten state. Normally, when a piece of metal is heated up to the melting point, molecular attraction pulls the metal into a globule or a flat ball. If a reducing flame is used on the torch, and if only a small part of the metal is melted at one time, and if the surface is well coated, the original form of the sheet metal will hold against the molecular pull, and the surface of the sheet metal will tend to ripple into a texture that varies according to chance and to the manner in which the surface has been coated. Too thin a sheet may not be used, because there is a tendency for holes to be melted into the metal. Practice will develop skill. The usual procedure is to prepare a larger sheet of metal and then use it as stock from which to cut out shapes for use.

left: Fig. 218. Philip Morton. Pin. 1945. Silver with chased design and torch texture, or reticulation. *above:* Fig. 219. Philip Morton. Bracelet. 1947. Sterling silver with torch texture, or reticulation.

Reticulation on Silver   Sterling silver may be used, but a somewhat lower grade of alloy seems to work better than sterling. Try making an alloy of silver from 800 to 925 parts fine silver. Roll this down to not less than 24-gauge thickness. Take this sheet through several stages of annealing and pickling in order to build up a good white coating of free silver oxide. It is best not to handle the silver with your fingers in order to avoid getting the surface greasy or marked. If you are planning to try a coating of loam or yellow ocher, now is the time to paint the sheet on both sides. Let the coating air-dry; otherwise it will flake off when the torch is applied.

To create the torch texture on the surface, the torch flame must be adjusted to a small to medium-hot flame. With the sheet of metal placed on a clean, flat asbestos block or bismuth block, play the flame on one place at a time until the metal is molten. Even with the utmost care small holes may sometimes appear. They may sometimes be used as a part of a design, however.

Reticulation on Gold   Reticulation works well on gold. Experiments should be performed on various alloys. Fourteen-karat gold can be readily textured.

Metal to be reticulated should be clean and well pickled. An even coating of oxide, loam, or yellow ocher should be applied and air-dried, and the metal should be placed on a clean, flat asbestos block. The torch texture is made with the small to medium flame, bringing to a molten state one small area at a time. A reducing flame, rather than an oxidizing flame, should be used.

8–11 Melting Metal Two rules should be observed when the nonferrous metals are melted to a molten state.

1. **The metal should not be overheated.** Overheating bronze or brass will vaporize the zinc content, thus changing the characteristics of the metal. Overheating silver or gold will increase the absorption of oxygen, thus making the metal more porous than necessary.
2. The flame used to melt the metal should be a reducing, or carburizing or nonoxidizing, flame if a hand crucible is used. An oxidizing flame is one with an excess of oxygen and is bluish in color. Such a flame, if played over the surface of nonferrous metal, will greatly increase the absorption of oxygen, and the cast metal will be full of small pits and pin holes. A reducing flame is yellowish in color.

Melting may also be done in a graphite crucible in a small melting furnace. In Cellini's time it was the practice to cover the surface of the metal with a layer of charcoal to seal off the oxygen of the air. In the casting of bronze today, it is the practice to throw a handful of a chemical called "phos" into the crucible and stir it well just prior to the pour, as a means of eliminating absorbed oxygen. This might be done with silver or gold.

When melting metal in the hand crucible, a large, feathery flame, in which the bright blue cone of gas has not been brought to sharp definition, will give a nonoxidizing melt. The flame should be held at a low angle into the crucible, so that the front pouring lip is heated at the same time as the metal (Fig. 220). As the metal scraps melt down, the surfaces become oxidized, and this prevents the metal from flowing together. For this reason a half teaspoon of borax flux should be added to a new crucible as a fluxing agent **(8–16)**. At each later melt a pinch of borax should be added if necessary.

When the proper melt temperature is approached, the nonferrous metals draw together into a liquid pool in the crucible, with a slightly convex surface

Fig. 220. Direction and position of flame into hand crucible, showing the bushy type of flame required.

Fig. 221. Jeweler's bench.

that becomes brilliantly mirrorlike. As this condition is reached, the crucible should be gently rocked, in order to stir up the metal and ensure an even mixture of even temperature. When the metal is liquid and well mixed, the flame should be specially directed to the pouring lip, so that it will become glowing hot. The pour must be made with the flame playing on the pouring lip, as well as upon the metal, until the last moment. Care must be taken to position the crucible properly, so that once it is tipped, the pour of molten metal will flow continuously into the mold. Any excess of flux at the pouring lip should be scraped away with an iron rod just before the pour. This is true also for the graphite crucible.

8–12 Casting Ingots Scrap metal and filings may be reclaimed by sending them into the refinery, where, for a reasonable milling fee, they are melted down, cast, and rolled into sheet or wire. Otherwise, scrap metal may be melted in the hand crucible and cast into an ingot mold. Scrap metal is preserved by the working jeweler in two forms. The jeweler's bench (Fig. 221) has a canvas, leather, or metal tray in which filings and silver and gold "sawdust" will fall as work is being done on the bench pin or V-block (Fig. 277). Periodically the jeweler scrapes out the filings, using a magnet to draw out any iron wire or broken sawblades, and stores them in a filings can. The small pieces of scrap silver and gold are picked out from the tray and placed in another scrap can. The reason for the separation is that the refining company pays less for mixed filings than for clean scrap metal.

Ingots may be required for projects of special dimensions, and a mold may be carved in a charcoal block (**14–6**) if the dimensions of the standard ingot mold are not suitable. The standard ingot mold is adjustable as to width. After being set to the desired dimensions, it should be placed on a gas burner and heated for half an hour. The metal is then heated in the crucible. Just before pouring, the ingot mold is removed from the gas burner and the inside of the mold is squirted with machine oil for lubrication. When the metal is up to temperature, it is poured into the mold. A hot mold will allow an even flow of metal into the mold and an even distribution of the crystal grains. The ingot should be removed from the mold, pickled, and cleaned. It should be forged once across the length and once along the width in order to pack the crystalline grains uniformly. The ingot is then ready for rolling (9–4).

8–13 Pickling When metals are heated, the surfaces become oxidized and dirty. The usual method of removing such dirt is to drop the heated metal into a *pickle solution,* which is usually made of sulphuric acid (C–19). When mixing the pickle solution, **always add the acid to the water.** Otherwise an explosion may take place. The pickle solution can be kept in a lead pan or a porcelain crock with a cover. Some jewelers keep the pickle solution in a Pyrex jar on a hot plate. A pickle crock with thermostatically controlled heating element is available from some supply houses. The pickle crock is kept near the sink, where pickled work may be easily rinsed off.

The pickle solution is not harmful to the hands, but care should be taken that it does not splash upon clothing. Metal pieces should be dropped into the crock on the near side, so that the splashes will move away. You may prefer to dip the piece into the pickle with copper or stainless-steel tongs. Rinse the pickled piece thoroughly with water. **Never put iron into the pickle,** including soldering tweezers (unless stainless steel), annealing tongs, or binding wire. Silver will come out of the pickle copper-plated at point of contact with iron.

A cold pickle solution reacts slowly to cold metal. For quick cleaning of metal, a small quantity of pickle may be heated on the hot plate in a pickle pan. The jewelry is placed in the pan with the pickle and heated until it begins to steam. After a few seconds, the pickle may be poured carefully back into the crock and the pan rinsed under the water tap.

8–14 Firecoat When gold or silver is heated to a low red color or hotter, the base metal of the alloy separates on the surface and forms a dark film on the surface of the metal. This is called *firecoat,* and it is difficult to remove. On a piece of silver that has been lightly polished it will appear as a dark shadow, against which the polished edges shine in contrast. You will be unable to get a good high polish on silver until this firecoat is removed. Silver on which the firecoat is allowed to remain tarnishes very rapidly. Firecoat can be most plainly seen if the back of the hand is held just below the piece of silver, so that it can be seen as a reflection in the surface of the silver.

There are several methods of removing firecoat.

■ Polishing with tripoli on a muslin buff is the most usual way of removing firecoat and works well if the surfaces are easily accessible. There is some danger of grinding off the edges or putting grooves in the silver if the work is overpolished.
■ Repeated annealing and pickling will build up a thick white coat of free silver on the surface. Such work should be burnished with the scratch brush.
■ The firecoat may be stripped by immersing the piece momentarily in a boiling solution of nitric acid and water (C–23). This is not a safe process

for inexperienced workers and requires a special blower installation to carry off the corrosive fumes.

■ The work may be stripped in an electroplating tank by reversing the direction of the current. The electroplating equipment usually has a cleaning, a stripping, and a plating tank (15–13).

■ The work may be given a quick silver plating to cover the firecoat.

■ The work may be painted with a yellow ocher solution (C–8), or it may be painted with Prip's Flux (C–9), which works very effectively to block out the firecoat.

■ Firecoat may be used as a color in itself.

SOLDERING

Soldering is the process of fusing two pieces of metal together with another metal of lower melting point. In nature metals are usually found combined with other elements in the form of ores. However, some deposits of free and relatively pure metals exist everywhere. From such deposits came man's first metal objects. Long before anything was known about the extraction of metals from ores, the Egyptians were making jewelry. They used free gold and a natural alloy of gold and silver, electrum. Through centuries of experience it was discovered that certain alloys of gold melted at a lower temperature than other alloys. This discovery made it possible to solder pieces of metal together (Pl. 11).

8–15 Hard Solders   Soldering with silver-alloy or gold-alloy solder is called "hard-soldering." The melting point of pure or "fine" silver is 1761° F. When a small amount of pure brass is melted with fine silver, the resulting alloy melts at a lower temperature. Five grades of silver solder are available on the market (C–21), and with these most soldering jobs can be done. I. T. solder melts at 1460° F. and is used primarily for soldering metal that is to be enameled. Hard-grade solder melts at 1410°F. Medium-grade solder melts at 1360° F. and is the grade most commonly used for general soldering. Easy-grade solder melts at 1310° F. It is used at the second stage of soldering when some parts have already been soldered with medium solder. Easy Flo solder melts at 1175° F. and is used for delicate and fine work when strength is not a factor, for repair work if stones cannot be removed, and for the third stage of a complex soldering project.

8–16 Fluxing   In order to solder one metal to another, the surfaces to be soldered must be clean and bright, and they must be kept clean during the soldering process. When pieces of silver are fused, they become covered with oxides, which prevent the flow of solder. Flux is a solution used to cover the solder seams and the solder in order to prevent oxidation while the metal is heated and soldered. Hard soldering requires a borax or fluoride type of flux (C–9). Soft soldering requires a different kind of flux.

8–17 Soft Solders   The term "soft solder" refers to solder containing lead in an alloy with tin. One standard soft solder, called "fifty-fifty," is made with equal parts of lead and tin and melts at about 400° F. For jewelry work, a special flux, zinc chloride, is used for soft soldering. This flux, also called "soldering salts," is made by mixing 1 oz. zinc chloride in 1 pt. water. Soft soldering is used to fasten ear wires and cuff-link backs to jewelry when the temperature of hard soldering might anneal the metal or burn up the steel spring in the clip. Soft solder is not used on gold. Be careful not to overheat the metal if you are soft-soldering. Use a small flame, and heat the work only to the melting point of the soft solder.

8–18 Special Soft-soldering Problems *Soft-soldering Ear Backs* All sterling ear backs are soft-soldered to the earring. They are never hard-soldered, since the high temperature required by hard solder takes the temper out of the ear back itself and also out of any spring that may be used to provide tension to hold the clip in place. Screw-back types often come apart when hard-soldered to the earring. For these reasons the low-melting-point soft solders are used.

Almost all ear backs are made with a small hollow cup to hold soft solder. The simplest way to solder these backs to the earring is to touch the hollow cup of the ear back first with the flux brush. Soft solder requires zinc chloride, or soldering salts (**C–9**), as a flux. Clip off a small piece of lead solder and place it in the cup of the ear back. The ear back is held in the self-locking soldering tweezers so that the cup is facing upward. A small flame is now played under the cup, as it is held by the tweezers, until the solder flows and fills the cup. With a little practice you can judge the right amount of solder just to fill the cup. Another way to fill the little cup is to set the self-locking tweezers holding the ear back on the soldering block, with the ear back projecting over the edge of the bench. Hold the torch in the right hand and a small length of soft solder in the left hand, and apply the solder as the cup is heated up. This is the strip method of applying solder (**8–20**). Solder should be fed into the cup so that it is just flush with the rim.

After solder has been put into each cup, place one ear back in position on the earring and place the self-locking tweezers in such a way as to hold the ear back there. Flux the joint between the earring and the ear back; then apply a small flame to the underside of the earring, playing the flame at the cup. As soon as the solder runs, dip the earring into a cup of water. This will immediately chill the solder and cool the earring. (If stones have already been set in the earring, it should not be dipped in water, as this may crack the stone. It must be allowed to cool slowly.) If the soldering has been properly done, there should be no excess solder to clean off around the ear-back cup.

Soft-soldering Cuff Backs to Cuff Links The same procedure is followed with soft solder in the case of cuff links. Cuff backs usually have a steel spring, which will be annealed if hard solder is used.

8–19 Paillon Method of Applying Solder When you receive a sheet of silver solder, take your scribe and cross-hatch it with lines on one side. If you are using three grades of solder, use a distinctive cross-hatching for each grade. One common system is single hatching for easy grade, cross-hatching for medium grade, and triple hatching for hard grade. Sad soldering failures occur when the wrong grade of solder is used.

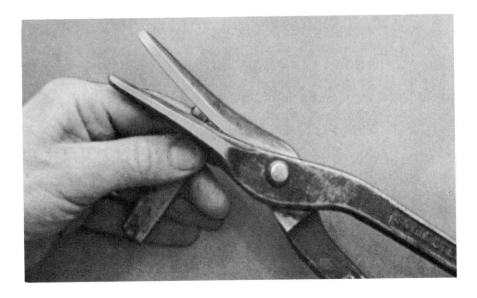

Fig. 222. Cutting a fringe
of solder to make paillons.

Cut a small strip, perhaps 1 in. wide, from your sheet of solder and fringe one end with the hand shears. Now, holding the strip in the manner illustrated (Fig. 222), with the forefinger across the top of the fringe, cut off a narrow strip of the fringe with the shears, and you will have a group of little *paillons,* or "panels," of solder. Your forefinger lies along the blade of the shears and on top of the fringe, to keep the paillons from flying away as they are cut off. The paillons should be oblong in shape, so that they will lie closely along the solder seam. Square pieces project out from the seam farther than necessary and may leave a trace when melted.

After fluxing the seam, place the paillons at intervals along the seam by picking each one up on the tip of the flux brush and setting it down in position. When doing this, wipe the brush against the neck of the flux bottle to remove excess flux. Only experience can tell you how much solder is enough for any given seam. Too little solder will leave open seams. Too much solder builds up and must be removed.

8–20   The Strip or Wire Method of Applying Hard Solder   A piece of wire solder or a narrow strip cut from sheet solder may be held in the soldering tweezers and applied to the fluxed seam at the moment when the work reaches the proper soldering temperature. The end of the solder strip should be dipped in flux before soldering begins. This is by far the most flexible method of applying solder, and with practice it becomes possible to apply quickly just the right amount of solder in each case. The difficulty of this method lies in the need to coordinate both hands so that the torch is removed instantaneously, just as the solder strip is applied. The beginner will find that, until he masters this particular bit of coordination, he will either forget to move his flame away while he is thinking about moving his solder strip into position, thus melting his solder into a bead, or he will move his flame away too quickly, thus allowing the work to cool down too much. This method is especially useful where it is difficult to place and hold little paillons in position.

8-21 The Pick Method of Applying Hard Solder   The paillon of solder, of proper size for the work, is fused into a ball and then picked up on the end of a sharply pointed iron rod, or *pick,* with which it is applied at the right place on the work. The pick may be dipped in flux and will then pick up the fused ball of solder. This method allows very precise positioning of the solder and avoids the accumulation of excess solder at the seam.

8-22 Sweating Surfaces Together, Sweat Soldering   When you wish to solder pieces of metal surface to surface, this method can be used to avoid applying excessive solder and putting solder where it is not wanted. Flux the surface of the underside of one piece, and flow over it, by the strip method, half enough solder to cover the surface. Now flux the surface of the second piece of metal and place them together, surface to surface, in the correct position. Heat both pieces slowly until the solder fuses them together.

8-23 Solder Filings   Another way of applying solder is to collect fine solder filings in a clean paper. This is best done by filing a heavier section of solder than is usually at hand, though the standard 26-gauge solder sheet may be used. The filings may be kept in a small bottle. A small portion may be placed in a shallow dish and Battern's or Prip's Flux added. The brush is then used to apply the flux and filings at the desired joints.

8-24 Solder Powder   Solder filings are well mixed with powdered borax in about equal portions and stored in a small bottle. This powder is applied by taking a small spatula (the flattened end of a piece of 16-gauge silver wire will serve) and dropping a small portion over the joint. Solder is applied in this way for filigree work (**9–23**), but may also be used in many other situations.

8-25 Rules for Soldering   The observance of the following rules will help you to solder successfully.

- The surfaces that you are soldering together should be scraped or filed clean and must fit together perfectly and squarely. Seams for sterling silver need not be finished too smoothly but must be square and exact. Seams for gold must be filed more smoothly. Sawed edges on silver will generally not require further finishing if the cut is true and even.
- The solder seam must be well fluxed, and the pieces of solder should be fluxed also.
- The heat must be applied to the metals that are to be soldered and hot to the solder. Only when the metals are heated to the right temperature will the solder flow properly along the seam.

Beginners encounter one common difficulty when soldering. Either the solder fails to flow, or the piece is melted up in the attempt to solder. A simple analogy may provide a practical theory to use. Think of each piece of metal as a volume that will soak up and hold a certain quantity of heat, depending upon its size. If you adjust a water tap to a certain constant flow of water, it will take twice as long to fill up a quart jar as it does to fill up a pint jar. This relationship applies to heating pieces of metal. Therefore, when soldering a small piece of silver to a large one, direct the flame to the larger piece first

and for a longer period of time, in order to bring both pieces up to temperature at the same time. If you heat the small piece first, the solder will fuse to it and fail to fuse to the larger piece.

Warning: Always keep lead and lead solder away from the annealing pan and the soldering blocks on which you work with silver (C–15). Lead will soak into silver or gold that has been heated to annealing or soldering temperature and cause holes to be eaten in the metal.

8–26 Methods of Holding Work for Soldering   The methods of holding work for soldering will be dealt with in relation to specific problems; however, certain basic methods should be understood.

If the work is self-supporting and need not be placed upon a flat or specially prepared surface, it is best placed in the annealing pan, upon a bed of pumice-stone fragments. Pumice stone is a good nonconductor of heat and allows the flame of the torch to flow underneath as well as around the work, thus making it possible to heat the work evenly. All work should be annealed in this pan, which is particularly useful when you are soldering a large, flat sheet, because the flame can be thrown underneath the sheet, rather than on top, where other small parts may be overheated before the large sheet is brought up to temperature.

A small charcoal block is excellent for supporting work to be soldered, because it, too, is a good nonconductor. It can be carved or shaped to fit irregularities of the work. Steel pins can be forced into it to hold work in place. It can be held in the hand and moved as the work is being heated. Its one disadvantage is that it breaks apart easily. It will hold together better if 10 or 15 turns of binding wire are wrapped around the edges.

A small square of asbestos sheet about 3/8 in. thick and 4 or 5 in. square also makes a durable soldering block. Jewelry supply houses also carry a number of specially prepared blocks that are good. One type is made of a coil of asbestos strip set in a sheet-metal pan. This one will last a long time. A bismuth block is remarkably good, because it is a nonconductor of heat and can easily be carved to fit work. However, it is somewhat messy and not very durable. A special soldering block should be kept for soft solder, in order to avoid getting soft-solder flux on your hard-soldering blocks, because the fumes from this flux will interfere with hard soldering.

The jeweler also uses a small tangle of fine iron wire (about 24-gauge) twisted up into a little pad and fixed to a wire handle that projects down underneath (Fig. 223). This is called a *"mop."* The wire should not be too fine, since it will fuse and burn in a hot flame. It must be soft iron wire, rather than a carbon-steel wire. Work is placed upon the mop, which is held in the left hand and rotated while the flame is played on and around the work. The advantage of the mop is that the wire allows the flame to come up underneath the work.

A heavy wire screen for holding the work is available from the supplier. The screen is usually set on a ring tripod.

Small pieces may be held in the soldering tweezers for soldering. **Never place your work upon cold-conducting materials such as transite, brick, or metal**. These materials will draw heat away from your work as fast as it is applied. As a result, the upper surface is likely to burn, while the lower surfaces remain cold.

Fig. 223. Top *(a)* and Side *(b)* views of a soldering mop.

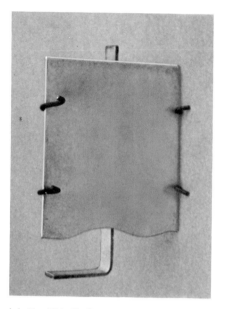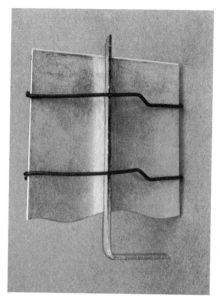

left: Fig. 224. Binding wire applied neatly to hold metal in position for soldering.
right: Fig. 225. Kinks in binding wire to allow for expansion while holding plate tightly in position.

8–27 Holding Work Together with Binding Wire or Steel Pins   If gravity cannot be utilized to hold parts together for soldering, or if they are likely to shift position when heated, soft iron binding wire can be used.

Never apply binding wire by wrapping it around and around. It should be applied precisely where it will hold the work together and in a manner that allows it to be easily removed after soldering for pickling. Notice in Figure 224 how the ends of the wire are carefully bent around the edges of the sheet and then bent up, with the excess wire clipped off. The bent-up ends can be gripped easily with pliers, after soldering, and pulled off quickly for pickling while the work is still hot.

The kinks in the binding wire are made firmly with squarenose pliers in order to tighten the binding (Fig. 225). As the silver heats, it will expand. The kinks allow the wire to expand with the silver. Otherwise the tightening binding wire will distort the work.

Strips, shapes, and wires that require fixed alignment for soldering may be held in place by setting up the work on a charcoal block and holding the parts in position with steel pins or small pieces of iron wire with sharpened points, which are pressed into the block (Fig. 226).

8–28 Holding Work in Position with Plaster of Paris   When a number of small parts must be assembled in the air (that is, without any supporting structure) and soldered together, they may be set in plaster of Paris. Assemble the pieces on a small cake of beeswax modeled to the correct shape. Press the pieces in about halfway. Then build a small wall around the wax and pour plaster of Paris over it to a depth of about 1 in. When it is set, remove the wax carefully, leaving the pieces embedded in the plaster. The plaster may be scraped away around the pieces until they are clean and open to one another.

Fig. 226. Steel pins holding parts together on block for soldering.

Solder may now be applied by the strip method or the paillon method and the work soldered together. Afterward the plaster may be removed. If further soldering is required, a hard solder should be used at this stage.

8–29 Preparation for Soldering Joints and Catches   Joints and catches are manufactured commercially in various designs and are satisfactory for use with many brooch designs. They come in two general types. Those for soft soldering have a small hollow disk attached at the base to provide greater surface contact for the softer lead solder. Those for hard solder need no such disk.

The catches are made with the slot opening either at the side or on the top (Fig. 434). If the piece of jewelry requires a short pin tong, the top-opening catch is better, since the pin can swing directly into the slot. When ordering catches, always specify the type. If only one type is stocked, the top opening is probably best, although some jewelers regard the side-slot catch as safer.

The joint usually comes with the flanges spread, and these should be squeezed parallel with the pliers. For a secure and permanent soldering job it is wise to hold each piece, the joint and the catch, with the pliers and file the bottom lightly with a fine file. This ensures clean surfaces for soldering. It also allows the joint, which will be slightly curved from bending, to sit flat upon the jewelry. The spot that the joint is to occupy should be scraped clean and fluxed with a small drop of flux. The joint is then set into position and a small paillon of solder placed on each side. The same procedure should be followed with the catch. Too much flux will tend to allow solder to run up into the slot of the catch. A small paillon of solder should be placed on each side of the catch. Do not place the paillon at the front or the back, because it will run into the hinge of the safety catch. Always adjust the safety catch so that the two little knobs are on top.

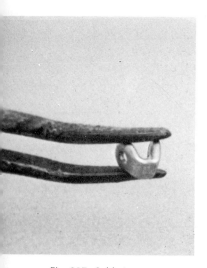

Fig. 227. Soldering tweezers set across slots of joint.

8–30 Soldering Joints and Catches Before soldering, the joint and catch should be carefully lined up so that when the pin tong is set, it will line up through the catch. When soldering, avoid directing the torch upon the joint or catch. Heat the work slowly and completely, moving the torch around the joint and catch until the last moment, when the solder is ready to run.

A more useful and flexible way to solder the joint and catch to a piece of work is to hold each one in the tweezers. Solder is applied to the fluxed bottom in the following manner. Hold the joint or catch in self-locking tweezers. The tweezers may be laid across the asbestos block so that the joint or catch extends out over the edge of the workbench. The bottom is fluxed and heated to a low red color, whereupon solder is applied in strip form, held in another pair of tweezers. Care must be taken not to apply too much solder. The work is now placed in position on the asbestos block, and the catch is taken up in the tweezers in such a way that the tweezer ends run across the safety-catch slot (Figs. 227, 228). The catch is positioned in the tweezers so that, when the heel of the hand is placed on the bench and the tweezers pivoted down, the catch is lowered into exactly the right position with respect to the piece of work and to the planned location of the joint (Figs. 229, 230). The hand must be located on the bench in such a comfortable position that it swings naturally into the correct position. The tweezers are then swung up out of the way of the flame while the piece is heated. The exact locations of the catch and joint are fluxed, and the piece is heated with the torch. When the work is up to soldering temperature, the catch is swung down into place and held steadily in position until the solder flows onto the work.

Now the joint is taken up with the tweezers. The ends of the tweezers should be across the open slot of the joint, and the joint should be turned in the tweezers so that, when the hand is positioned and swung down, it, too, will land on the piece of work in exactly the correct position and aligned with the catch. **The slots of the joint and catch must line up** (Fig. 231).

Descriptively, this may seem to be a laborious process, but, when mastered, it can save a great deal of time. Joints and catches often must be placed on narrow or rounded edges where they cannot be made to stand. This process permits quick and exact placement. The important thing is to set your hand on the bench in just the right position with respect to the work and leave it there, using the heel of the hand as the pivot.

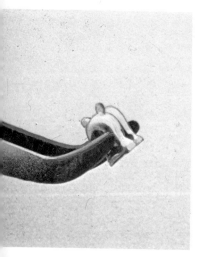

Fig. 228. Soldering tweezers set across slot of catch.

8–31 Fastening the Pin Tong to the Joint Although this operation is not soldering, it is the final necessary step to soldering on the joint and catch. The tong has a small rivet pin at one end. This may be squeezed out with the square-nose pliers and set carefully to one side. The tong is placed in position in the joint, and the stop flange, which should point downward, is checked to see whether it needs filing down in order to allow the pin to swing into the catch and be stopped at the correct "spring" position. The stop flange usually requires some filing. In case the stop flange should not extend far enough down to cause some slight spring tension of the pin in the catch, the flange may be planished on the side with a small cross-peen hammer to stretch its length. It is then filed to finish and shape. The pin tong is set in the hinge of the joint, and the rivet is taken up in the squarenose pliers and started into the hinge hole. Then the pliers are used to squeeze the rivet all the way through the

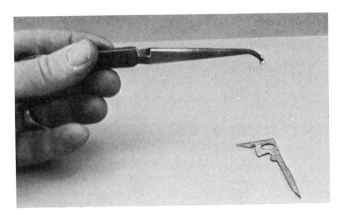
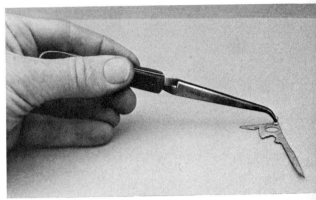

above: Fig. 229.   Hand in position to swing down catch in exact position for soldering.
above right: Fig. 230. Catch in position for soldering.
right: Fig. 231. Slots of catch and joined lined up so that pin tong fits.

hinge holes (Fig. 232). **To** set this rivet, grasp the joint at the base of the pliers, where the leverage is greatest, and squeeze strongly. If the pin tong is found to point slightly out of line to the catch, take the hinge in the pliers and twist gently until the pin is in line.

Never solder a joint onto the work with the pin in the joint, since this will anneal and soften the pin tong.

If the rivet pin is missing, it is easy to make one from nickel-silver or sterling wire by filing a flat taper in the pin vise. This tapered end should be inserted in the hinge from the top downward and the excess clipped off underneath. File the snipped ends flat, leaving a small amount projecting beyond the hinge on each side, and then squeeze firmly with the pliers, as has been already described.

8–32   Soldering Jump Rings, Rings, and Ring Shanks   In the section dealing with bending you learn how to prepare and close jump rings (**9–14**). Soldering the jump ring closed is a delicate process, but it can be done easily if the correct technique is used. The ends must touch each other.

Fig. 232. Fastening pin tong by squeezing with pliers.

1. Clamp the tweezers at the lower end of the jump ring, at the opposite end from the seam. If another ring is attached to the ring, or if it is a part of a chain, the attached ring and tweezers must be held as far away from the seam as possible. Hold the tweezers in a vertical position, with the jump-ring seam on top.
2. Flux the seam with a touch of the flux brush, and pick up a small paillon of solder. This paillon should be very small in size, since a wire ring seam will require very little. Place the paillon on top of the seam so that it lies across the seam and touches both sides.
3. A small torch tip should be used for soldering. A tip with a hole about the size of a No. 57 drill is about right for small jump rings. The flame will be extremely small and will heat the ring without heating up a large section of chain.

Introduction to Processes: Fusing and Soldering   147

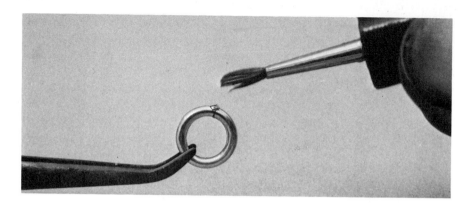

Fig. 233. Paillon on seam
of jump ring, ready to solder.

4. Place the flame near the seam, not touching the solder or the jump ring but heating the air. The heat will evaporate the flux without flipping off the paillon.

5. Now hit the seam with the flame once or twice with a quick motion—on and away. With a little practice you will find that this can be done quickly the first time. If you allow the flame to linger, the ring will melt down at both ends. The purpose of the hot flame is to heat the ring quickly and yet avoid heating or melting other attached rings. The flame should be directed onto the ring in such a way that it is also directed away from attached rings or other parts. This technique will require a little practice, but by the time you have made a foot of chain, you will be an expert.

Soldering ring shanks, jump rings, or circles of wire or strip may be done by the following method.

1. The two ends of the shank or circle must be brought squarely together in the curved line of the circle and under spring pressure, which holds them together (9–14). If this is not done, the ends may separate while being soldered.

2. Clamp the tweezers across the lower end opposite the seam. Flux the seam and, for a ring band, place in between the two ends a paillon of solder that is a little longer than the band is wide, and a little wider than the band is thick. The solder paillon should project lightly all around. If the ring is of heavy strip, it is easy to spread the seam apart by sliding the ring up the ring mandrel until the seam opens far enough to allow the paillon to be inserted. When the solder is in position, the seam should be thoroughly fluxed. For a jump ring, place a small paillon of solder on top of the seam (Fig. 233).

   When a ring is stamped or textured, solder can be prevented from running into the depressions if the paillon is kept flush with the outside surface and the ring held so that the seam is upward. Excess solder will then run downward to the inside of the ring, where it may be filed off.

3. Holding the tweezers up, throw a medium-size, medium-hot flame over and around the entire ring. As the ring band comes up to temperature, the solder will flow quickly. Remove flame immediately and drop the ring into the pickle. For soldering a jump ring, use a very small, rather tight flame. It may be desirable to switch to a smaller torch tip if possible.

Plate 11. Philip Fike. Fibula. c. 1968. Gold and Grenadilla wood.

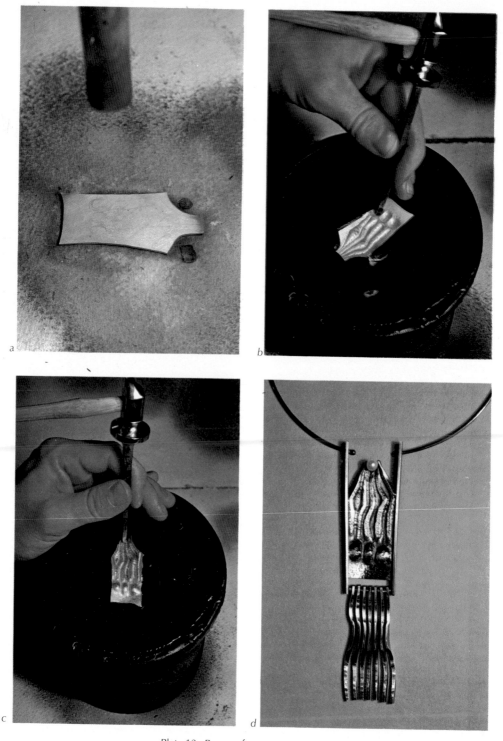

Plate 12. Repoussé process, performed by John Jauquet, graduate student
of Fred Fenster, Madison, Wisc. a. Annealing basic blank of sterling silver.
b. Roughing out form in softened pitch. c. Refining form after annealing work-hardened metal.
d. Finished pendant assembled with pearl.

9

FORMING

DRAWING WIRE AND TUBING

The size of wire, as well as of sheet, is measured by the Brown & Sharp standard gauge plate (Fig. 234). A variety of gauge sizes of wire is available on the market, but it is useful to know how to draw wire down to small diameters from large sizes. Also, in a well-equipped shop carrying on production operations it is cheaper to buy large quantities of 6- or 8-gauge wire and draw down all smaller sizes as required. Sterling scrap may also be saved up and cast into ingots of rod, which may be rolled down to a size suitable for drawing (9–2).

As you carry out the simple process of wire drawing, you will enjoy reflecting upon how the Egyptians prepared the wire for their exquisite jewelry. Having hammered out their sheets of gold between polished stone boulders, they cut narrow strips with stone knives. The strips were then rolled into a tight

Fig. 234. Front *(left)* and back *(right)* of Brown & Sharpe standard gauge plate.

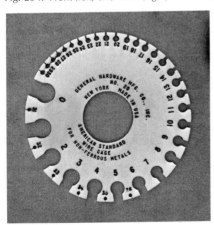
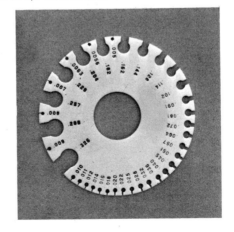

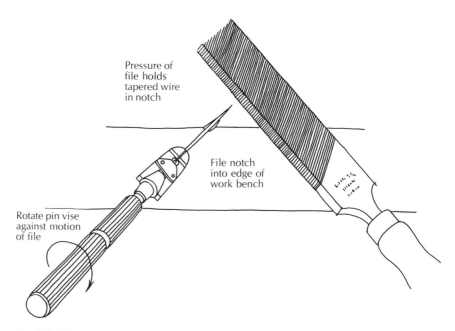

Pressure of file holds tapered wire in notch

File notch into edge of work bench

Rotate pin vise against motion of file

Fig. 235. Wire in pin vise being filed to a taper. Arrow shows direction of movements.

spiral, just as paper drinking straws are made to form a tube. The spiral seams were soldered, and the tube was pulled through a stone drawplate to reduce it in size to a fine hollow wire. This long, tedious preliminary work may seem arduous to us, yet it undoubtedly gave the Egyptians a deep understanding of the nature of metal, its capacities, and its limitations.

You should make two observations about the process of wire drawing. First, metal is extremely malleable, when dealt with properly, and can be reduced in size merely by drawing it through a tapered hole. As you squeeze the metal in this way, you pack its crystals closer together and displace some of the metal, thus increasing the length. Second, whenever you do work upon metal, by drawing it for instance, it becomes less malleable and more springy and brittle (8–3).

Compare a piece of drawn wire with a piece of wire that has been annealed. This hardening characteristic can be utilized in jewelry. For example, if you wish to make a sterling brooch or ear clip of wire, you would find it desirable to use drawn wire, since it is hardened and springy and will hold its shape better than a piece of annealed wire. To maintain this springiness, you should avoid heating or soldering the wire and devise some other means of fastening (Chap. 13).

9–1 Preparing Wire for Drawing   Take a length of wire (about 12 in. of 12-gauge sterling wire) and place it in the pin vise, so that about 1 in. projects beyond the jaws of the vise (Fig. 235). Holding the pin vise between the thumb and the four fingers of the left hand, place the wire end in a V-shaped notch that has been filed into the edge of the bench pin or workbench with the edge of a half-round file. Use a hand file that is not too coarse. Place it on the wire and, with a forward stroke of the file, rotate the pin vise against the direction of the file stroke. At the end of the file stroke, reverse both directions, keeping

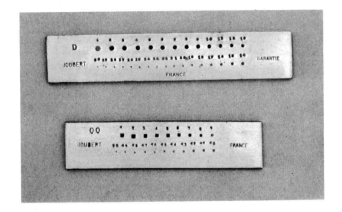

Fig. 236. Drawplates.

the pin vise rotating always against the direction of the file. Suitable pressure of the file will hold the wire in the slot as you rotate the pin vise. A fine-cut file will work better on fine wire. File a long, flat taper in the wire, so that, as you reduce the size of the wire by drawing, the taper will remain long enough to go through the drawplate (Fig. 236). You will probably have to refile the taper as the wire is reduced in size. Rub the tapered point with beeswax for lubrication.

9–2 Drawing Wire   Place the drawplate in a horizontal position in the draw bench or bench vise, with enough clearance above the vise jaws to allow the drawtongs to be centered on the row of holes you are using (Fig. 237). Find the hole that just fits the size of wire you are using. Place the tapered end snugly into the next smaller hole. The wire goes into the tapered-cone side of the drawplate and is pulled out the numbered side. Grasp firmly with the draw-tongs as much of the tapered end of the wire as you can get hold of and, with both hands holding the tongs closed on the wire, draw it completely through the hole. Pull with your entire body, not just your arms. The numbers stamped near the holes do not correspond to gauge sizes but enable you to keep track of the hole you are drawing through. To avoid curling the wire, always draw straight away from the plate.

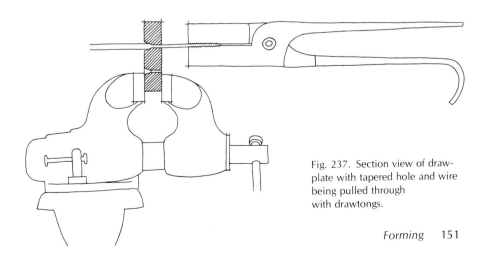

Fig. 237. Section view of draw-plate with tapered hole and wire being pulled through with drawtongs.

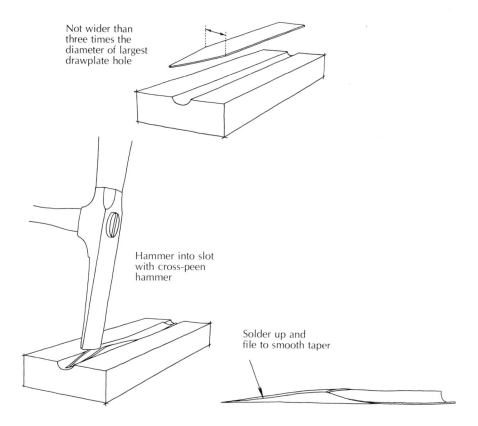

Not wider than three times the diameter of largest drawplate hole

Hammer into slot with cross-peen hammer

Solder up and file to smooth taper

Fig. 238. Tapered strip with channel being formed in a slot with cross-peen hammer.

Fig. 239. Burnisher.

Drawplates can be purchased that are cut for drawing square, rectangular, and half-round wire. Half-round wire may also be drawn in the regular draw-plate by soldering the ends of two wires together, filing the taper, and drawing them down together. In order to prevent their twisting, a burnisher or smooth mandrel must be held in a fixed position between the wires and against the back of the drawplate. Triangular wire can be made in a similar manner by drawing two wires through a square-hole drawplate.

9–3 Drawing Tubing   The drawplate can also be used for making tubing of a diameter slightly smaller than the largest hole. This is done by cutting a strip of sheet metal, 20-gauge or less, to a width slightly less than three times the diameter of the largest hole in your drawplate. The point is that you must be able to draw your tube through the largest hole and cannot make a tube of larger diameter, though one of smaller diameter can be made.

With the shears, cut a taper that runs back about 1½ in. on each side of one end. Then, with a small cross-peen hammer, form the tapered end into a gutter-shaped channel on the tin block or in a groove of the right size (Fig. 238). The strip beyond the tapered end must also be curved into the start of a channel. Now, with the small hammer, close the channel a short distance beyond the taper. Then solder this tapered end and file it into a smooth tapered point.

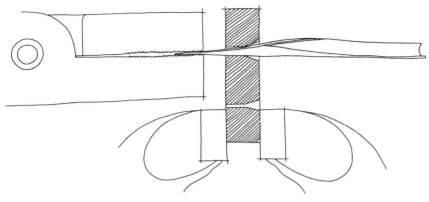

Fig. 240. Strip being drawn through drawplate to make tube.

Now you are ready to rub the taper with beeswax and begin the drawing operation. Place the point of your burnisher (Fig. 239) in the channel and snugly into the tapered cone at the back of the drawplate and hold it firmly in position as you draw the strip through (Fig. 240). At this first draw, the tube will begin to form. Draw the tube through successively smaller holes until the sides have closed and the tube is the desired size. The seam may then be soldered. You will note that as the tube size decreases, the wall thickness increases.

ROLLING METAL

In earlier times, metal was formed into sheets by the laborious process of forging cast ingots down to size and planishing them smooth. This slow process undoubtedly taught metalworkers a great deal about the qualities of metal. It would be desirable for all jewelers to try this as a learning experiment. Even though we can easily buy sheet metal of every gauge, it is convenient to be able to roll pieces of metal to special sizes by means of the rolling mill (Fig. 241).

Fig. 241. Rolling mill.

Fig. 242. Scrapers.

9–4 Rolling Ingots into Sheet Metal

If you have at hand a silver ingot to be rolled, the first step is to forge the ingot once over on each side with the forging hammer. This serves to pack the crystals more tightly together. Then smooth the surfaces by planishing evenly **(12–5)**. Now take the scraper (Fig. 242) and clean out any pits or imperfections that appear on the surface or along the edges. If these are not scraped out, they will spread as the metal is rolled. Now anneal the ingot.

The ingot is placed between the rollers, and the rollers are screwed down snugly upon the metal. The metal is then removed and a small additional turn is given to the mill until, by trial, you find that the ingot is being pulled into the rollers. The ingot is then rolled through the mill. Be careful to note which end leads through the mill. Turn the ingot over end for end, so that the same sides are in the same relative position to the mill. At the same time you should observe whether the ingot has begun to curve to the right or left. If one side of the rollers is tighter than the other, that side will squeeze the metal harder and lengthen it farther. If this has happened, the screw on that side must be released a bit or the screw on the other side must be tightened slightly. As the ingot is rolled through, the screws are tightened a bit after each pass. Do not try to take too big a bite at one time. After the ingot has been put through three or four times, it will have work-hardened and must be annealed **(8–3)**. Soft metal will roll much more easily.

As you roll the ingot, watch for cracks along the sides. Cut them out at once, right up to the end of the crack. Watch also for blemishes on the surface and scrape them out.

9–5 Rolling Wire

Special dies can be bought or made to fit the rolling mill, and many simple and complex designs and shapes of wire can be made on the rolling mill. Such wire is called "gallery wire" **(12–11)**.

If silver wire is to be made in the workshop, long rods of ½-in. or ¼-in. diameter may be cast. These may be rolled down, between rollers with specially sized grooves, to smaller diameters until they can be accommodated in the drawplate.

BENDING METAL

Bending is one of the fundamental processes of metalwork. Though it is a simple process, jewelry construction demands many special techniques, of which the most basic and typical are described below.

9–6 The Mechanics of Bending

A knowledge of the simple mechanics of bending will help you to think correctly about all bending problems. When a piece of metal bends, its internal structure is placed under strain on the outside of the bend and compressed on the inside of the bend. These strains are relieved because the crystals of the metal shift along slip planes and take up new positions, thus allowing the metal to stretch on one side and contract on the other side. The thicker the metal, of course, the greater is the resistance to deformation, and also the greater is the radius of displacement. For this reason a

Fig. 243. Making square bend with squarenose pliers.

thick piece of metal, when bent sharply, will break. Bending hardens the metal and reduces its capacity for further bending. Repeated bending eventually results in failure or breakage of the metal. It is advisable to anneal metal when construction processes require successive bending at the same location.

When metal is rolled or bent in a curve, the true length of the metal around the curve must be calculated by the radius, which extends to the center line of the thickness of the material. If you wish to calculate the circumferential length needed for a piece of 12-gauge silver to roll up into a ring with a diameter of exactly 2 in., you will use a radius figure equal to 1 in. plus half the thickness of 12-gauge material **(C–10)**.

9–7 General Bending Techniques

1. Whenever possible, use your fingers to bend wire, strip, or sheet metal. You will thereby avoid putting unwanted kinks or nicks into the metal.
2. To make a right-angle bend in wire or strip, place the edge of your square-nose pliers exactly at the point of the bend and push the metal against the side of the pliers with your thumb (Fig. 243). This will not yet give you a right angle. Therefore, place the pliers on the other side of the bend, with the edge of the pliers in the nick made by the first operation, and again push the metal against the side of the pliers. By working back and forth a time or two, you should get a perfect bend. You will not get a sharp corner, naturally, because of the bend curve around the corner. If you still fail to get a square bend, take your snipe-nose pliers, place the edge in the *single* nick you have made, and press the metal until you have brought it past square. Then with the squarenose pliers squeeze the wire of strip close up against the bend until it comes to square.
3. Never try to bend a curve in wire or strip with a flat-faced pair of pliers. The sharp edges of the pliers will make unwanted nicks. Use half-round pliers, placing the curved face of the pliers on the inside of the curve you wish to make. For small-radius curves use roundnose pliers.
4. Always estimate carefully the location of a sharp bend, place your pliers in the right place, and make the bend perpendicular to the wire or strip.

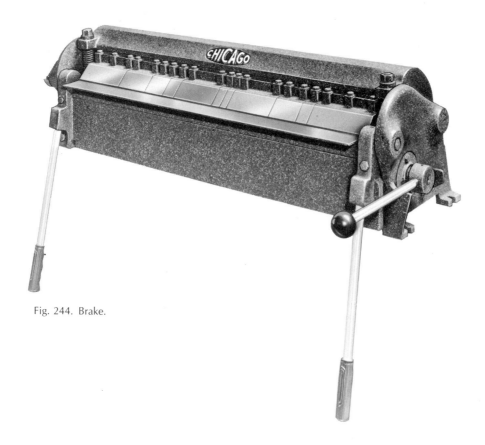

Fig. 244. Brake.

5. Always approach your work experimentally. If you are trying out a design idea for the first time, consider the work to be an experiment, which you carry out to discover and solve the problems involved so that you can execute the final version perfectly.
6. Kinky wire can be smoothed out by drawing it through the next smaller hole in the draw plate. Kinky strip can be smoothed out by annealing it and then tapping it all over on both sides with a rawhide mallet on a smooth, flat anvil.

9–8 Bending a Wide Strip of Sheet Metal   Sheet-metal shops have a machine called a brake (Fig. 244) with which bends can be made in sheet metal. If a brake is not available, the jeweler must accomplish this operation with hand tools as follows:

1. Scribe a light, straight line at the bend point on the back of the sheet.
2. Place the sheet in the jaws of the vise with the bend line set to the top surface of the vise jaw. If your vise jaw is not smooth, you must bend small copper sheets over each jaw to protect your sheet metal.
3. Take a smooth hardwood block, set it with the edge on the scribed line, and press the metal over. Then take a mallet and pound the block in order to set the bend sharply (Fig. 245).

9–9 Bending a Strip to any Circular Radius   Ring bands and other circular strips may be made as follows:

1. From the required diameter calculate or estimate the circumference required **(C–16)**. Always allow extra length, especially for sheet metal that is 14-gauge or heavier.
2. Thin strips of metal may be rolled around the ring mandrel (or a mandrel of suitable size) with the fingers. Hold one end in place on the mandrel at the desired size and roll the strip around and over the beginning end (Fig. 246). With the rolled strip held snugly around the mandrel, make a small mark on the outer end of the strip at the point just above the inside strip end.
3. Set the circle of the strip in a flat position on the V-block and saw vertically straight through the outside strip toward the center of the circle (Fig. 247). The edges at both ends must be cut squarely. It is well to allow a bit of extra material on this first cut.
4. With roundnose pliers adjust the edges until the ends come perfectly and squarely together in all planes.
5. Thick strips of metal, such as ring bands, need more elaborate treatment of the ends, and the bending must be done with a rawhide mallet.
   a. Hold each end of the strip over the mandrel and hammer it down with the mallet (Figs. 248, 249).
   b. Hold the strip on the bench or on an anvil, on one of the curved ends, and tap it into a circle with the mallet (Fig. 250). When the ends are brought near together, slide the ring on the mandrel and strike it around and around to smooth out the irregularities. This process may need to be repeated several times.

Fig. 246. Bending strip ring around a mandrel.

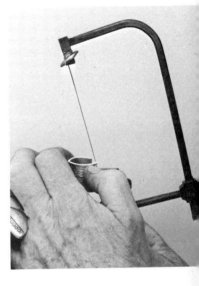

right: Fig. 247. Ring set on V-block and sawed vertically through toward center.
below left: Fig. 248. Starting to roll ring band around mandrel.
below center: Fig. 249. Ring band after hammering each end over mandrel.
below right: Fig. 250. Hammering ring band round on bench with rawhide mallet.

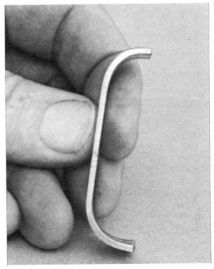

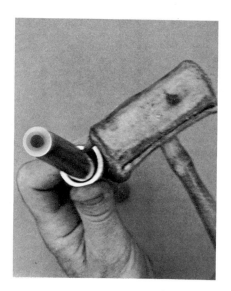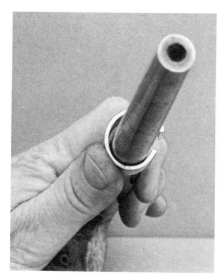

left: Fig. 251. Ring band held against mandrel while being struck to close gap.
right: Fig. 252. Displacement of one side of ring band after being struck.

c. The ends of the strip often become separated by this process and must be closed again. Place your left hand so that the ring is pressed up and supported against the mandrel on the underside, with the left thumb pressing the strip against the mandrel (Fig. 251). One end of the strip should now project above and to the right of the mandrel (Fig. 252). Strike the strip with the mallet at a point very close to the thumb. This will bring the end down to the mandrel. Now slip the ring off, turn it over, and repeat the process on the other end. Repeat this sequence until the ends are touching snugly.

d. Another method of bringing the ends together is to place the ring on a V-slot cut in a hardwood block with its ends at the top of the ring. Place the small end of the ring mandrel in the ring and strike it a sharp blow with the rawhide mallet. This will squeeze the ends together. The ends may be evened up by shifting the position of the ring to one side or the other, as required, and tapping the mandrel so as to pull one end into line with the other.

e. Measure the exact size of the ring on the ring mandrel and estimate the amount of material that must be cut from the ends to reduce the ring to the size wanted. Experience will assist you to make this estimate. Meanwhile, figure that about 2 mm. of length will equal one ring size on the mandrel. You will approach the correct size by successive approximations.

f. Place the ring flat on the V-block and saw one-half the reduction off each end. In sawing (11–3), line your jeweler's saw so that you saw in a plane that runs through the center of the ring circle.

g. Now carry out operation c again until the ends are brought into snug contact. If your cuts are square and true to the center of the ring, the ends should butt together perfectly. If they do not fit perfectly (Fig. 253),

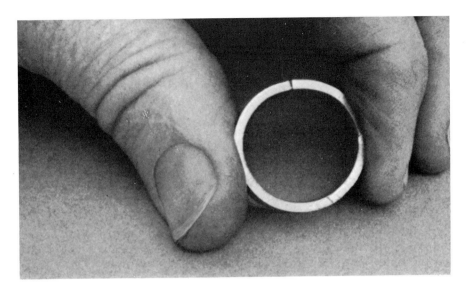

Fig. 253. Ring band closed. V-shaped gap may be sawed out.

you must saw through the open wedge of the seam repeatedly until the excess material is removed and the ends do butt snugly. After each saw-cut, the ring must be sprung closed again by the method described in *d*. You will not be able to fill up a gap in the seam with solder.

h. Measure the actual size of the ring again. If it is still too large, saw a lit-tle more off one end as you did in *f*. Repeat this procedure until the cor-rect size is reached.

i. If the ring is too small, but not excessively small, solder the seam and then place the ring in the ring stretcher or planish the ring to stretch it to the correct size. In planishing, strike light, even blows all around the ring, holding the planishing hammer loosely in the hand so that the ham-mer face will of its own accord find the flat plane of the strip surface. Begin by hammering directly on the seam. If too much solder has been applied and has collected on the inside of the seam, you must take a half-round file and remove it before planishing.

If a ring enlarger is available, sizing is much simpler. Merely solder the ring to a size somewhat smaller than that desired. After soldering stretch the ring to the correct size in the ring enlarger.

9–10   Rolling a Wire Ring

1. Wrap the wire around a mandrel of suitable size, allowing the ends to over-lap. Slide the loop off the mandrel, lay it flat upon the V-block, and saw through both ends.
2. To close the ends of such a ring, no matter what size, grasp each of them in a pair of pliers, push them past each other while still in the displaced posi-tion of the spiral, and then pull them back in line and a little past alignment so that they spring into an exact meeting.

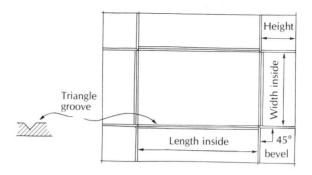

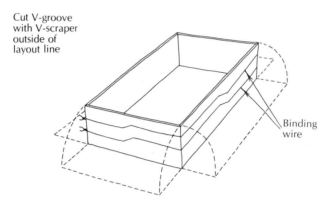

Fig. 254. Procedure for bending up a square box.

When this is done correctly, the wire ends will be in spring tension against each other, so that there will be no problem in getting the solder to flow into and close the seam. If the ends are not together, the ring cannot be soldered.

9–11 Bending Oval Strip Rings or Wire Rings When it is possible to do so, oval rings of strip or wire are more easily made by rolling up and soldering perfect circles and then bending the circles into proper oval shapes. They may be bent on an oval mandrel or in a jig. Specific sizes can be made by calculating the circumference of the oval **(C-16)**. This length is then used to make the circle.

9–12 Bending a Rectangular Box from Sheet The process of making a box requires precise layout. Lay out a sheet of metal in a rectangle equal to the width plus twice the height of the box and the length plus twice the height. Lay out the sides and the ends of the box, using a divider to scribe the lines along all four edges (Fig. 254). The squares at the four corners should be sawed out carefully, leaving the scribed lines on the end and side pieces. They should be sawed with a 45° bevel to the lines, so that, when the sides and ends are bent up, they will come together with mitered ends. Now take a V-scraper and

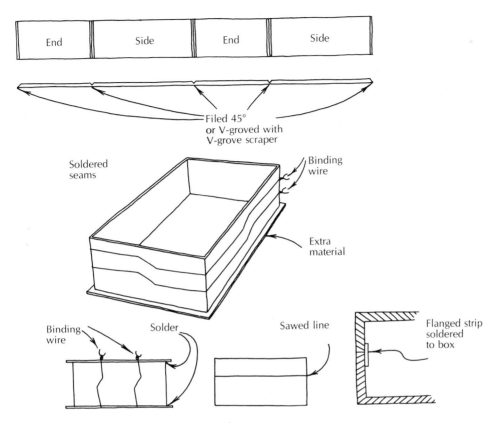

Fig. 255. Alternate method for making a square box.

cut a V-channel along each bend line around the box base. This channel must be cut just on the line and to half the thickness of the material.

Bend up the sides and ends squarely. If properly prepared, the sides and ends should fit evenly together at the corners. The seams are now soldered evenly, and a flat top is made to fit.

If the lid must be part of the box (Fig. 255), the box can be made either from a strip that is bent around for the sides or from separate strips, each of which has beveled ends. These strips are soldered together squarely and finished up. With dividers scribe a lid line at the proper height around the side strip and then fasten on a top and bottom plate, each cut with just a slight amount of extra material all around. Binding wire of 20-gauge is used for holding them in position. Before soldering, make a small cut on one corner of the box at the lid line to allow gas to escape during the soldering process. The top and bottom plates are then soldered to the side strip. Afterward, the excess metal on the top and bottom plates is filed off and the sides finished. Then the box may be sawed apart at the lid line and the sawed edges filed and finished. A flange strip soldered to the box as shown serves to hold the lid in position.

9–13 Bending a Corner for a Solder Joint in a Strip Shape   Closed shapes made of strip should, whenever possible, be soldered together at a corner

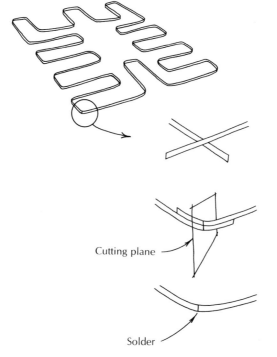

Cutting plane

Solder

Fig. 256. Ends of a strip shape brought together at a corner, with half bend on each side.

rather than at a point on a flat side, but this corner seam should be made in such a way as to correspond to other bent corners of the shape. This means that each end of the strip should be bent completely around the corner. The excess material at each end, running past the mid-point of the corner, should be cut with the saw on a plane that bisects the interior angle of the corner (Fig. 256). When the ends are then brought together, a perfect corner, identical with the others, will be attained.

9–14 Bending up Jump Rings   Jump ring is the trade name for a perfect circle of wire. It is used as a connector and in chains of various kinds.

For bending up jump rings, select a round mandrel of the proper diameter. The mandrel may be made of welding rod, carbon-steel drill rod, the back end of a drill bit, or a nail with the head and point cut off. Place the end of the mandrel in a hand drill, and set the handle of the drill in a bench vise so that the mandrel points upward. Make a right-angle bend about ¼ in. from the end of the wire and hook this down against the mandrel between the jaws of the drill chuck. Place your left thumb against the wire at the drill chuck (Fig. 257). Place the end of your forefinger against the mandrel and squeeze the wire between the finger and thumb. Now crank the hand drill to wind the wire around the mandrel. With a little practice you will find how to control the wire so that each loop lies snugly against the loop below. There should be no space between loops. When you have sufficient loops, slide the spiral off the mandrel.

If you are using annealed wire, you may have difficulty in doing this. Therefore, it is good practice to wrap about two layers of tissue paper smoothly around the mandrel **in the direction you are going to wind the wire**. Wind

162   *Fundamental Processes and Practical Procedures*

the wire over this paper. After the spiral has been made, the mandrel is removed from the drill, placed in the annealing pan, and heated with a torch. As the wire is annealed, the paper will burn away and the spiral can easily be removed. If you are winding wire around an oval or square mandrel, it is absolutely essential to wrap three or four layers of tissue paper around the mandrel.

To cut the rings apart, grasp the upper end of the spiral firmly between thumb and forefinger, resting your hand against the file block or edge of the bench (Fig. 258), and saw at a shallow angle straight down the center of the spiral. The angle of the saw should be flat enough to saw through three or four rings at the same time. Fine saw blades should be used on fine wire.

In order to close the jump ring, seize each side with a pair of squarenose pliers and press the ends past each other; then pull them back into alignment so that they spring against each other. (Figs. 259, 260).

left: Fig. 257. Wire being wound around a mandrel in a hand drill.
center: Fig. 258. Cutting jump rings from a spiral of wire.
above right: Fig. 259. Displacement of the ends of a jump ring made by winding spiral wire on a mandrel.
below right: Fig. 260. Bringing ends of jump ring into spring tension and alignment with two pairs of pliers.

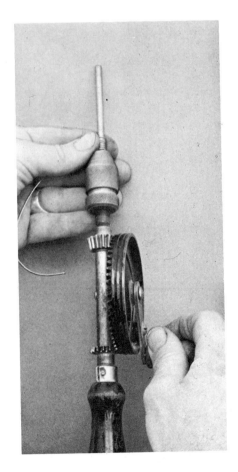

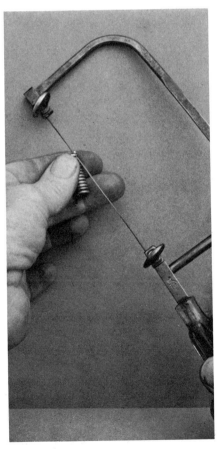

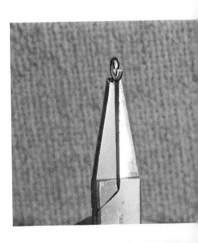

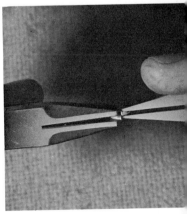

FORMING METAL

Forming is distinguished from bending, as a process, by the fact that formed metal is warped out of a flat plane by stretching the metal. Metal hemispheres, spoon bowls, and hollow ware are examples of formed metal.

9–15 Repoussé

For jewelers, the process of repoussé is probably the single most important means of shaping metal. The term comes from the French verb meaning "to push," and the process consists of pushing metal out from the back with hammers and punches. For jewelry, this work is usually done in a pitch bowl, full of pitch (Fig. 261). The sheet of metal is annealed and then placed upon the flat surface of the pitch and gently warmed with the torch until it sinks slightly into the pitch. When starting a new sheet of metal, it is sometimes useful to bend the corners down so that they penetrate into, and are held by, the pitch. After the metal has cooled and the pitch has become hardened, special repoussé punches are used with the chasing hammer to press the metal down into the pitch. The pitch gives the metal support, yet yields where the punch drives the metal down.

In general, the full depth of a given form is made with larger rounded punches in the first step. The metal is then heated up and removed with tongs or soldering tweezers and annealed to soften the work-hardened metal (8–3). In the annealing process the adhering pitch is also burned away.

After pickling, rinsing, and drying, the hollow that has been made in the first step is filled with pitch and the shape is set in the center of the pitch, with the pushed-out form upward. Punches and chasing tools (Fig. 262) are now used to work the metal back and to define the boundary of the shapes. By working in this manner, back and forth, any form may be developed. Details are finally added with chasing tools, and lines or edges defined as required. The main steps of the process are shown in Plate 12.

Fig. 261. Section view of repoussé
punch pushing metal down into pitch.

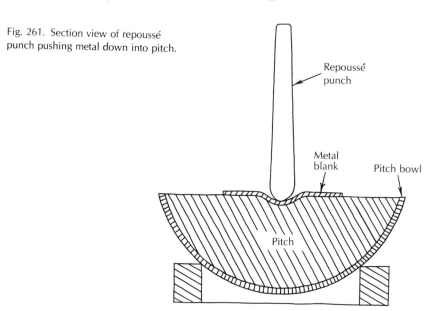

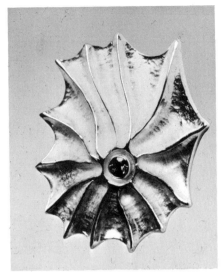

left: Fig. 262. Chasing hammer
and chasing tools.
right: Fig. 263. Fred Fenster.
Repoussé pin. 1967.
Sterling silver with stone.

The development of special forms, such as hollow rings, requires considerable practice and experience, but this is the basic approach that is required in repoussé. Bear in mind that, as you stretch the metal down into the pitch, you are also thinning the metal. Therefore you must learn to use the punches in such a way as to stretch and thin the metal evenly over a larger surface. You cannot make a deep hollow by driving the punch directly down the full depth. The deeper the hollow is to be, the farther out from the center must you gather in metal. To push down a deep hollow, you first push down a broad area to perhaps half the depth. Then from the other side the pushed-up metal is driven toward the center. At the second or third stage, the final shape and depth is achieved (Fig. 263).

9–16 Sandbag Forming   Metal may be shaped also by using a canvas or, better yet, a leather bag filled with fine sand. The sandbag does not allow the delicate forming possible with the pitch bowl, but it can be used for larger, more generalized hollows and simple warped shapes.

9–17 Block Forming   Depressions or hollows may be carved in wood, or stone, or in a tin or lead block. The metal is then shaped by driving it into the hollow with rounded punches. Thin sheets of metal may be pressed into such hollows.

9–18 Embossing and Dapping   Embossing is a shaping process in which small punches are used to drive simple forms into sheet metal from the back. Embossing may be done on a pitch bowl, a wood block, a tin block, or a lead block. Hollow beads were traditionally made by dapping out hemispheres of sheet metal and soldering two halves together. Special round-headed dapping punches are available, together with a dapping block. With this outfit hemispheres of various sizes may be made. These are made by cutting disks of appropriate size, starting them in the larger depression in the dapping block, and then moving the curving disk to successively smaller depressions. A dapping block is made of soft steel and must be treated carefully so that nicks are not put into the depressions.

When making beads or any hollow form, by soldering two halves together, always drill an air hole in the center of one hemisphere to allow air to escape during the soldering operation; otherwise the work may explode as a result of air expansion.

After pickling such hollow beads, the pickle must be removed by boiling them in soapy water. The water may then be removed by warming the beads with the torch so that the water is driven out. Also, when oxidizing hollow forms, be sure to remove the sulphur solution in the same manner.

9–19 Electroforming   The process of electroforming is a mode of electro-deposition utilizing the electroplating equipment and following the technical process of electroplating **(15–13),** although special plating baths must be used. The steps of the process are shown in Figure 264.

Prepare a pattern from wax, expanded polystyrene, or some other suitable material **(6–4).** Then a piece of fine copper, silver, or gold wire should be embedded into it quite firmly. This piece of wire may be bent into a small ring at the end for fastening to the cathode connection, which should also be of fine metal wire, depending upon the metal being used for plating. Stanley Lechtzin uses a frame around the outside of his matrix to increase conductance. Both cathode and anode wires should be annealed.

Then the pattern is sprayed or painted carefully with a conductive silver coating. The silver lacquer used for printed circuits and sold in radio shops can be used. The matrix is then dipped in an acid copper solution to deposit a thin coating of copper, which protects the silver coating from being dissolved by the silver-cyanide bath. Afterward the matrix is rinsed and placed in the silver electroforming bath, where a silver coating is deposited.

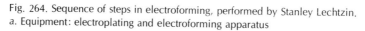

Fig. 264. Sequence of steps in electroforming, performed by Stanley Lechtzin.
a. Equipment: electroplating and electroforming apparatus

Fig. 264b. Equipment: rectifier and periodic reverse unit.

Step 1, drawing and wax matrix for electroformed pin.

Step 2, forming silver wire frame for pin.

Step 3, soldering handmade tube catch to wire frame.

Step 5, attaching frame to wax matrix with electric waxing tool.

Step 4, fitting frame to wax matrix.

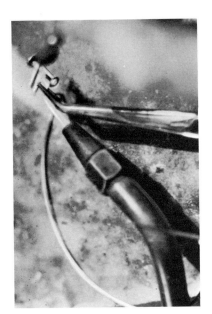

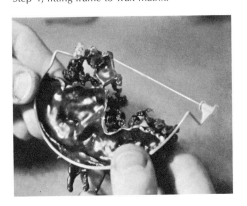

Step 6, forming additional wax elements to be attached to matrix.

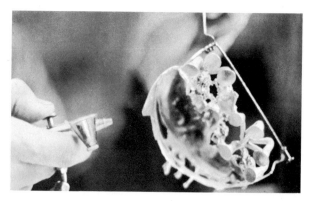

Step 7, spraying conductive silver lacquer on wax matrix with airbrush. Pin stem and catch have been stopped out with red lacquer.

Step 8, electroplating baths (left to right): gold electroforming bath, acid gold-plating bath, and copper bath.

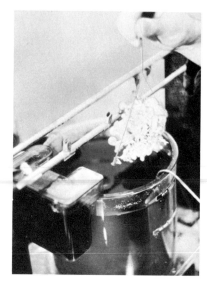

Step 10, removing pin from silver bath after partial build-up of silver.

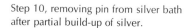

Step 9, placing matrix in copper bath.

Step 11, melting out wax matrix in boiling water.

Step 12, electrocleaning pin after wax removal.

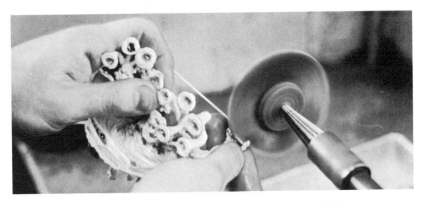

Step 13, scratch-brushing pin after final silver build-up and before gold-plating.

Step 15, brushing pin with bicarbonate of soda to burnish gold plate.

Step 14, removing pin from gold-plating bath.

Step 16, attaching pearls to pin.

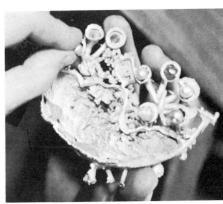

Step 17, finished electroformed pin.

169

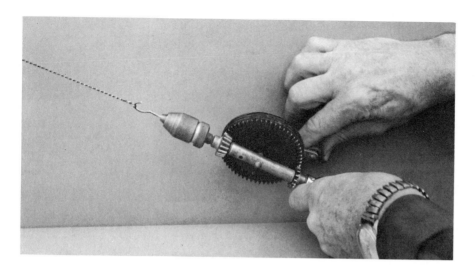

Fig. 265. Wire being twisted in hand drill.

If it is desired to carry out electroforming in gold, the silver-coated matrix may be transferred, after cleaning, to a gold-cyanide bath. If a sufficiently heavy coating of silver has been built up, the matrix may be removed before the gold plating takes place. The jeweler must distinguish, however, between solid gold electroforms and gold-veneered electroforms.

If it is desired to prevent the deposition of metal at certain points on the pattern, copal varnish with a small amount of chrome coloring can be used for cyanide solutions. This is known as *stopping off*.

Following the electroforming process, the piece is rinsed thoroughly and the matrix removed at this time if it has not been removed at an earlier stage (6–4). Gold and silver are usually finished by scratch-brushing with a brass or nickel-silver scratch brush, which has the effect of burnishing or smoothing the surface.

The electroform, once cleaned, may be treated like any other piece of metal—sawed, drilled, or soldered. Electroforming seems to result in an unusually dense metal. Annealing should soften it and release its compactness somewhat. One of the great advantages of the electroform is its unusual lightness.

9–20 Hardening Wire by Twisting   When you need wire to be rigid or springy, as, for example, in the case of a wire pin tong (Fig. 434) it may be hardened by twisting. Twisting is a special aspect of bending, in which the metal is bent around its own axis. This is done by grasping each end of the wire with a pair of pliers and twisting by turning the pliers in opposite directions, meanwhile pulling on the wire to keep it in tension. For a long piece of wire, one end may be placed in a vise and the other end attached to a hook that is bent up and placed in the chuck of the drill. The wire is then twisted by cranking the hand drill while pulling on the wire to keep it tight (Fig. 265).

9–21 Twisted Wires   Elaborate twists of wire have been used in traditional jewelry. Contemporary jewelry has not utilized this technique to any great extent, but it deserves exploration. Interesting experiments can be carried out with wires of various gauges or shapes—square wire, triangular wire, rectangular wire, oval wire—arranged in different combinations (Fig. 266). They are twisted with the hand drill, as described in the preceding section. Wires must be kept tight and of the same length. Square, triangular, and rectangular wires may be twisted individually before combining with other wires, to form complex patterns.

9–22   Making Chain   Chain making is probably as old as the process of wire-drawing, and a study of jewelry history will reveal many fascinating and elaborate chains. The contemporary jeweler has yet to explore the full range of possibilities residing in this process. Exploration of chain making may start with the assembly of simple, circular jump rings (**8–32, 9–14**). Since all rings in a chain must be soldered, chain making is a wonderful procedure for mastering delicate soldering operations.

To make oval rings or links for a chain, an oval mandrel should be used. Wrap the mandrel with three layers of tissue paper before rolling the wire up in a spiral. After the mandrel has been filled with the spiral of wire, it is annealed with a soft flame. This annealing will burn off the tissue paper and allow the oval spiral to be drawn off the mandrel. The oval rings are then sawed apart.

To make a chain from any kind of link, solder half the links closed, and then attach each two closed links with an open link. This cuts in half the number of links which must be soldered in place in the chain.

There is no limit to the variety of relationships that can be attained by varying size of link, size of wire, and shape of links or by using multiple links, interlocking links, textured links, massive links (Figs. 267, 268). The field is open to the curious and interested jeweler.

Fig. 266. Twisted wires.

Fig. 267. Examples of chain variations.

Fig. 268. Mario Pinton. Long chain necklace. 1966. Gold.

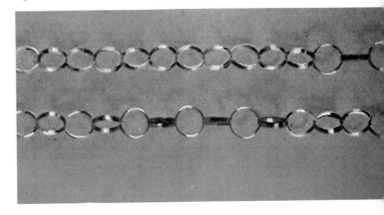

Cut filigree wire with a sharp chisel.

Gum tragacanth for cementing filigree pieces in place.

Fig. 269. Example of filigree process.

9–23 Filigree   Filigree is a process in which small wires are fastened together by means of soldering. This technique has been greatly used in the past, and is still a dominant means of jewelry making in some parts of the world, such as India and China. In this process, flattened wires are arranged in complex designs, usually within a frame of heavier flat wire. The pieces are assembled in position and held by means of pins or binding wire embedded in plaster of Paris **(8–28)**. Solder filings are applied in a solution of flux **(8–23)**. Very beautiful work can be done, and there are great possibilities for contemporary jewelry in this technique.

Filigree wire must be annealed soft. It is bent with the fingers or pliers, and pieces are cut apart with a sharp chisel by pressing the cutting edge against the wire supported by a copper plate. The pieces may also be assembled on a clean iron sheet. As the pieces are put together, a small drop of gum tragacanth is applied with a camel's-hair brush (Fig. 269). Before the tragacanth is dry, sprinkle a little soldering powder on each joint **(8–24)**. When the assembling is complete, the iron plate is warmed gently to evaporate the tragacanth and then placed in a furnace until the solder fuses. The work is then removed and pickled.

ELEMENTARY LAYOUT FOR JEWELRY

Layout is the graphic division and subdivision of circles, ellipses, squares, rectangles, lines, and other geometric figures into spaces of various sizes and proportions. Often the jeweler must divide a circle into equal space divisions or lay out an ellipse of a certain size. Geometry is a complex subject that cannot be extensively covered here, but certain basic geometric constructions should be mastered.

10–1 Basic Geometric Constructions   *To Divide a Line AB into Two Equal Parts* (Fig. 270a): Using the ends of the line *AB* as centers and a radius greater than half the length of the line, draw circular arcs with a pencil compass that intersect above and below the line *AB*. Through these intersections draw line *CD*, which divides *AB* into two equal parts and is also perpendicular to *AB*.

To Draw a Perpendicular to a Straight Line from Point A on That Line (Fig. 270b): Using *A* as the center, draw a circular arc on each side across the line, locating *B* and *C*. Then using *B* and *C* as centers, draw intersecting arcs above the line. A line drawn from this intersection through *A* will give a perpendicular to the straight line.

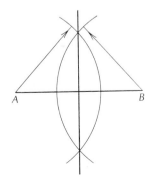
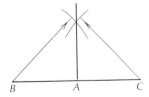

Fig. 270. *a.* To divide line *AB* into two equal parts.
b. To draw a perpendicular to a line *BC* from point *A* on the line.

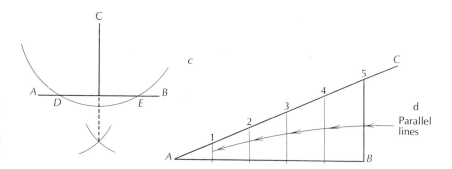

Fig. 270. c. To draw a perpendicular to line *AB* from point *C* above the line.
d. To divide straight line *AB* into any number of equal parts.

To Draw a Perpendicular to a Line AB from a Point C above the Line (Fig. 270c): Using *C* as the center, draw a circular arc that intersects line *AB* at *D* and *E*. Using *D* and *E* as centers, draw intersecting arcs below the line *AB*. A line from *C* through the intersection of the arcs will be perpendicular to *AB*.

To Divide a Straight Line AB into Any Number of Equal Parts (Fig. 270d): If, for example, it is desired to divide line *AB* into 5 equal parts, draw a line at an angle from *A* to some point *C*. With the dividers, set off five equal parts of a convenient size from *A* along line *AC*. Draw line B5 first, then draw lines parallel to B5 which run through the other division points on *AC*. Where these parallel lines intersect line *AB*, equal division points are established.

10–2   General Layout Rules   To duplicate one or more shapes, cut and file-finish one shape perfectly; then use it as a pattern to trace the other shapes with a sharp scribe. The resulting outline will be slightly larger than the original. Therefore, saw *on* the line, rather than outside the line, as in normal practice.

Always center-punch the location of holes to be drilled. The center-punch hole will hold the drill exactly in place.

When laying out shapes on a piece of sheet metal, always locate the shape on or near the edges of the sheet, in order to reduce waste.

Lines on metal sheet are often difficult to see, whether scratched with a scribe or dividers, drawn with a pencil, or traced with carbon paper. To make scribed lines more visible, prepare a solution of whiting in alcohol. This solution may be painted over the surface and dries quickly. A scratch line will then show clearly.

Lines and shapes may be transferred from a design drawn on paper by the following methods:

1. Trace the design, using carbon paper and a hard-pointed pencil.
2. Lay the design in position on the sheet metal and make pin pricks along the lines with a sharp scribe.
3. If duplication is necessary, make an accurate template from 24-gauge brass sheet and trace the template with a sharp scribe.

Use of the Dividers   Dividers are very useful to the jeweler for laying out dimensions, as well as for drawing circles. Lay out measurements on metal by

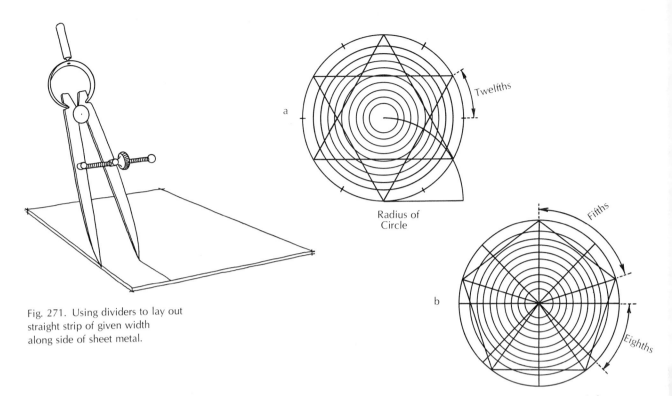

Fig. 271. Using dividers to lay out straight strip of given width along side of sheet metal.

Fig. 272. a. Drawing circle template into equal thirds, sixths, and twelfths. b. Drawing circle template into equal fifths and eights.

setting the dividers to the exact measurement on the scale or steel rule, placing one point of the dividers on the metal at the beginning edge and scratching a short mark with the other point.

To lay out a straight strip of given width along a straight side of sheet metal, lay out the correct width from the exact edge of the sheet. Then, with the sheet laid flat on the workbench, place one point of the dividers against the edge of the sheet, opposite the dimension you have made, and reset the other point of the dividers to that mark. Now draw the dividers along the edge of the sheet, thereby scratching a straight line parallel to the edge of the sheet (Fig. 271).

10–3   Circle Division: The Circle Template   *To Divide the Circumference of a Circle into Equal Thirds, Sixths, and Twelfths*   Pick up the radius with the dividers and step this distance around the circumference carefully (Fig. 272a). Bisect the one-sixth arcs to get twelfths.

To Divide a Circle into Eighths   Prepare a circle template as follows (Fig. 272b). Take a small disk of brass about 4 in. in diameter and of 18- or 20-gauge. Center-punch the center and inscribe concentric circles about ⅛ in. apart all the way to the outside edge. Lay off a diameter through the center, carefully, with a scribe. Erect a perpendicular to this line through the center. Bisect the upper left and right quadrants and scribe lines very accurately through the center of the circle from these points. You now have a small circle template divided into eighths and quarters.

If you wish to divide any small piece into halves, thirds, fourths, sixths, or twelfths, you merely set the piece in the center of the nearest scribed circle and mark off the proper dividing lines.

a   b

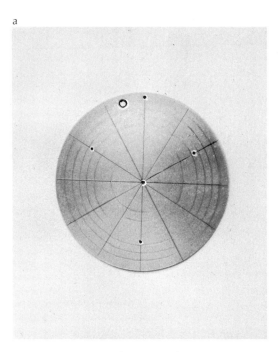 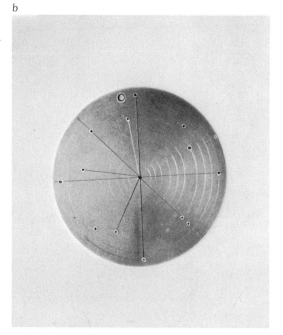

Fig. 273. Finished circle templates. *a.* Thirds, sixths, twelfths, fourths, and eights. *b.* Fifths and tenths.

To Divide a Circle into Fifths   Prepare a circle template as above (Fig. 273). It is usually better to keep a separate template for eighths and fifths. For dividing the circle into fifths, it is most convenient to secure a protractor and mark out the circle into units of 72°.

10–4   Ellipse Division and Construction   The templates described above may be used for dividing ellipses into symmetrical parts.

Templates are now commonly available with an assortment of ellipses that may be traced. You may, however, wish to construct an ellipse with a specific major and minor axis. If so, proceed as follows (Fig. 274):

Fig. 274. Drawing ellipse with string and two pins.

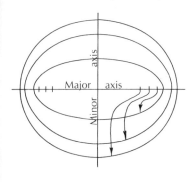

1. Draw a straight line on paper and call it the major axis. Erect a perpendicular line across the major axis and call it the minor axis.
2. Set two pins at an equal distance from the intersection of the major axis, say 12 mm. apart. Tie a loop of string that is, say, 15 mm. long. Place this loop over both pins.
3. Take your sharp pencil and push the point against one part of the loop, pushing it taut along the upper minor axis as far as the pencil will go.
4. Now draw a line by moving the pencil against the string, allowing the string to guide the pencil. An elliptical path will be produced.
5. To make a narrower ellipse, the pins must be set nearer to the ends of the desired major axis size. To make a wider ellipse, move the pins along the major axis nearer to the center of the ellipse.

10–5 Layout of Ring-band Lengths The circumference of a circle is 3.14159 times the diameter, but to calculate the circumference of a ring band, you must add to the diameter, as measured in inches, the thickness of the band, also measured in inches, and multiply this by 3.14159. For example, for 12-gauge silver the following approximate sizes will require these lengths:

Size	Inches
4	$2\frac{1}{8}$
6	$2\frac{3}{8}$
8	$2\frac{1}{2}$
10	$2\frac{3}{4}$
12	$3\frac{1}{4}$

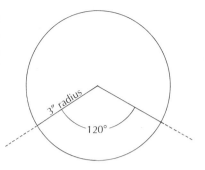

Fig. 275. Practical limits of a necklace array.

A simple and direct way of getting the approximate size is to wrap a strip of paper around the ring mandrel at the desired size and mark the actual circumference. Then you must add about $\frac{1}{4}$ in. extra length, because as metal is rolled around, the true length must be measured along the center of the thickness rather than along the inside surface. Thus, if you roll the edge of a ruler along the size-10 line on the ring mandrel, it will measure about $2\frac{7}{16}$ in. In the table above there has been added $\frac{5}{16}$ in. for bend loss, plus a little extra to work with. If you roll the edge of your ruler along the size-6 line, it will measure about $1\frac{3}{4}$ in. In the table $\frac{5}{16}$ in. has been added to this measurement also.

For 18-gauge, less additional length will be required. It will be well for the jeweler to make up his own table from his practical experiments. Actual measurements on the author's ring mandrel give the following practical circumference dimensions:

Size	Inches
4	$1\frac{7}{16}$
6	$1\frac{3}{4}$
8	$2\frac{1}{16}$
10	$2\frac{3}{8}$
12	$2\frac{5}{8}$

To these circumference lengths must be added extra material, as indicated above.

10–6 Layout of Necklace Arrays Draw a circle of 6-in. diameter and drop a line straight down from the center. Lay off 60° divided equally on each side of this line to mark the practical limits of an array to be suspended around a chain (Fig. 275).

A woman's neck will range from about 12 to 15 in. in circumference. Only with a snug-fitting choker can an array be carried around the neck. Such a choker will fit higher on the neck and pass above the shoulders, whereas a chain type of necklace will pass over and rest upon the shoulders.

A necklace array that is flexible and consists of a lattice of spacing elements will drape well across the shoulders. But a necklace consisting of pendant elements hung from a single chain will not hold an array pattern. The pendants will hang toward the ground in parallel relation.

CUTTING

Cutting metal is one of the most basic and most important of the metalworking processes. With all the effective and convenient means of cutting metal that we possess today, it is hard to imagine the primitive metalsmith cutting his shapes and strips with a stone chisel.

11–1   Shearing, Clipping, and Chisel Cutting   Shearing is the simplest and most rapid means of cutting simple curved or rectangular shapes or strips of sheet metal. When using the hand shears, always cut **on** the line. Gauges up to about 16 (**C–10**) can be cut quite easily with hand shears having a 4 in. blade or with the bench shears.

One disadvantage of cutting with any shears is that the sheet metal is usually twisted by the action of the blades if narrow strips are cut. This twist can usually be taken out with the fingers or pliers. A long strip should be seized at each end with a pair of squarenose pliers and pulled during the twisting. Another disadvantage to shearing is that one face of the cut is beveled by the action of the shears and this face must be filed square. A large workshop will have squaring shears (Fig. 276) and a cutter which has a blade 30 in. long, or more, and is operated by a foot pedal.

Clipping is simply the process of cutting strip or wire into lengths with cutting pliers.

Chisel cutting is a method not generally used today, but it is useful for many purposes. Cloisonné wire is usually cut with a chisel, for example. At one time, chisel cutting was the sole method available. The chisel should be very sharp and ground with a single bevel on one side. Place the chisel exactly on the line, with the bevel side facing away from the piece to be saved. Strike the chisel a blow that carries it about halfway through the metal. Shift the chisel along this slot half or three-quarters of the way, so that part of the chisel is held in line, and strike again. Continue this process along the line. To follow an outside curve the chisel must be placed tangent to the curve at every point. For inside curves a curved chisel is required. After the boundary has been traced, it is retraced by striking the chisel through the sheet. The work should be done on a soft iron anvil.

SAWING WITH THE JEWELER'S SAW

Sawing is by far the most accurate and the most generally used method of cutting metal. To handle the jeweler's saw accurately and easily, a very precise form must be developed. The following instructions should be studied thoroughly and applied consistently if you wish to saw effectively.

11–2 Stringing the Saw Frame   The jeweler's saw blade is always placed in the frame with the teeth pointing toward the handle. Jeweler's saw blades are graded by number from fine to coarse as follows: fine, 8/0 to 0; coarse 1 to 14.

With fine blades it is difficult to see the teeth, but you can determine the direction of the teeth by running your finger lightly over the blade. For most silverwork a No. 3 blade is good; No. 0 or finer should be used on goldwork. Place the upper end of the blade in the upper clamp of the frame. Make sure that the end is set in as far as it will go and that it is set in a straight line toward the handle, so that it will not be twisted and break.

There are two ways of setting the blade in the handle clamp. One way is to adjust the handle piece of the saw along the front piece by loosening the slide clamp on the back and sliding the handle piece to such a position that the blade lacks about 3/8 in. of reaching the back of the clamp. The slide clamp is then tightened. The front clamp of the saw is held against the edge of the bench, and by leaning against the handle with your chest, you will be able to bring the back clamp into position while the blade is set and tightened in the handle clamp.

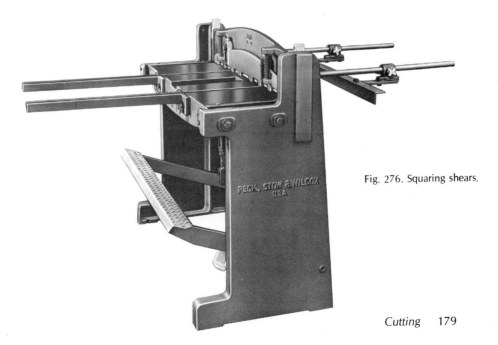

Fig. 276. Squaring shears.

Cutting   179

The other method is to loosen the back slide clamp and set the handle piece so that the blade may be fastened into the handle clamp. Then, by squeezing between the handle clamp and the end of the front piece, the blade is brought under tension and the back slide clamp is tightened.

The purpose of both methods is to place the blade under tension. When properly strung, the blade should give a high ping when plucked with the finger. **A slack blade will always break**. Never tighten the clamp screw with pliers, or you will strip the threads.

11–3 Position for Sawing For general sawing, it is necessary to arrange a V-block at the proper height in your jeweler's vise or at the edge of the workbench, so that it is not more than about 6 in. below the level of the eyes when you are in a normal sitting position (Fig. 277). This allows you to view your work closely without bending over or straining at the back and neck. It also places your arms in a natural and easy position for sawing. If the height of the bench is fixed, you may make the proper adjustment by sawing off the legs of the stool or chair. With the V-block set in position, you should sit so that your arm and right shoulder (left shoulder if you are left-handed) are lined up in a normal and relaxed position to the block. Relaxation is important, because a strained position is difficult to hold for long periods of time and leads to muscular tension.

The saw handle is held firmly at its throat, between the inside joint of the thumb and the inside joint of the index finger. The remaining fingers should not grasp the handle but merely lie against it to keep the saw in a vertical position.

The saw blade must be held always in a vertical position, perpendicular to the plane of the work, unless you are purposely sawing a beveled or slanting edge along the saw line. The metal you are sawing is held clamped to the V-block with the four fingers of the left hand on top and your left thumb beneath the block. If you allow the metal to be pulled up or out of this position, you will be likely to break the blade.

11–4 Form for Sawing The reason for these detailed instructions, which will enable you to develop a correct form in sawing, will become more apparent to you after you have broken a number of saw blades. Do not let the breakage discourage you, however, because it seems to be a part of the learning process.

The following suggestions will help you perfect your form.

- Always keep your saw blade under tension.
- Always keep your saw blade vertical.
- Always keep your arm, wrist, and hand relaxed.
- Avoid twisting the saw blade sideways in the metal.
- Take long, steady strokes, using the full length of the blade.
- Always keep the saw in motion up and down, both when you are sawing and when you are backing the blade out of a cut. To save saw blades, unstring the blade and pull it through, instead of backing out.
- The saw blade is a delicate and subtle tool. Think of each saw tooth as chiseling out a small piece of metal. This thought will place you in the correct psychological relation to the process.

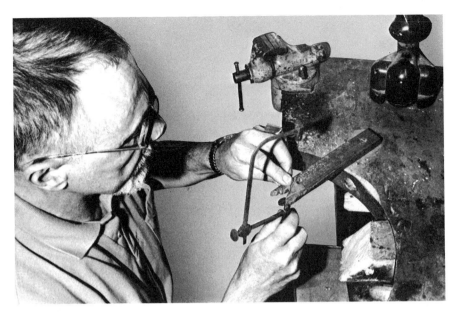

Fig. 277. Position for sawing. Sit up to V-block at jewelry bench, with right arm and shoulder aligned comfortably to V-block.

■ In order to saw a curved line, swing the back of the saw around in the correct direction **as you saw**.

■ To change directions at a corner, hold the blade in the location of the corner and swing the back of the saw around in the correct direction as you saw **at that stationary point**. Twist the saw frame around slowly, since the saw teeth must cut their own space for turning. Otherwise, you will only twist the blade, and it will break.

■ When sawing, always saw along the outside of the layout line, **leaving the line on the work**. This will allow you to file-finish right to the line.

■ Run the saw blade through a lump of beeswax now and then for lubrication.

Most broken saw blades result from undue haste or from failure to hold the blade vertical, which causes pinching or kinking.

You will save yourself many additional broken blades if, when you remove broken ends from the frame clamps, you tap the frame against the bench. This shakes small broken ends out of the clamps. If they are allowed to remain, a new blade will immediately slip out of the clamp and break.

11–5   Sawing an Inside Hole in Sheet Metal   Drill a small hole near the boundary line of the inside hole or shape. String the blade through the hole and fasten it to the saw frame. Set the work on the V-block and saw in the usual manner.

11–6   Piercing   Piercing is elaborate cutout work done with the jeweler's saw. Such work involves careful layout of lines and accurate cutting with the saw (**6–9**).

DRILLING

Drilling holes in metal is usually performed by a hand drill or an electric bench drill or a flexible-shaft drill (Fig. 278). A hole may be made by driving a properly tempered and tapered punch through the metal, which must be supported on a wood or lead block. This method spreads the metal around the hole, an effect which can be used in some design situations.

11–7 Form for Drilling   Drilling is a process of cutting the metal away with a spiral drill. The following suggestions will assist you to drill successfully.

■ Always use a center punch to locate the position of the holes you wish to drill. The small depression made by the center punch will hold and position the point of the drill.
■ Never place the metal to be drilled on a metal anvil. Use a wood support in order to protect the point of the drill.
■ To drill a large hole through metal, drill a small lead hole first.
■ To avoid raising a burr on the metal when using a large drill, a lead hole should be drilled first, and then the metal should be drilled part way from each side.
■ Never apply too much pressure to the drill. Allow it to cut its own way. If it will not cut, the drill needs sharpening.
■ Fine-number drills will break easily. Therefore, brace and support the hand drill carefully as you drill, or snap the drill in half to reduce its length.
■ Holes may be drilled through wire by flattening the wire slightly with a planishing hammer and then center-punching exactly in the center.
■ When drilling through thick metal, thrust the drill point into a lump of beeswax first for lubrication.

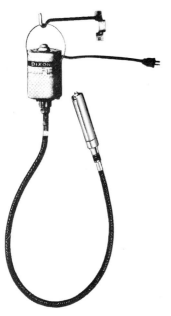

Fig. 278. Flexible-shaft and motor outfit.

left: Fig. 279. Scorpers.

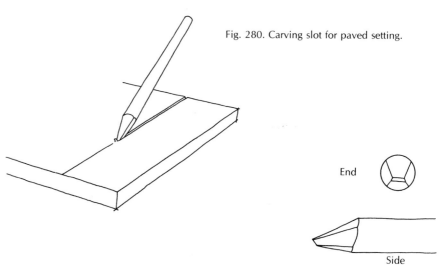

Fig. 280. Carving slot for paved setting.

End

Side

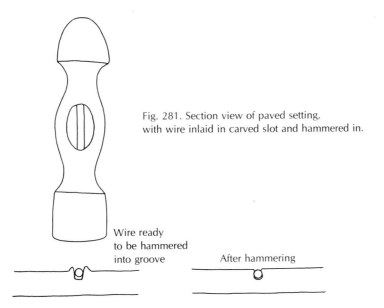

Fig. 281. Section view of paved setting, with wire inlaid in carved slot and hammered in.

Wire ready
to be hammered
into groove

After hammering

11–8 Carving with Scorpers Carving can be done directly in the surface of the metal by means of scorpers (Fig. 279), or chisels, which are used with the chasing hammer. This is a delicate and refined process requiring considerable practice. Paved settings (Fig. 362) can be made with scorpers **(17–3)**. Scorpers may be made and hardened and tempered to a deep straw color **(18–5, 18–6).**

Wire may be inlaid in sheet metal by chiseling the patterns as shown in the illustration (Fig. 280). Wire is then bent to fit into the cut and hammered in (Fig. 281). Niello **(C–18)** may also be fused into chiseled patterns (Fig. 282).

11–9 Scraping Metalworkers use an assortment of very sharp scrapers for cutting away metal. The scraper is usually used to clean metal along seams to be soldered, to cut away excess solder, or to clean out pits or imperfections in the surface of metal that is being planished, forged, or rolled. A scraped surface may be quite rich texturally, too.

Fig. 282. Mario Pinton. Ring. 1967.
Gold with niello and pearl.

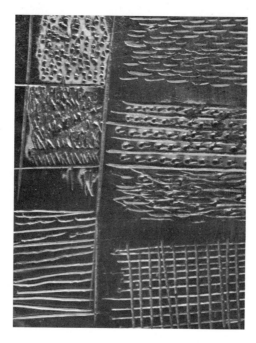

Fig. 283. Graver textures.

ENGRAVING

Gravers are made in a wide range of shapes, each with a distinctive name. Engraving is an extremely delicate and complex skill, requiring long training and practice. The jeweler will not usually expect to do more than acquire an ability to perform simple engraving processes. Simple line engraving and simple line textures are possible (Fig. 283).

11-10   Form for Engraving   For elaborate and skilled engraving a jeweler's engraving block (Fig. 284) is required. For our purposes the sheet metal may be cemented to a shellac stick or a shellac block, or placed in a diemaker's ball.

To cement the metal to a shellac stick or block, place a small handful of shellac chips on the block or stick, melting them down with the torch. Place the metal on the shellac and heat it with the torch until it sinks into the shellac. Allow it to cool and, if you are using a block, place the block in a vise or diemaker's ball. The metal may be removed from the shellac block by striking the block sharply with a mallet. Shellac is scraped or burned off the metal or dissolved away in alcohol if other methods may be damaging.

Procedure for engraving is as follows:

1. The graver is held in the hand as illustrated (Fig. 285), with the handle well back against the heel of the palm. The end of the thumb is placed against the block and pressure is applied. This pressure is released from the thumb and applied to the graver by using the hand muscles to push the graver forward.
2. The angle of the graver must be adjusted in relation to the plate so that with a given pressure the point will be driven into the metal at a constant depth, neither going deeper nor slipping up.

Fig. 284. Engraving block.

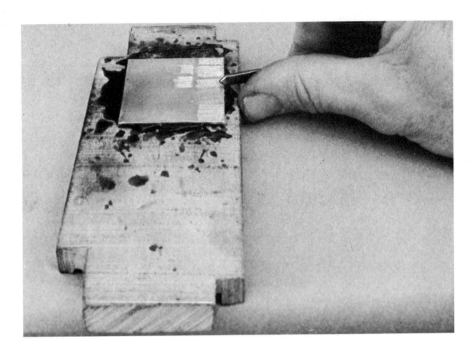

Fig. 285. Position of graver in hand, with thumb against block to hold work.

3. The advantage of using the hand muscles to adjust the pressure is that you have complete control of the graver. At any point it may be halted merely by shifting the pressure from the graver to the thumb.

4. To assist you in the beginning to prevent the point from slipping out and across the metal you may place the index finger of your left hand on the end of the graver. A slight pressure will hold the point down.

5. When you engrave, always keep your fingers and hands **both** on the handle side of the point.

11–11   Adjusting and Sharpening Gravers   New gravers, when fitted into the graver handle, may be too long for some hands. When the graver is held as described above, the point should not extend much beyond the end of the thumb. If it does, the excess should be taken off. This is done by setting the graver point up in a vise, so that the excess length is above the vise jaws, draping an old piece of heavy cloth over the graver end, and striking the graver end sharply with a ball-peen hammer. It should snap off readily. A bevel is then ground on the end of the graver at the angle of the original tip. This should be done on a coarse grindstone. **Be careful not to burn the steel** by grinding too fast. When the correct bevel has been attained, shift to the fine grindstone for a careful smoothing. Be sure you keep the bevel in a single true plane. Then transfer to the hand stone for sharpening and finally the Arkansas stone for polishing.

Fig. 286. Graver sharpener.

The graver is normally sharpened **only on the beveled face**. If gravers are kept oiled and dry, there should be no rusting and consequently no need to smooth or grind the sides. Sharpening a graver consists in grinding a perfectly smooth **flat** surface on the end bevel. This can best be done with a special tool called a graver sharpener (Fig. 286). Otherwise it can be done by hand in

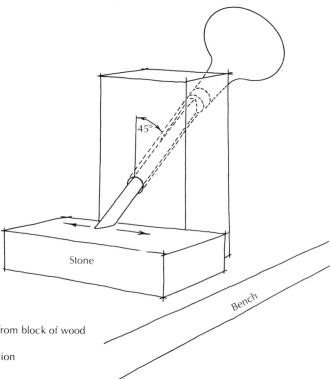

Fig. 287. Graver sharpener made from block of wood
with hole drilled at proper angle
and graver inserted in correct position
against sharpening stone.

the following manner: Hold the graver in your right hand so that the heel of the hand rests on the table and the end bevel is pressed against the face of the sharpening stone. Now carefully slide the graver point sideways along the stone, keeping the end bevel surface flat. A drop of oil should be used on the stone. Grind the bevel until a clean, uniform plane has been attained. A simple graver sharpener can be made from a block of wood by drilling a hole through it at the proper angle. This angle would be identical with the angle of the face of the graver point. The graver is inserted through the hole and thus held in fixed position (Fig. 287).

When a new graver is to be fastened into a handle, a hole must be drilled into the handle. This hole should be of a diameter about equal to the width of the tapered end about halfway up the taper. The point is then set against a hardwood block and the handle driven on with light blows of a mallet.

12

HAMMERING

Beating metal with a hammer is a subtle and exacting process, although it is often considered to be a gross muscular activity in which the arm is swung up and down with great force. This is perhaps true of blacksmithing. It is not true of most nonferrous metalwork. In silversmithing and jewelry the hammer must be used as delicately as the jeweler's saw or the needle file.

12–1 Form for Hammering The primary problem of hammering is that of control. Complete control can be achieved by the development of form, and form can be learned by careful observation of the following general rules.

■ Adjust the height of the stake, or anvil, so that when the hammer face is resting in a plane normal to the surface of the stake, your forearm is in a natural and horizontal position. This allows you to take a relaxed position that you could hold all day, if necessary.

■ Stand or sit so that your right shoulder, arm, and hammer are in line with the stake. (Left-handed craftsmen will adjust their position appropriately.)

■ Set your upper arm against your side and do not move from that position except to alter the relationships of the hammer face to the anvil, or stake.

■ Grasp the hammer firmly, but not tensely, at the end of the handle. Do not hold the hammer close to the head and push the hammer head up and down. **Swing** the hammer head up and down.

■ Use your wrist, not your elbow, as the pivot of your hammer swing. Do not try to strike extremely heavy blows, but allow the weight of the hammer head to do the work, accelerating the downward fall of the head with a slight snap of the wrist.

■ Pick up the hammer head on its bounce after it strikes the metal.

■ The force of the blow will vary with the arc of the distance the hammer head travels. For a light blow, use a short arc. For heavy blows, use a longer arc. For a hammer head of a given weight, the rate of hammer blows will

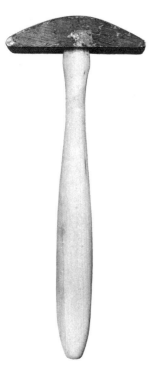

Fig. 288. Forging hammer.

vary with the arc of travel. The force can, therefore, be controlled by controlling the length of the arc. You do not need great strength to hammer.

■ Pay attention to the angle of the face of the hammer to the anvil. To change this angle, you either twist your forearm slightly or shift the position of your arm and shoulder to another set position.

■ With practice you will develop a feeling for position, and the meaning of these rules will be incorporated as a habit pattern.

There are four general types of hammering: striking, punching, forging, and planishing.

12–2 Striking   The term "striking" includes all uses of the hammer other than forging or planishing. Forming, or bossing, is considered here as a way of shaping by means of striking.

12–3 Punching   The use of punches is important in jewelry making. Many special punches can be purchased, but every jeweler should learn how to make his own punches for special design purposes **(18–9)**. The striking of all punches, as well as of chasing and repoussé tools, should be done with a chasing hammer or a ball-peen hammer. Never use the planishing hammer for this purpose, because such use will mar the polished face of this hammer. Punches with a large surface area may require a heavy ball-peen hammer.

12–4 Forging   Forging is the process of shaping, thickening, or thinning metal by the impact of the hammer head. The primary forging hammer (Fig. 288) has a head with a cross-peen face. When the cross-peen face is driven down into the metal, it spreads in both directions perpendicular to the direction of the cross peen (Fig. 289). Forging, therefore, moves the metal and thins it between the hammer head and the stake, or anvil.

Forging hammers are of many sizes and weights. A round-faced or slightly crowned-faced hammer may also be used for forging. In forging heavy wire or rod such a hammer may accomplish a specific operation more effectively. A short-handled sledge hammer (Fig. 290) may be converted into an effective forging hammer with one crowned face and one cross-peened face.

Forging is a subtle operation in that sensitive variations in the weight of blows must be distinguished. To develop a smooth, tapered form, the weight of the blows must be "tapered" to suit the form.

Fig. 289. Cross peen of hammer penetrating metal and spreading it, and disk spread by forging in a ray pattern.

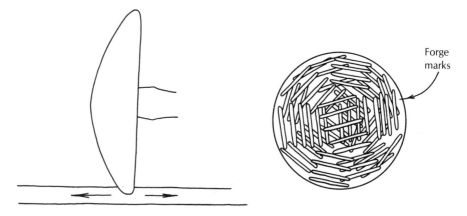

Forge marks

In forging, the angle of the hammer-head axis must be controlled. The axis should always be perpendicular to the surface you are hammering. If the forging hammer is tipped slightly over to the right side, the effect will be to spread the metal on the right side more than on the left. If a strip or wire is being forged, the result will be a curving of the metal to the left. Unless such curvature is desired, the axis of the hammer must not be allowed to depart from the vertical. Tipping of the hammer thus is a means of controlling the curvature of a strip or wire. Forging hammers should be used only for forging.

12–5 Planishing Planishing is the process of smoothing the surface of metal by beating down the hills and bumps with a hammer that has a flat hammer face on one end and a slightly crowned face on the other end. The effect of planishing also thins the metal. The faces of the planishing hammer should be kept highly polished and protected from moisture, nicks, and scratches. Every nick or scratch in the face of this hammer will put a corresponding mark in the metal. Properly planished metal surfaces should require no further polishing. Many jewelers make little copper caps to snap on over the faces of their planishing hammers for protection. What is true of the planishing hammer is true for all hammers that are applied to metal. Never use the planishing hammer for anything but planishing. Keep a bit of crocus cloth handy to polish your hammer faces each time they are used. Polish the faces on the tripoli and rouge buffs occasionally.

12–6 Stakes and Anvils Almost all hammering is done on some kind of anvil or stake. The jeweler usually has one or two small bench anvils on which to do general hammering work. He will also have one or two stakes that are kept highly polished and free from nicks, on which he can forge or planish work without marring the underside. The T-stake is one of the most generally useful stakes for both silversmiths and jewelers. An assortment of small stakes and anvils is useful to have on hand.

Fig. 290. Short-handled sledge hammer.

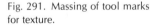

Fig. 291. Massing of tool marks for texture.

TEXTURING METAL

A tool texture (Fig. 291) is the visual result of massing tool marks closely enough together over an area to create a visual effect independent of the visual appearance of any single tool mark. Tool textures result from the normal application of tools to materials and have always been used in design. Textures may be created also for specific purposes in controlled relationships, as explained below.

12–7 Exploration of Tool Marks Every tool makes its own unique marks, which may be used for making controlled textures. You should experiment on pieces of scrap copper or bronze or brass and discover the characteristic mark of every possible tool. Remember, this is a creative search for textures. Try methods of handling that go beyond the obvious and normal ones of using tools. For instance, the edge of a hammer makes a mark ordinarily avoided in planishing. Perhaps it could be used as an interesting texture. The teeth of an old broken file may be hammered into the surface of metal. A rasp might give

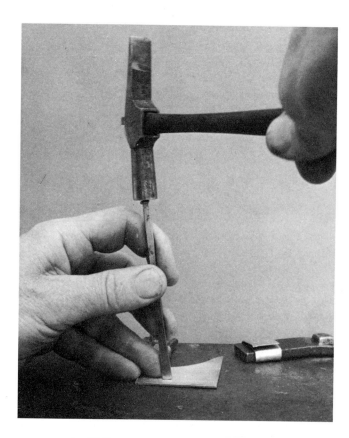

Fig. 292. Chasing tool tipped slightly
for hammering.

just the right quality of texture for some surface. These experiments should, of
course, always be carried out with regard for the safe use and proper care of
the tools used. For example, files are brittle and will break under the force of
a sharp blow. Therefore, good files should not be used in these experiments.

12–8   Chasing Tools and Punches   A wide range of textures can be achieved
by the use of chasing tools and punches. These tools are specifically designed
and used for making marks in metal. Chasing is usually done on sheet metal
prior to any further construction or soldering operation. The sheet of metal is
placed on a chasing plate (see Fig. 292), which is a soft iron plate of any reasonable dimension and about 1 in. thick. The plate is provided with clamps
which may be screwed down to hold the sheet metal in place during chasing
or texturing operations.

12–9   Form for Chasing   Chasing requires the development of form, which
can be mastered by observance of the following rules:

■ Hold the chasing tool firmly, but not tightly, in the left hand (Fig. 292).
Notice that the little finger rests upon the surface of the sheet. The other
three fingers are spread along the tool, one finger near the top, one at the
middle, and one near the bottom of the tool. The tool is tilted slightly back,

away from the direction you wish to move, but it is vertical in the side directions.

■ Using a chasing hammer or a small ball-peen hammer, strike the upper end of the tool steadily and continuously with light blows.

■ As each blow strikes the tool, it will drive it into the metal, and, if the angle of the tool is adjusted correctly, will also move the tool along the surface of the metal.

■ As the tool moves along, the impression helps to hold the point of the tool in line. It is a good practice to chase your lines lightly at first, going over them a second time for more depth.

■ Straight lines should be chased with a straight "liner." All but very flat curves must be chased with a curved "liner." All flat curves can be made by gradually rotating the straight liner as you move the tool along.

■ Do not expect too much from yourself at first. Chasing is a delicate technique and requires much practice. Skill will increase in relation to time spent.

■ When striking with the hammer, remember that the face of the hammer must always be held in normal relationship to the axis of the tool; otherwise, each blow will deflect the tool out of line and the force of the blow will be lost. When the hammer and the tool are held in the proper alignment, the force of the blow goes directly into the metal.

12–10   Form for Texturing   When areas must be closely covered with tool marks, a slightly different method is useful.

■ Hold the tool in your hand with the same firm grasp, but keep the little finger on the sheet metal and hold the tool slightly above the surface of the metal.

■ As you strike the tool with the hammer, the point is driven into the surface of the metal but is lifted out each time the hammer rises.

■ This method increases the rapidity with which an area may be textured, since it eliminates two additional motions: that of placing the tool in each new position and that of removing the tool afterwards.

■ This method also allows a flexible movement of the tool over the surface and permits the tool to be rotated between the fingers in order to create varying effects.

12–11   Stamping Sheet and Gallery Wire   Both areas of sheet metal and the surface of wire (Fig. 293) can be enriched by stamping with punches made especially for that purpose **(18–9)**. The punch mark of a stamp may be used as a border or to create a textural area. Experiment with punch marks on a thick sheet of lead or aluminum. Try rotating the punch 90° or 180° every time or every other time. Try all the positional relationships to see whether more interesting patterns arise. When punch marks are grouped, you will discover that the area between the punch marks becomes a significant design pattern. Explore the variations of this area.

If a sheet of sterling is to be stamped, it should be clamped in the chasing plate so that one side or part of the area is accessible. When a border is wanted, a light line should be scribed along the edge with the dividers, and the punch

Fig. 293. Examples of gallery wire stamped with punches.

should be carefully positioned each time. It is important to keep the punch marks straight and even along the guideline and equally spaced apart (Fig. 294).

Two observations will be of use to the beginner. First, punch marks will be sharp and deep if the gauge of metal is fairly thick — 16-gauge, at least, and preferably 14-gauge or thicker. Second, punch marks will be sharp and deep if the area of the face of the punch is not too great (Fig. 295). Probably a punch face that is ¼ in. square will fail to make more than a bare imprint in a piece of 18-gauge silver, even with a heavy hammer. A punch face ⅛ in. square, more or less, should make a satisfactory mark in 16-gauge sheet. The weight of the hammer head is important in attaining good imprints. A little experience will provide a basis for judgment.

Gallery wire may be made by stamping nonferrous wire with any punch or chasing tool. Punches especially made for the purpose will give the most interesting effects. The punch face should be as wide as the wire, or wider. If a groove is filed across the punch face before the pattern is filed, the punch will stay on the wire in a constant position. It is useful to planish your length of wire so that it is slightly flat along the top edge; this will help prevent the wire from rolling as it is stamped. The stamping should begin at the clamped end (in the chasing plate) and move away so that the preceding mark is visible for positioning of the punch for the next mark.

Gallery wire may be used as a border around a high bezel, around a shape, or in combination with plain wire for a ring.

Fig. 294. Border stamped with a punch.

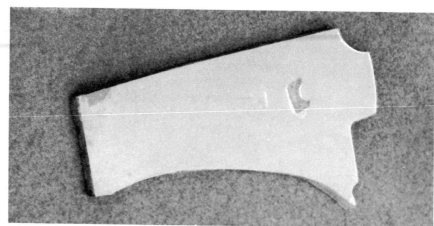

Fig. 295. Deep punch and shallow punch mark controlled by area of punch face.

FASTENINGS

Historical practice has developed an infinitely broad range of fastening methods that ordinarily cannot be surpassed in effectiveness, and the possibility of developing new methods of fastening arises usually only when new materials or new techniques are developed. Nevertheless, experimentation may reveal unsuspected possibilities in specific design relationships that you devise. Also, historical practice is often confined to conventional or well-established methods. New solutions therefore lie within a fresh or unconventional approach to old problems.

In jewelry a fastening is not successful unless it is both durable and simple, as well as being visually suitable. Fastenings that can be incorporated into the form of the design are to be considered superior to those which are "stuck" on. For example, devising the catch for a necklace is usually regarded as simply a functional problem, the featured part being conceived as the front. Why should not the catch be made the featured design of a necklace, wherein the mode of fastening becomes the form of the design? The creative jeweler makes a constant reappraisal of his ideas about what a piece of jewelry should be.

DIRECT METHODS OF FASTENING

Methods of fastening in which material is set in opposition to material are the simplest and most effective solutions. Examples of this type are flanges, clips, rivets, interlocking joints, catches, and hinges. The following solutions are presented as a basis for working out your own particular methods.

13–1 Flanges   Flanges are so simple in design and construction that they are used wherever possible in all types of metal construction. A flange is a rim of metal allowed to extend beyond the normal boundary line of a sheet-metal shape sufficiently to permit bending it up and around or over another

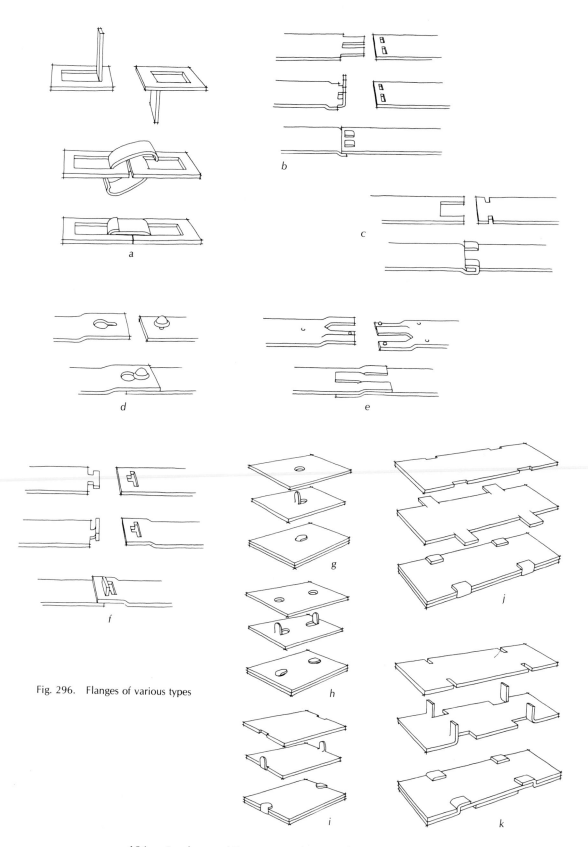

Fig. 296. Flanges of various types

shape of metal. Great variation is possible in size, shape, and location of the flange (Fig. 296). No additional, separate pieces are required, and the mechanical process is simple and suitable for either hand or machine fabrication. All the basic positional relationships can be accommodated: edge-to-edge, edge-to-surface, or surface-to-surface. In jewelry the flange method has many creative applications and could probably be used more than it is. The claw setting is a special variation of the method.

13–2 Clips   Clips are small pieces of metal which, when fastened to one piece of metal, hold another piece in position (Fig. 297). The spring clip is a special variation, in which the clip is a spring or is fastened to a spring that allows displacement of the clip for attaching or releasing one piece of metal to or from another piece. The spring clip is part of a catch. In almost all the ancient cultures brooches were used to hold garments closed. These utilized a wire spring clip. We retain the same idea in the safety pin.

Fig. 297. Examples of clips.

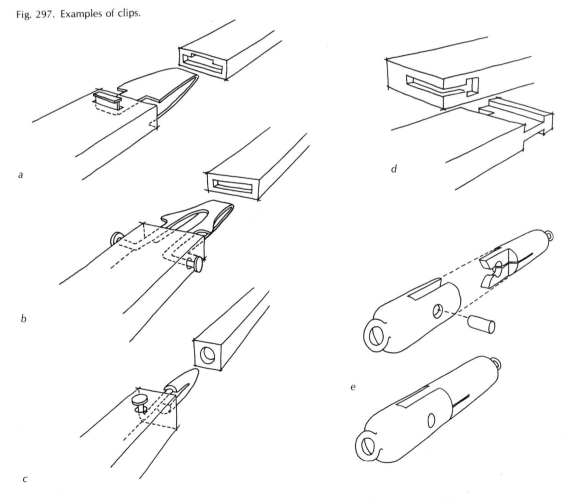

a

b

c

d

e

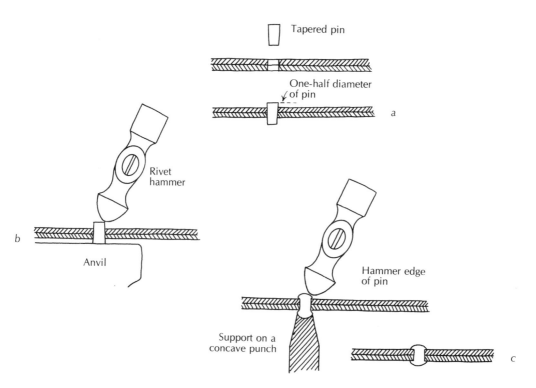

Fig. 298. Procedure for setting rivets and hammering heads.

13–3 Rivets A rivet is a small pin used to hold two sheets of metal together in a surface-to-surface relationship. The rivet pin runs through holes in the two plates, and the ends of the pin are flattened carefully to form heads, which prevent the two pieces of metal from separating.

Select an appropriate size of drill and drill a hole through the pieces of metal to be fastened together. Choose a wire that is just slightly larger than the hole, and, using a pin vise, file a fairly long taper, so that the tapered end will wedge snugly through the hole (Fig. 298). Clip the ends off on each side of the metal with the cutting pliers, leaving a length of wire projecting beyond the surface of each side that is about equal to half the diameter of the wire. The pliers pinch a crest in the end of the wire, which should be filed flat. Now set the rivet on an anvil and, with a small rivet hammer, strike very light blows around and around the edge of the rivet. As soon as the wire end has begun to spread over the edge of the hole, turn the work over and repeat the same process on the other end of the rivet. Work back and forth until the rivet heads are driven down snugly and tightly against the surface of the metal.

If the rivet wire that you use is too long, if it does not fit the hole in the metal snugly, or if you strike too heavily with the hammer, the rivet is likely to bend over.

13–4 Flush Rivet If an invisible rivet is desired, a countersunk hole is drilled to an appropriate depth (Fig. 299a). The rivet head, which may be made by fusing the end of a wire into a bead **(8–6)**, may be filed to a cone that fits

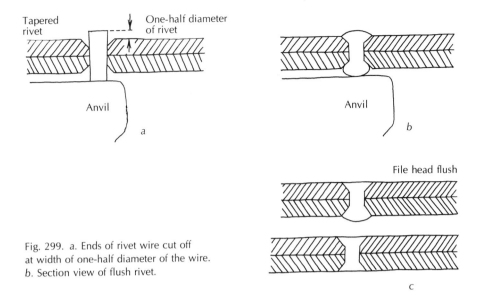

Fig. 299. a. Ends of rivet wire cut off at width of one-half diameter of the wire. b. Section view of flush rivet.

the countersunk hole or may be placed directly in the rivet hole. In either case the rivet is closed by hammering until the rivet metal fills the countersunk hole uniformly and completely (Fig. 299b). Excess material is filed away, and the surface of the plate finished off. Such rivets, when properly made, are completely invisible.

13–5 Tube Rivet   In certain situations a tube rivet may be the necessary solution. A tube of metal of the proper diameter is placed in the rivet hole. The ends of the tube should be cut off to extend above the surface sufficiently so that, when the sides of the tube are bent over, they grasp the edges of the hole securely (Fig. 300). Bending the edge of the tube may be started by twisting the point of the burnisher in the end of the tube, gradually pressing farther down as the sides are pressed out until they finally rest snugly against the surface of the metal.

Fig. 300. Section view of tube rivet.

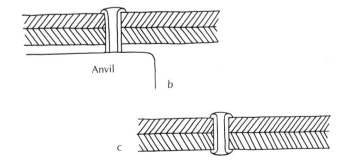

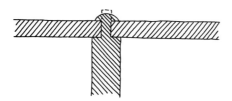

Fig. 301. Section view of integral rivet.

13–6 Integral Rivet The integral rivet is made from a part of one piece of material which projects through another piece (Fig. 301). The projecting end is then closed in a typical rivet fashion, flush or domed.

13–7 The Rivet Set When the rivet has been set in place, cut, and filed to the proper height, the rivet heads may be made with a rivet set. This is a small punch with a tapered end in which a smooth, round hemispheric hole has been made. The point is set over the rivet, and the rivet set is rotated as it is struck lightly with a hammer (Fig. 302). The rivet head is thus rounded and polished.

13–8 Interlocking Joints Interlocking joints are fasteners designed to block the separation of two pieces of metal in every direction except the one along which the pieces must move to be joined or parted (Fig. 303). Usually the direction of the joint opposes the normal pull or movement of the pieces away from each other. When a spring clip is added, this joint becomes a clip-catch. The Egyptians made beautiful interlocking joints for their bracelets and necklaces.

Fig. 302. Using rivet set to round rivet heads.

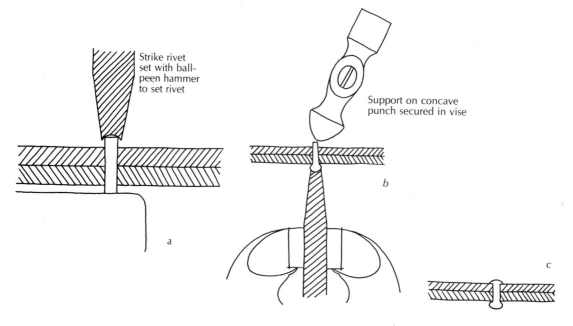

Strike rivet set with ball-peen hammer to set rivet

Support on concave punch secured in vise

a

b

c

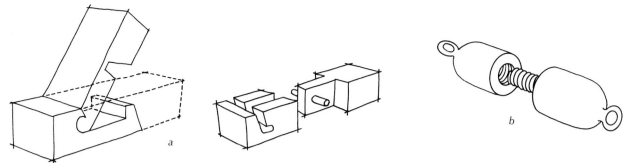

Fig. 303. a. Interlocking joint. b. Screw-lock fastener.

13–9 Catches   Catches involve all the methods of fastening that can be applied to closures which are temporary rather than permanent (Fig. 304). The basis of the catch is displacement of one piece of metal to allow two pieces of metal to come together in position, after which the displaced piece of metal moves back to its original position, where it blocks separation of the two pieces. Displacement may be made possible by a slide, hinge, twist, radial rotation, or a spring.

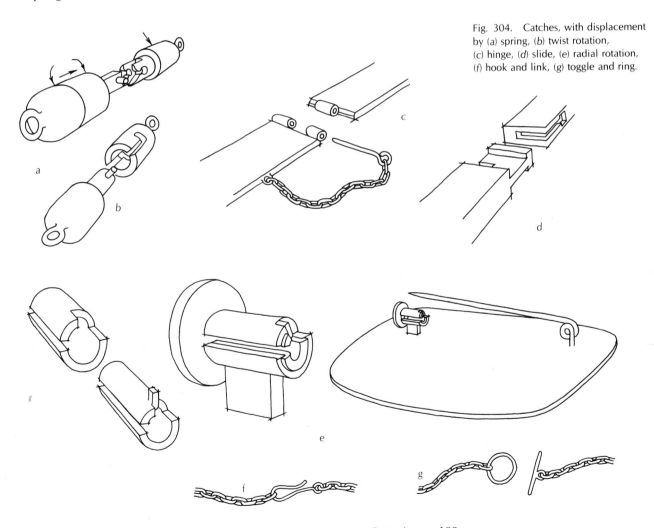

Fig. 304.   Catches, with displacement by (a) spring, (b) twist rotation, (c) hinge, (d) slide, (e) radial rotation, (f) hook and link, (g) toggle and ring.

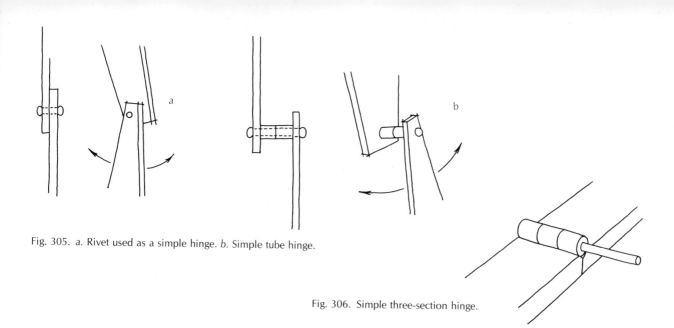

Fig. 305. *a.* Rivet used as a simple hinge. *b.* Simple tube hinge.

Fig. 306. Simple three-section hinge.

13-10   Fastening Wire   The ends of wire may be fastened to metal by running them through a hole and either fusing a bead on the end, or hammering a rivet head to close the end, or merely by spreading the end of the wire that projects beyond the hole.

HINGES

The hinge is a device which allows one part of a piece of jewelry to swing on an axis fastened to another part. One might regard the jump ring between two links of a bracelet as a hinge. The hinge, as a structure, however, is usually more complex than this. The construction of the hinge may be simple or complex. Both types are presented here, even though the complex hinge is not often used.

13–11   Simple Hinges   The simplest type of hinge is probably achieved by riveting one piece of metal to another (Fig. 305a). Another simple type of hinge is the use of a supporting tube through which a rivet runs and fastens to another piece of metal.

A slightly more complex hinge can be made by soldering a small tube to each of two pieces of metal, drilling a hole through the metal to which the tube is soldered, and fastening the two tubes together with a rivet (Fig. 305b).

The simplest complete hinge consists of three sections of tubing in line on a rivet or hinge wire (Fig. 306). The outside tubes are soldered to one piece of metal, the inside tube is soldered to the other piece of metal.

13–12   The Joint Tool   You will find it difficult to file the ends of a short piece of tubing exactly square, as they should be in order to fit well together. In practice, the jeweler and silversmith use a joint tool (Fig. 307), which holds the tubing squarely while the filing is done across the surface perpendicular to the tube (Fig. 308).

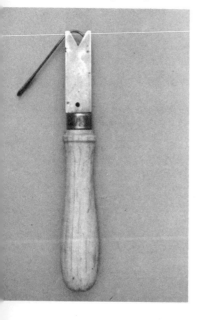

Fig. 307. Joint tool.

13–13 Procedure for Soldering Hinge Joints Certain precautions must be taken to avoid soldering the sections of the tube together.

1. When the sections have been cut to size and their ends filed square, they are strung together on a straight iron wire that snugly fits the tube hole.
2. The tubes are set between the edges of the two pieces of metal which are to be hinged together. A more accurate and pleasing job can be done if the edges of the pieces to be hinged are either beveled or filed with a hollow to fit the curvature of the tubes (Fig. 309). The individual hinge knuckles should be beveled where they touch the metal pieces, so that solder does not flow between the knuckle joints.
3. When the work is in position, the seams are fluxed, and a single piece of solder is set in the center of each hinge section at the seam. The work is now heated until the solder just begins to flow and has tacked the hinge section to its proper piece of metal. This can be done by heating the large piece of metal to a temperature just below the melting point of the solder and then using a very small, hot flame at the location of the particular hinge joint to melt the solder. The soldering process is stopped just after the joint has been tacked and before it has a chance to spread along the entire seam. After all the sections have been tacked in place, the iron wire is withdrawn and the hinge is taken apart. The hinge joints are now correctly located and the soldering can be completed (Fig. 310).
4. Care must be taken that the relative position of the hinge joints is not disturbed or allowed to slip when the final soldering is done. A special setup is sometimes required on the soldering block to hold the hinge sections and the piece of metal in relative position.

13–14 The Full Hinge The full hinge traditionally involves five hinge sections (Fig. 311). The two outside sections and the center section are soldered to one side. The other two sections are soldered to the other side.

Any of the above hinges may also be made by using flanges on each piece of metal. These flanges are cut out to correspond to the joints of the tube hinge and are rolled around a rivet or hinge pin. Such hinges are characteristic of cheaper construction but may have a legitimate design use.

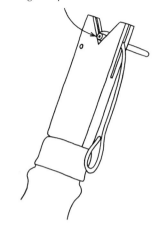

Fig. 308. The joint tool used for filing tube square.

File flush
to face
of tubing clamp

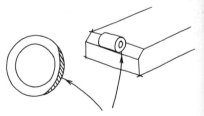

Fig. 309. Bevel on tube where it fits against hinge position.

Bevel where tube
section meets base

below left: Fig. 310. Sections of three-section hinge tacked in position.
below right: Fig. 311. Construction of five-section hinge.

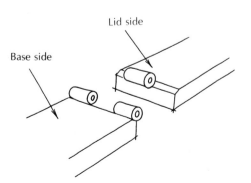

Lid side

Base side

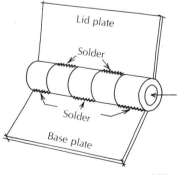

Lid plate

Solder

Solder

Base plate

Hinge pin

Fastenings   201

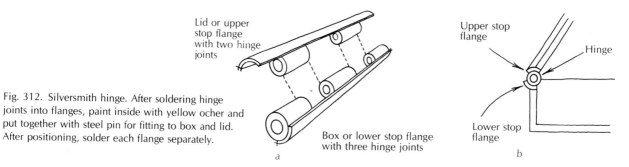

Fig. 312. Silversmith hinge. After soldering hinge joints into flanges, paint inside with yellow ocher and put together with steel pin for fitting to box and lid. After positioning, solder each flange separately.

13–15   The Silversmith Hinge   The silversmith hinge (Fig. 312) is the lord of all traditional hinges, consisting of stop plates and requiring considerable skill to construct. Two tubes are prepared, the one fitting snugly into the other one. The outer tube is split lengthwise into equal thirds and finished accurately and perfectly. The inner tube is cut into five, seven, or nine sections. They are then fitted into two-thirds of the outer tube, and these two pieces are cut and finished to length.

The two pieces of metal to be hinged together are now cut to receive the lengths of outer tubing. The cuts must be made with exactness and in relation to the relative positions of the two pieces to each other when assembled with the hinge joints. When this is completed, each outer shell is soldered to its respective piece.

Now the hinge sections are placed accurately in position in one outer shell and the appropriate alternate sections tacked in place. The sections of the hinge belonging to the other piece are removed and placed in their positions, being tested by matching against the tacked sections. Then they are tacked in position.

The hinges are tested by assembling. When the hinge assembles perfectly, the soldering is completed on each piece separately. The purpose of the shell sections of tubing is not only to cradle the hinge sections but also to provide a stop as they come together when the hinge is opened. The position of the pieces, when opened, should be checked against the size and position of the stops before final soldering.

13–16   Cementing   Cementing is seldom used in jewelry except in "junk" jewelry. One exception is in the case of pearls, which are too soft to be set by means of claws or bezels. The pearl is usually drilled halfway through and cemented on a small metal post. For cementing pearls, litharge mixed with glycerin into a paste is a traditional and effective means. This cement is impervious to water, once it has set. Epoxy cement, of course, is universally used these days for almost every kind of cementing job.

13–17   Riveting Metal to Soft Materials   Riveting may be used successfully for fastening almost any material to metal. In the case of soft materials, such as bone or wood, a small washer of metal (this can be part of a metal shape) comes between the material and the rivet head for protection. Also, a metal shape that is to be placed over a stone may have rivets soldered to it so that they penetrate through holes drilled in the material and through another metal shape upon which the rivet heads are formed.

14

CASTING

Casting is the process of forming molten metal into a mold that has been fashioned to a predetermined form. It is one of the major processes of working metal, as well as one of the oldest. No doubt it arose out of the earliest discovery of smelting metals.

14-1   Equipment and Methods   Metals melt at relatively high temperatures, so that some specially devised equipment is required. The container, or crucible, must withstand this high heat without cracking or breaking apart. The fire must be concentrated around the crucible and raised to 2000° F., more or less. When both of these problems were solved by ancient man, casting became possible. In primitive times crucibles were made of clay or loam mixed with roughly ground charcoal and organic matter such as straw. When baked, this material became refractory, that is, able to withstand high temperatures without cracking. Although much early casting was done in steatite molds, just as the Navajo Indians do today, lost-wax molds were made of the same mixture of clay and charcoal.

Today a graphite crucible is usually used in the melting furnace, and the hand crucible is made of a ceramic material.

In the jewelry shop of today a number of different ways of casting may be used. If these ways are classified according to the method of pouring the molten metal into the mold, there are four ways of casting:

1. *Gravity Casting.* The molten metal is drawn into the mold by gravity.
2. *Centrifugal Casting.* The molten metal is thrown into the mold by centrifugal force (Fig. 313).
3. *Vacuum Casting.* A vacuum applied at the base of the mold helps to draw the air and gas out of the mold and the molten metal into the mold. This way is usually combined with one of the other ways (Fig. 314).
4. *Pressure Casting.* Air or steam is applied at the sprue of the investment to force the molten metal into the investment cavity.

Fig. 313. Kerr centrifugal casting machine.

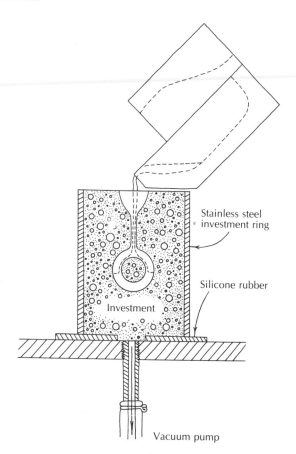

Stainless steel
investment ring

Silicone rubber

Investment

Fig. 314. Vacuum casting.

Vacuum pump

If the ways of casting are classified according to the type of mold used, there are at least six ways of casting:

1. Stone mold, which uses gravity casting.
2. Cuttlebone mold, also gravity casting.
3. Plaster mold, gravity casting.
4. Charcoal mold, gravity casting.
5. Sand mold, gravity casting.
6. Investment mold, which utilizes gravity or centrifugal casting, with or without vacuum casting.

14–2 General Casting Principles   Sand casting, by means of gravity, and investment-mold casting, by means of centrifugal force or gravity force, are the major methods of casting jewelry, and they will be described in detail in the sections to follow. This does not mean, however, that other methods might not offer interesting design possibilities to the contemporary jeweler, particularly if expensive casting equipment is lacking. For this reason all the methods will be discussed.

Regardless of the method used in casting, there are certain general principles to be kept in mind and followed.

1. The metal should not be overheated (**8–11, C–17**).
2. A slightly yellowish, or nonoxidizing, flame should be used in order to avoid absorption of oxygen by the molten metal.
3. The investment mold should usually be hot when the metal is poured into it. This is true of gold and silver. In some cases a sharper impression is made by bronze when poured into a cool mold.
4. The lost-wax investment mold should be heated to not much over 1000° F., and certainly not over 1300° F. In the author's experience a temperature of 1000° F. will vaporize all the wax fumes. The time of burnout varies with the size of the investment. Investment manufacturers always supply technical information as to temperatures for burnout and the best temperatures for pouring of various metals. For sterling the investment mold can be cooled down in the furnace to about 600° F. before casting. For white gold the mold should be allowed to cool to 1100° F., and for yellow gold, to 850° F. The cooling prevents the possibility of boiling the metal in the mold and yielding rough castings. Overheating tends to expand the investment mold excessively, and this causes cracks during the cooling stage and produces flashings on the pattern.
5. A flux, usually ordinary borax, must be melted into the crucible with the metal. The flux keeps the molten metal free-running, gathers together the impurities in the metal, and helps to prevent it from oxidizing.
6. When pouring, skim the flux away from the pouring lip, so that it will not run into the mold.
7. Once started, the pour must be uninterrupted, so that a continuous flow of metal runs into the mold.
8. A large investment mold should be supported by a steel shell, or by being buried in a box of loam (not sand), or by being buried in the ground up to its neck, so that molten metal will not leak out through cracks or break the mold apart by its pressure.

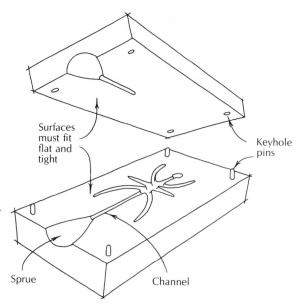

Fig. 315. Open stone mold, showing pattern, sprue, channel, and key pins.

Surfaces must fit flat and tight

Keyhole pins

Sprue

Channel

9. Safety precautions should be observed whenever molten metal is handled. Large pours should be made close to the ground, and safety goggles, shoes, gloves, and aprons should be worn. Small pours may be made at table height but should be made over an annealing pan in case of spilling. If a centrifugal casting machine is used, it should be installed in a countersunk box below the surface of the counter, or a sheet metal shield should be installed around it.

Fig. 316. Olaf Skoogfors. Ring, cast from cuttlebone, constructed, and gilded.

14–3 Steatite-mold Casting   No method should be automatically excluded from consideration by the contemporary jeweler. The Navajo Indians have done some exquisite bracelets and buckles cast in stone molds, and there is nothing to prevent the contemporary jeweler from exploring the possibilities of using steatite and chiseling and carving out his own designs. The mold is made of two halves (Fig. 315). The pattern, the pouring channel running to it, and the sprue are carved in the lower half. The other half of the sprue is carved in the upper half of the mold, which must be keyed to the lower half. Keying is done by drilling matching holes in each half for keying pins.

14–4 Cuttlebone-mold Casting   Cuttlebone is a traditional mold material for casting duplicates of small jewelry items, such as emblems, or even rings having no undercuts (Fig. 316). The perfect detail that can be reproduced is almost unbelievable. *Cuttlebone* can be secured from jewelry supply houses in sizes from 4 to 9 in. long.

Two bones are filed flat on one side with a coarse file until the filed sides fit together evenly and perfectly (Fig. 317). Two pins of appropriate length are made of 8-gauge wire. One pin is pressed into the lower bone at the upper left-hand side. The other pin is pressed into the lower bone at the lower right-hand side. The pattern **(14–8)** is placed in the center of the lower bone, where the thickness of the bone is greatest. The upper bone is now placed in a corresponding position over the lower bone, and the two are squeezed together gently but firmly. The pattern presses into each half of the mold, and the key pins press into the upper mold. Now the bones are carefully separated and the pattern delicately removed. A small channel is cut from the pattern up to the top end of the lower mold, and at this top end a half of the sprue is carved out. Knife cuts around the pattern, as shown in the illustration, serve as air vents. The upper mold is now placed on the lower mold, carefully, aligned by the key pins, and the position of the half-sprue is marked on the upper mold. The parts are separated again, and the other half of the sprue is carved on the upper mold.

The pattern cavity and the channels are checked to be sure they are clean, and the two molds are put together and fastened by binding wire. Now a piece of charcoal is carved to fit snugly against the upper end of the mold, and a cavity is carved into the top, with a small channel running over and into the sprue in the cuttlebone (Fig. 318). This piece of charcoal is wired to the mold in such a position that the metal, placed in the cavity and melted, will run into the sprue when the mold is tilted. This charcoal, then, becomes the crucible, and the process of melting the metal and pouring it into the mold is facilitated (8–11, 8–12). Cuttlebone may also be carved directly.

14–5 Plaster-mold Casting   For the plaster mold two halves must be prepared, with the pattern centered at the parting line. The mold is begun by embedding the pattern halfway into the center of a small smooth pad of water clay or Plasticine. Build a wall of clay around the pad and possibly an inch higher than the surface of the clay. Into this may be poured a smooth, creamy mixture of plaster of Paris that has been made by sifting plaster into a small pan of water. If the volume of your mold, within the clay wall, is about 2 in. in diameter, about ½ cup of water should be sufficient to mix enough plaster to a creamy mixture. The plaster must be thin enough to flow around the details of the pattern.

Fig. 317. Open cuttlebone mold, showing pattern, sprue, channel, air vents, and key pins.

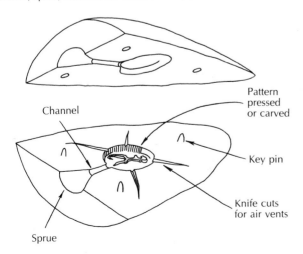

Channel

Pattern pressed or carved

Key pin

Knife cuts for air vents

Sprue

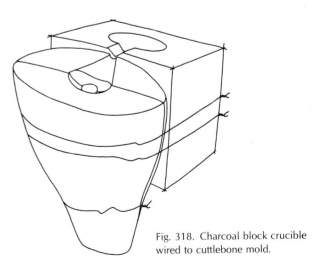

Fig. 318. Charcoal block crucible wired to cuttlebone mold.

Fig. 319. Vacuum pump.

After the lower half of the mold has set—at least four hours later—the clay may be removed from the plaster mold. The surface should be trimmed, if necessary, and shellacked with a mixture of shellac and alcohol in equal proportions. After the shellac has dried, paint the surface with a mixture of equal parts of stearic acid and kerosene. The stearic acid is melted in a small pan on a hot plate. This will keep the plaster of the second half of the mold from sticking to this one.

Place your mold on the table, with the pattern in it, and build a clay wall around it. Then pour plaster over the mold and flush with the top of the clay wall. If available, a vacuum pump (Fig. 319) may be used to exhaust the air bubbles from the plaster in the mixing bowl just before it is poured, each time. After the mold has set, the two parts are separated gently and the pattern removed. The mold is shellacked on the surface but not in the pattern cavity. Now a channel and a sprue must be cut into the surface of the mold, as is done for steatite molds (14–3).

Plaster molds can be used only for casting metals with low melting points, such as pewter, with its melting point at 400° F. Molten lead, with a melting point at about 620° F., will usually crack a plaster mold. One precaution must be observed if molten metal is to be poured into the plaster mold. **The mold must be completely dry**. A wet plaster mold will explode molten metal dangerously. Therefore, either bake the mold in an oven or allow it to dry for several days before casting into it.

14–6 Charcoal-mold Casting Since charcoal-mold casting is similar in method to stone-mold casting, no further description is needed. The problems of design for casting by this method are discussed in Chapter 6 **(6–20)**.

14–7 Sand-mold Casting Sand casting is done by gravity pour into a sand mold that consists of two halves. The casting flask is made in two parts, the cope and the drag, which are keyed together by pins at each end of the cope (Fig. 175). The process for preparing a sand mold for casting is performed as follows:

1. Place the lower frame (cope) upside down (with the pins pointing down) on the molding board. This board is just the size of the outside dimensions of the casting flask. Set the pattern in the center of the cope, but toward the lower end if the flask is of cast iron, with sprue opening at the upper end.
2. Sift parting powder over the pattern and the molding board within the cope.
3. Sieve sand over the pattern and within the cope to the top of the cope. Take a rammer, which can be the end of a wooden mallet or a 1-in. dowel, and tamp the sand around the pattern and along the sides of the flask, being careful not to press into the pattern itself.
4. Sieve more sand into the cope until it is heaped overfull. Pack this sand firmly but gently, and then with a straightedge strike off the excess sand by drawing the straightedge diagonally across the top edges of the cope.
5. Holding the cope firmly to the molding board, tip them over away from you and set the cope right side up on a smooth surface.
6. Remove the molding board. Then take a small spatula and clean the sand around the pattern right down to the parting line (Fig. 320). The parting line is that line at which the pattern is at its farthest outward extension from the center. Sand may need to be trimmed at a slant from the surface down to that parting line, or it may be pressed gently and smoothly down to the parting line. When the sand is smoothed out all around the pattern, cover the surface evenly with parting powder.

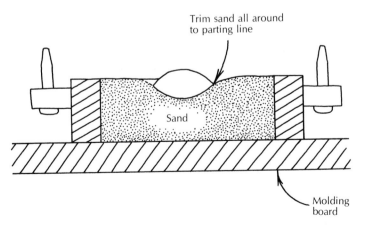

Trim sand all around
to parting line

Sand

Molding
board

Fig. 320. Sand trimmed on cope
to parting line of pattern.

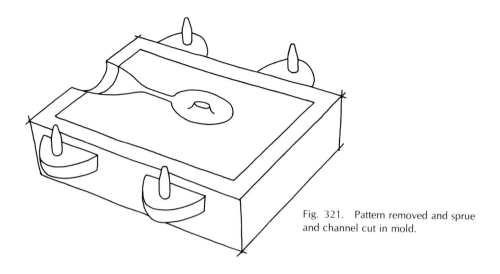

Fig. 321.   Pattern removed and sprue and channel cut in mold.

7. Place the drag in position on the cope and sieve the drag full of sand. Pack this down, as was done with the cope, refilling and then striking off.

8. Carefully lift the drag away from the cope and set it upside down on a smooth surface.

9. Gently remove the pattern. Clean up any parts of the mold that break away. Gently blow away loose sand. A hose with compressed air is used at a foundry.

10. Carve a channel with the spatula from the sprue at the upper end of the flask to the pattern cavity (Fig. 321). This can be a V-channel. The sprue is carved and pressed smoothly to join the flask sprue. Blow away all loose sand.

11. Carefully replace the drag in its proper position.

12. Place a small board cut to fit on each side of the flask and apply a C-clamp on each side to hold the cope and the drag together. Stand the flask on end, sprue up, for casting. Molten metal may now be poured into the sprue.

13. After the pour the C-clamps are removed and the sand is knocked out of the frames with a mallet.

14. The cast pattern (Fig. 322) is removed and pickled and cleaned, after which the channel may be cut away and that cut finished.

Fig. 322. Cast pattern with sprue and channel.

The casting of rings in the ring casting outfit, which is available from jewelry supply houses, is done in the same general manner, although there are many special parts to the outfit. Adequate instructions come with it.

14–8   Making Patterns for Casting   Jewelry patterns for casting are usually made of metal, although many other materials may be used under special circumstances. Patterns for sand casting might be made of metal, plastic, wood, paper, or even wax. Wood patterns should be sanded and shellacked.

Patterns for lost-wax casting are made directly in wax by some jewelers (**14–10**). The wax pattern is invested and cast, and the cast pattern is then either finished as a final piece of jewelry or prepared as a metal pattern (Fig. 323) for making a rubber mold (**14–9**).

Otherwise, patterns for lost-wax casting are usually made of metal. Usually silver is used for sterling or gold jewelry, but sometimes tin is used because it works more easily. The metal pattern for lost-wax casting should always be made about 10 percent, or more, larger than the final casting because of the shrinkage that takes place. Because of its softness, sterling jewelry should be made somewhat more massive than gold jewelry. Prongs, particularly, and ring shanks should always be made larger for both gold and silver in order to allow for filing and finishing. When the pattern is finished, a sprue channel of 8-gauge sterling wire should be soldered to the pattern at a point from which (1) it can most conveniently be removed from the cast pattern and finished, or (2) the molten metal will most logically flow into the entire pattern. Patterns should never be set up on the sprue channel in such a way that a backward flow of metal must take place to fill the mold (Fig. 324). If this situation cannot be avoided, a separate channel must be led directly into the part from the sprue.

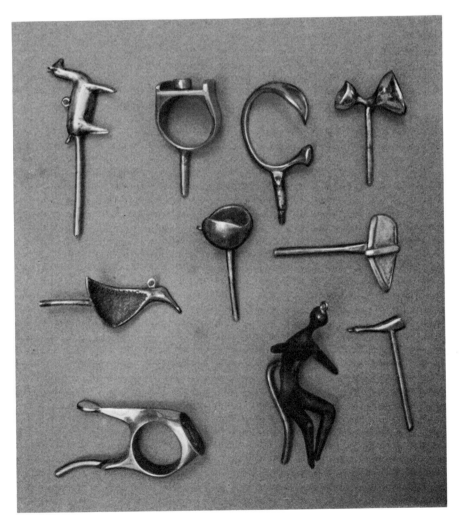

Fig. 323. Patterns with sprues attached.

Fig. 324. Pattern setup to be avoided because it requires back flow.

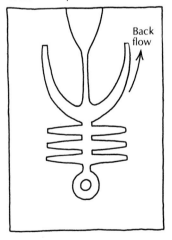

Back flow

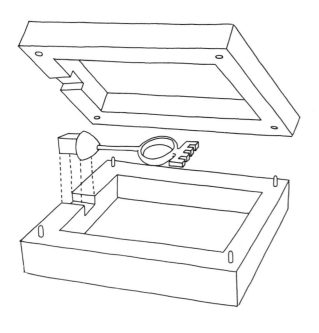

above: Fig. 325. Pattern set into vulcanizing frame.
right: Fig. 326. Vulcanizing Press.

14–9 The Rubber Mold   A metal jewelry pattern is used to make a rubber mold in which wax patterns can be formed. These wax patterns are then invested in a casting flask.

The rubber mold is made in an aluminum vulcanizing frame. The vulcanizing frame is made of two pieces, similar to the sand-casting flask but much smaller. At one end of the frame is a small hole into which the sprue channel of the pattern is set in order to suspend the pattern at the center of the frame (Fig. 325). The length of the sprue channel may need to be adjusted in order to place the pattern at the center of the frame.

There are two methods of making a rubber mold. In the first of these the lower part of the frame is filled with Plasticine so that the pattern is half embedded along a logical parting line. The upper frame is then placed in position and plaster of Paris is poured in to fill the upper frame. After the plaster has set, the lower frame is cleaned out and the plaster around the pattern is cleaned up where necessary. Two or four small depressions are carved into the plaster to serve as keys. The mold is turned over so that the plaster and the pattern are in the bottom frame. The upper frame is then filled with sheets of mold rubber cut to fit snugly in the frame. The vulcanizing frame is then placed in the electric vulcanizing press (Fig. 326). The upper press is screwed down tightly upon the frame and the mold is vulcanized. The time of vulcanizing depends upon the size of the mold; recommendations for vulcanizing times come with the vulcanizer.

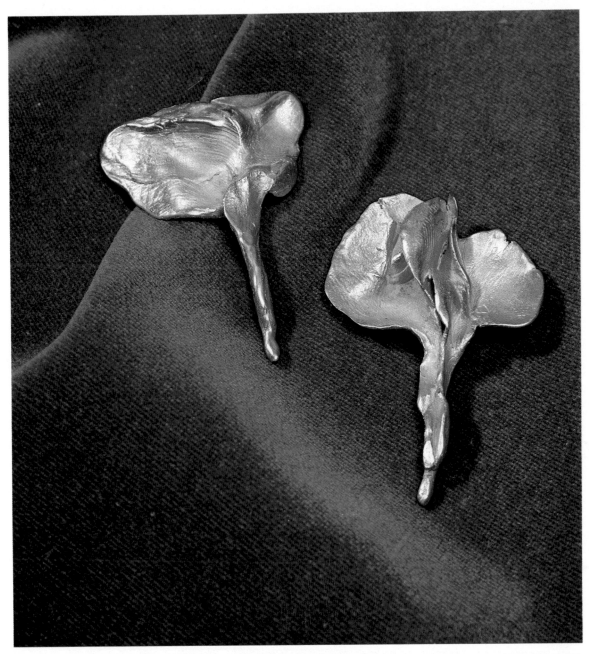

Plate 13. Michael Jerry. Brooches. 1967. 14-kt. gold, modeled in soft wax and cast.

Plate 14. Philip Morton. Brooch. 1969. Cast sterling with gold, ruby, and rhodochrosite.

After the rubber mold has been vulcanized, the frame is removed and opened, the plaster is removed from the lower half of the frame, the surface of the rubber is sprinkled with talc, and sheets of rubber are placed in the upper half. The frame is again placed in the vulcanizing press, and the other half of the mold is vulcanized.

After vulcanizing, the two halves of the rubber mold may be removed from the frame and opened and the pattern extracted. When cool, the mold is ready to use.

The other way to make a rubber mold is somewhat simpler. The metal pattern is placed in the vulcanizing frame and both sides are filled with rubber sheets cut just to size. The frame is then placed in the vulcanizer in the usual manner. After vulcanizing, the rubber mold is removed from the frame. It is in one piece, however, and the pattern is embedded within. A very sharp knife, such as the Exacto knife, is used to cut the mold in half. This is somewhat complicated, for keys must be cut into one half at all four corners, as the mold is cut along the sides. The cutting begins at the sprue channel, comes down along that channel on one side, exactly along the center, then along the high edge of the pattern, all around, and up the other side of the sprue channel. When the mold is finally cut in half, the pattern is easily removed.

14–10 Wax Patterns, Direct Modeling   Though many casting patterns are made directly in metal, it has become increasingly the practice to model patterns directly in wax. The wax used for direct modeling is fairly soft, though combinations of harder and softer waxes are likely to be used. Southwest (**B–2**) supplies a Mold and Carve wax that is pliable with light heat. A mixture of beeswax and paraffin in equal proportions is a good pattern wax. Adding powdered rosin and lampblack gives this wax a better working color. Kerr (**B-2**) puts out a Utility wax that is plastic at room temperatures. These waxes or combinations of them work well for direct modeling (Pls. 13, 14).

It does not take long to discover the peculiarities of wax. Bear in mind that wax has a crystalline structure. When it is melted, this structure disappears. It becomes rigid only when it has cooled down to a point at which recrystallization takes place. For this reason, when wax has been welded to another piece of wax, it must not be disturbed until the melted wax has cooled down to the point of recrystallization. If it is disturbed, the joint will break apart. The term "welded" refers to the process of fastening two pieces of wax together with melted wax. Either liquid wax from a heated wax pot can be introduced between the two pieces, or a hot knife blade may be inserted briefly between the two pieces, causing them both to melt and fuse together.

A wax pattern modeled solely with the fingers will tend to be organic in quality, rather than geometric.

Southwest sells a water-soluble wax called Solu-Wax that can be used to build up hollow forms of modeling or casting wax. The Solu-Wax is built up into the matrix form that is desired, and then casting or modeling wax is painted over it and built up as desired. Or the Solu-Wax form may be dipped in wax. When the form has been completed, it is soaked in water to dissolve out the Solu-Wax. The hollow wax pattern can then be invested as usual and cast.

The above-mentioned waxes can be modeled just with the fingers, but it is usual to use a heated tool along with finger modeling.

14–11 Wax Patterns Modeled with Heated Tool A wax pattern made directly is usually completed by using a small spatula, knife, or carver to shape and form it. These tools are sometimes heated in a bunsen burner for carving, cutting, or texturing action. Now available on the market are wax welders, which are adaptations of the electric soldering iron, with a small, electrically heated tip at the end of a light hand piece. This hand piece is wired to a box having a temperature regulator, switch, and on-off pilot light. The wax welder is more convenient to use than the spatula that requires constant heating and reheating in a flame.

A ring pattern is made by pouring wax sheet to a thickness of about 12-gauge and then cutting a strip of the correct width and length for a ring band. This is rolled around a thin brass tube. The size of the tube should be about size 6 for a woman's ring and size 10 for a man's ring. The rest of the ring is then built up on this band. It is useful to have a little pot of melted wax at hand for modeling. A special bunsen burner on the market has a small wax pot built into it.

When the wax pattern is finished, a short channel about ⅛ in. in diameter is attached to it for attaching to the "tree" (**14–14**).

14–12 Wax Patterns, File-Wax Carving File-Wax is a very hard, brittle wax that can be sawed, filed, or cut. It is not sticky and does not foul up a file but comes away in clean filings. The wax-filing method of designing rings has become extremely popular in the past ten years. Such rings are made by cutting a slab of the right thickness, drilling out the ring center to the proper ring size, and then shaping the form with saws and files. Very accurate surfaces and edges can be attained, and for this reason most File-Wax rings tend toward geometric forms. The sequence of illustrations in Figure 327 illustrates the steps in the process.

Fig. 327. Sequence of operations for File-Wax casting, performed by Olaf Skoogfors. Step 1, cutting File-Wax on band saw. Step 2, drilling wax to nearest ring size on drill press.

 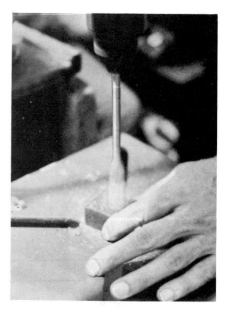

Step 3, marking off shape of ring pattern.

Step 4, filing out shape.

Step 5, further shaping.

Step 6, painting on "debubblizer" or "conditioner" before investment.

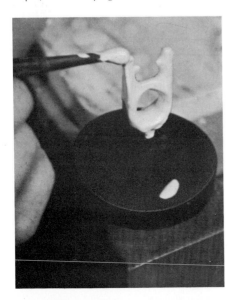

left: Step 7, painting on face coating of investment to make sure no air bubbles are trapped.
right: Step 8, pouring investment into flask.

Step 9, inserting flask into kiln for burnout.

Step 10, melting gold on casting machine.

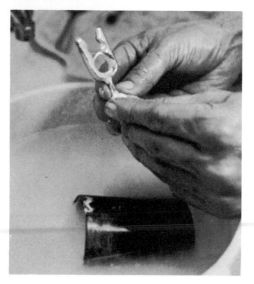

left: Step 11, removing cast ring from investment.
below: Step 12, polishing the casting.

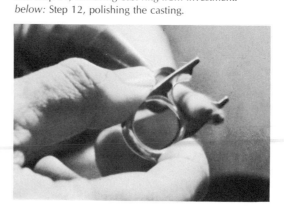

Step 13, constructed "bearing," stone,
and cast gold ring ready for assembling.

Step 14, soldering the "bearing" to the ring.

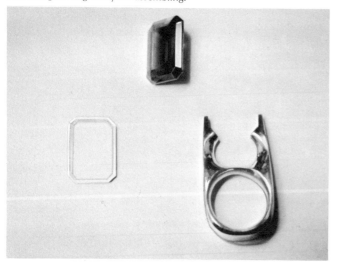

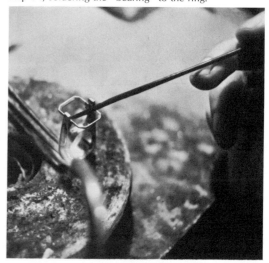

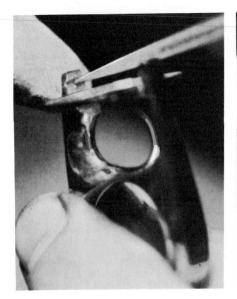

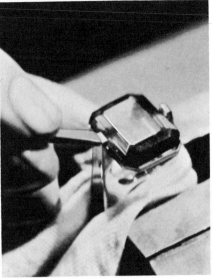

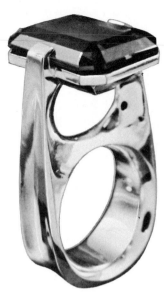

Step 15, filing groove
in prongs to hold stone.

Step 16, pushing over prongs
to hold stone.

Step 17, completed ring,
14-kt gold with synthetic
blue zircon.

File-Wax comes preformed in many kinds of ring forms (Fig. 328), which can be cut off in small slabs. It can also be procured in rods and bulk slabs. File-Wax cannot be modeled well, but it can be formed with the wax welder or a heated spatula.

14–13   Wax Patterns Cast in a Rubber Mold   There are two ways to cast wax patterns. The old way is to place the mold in a small rubber-mold frame, which supports the mold and prevents distortion. The frame is then put into a centrifugal casting machine (Figs. 313, 329), used only for casting wax patterns, which has an aluminum crucible. The machine is wound up on its spring, liquid wax from a wax pot is put into the crucible, and the arm of the machine

Fig. 329. Thermatrol
casting machine.

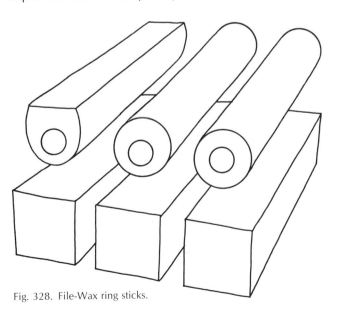

Fig. 328. File-Wax ring sticks.

Fig. 330. Wax pressure injector.

is spun to throw the wax into the rubber mold. The crucible of the machine has to be kept warm to prevent the wax from cooling down. This is usually done with a torch, in between castings. After each casting of the pattern, the mold is removed from the machine and from the rubber-mold frame, and the wax pattern is extracted.

A newer method of casting wax patterns utilizes a wax pressure injector (Fig. 330). A cast-aluminum pot is electrically heated and thermostatically controlled to hold the temperature constant. Air pressure forces the wax into the rubber mold. The rubber mold is placed in a rubber-mold frame and then pressed against a nozzle; the air pressure forces wax into the mold. It is important to hold the wax at the lowest temperature that will keep it molten. If the wax is too hot, the mold becomes heated, and then it becomes more difficult to extract the wax patterns, since they do not cool sufficiently to solidify.

There are several kinds of casting wax available, each with its special qualities. A hard, brittle wax is more desirable for use with simple patterns that are easily removed from the rubber mold. The dark-green casting wax is quite brittle and casts well but will break easily. The light-green wax is tougher and less brittle. The blue casting wax is tough and somewhat flexible. A red wax from Denton Precision Casting Co. is an ideal casting wax, also. Fragile and complex patterns require a tough, less brittle wax.

Temperature and pressure are both extremely important factors. These waxes melt at anywhere from 90° F. to 165° F. Each wax must be held at its lowest possible molten temperature in order to avoid excessive expansion of the molten wax, which in turn leads to excessive shrinking of the cooled wax pattern. Injection pressure, if excessive, will tend to bulge the wax pattern in the rubber mold. Optimum temperatures and pressures are always specified by the manufacturer.

14–14 Setting up the Wax Pattern

Wax patterns are always set up on a sprue base, which is usually made of rubber. These come in sizes to match the stainless-steel casting flasks in which the patterns are invested. They range in size from 2½ to 4 in. in diameter, and 2½ to 7 in. in height. The small flask is used for single patterns. The larger flasks are used when patterns are set in a "tree" (Fig. 331), that is, when wax patterns are set circularly around a small tapered wax "trunk" at an angle of about 45° and two or more rows are placed one above the other. Up to twelve pieces may be cast at once in such a "tree."

The sprue base has a small, conical sprue form at the center, in which there is a small hole. This hole is filled with wax, to which the sprue channel or the tree "trunk" is attached. Wax pieces are welded to each other by using a heated narrow blade to melt the surfaces that are to be joined. With practice these welds can be made solidly, so that the joints will not break apart when the investment is added. Wax patterns can be set up so that they come within ½ in. of the sides of the casting flask. They should not come closer than ½ in. to the top of the flask (Fig. 332).

Fig. 331. Patterns set up on a tree.

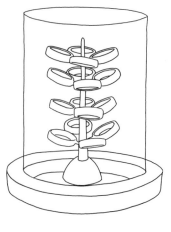

14–15 Investing the Wax Pattern

After the wax patterns are set up, the casting flask is placed on the sprue base. A 1-in. strip of asbestos sheet is placed around the center of the flask on the inside. It will stay in place if it is moistened first. This strip allows for easier removal of the investment material.

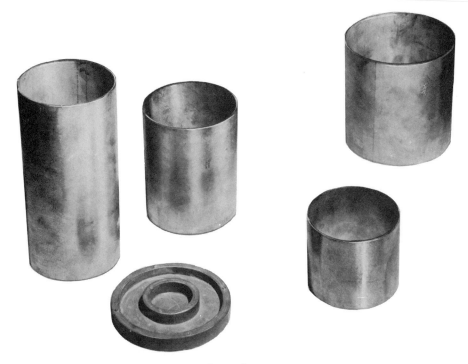

Fig. 332. Flasks for investment casting and sprue base.

The investment material must now be mixed in a rubber bowl. This material will consist of one of the special powdered investments prepared by various manufacturers. All of them are developed to maintain a minimum expansion at burnout temperature, which is about 1000° F. Most manufacturers have made elaborate tests to determine exactly the correct proportion of water to investment powder that will yield the maximum strength and the lowest expansion. Most of these investments were developed for dental or commercial work, in which the finished size of the casting is critical. Hence the extreme concern for expansion. It is advisable for the jeweler to follow closely the recommended proportions of water to investment. Once measured out, the mixture is stirred until the investment is smooth and creamy.

The bowl of investment is then placed under the bell jar of the vacuum pump for "debubblizing." A properly equipped casting shop will have a machine that pumps air out from a bell jar. When the bowl of plaster is placed under the bell jar and a vacuum created therein, all the bubbles of air trapped in the investment plaster are drawn out. This prevents bubbles from forming on the wax patterns and appearing as part of the cast patterns.

It is standard practice to paint the wax patterns with a degreasing or "debubblizing" solution, so that the liquid investment will flow freely around the surfaces of the patterns. Sometimes, if there is a great amount of detail in the patterns, investment is painted over the surface of the patterns before the casting flask is placed on the sprue base, or the patterns may be dipped in the investment.

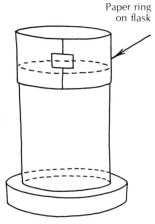

Paper ring
on flask

Fig. 333. Flask with
paper-strip extension.

Otherwise, the investment, after "debubblizing," is poured into the flask, but to one side, so that it flows to the bottom and rises up and around the patterns. The flask must be filled up to the top. This is best accomplished by taping a strip of paper around the top of the flask so that it projects about 2 in. above the top of the flask (Fig. 333). Investment must be poured to at least 1/2 in. above the flask.

The flask is then placed under the bell jar and the vacuum pump turned on again, in order to exhaust any air trapped in the plaster around the patterns. This will froth up the plaster, but it will not run over and down onto the table of the bell jar, because the paper strip retains it.

When the investment plaster has set, the paper strip can be removed and the sprue base pulled off. Plaster investment now extends past the top of the investment. This excess is necessary, because, when it is cut off with a hacksaw blade (Fig. 334), the top surface is flush with the edges of the flask. If any depression is allowed in this surface, the investment will be likely to cave in from the weight and pressure of the molten metal when it is cast in the centrifugal casting machine. Then the metal will leak out the back end of the investment and the cast will be lost.

14–16 Investment Burnout   A gas burnout furnace is superior to the electric furnace, because the vent of the gas furnace will carry off the wax fumes. The investment calcinates at about 800° F., but burnout temperatures should not exceed 1300° F. The length of burnout depends upon the size of the furnace and the size and number of investments. Burnout should be continued until an inspection of the sprue shows no trace of odor and the color is a pure rose red with no patches of black carbon. It is desirable to burn out at the lowest possible temperature in order to avoid unnecessary expansion cracks. The author employs a temperature of about 1000° F. and a burnout time of from one to four hours. The investment is placed in the furnace, sprue down. The bottom of the furnace is ridged, so that spaces are provided under the investment where wax may drip out or fumes escape. In jewelry casting no attempt is made to save wax. The hot investments are removed from the furnace with special casting-flask tongs that fit around the flask.

Investments should be allowed to cool somewhat before casting. For white gold, many jewelers cool the investment down to 1100° F.; for yellow gold, down to about 850° F. Silver can be cooled down to about 600° F. Some jewelers burn out for 8 hours, cool down for casting, and then, after casting, leave the investment overnight before opening.

14–17 Centrifugal Casting   Centrifugal casting should be carried out quite systematically if consistent results are to be obtained.

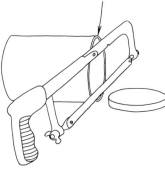

Cut surface
flush with
edges of ring

Fig. 334. Casting ring with bottom
cut off flush by a hack saw.

1. First, the casting arm must be balanced. One end of the arm carries a crucible. The other end carries an adjustable weight that may be moved forward or backward along the arm to balance the extra weight of the casting metal and the investment. The investment is placed in its frame at the end of the casting arm. The crucible is moved up against the investment.

    Sufficient metal is then placed in the crucible to make the pour. This quantity must be estimated in relation to the size and number of patterns to be cast and must include enough metal to fill the sprue. The estimate may be made by guess, or it may be made by calculating the weight of the wax patterns and the casting channel. Silver is about 14 times heavier than wax. The specific gravity of silver is about 10.5, while that of gold is about 19.3. Gold is therefore about 20 times heavier than wax. The specific gravity of wax is somewhere under 1.0, since wax is lighter than water, which has a specific gravity of 1.0. When the correct amount of metal is in the crucible, the weight at the opposite end of the casting arm must be turned toward or away from the crucible until the two ends balance.

Balancing is easier to do on a machine that rotates vertically. It can be done just before each investment is cast. For systematic casting, the investments are numbered and the balancing of each is done in advance, so that the exact amount of metal can be recorded for each one. The machine is usually wound up on its spring before the investment is placed in position for the casting, but not until after the balancing has been done. Balancing is less critical for the horizontal casting machine than for the vertical casting machine.

2. Heat the metal in the crucible. If the amount of metal required is known in advance, the metal is usually heated with the torch to the melting point before the investment is removed from the furnace and placed in the machine. After the investment is in the machine, which has already been wound up on its rotating spring, the metal is brought to melting temperature (C–17). At the proper moment the torch is pulled away from the crucible, and at the same time the rotating arm is pulled away from the catch and then released. This process is done in one sweeping movement. The rotating arm will now spin around, throwing the metal into the investment. It should be allowed to come to a stop, so that the metal will have some chance to solidify.

The investment is removed with the tongs and placed in a bucket of water. When casting silver or gold, this may be done as soon as the red glow of the sprue is no longer visible. When casting bronze, a little time must be allowed to elapse for the bronze to solidify. Bronze seems to cool more slowly than silver or gold. Plunging the investment into a bucket of water breaks out the investment quickly and frees the casting. The casting is then pickled and cleaned, and the channels are clipped away.

There are several variations in the process of centrifugal casting, depending upon the type of machine used. Some machines are spun by an electric motor. Some have an electric crucible built into the casting arm. Manufacturers provide detailed instructions for the operation of their own particular machines.

The great advantage of centrifugal casting is the delicacy and complexity that can be attained. Commercial precision casting is an extremely technical process, wherein variable factors must be exactly controlled.

The foregoing description of casting is at best a brief summary of the process. Those who wish to pursue casting seriously should research the field thoroughly.

14–18 Vacuum Casting   Vacuum casting is not new, but it is becoming increasingly popular with contemporary jewelers for three reasons. First, there is a growing opinion that the castings are more uniform with this process. Sec-

Fig. 335. Vacuum casting machine.

ond, the cost of equipment is lower. And, third, the casting operation is simpler and, therefore, faster.

Vacuum casting requires a table with a hole in the center over which the investment is placed. A pipe leads from the hole to a vacuum pump. A heavy silicone rubber mat that can withstand temperatures up to 1000° F. is used under the investment on the casting table, so that a tight air seal will be possible when the vacuum is applied to the flask.

1. When the investment has been properly burned out and has cooled to the proper temperature, the metal is melted in the hand crucible or bench furnace.
2. When the metal is molten, the jeweler removes the investment from the furnace and places it on the casting table and turns on the vacuum pump. Then he takes up the crucible and makes the pour. The vacuum is already drawing air out of the flask, and as the metal enters the flask, vapors and gases are withdrawn, enabling the molten metal to flow in with decreased resistance. In his experience, Ronald Hayes Pearson has found that, with a 4-in. flask, the rubber mat should have about a 3-in. hole under the flask for best results.

An excellent vacuum casting outfit, which includes also a vacuum bell-jar table, can be procured from Southwest Smelting (Fig. 335).

14–19 Pressure Casting   Pressure casting utilizes pressure to force molten metal into the investment mold. At a primitive level pressure casting can be tried by placing the burnt-out investment right side up on an asbestos block and putting the unmelted metal into the sprue. For pressure casting, the sprue channel should not be larger than about $\frac{1}{8}$ in. in diameter. A torch is then applied to the metal. When the metal is molten, a board covered with a thick layer of wet cloth is pressed firmly against the top. The steam generated by the heat of the metal exerts the pressure that forces the molten metal into the mold.

A more sophisticated device for pressure casting can be made from a small tin can that is a bit larger than the casting ring. A wooden handle is nailed to the center of the back end of the can. The back end is filled with about a $\frac{1}{2}$-in. layer of wet asbestos sheet cut to fit the diameter of the can snugly. When the metal in the sprue is molten, the can is quickly pressed down upon the casting ring, and the generated steam forces the metal into the casting flask.

The Wilkinson Company offers a small air-pressure casting outfit (Fig. 336) suitable for very small castings. (The largest casting flask is only $1\frac{1}{2} \times 3$ in. in size.) One reason for the diminutive size of this outfit may be that only a small channel is permissible from the sprue; otherwise, the metal would run down the channel from the sprue at once when it becomes molten. This outfit, however, has a small cylindrical casting machine containing an air pump with which to pump up air pressure; it is placed over the investment when the metal is molten. When the machine is pressed down against the flask, the compressed air is released and the molten metal forced into the mold.

Fig. 336. Pressure casting outfit.

15

FINISHING METAL

Finishing should always be a systematic process wherein successively finer tools are used upon the surface of the metal. In general, coarse cutting tools should be used first. A coarse file smooths the surface form but leaves coarse file marks. These should be removed by a finer file and the finer file marks by a still finer file or a coarse emery stick.

Coarse emery scratches should be removed by a medium emery stick, and these by a fine emery stick. In carrying out this entire process, it is well to work across the preceding file or scratch marks, rather than parallel with them.

After the fine emery process the piece is ready for the buffing or polishing lathe.

15–1 Files The file is often considered to be the most important single tool of the jeweler. Without it he could do little metal forming or finishing. A great many different types of files are available in many sizes and cuts. A supplier's catalogue should be consulted by the beginner in order that he may become familiar with the full range of files. The general types are:

Hand File This is a flat file with parallel edges. One edge is cut, and one edge is smooth and therefore called "safe." In a good deal of filing the thumb is used as a guide to control the position of the file on the work. The "safe" side of the file is always put against the thumb. The hand file is used on convex surfaces and on flat surfaces.

Half-round File This file has one flat face and one round face. The side edges are sharp intersections of the two sides and run to a tapered point. This tool is used chiefly for working on concave surfaces.

Half-round Ring File The size of this file is in better proportion than the regular half-round file to fit inside ring bands for filing and finishing.

Actual Size Illustrations					
Teeth per inch (up cut)	30	38	51	64	79
Length of files 10″ and over	00	0	1	2	3
Length of files 4″ to 8″	00		0	1	2
Escapement files				0	
Needle files 4″ to 7¾″				0	
Regular rifflers				0	

Actual Size Illustrations					
Teeth per inch (up cut)	97	117	142	173	213
Length of files 10″ and over	4		6		
Length of files 4″ to 8″	3	4		6	
Escapement files	2	3	4		6
Needle files 4″ to 7¾″	2	3	4		6
Regular rifflers	2	3	4		6

Fig. 337. File cuts from 00, coarse, to 6, fine.

Round File   As the name indicates, this is a round, tapered file, also called "rattail file."

Barrette File   This file has one flat face and very narrow, thin edges, making it possible to file up closely against a corner. The back is smooth.

Needle Files   As the name implies, needle files are very small, slender files. They are available in many styles, such as barrette, crossing, equaling, half-round, knife, round, square, triangular or three-square, marking, and slitting.

File cuts (Fig. 337) are numbered from 00, the coarsest, to No. 6, the finest. The jeweler eventually selects according to his own preference, but the beginner might well begin his shop with two cuts for large files—a No. 1 for rough shaping and finishing and a No. 3 or 4 for final smoothing and finishing. Needle files, too, should be selected on this basis – a No. 1 for rough filing and a No. 4 or 6 for final smoothing.

15–2 Position for Filing   Your workbench should be provided with a file block or bench pin set about 6 in. below the level of the eyes when you are in a normal sitting position. This places your work at a comfortable working distance from your eyes. In most cases filing should be done by holding the work in your left hand, which is supported on the bench pin. Small work, as well as rings, may be held in either end of the ring vise or in the hand vise.

15–3 Form for Filing   The file is made with teeth which cut only on the forward stroke; therefore there is no point in drawing the file across the work on the backstroke. Pressure should be applied on the forward stroke and the file lifted up on the backstroke. All files should have handles and should be held by the handle. Files on the shelf should not be allowed to rub against each other, since this will eventually dull them. They should be kept clean and dry to avoid rust. Do not put your fingers on the fine files, because the grease from your hand will make the file slick across the metal. Never use your regular files for filing lead or solder for this will clog the teeth. Keep old files for this purpose.

■ When filing, always take a full stroke of the file.
■ Hold the arm and wrist relaxed, and let the file follow the work if the shape is curved.
■ When filing the edges of a sheet or strip, slap the file gently against the edge so that it will find the flat surface. Thus you will avoid filing new planes across the edge.
■ The coarsest appropriate file should always be used to begin a cutting or smoothing operation. When filing across the edge of a sheet, however, select a file with teeth somewhat smaller than the thickness of the sheet.
■ Flat files should be used for straight edges and outside curves. Half-round files are necessary for inside curves. When filing an inside curve, slide the file along the length of the curve as you make the forward stroke. This will help to avoid filing irregular grooves in an edge, particularly when needle files are being used.

15–4 Flexible Shaft for Grinding, Emerying, and Polishing   One of the most useful tools for cutting away metal, smoothing with emery, and polishing is the flexible shaft (Fig. 278). This tool consists of a small motor to which a flexible shaft is attached. Several designs of chucks are available for the flexible shaft, to which drills, burs, grinding stones, and polishing buffs may be fastened. In some models one end of the motor is geared down so that the flexible shaft can be operated with more power at lower speed. The motor is operated by a foot rheostat to provide variation of speed.

Most suppliers' catalogues carry a wide selection of small tools that can be used with the flexible shaft. Burs are made in many shapes: round, cone, bud, wheel, reamer, tree. The setting bur **(17–3)** is designed to cut a shoulder in the metal in which a stone may be set. Small grinding wheels, brushes, and crystal and pumice wheels, as well as small muslin buffs, can be attached to mandrels for use with the flexible shaft.

Some experiment is necessary to learn control of the cutting burs. Cutting is done on a forward stroke, and it is well to use the thumb in a solid position to anchor the hand piece to the work. The speed of the bur must be adjusted so that the momentum of the cutting balances the pressure exerted on the metal. If too slow a speed is used, or if a backward stroke is taken, the bur is likely to run over the work.

15–5 Emery Paper   Emery paper is a refined type of abrasive sheet available in many grades. Hubert's emery paper from France has always been preferred by many jewelers but does not seem to be available these days. Behr-Manning emery papers are listed in most supply houses.

Emery paper comes in grades from No. 3, coarsest, through Nos. 2, 1, 0, 2/0, 3/0 to No. 4/0, the finest. It is useful to have three grades: No. 3 or 2 can be used for roughing off filed forms; No. 1 can be used for medium finishing; and No. 3/0 or 4/0 can be used for fine finishing.

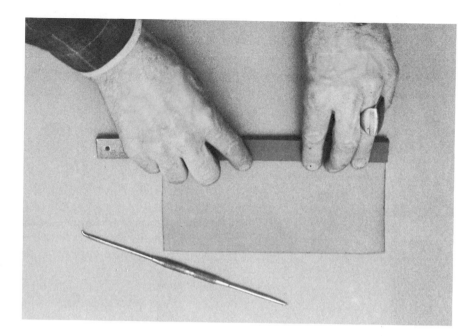

Fig. 338. Preparing emergy stick by folding paper over stick and using scribe to sharpen crease at corner.

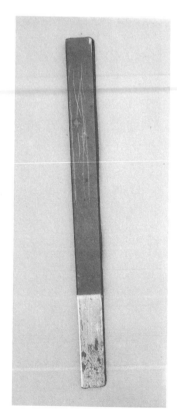

Fig. 339. Completed emery stick.

15–6 Emery Sticks   The jeweler uses emery paper fastened to a flat stick called an emery stick or emery buff. The emery stick may be purchased in all the grades. The jeweler may make his own with strips and dowels of various sizes. A good size for an emery stick is about 1 in. wide, ¼ in. thick, and 12 in. long. Smaller and thinner flat sticks may also be useful, as well as dowels of from 1 in. diameter down to ¼ in. diameter.

For flat sticks, use a piece of soft wood with smooth surfaces and sharp edges. Lay the stick on the paper and line up the outside edge of the stick exactly on the narrow edge of the paper (Fig. 338). With a scribe scratch a line along the inside edge of the stick. Fold the paper up along this scratched line. Place the stick snugly against this fold and scribe a line along the other edge of the stick. Fold the paper along this line also. Place the stick snugly in these folds and continue the process until you have wrapped three or four layers around the stick. The paper should be cut off so that the last layer ends across one edge of the stick. Three small round-headed nails or three staples will hold this edge against the edge of the stick and be out of the way when you emery on the flat sides or the opposite edge (Fig. 339). The emery paper may be cut by drawing the scribe several times along the same line. As each layer wears out, it can be trimmed off, always along the nailed or stapled edge.

When using the emery stick (or files, for that matter), always work across the scratches made by the preceding tool. Emery finishing is never completed properly until all file marks have been removed. A file mark left in the work will show up immediately when polishing is done on the buffing lathe. Do not attempt to polish out a deep file mark. Always go back to the emery stick until the file mark is removed. This way you will achieve perfect finished work.

Round and oval emery sticks of various diameters can have two or three layers of emery paper rolled up and stapled along the edge.

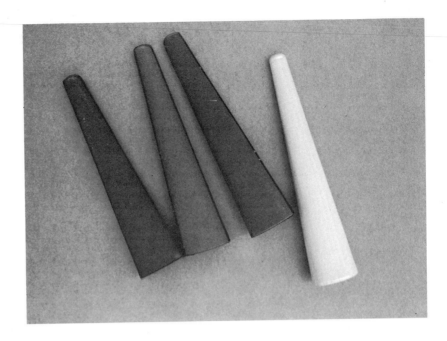

Fig. 340. Ring sticks.

15–7 Emery Shells for Ring Sticks   Emery shells which fit on conical ring sticks (Fig. 340) are commercially available, also. The stick is placed on the buffing mandrel, a tapered spindle, and the shell slipped on the tapered stick. These shells can easily be made by cutting the emery paper in the proper arc and gluing together.

When using the ring stick, never bring the ring up on the cone to where the diameter of the stick is equal to the ring size. The ring will be likely to catch and tear out of your hands. Always work just below that point. This will require that you continually rotate the ring as you press it against the stick, in order to avoid cutting a groove in the ring. Finishing the inside of a ring should also follow a sequence from coarse to fine emery and finally to a ring buff.

15–8 Cutting and Polishing on the Buffing Lathe   The process of polishing with the buffing lathe is a modern improvement that replaces the slow traditional method of working the metal smooth with scotch stone and polishing with burnishers. If you consult a jewelers' supply-house catalogue, you will find a wide range of specialized buffs. These can be classified as (1) cutting buffs, (2) polishing buffs, (3) brush buffs, (4) laps, (5) scratch brushes, and (6) ring buffs. Although there are many others, they are not of particular importance to the jeweler.

Cutting buffs are usually made of layers of coarse, hard materials such as wool, muslin, or leather, which are sewn together. Leather buffs are commonly used with pumice and are called "sand bobs." They are made of walrus hide and used mainly by silversmiths for fast cutting. Wool buffs are used with coarse cutting compounds such as Hard White or Lea Compound. Muslin buffs are usually used with tripoli or White Diamond Compound for jewelry. This buff will give a "butler finish" to the silver, rather than a high polish.

The "butler finish" is often preferred to the high polish, because silver scratches readily. Tripoli is a cutting compound. It consists of fine, sharp particles, which put very fine scratches into the metal, thereby taking out the coarser emery-paper scratches.

Polishing buffs are made of flannel and used with white or red rouge for imparting a high polish to silver or gold. Rouge is not a cutting compound but, being made of flat particles, has a burnishing or smoothing effect on metal.

Brush buffs are used wherever the work is irregular or has deep corners or crevices that cannot be reached by cloth buffs. They are small wooden disks with one or more rows of bristles around the circumference. Both tripoli and rouge are used with them.

The scratch brush is made of fine brass or nickel-silver wire and gives a burnished, mat finish. The work is usually pickled several times for scratch brushing. By tradition, Scandinavian silversmiths dip their work in stale beer for scratch brushing and believe that this gives a superior finish. The scratch brush should be run at a speed of not more than 600 r.p.m.

The ring buff is a tapered cone of wood covered with a layer of felt. Tripoli or rouge is applied for polishing the inside surface of the ring band.

15-9 Buffing Practice

While most of the compounds have been named, some further description may be useful. Most of them consist of a cutting or polishing material mixed with a thick grease or wax. When leather buffs or sandbobs are used, however, the work is held against the bob with one hand, and a handful of pumice sand is fed into the buff. To help hold the pumice sand from dusting into the air, a small amount of oil is mixed with the sand.

For usual jewelry work, it is useful to have three types of compound on hand: a coarse compound such as Hard White, a finer compound like tripoli, and a stick of red rouge for high polishing.

For ideal buffing practice, your buffing lathe should have three speeds—a slow speed for scratch brushing, a medium speed for tripoli or other cutting compounds, and a high speed for rouge polishing. For a permanent workshop a dust collector should be hooked up to the buffing lathe, so that dust and lint are carried off instead of being thrown into the face of the craftsman.

The following general buffing rules will assist the beginner to polish correctly.

- Use separate buffs for each compound. Do not mix them.
- A 4-in. or 5-in. buff is large enough for ordinary small polishing. As buffs wear down, a row of stitching may be cut out.
- Apply compounds frequently, as you polish, by lightly touching the spinning buff with the compound. Do not apply too much at one time; the excess will merely fly off the wheel.
- Hold your work with the edge toward you covered over by your thumbs. This will prevent the buff from catching this edge and tearing the work out of your hands.
- When cutting with tripoli, keep shifting your work around so that the buff works across the metal in many directions. If you continue holding the work in one position, the buff will cut wavy marks into the surfaces of the metal.

- As you hold the work up against the buff, keep it sliding back and forth.
- It is dangerous to polish long lengths of wire or chain, or long jewelry pieces such as necklaces or bracelets, without following a special practice: Each end of the chain should be held closed up in one hand, with but a very short length of not more than 1 in. running out from under the thumbs and across the two forefingers. The fists are held together with the thumbs up and pointing toward the buff. The chain is exposed to the buff and supported by the forefingers, which curl back under the thumbs, pointing away from the buff. A small length of chain is thus polished, and since it is held tightly in the fingers, it cannot be caught and twisted around the buff. If this practice is not followed, there is danger that the chain will catch the fingers and cut or break.
- Small pieces of metal sheet or wire may be supported on a strap of leather, cardboard, or wood and thus be brought up against the buff. The upper end of the piece is pinched to the leather between the thumb and forefinger.

15–10 Burnishing   A traditional manner of smoothing and polishing the surface of metal is performed with burnishers. The burnisher is a tool with a smooth and highly polished end. It is used by pressing the polished end against the surface of the metal and rubbing it smoothly back and forth. The effect is to compress and smooth the metal. The burnisher is used today almost exclusively to press the surface of the closed setting snugly and smoothly around the cabochon, but there is nothing to prevent the jeweler from experimenting with the special surface that the burnisher produces on metal.

15–11 Finishing with Powdered Pumice   Whereas much traditional jewelry and most trade jewelry is finished to a high polish, the contemporary jeweler finds greater emotional richness in other types of finishes on certain designs. "Flash," or shine, is but one characteristic appearance of metal. When metal is rubbed with fine pumice, a more subtle quality may be produced. This is done after the final pickling of the piece, or after oxidation if the piece is colored (see below). Powdered pumice comes in coarse and fine grades. One way of using it is to dip the thumb in water and then in the pumice powder and rub the surface of the piece. This operation is repeated until the desired finish is attained.

15–12 Coloring Metals   While there are many methods of coloring metal to different tones, the most successful and most commonly used process for silver, copper, and bronze is to oxidize the metal with liver of sulphur dissolved in water or with barium sulphide dissolved in water. The solution is prepared by adding a small amount of the chemical to a cup of water. This solution must be kept in a tightly closed jar, since it deteriorates when exposed to the oxygen of the air.

The solution may be used in two ways. The piece of jewelry is placed in the jar for a period of time until the proper color is reached. This time may be from 15 minutes to an hour. If you wish to color the jewelry more rapidly, the solution is poured into a small pan and heated to the boiling point. The piece is then dipped in the boiling solution and rinsed off immediately. The longer the metal is left in the hot solution, the thicker the coat of oxide becomes. If you

Fig. 341. Electroplating equipment.

wish to shade the color with pumice powder, do not allow a heavy coat to form, because it will tend to flake off. On the other hand, a heavy coat of oxide gives a deep, rich color. The solution is not poisonous to the hands, though it should be washed off to avoid staining the fingers. The boiled fumes should not be inhaled.

Barium chloride works just like liver of sulphur, except that it is somewhat stronger in its reaction.

Silver may also be oxidized by painting the surface with a solution of chloride of platinum. The proportions of this solution are 1 oz. chloride of platinum to 1 gal. water. Only a small quantity is required, however. It should be kept in a small stoppered bottle and applied with a small brush.

Silver may be colored green by applying, or soaking it in, a solution consisting of three parts hydrochloric acid, one part iodine, and one part water. The metal is soaked in the solution until the desired color is reached.

Bear in mind that all coloring processes affect the surface only and that the color can be more or less easily rubbed away.

15-13 Electroplating   Electroplating is the process of depositing a thin layer of metal by means of electrolytic action. The process requires:

1. Plating bath, consisting of a metal compound in solution.
2. Source of direct current (D.C.).
3. Bar of plating metal.
4. An object to be plated.

Electrolysis is the passage of an electric current through a substance in liquid solution, accompanied by definite chemical changes. The process is made possible by a salt dissolved in the solution, which permits the passage of a current of electricity through the solution because of the dissociation of the salt into negative and positive ions. These ions migrate through the solution to the positive and negative electrodes. When sodium argentocyanide is used in solution, silver connected to the positive terminal (the anode) passes into the solution, and silver ions in the solution are deposited on the object to be plated, which is attached to the negative terminal (the cathode). This process is called electrodeposition. In this way a coating of metal may be built up in a thin, even layer. Theoretically the thickness of a plated coating is determined by the time of plating and the current density. The current density is measured as amperes per square foot of cathode surface. Thus, if an electric source of 5 amperes is used to plate an object with a surface of 0.1 square foot, the current density is 50 ampere-feet.

Several types of power source may be used, depending upon the size of the plating operation. For small-shop operation, storage batteries yielding up to 5 amperes may be satisfactory; for a medium-size operation, 5 to 1000 amperes. Copper oxide, copper sulphide, or selenium rectifiers may be used to convert alternating current into direct current and are suitable sources for a jewelry shop.

Practical electroplating equipment for a small shop and plating solutions are available from many supply houses (Fig. 341).

Procedure for plating begins with a thorough cleaning of the object to be plated. It must be free from grease, dirt, oxides, or other foreign matter. Scrubbing the object with a brush and soapy water can be followed by pickling to remove any oxide deposits. Then the piece may be immersed in the Ultrasonic cleaning machine (Fig. 342), which uses a detergent solution. Finally, the piece can be electrocleaned in the cleaning bath.

The actual plating process is done by suspending the object in the plating solution by the cathode wire (negative terminal) and the plating bar by the anode wire and running the current through. During the plating the current should be periodically reversed for a short time. In simple, permanent operations this can be accomplished by installing a d.t.d.p. switch, which can be

Fig. 342. Ultrasonic cleaning machine.

secured at any radio supply shop. Periodic reversing of the direct current improves the smoothness and uniformity of the plating.

After plating, the work is rinsed thoroughly in water. Care must be taken to avoid splashing the solution of cyanide on the work. It may then be boiled in soapy water and polished on the scratch brush, which burnishes the deposited metal. Afterward a rouge polishing may be given, if desired.

For a very small shop or for initial experimentation all that is required is a small glass container about 8 in. in diameter and about 5 in. deep; a storage battery with two copper leads, which can hang down from a battery above the container into the solution; the plating solution; and a piece of metal for the anode.

The plating bath for gold and silver is a deadly poison, consisting of salts of cyanide. For this reason the **process must be handled carefully.** It must be used only if the equipment can be kept out of the way of children or unwary visitors, preferably in a locked room or locked cabinet. The equipment should never be set up at higher than bench level. Extreme care must be used to avoid splashing the solution onto the bench or into the mouth, eyes, nose, or ears, and it should not be contacted directly with the hands. Rubber gloves and a rubber apron should be worn, and the hands should be washed thoroughly after every operation. Only advanced students or mature and carefully precise craftsmen should attempt this process.

The plating bath always consists of a compound of the metal to be plated, mixed with a colloidal "addition agent," which appears to act in a catalytic manner. The "addition agent" is usually glue, gelatin, albumin, or, in some cases, an aldehyde or ketone. The temperature of the plating bath is critical for commercial operations, though room temperature in a comfortable shop is probably satisfactory for the individual craftsman.

Formulas for typical electroplating baths are given in Appendix C (**C−7**).

15–14   Cleaning Jewelry   There are a number of methods of cleaning jewelry. Usually, after polishing, the piece must be washed to remove the grease of the polishing compound. Actually jewelry should be washed thoroughly after each stage of polishing. In many shops a pan of soapy water is kept boiling on the hot plate with a strainer set in the pan to hold the jewelry. As the jewelry is finished, it is put in the strainer and allowed to soak. When taken out, it is scrubbed with a soft-bristle brush. A covered jar of alcohol is kept nearby for drying the jewelry. After scrubbing and rinsing, the jewelry is dipped in alcohol. This removes the water, and the piece can be wiped with a soft, clean cloth.

In professional shops the Ultrasonic cleaner is increasingly used.

16

GEMS AND SEMIPRECIOUS STONES

Gems and semiprecious stones have been an inseparable part of jewelry throughout history. From the very beginning they have been valued for color, pattern, texture, and transparency, as well as for the magical and protective qualities attributed to them in the past.

Until the Renaissance stones were used *en cabochon* or carved. The faceting of stones waited upon the development of technology and was begun by Louis Van Berquem at Antwerp, as was noted in Chapter 3, although some faceted stones had been brought into Europe much earlier. From the Renaissance onward, the qualities of transparent gems, enhanced by the technique of faceting, lifted them to the highest value in jewelry. The technical purpose of faceting is to establish reflecting planes in such relationship that every light ray entering the gem from above will be reflected back through the top, creating the maximum amount of light or fire and the fullest illumination of the color. Beauty, durability, and rarity have always been the criteria for evaluating gems.

The contemporary view of gems and semiprecious stones is somewhat different from that of the preceding tradition. The contemporary jeweler places as high a value on color, pattern, and texture as on brilliance alone, for he is interested in the integration of the stone with the form of the jewelry. We have noted that one current tendency in contemporary jewelry is a renewed interest in faceted stones. However, the contemporary jeweler is particularly interested in exploring other aspects of faceting than the traditional one of pure brilliance. Margaret De Patta pioneered the contemporary search for such aspects as transparency, refraction, displacement, and distortion, as well as experimenting with freer transparent volumes and other facet relationships. Asymmetrical volumes and structural settings have been emerging in the postwar period.

Plate 15 shows a selection of commonly available gemstones, and Appendix D lists the names of the most useful gemstones and other substances suitable for jewelry settings.

233

16–1 The Forms of Gemstones   The natural forms of gemstones have always aroused the interest of the jeweler. In contemporary times the appreciation of the found object as an expression of nonrational expressive values has extended to coral, petrified wood, and bone, as well as gemstones. The baroque pearl, so popular in an earlier period, is again utilized.

Tumbled stones have become popular since the development of the tumbling machine, which, by rolling the stones together, effects a mutual abrasion and gives a high polish at an extremely low cost. Technology and tourism in America have greatly increased the popularity of "rocks," and multiplied the ranks of "rock-hounds." Though tumbled forms are frequently used in tourist jewelry of little esthetic value beyond the stone itself, this does not prevent the sensitive contemporary jeweler from utilizing the unique tumbled gemstone in an original and expressive way.

Cabochon forms are the oldest forms to be fabricated from rough natural stones. There are four styles of cabochon: low, normal, high, and double (Fig. 343).

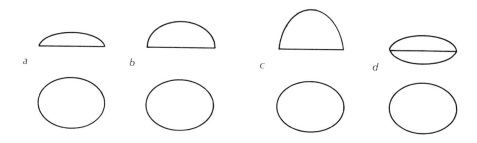

Fig. 343. Top and sectional views of (a) low cabochon, (b) normal cabochon, (c) high cabochon, and (d) double cabochon.

Fig. 344. Special shapes of cabochons. *below:* (a) Rectangular cushion, (b) oval, (c) round, (d) octagon, (e) antique (top views).

bottom: (f) Flat top, (g) buff top, (h) cabochon, (i) double cabochon (sectional views).

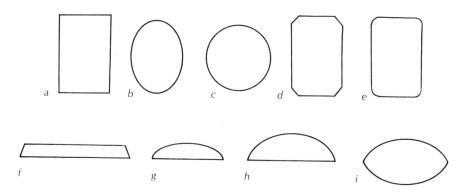

0   1   2   3   4   5

Fig. 345. Standard millimeter scale, 50 mm. = 5 cm.

The cabochon may be round, oval, rectangular, or square, but almost any special shape can be cut and polished into a cabochon style (Fig. 344).

The contemporary jeweler is likely to use small gemstones as accents where only color or contrast is required and larger forms when the stone possesses exciting pattern as well as color (Figs. 345–348).

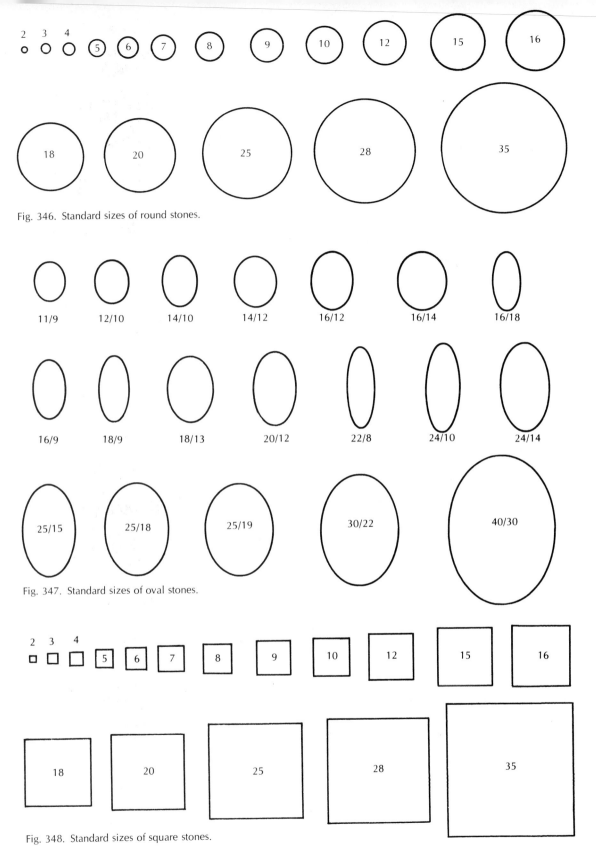

Fig. 346. Standard sizes of round stones.

Fig. 347. Standard sizes of oval stones.

Fig. 348. Standard sizes of square stones.

Faceted gemstones in traditional styles offer design restrictions that many contemporary jewelers are unwilling to accept. They may prefer to design their own shapes and forms of gemstones, and if they are interested in faceted stones, they will sooner or later explore the problem independently of tradition. Some of the common and popular forms of faceted stones are illustrated in Figure 349.

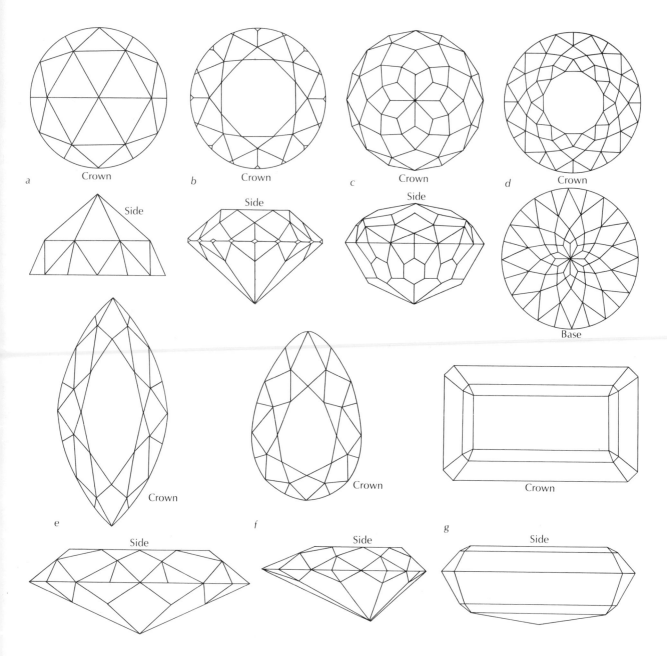

Fig. 349. Typical standard faceted gem shapes and forms: *(a)* rose cut, *(b)* brilliant cut, *(c)* jubilee cut, *(d)* star cut, *(e)* marquise cut, *(f)* pendeloque cut, *(g)* step cut.

16–2 Selecting Gemstones for Contemporary Jewelry   Pictures of gemstones are interesting to look at and will be of help to the beginning jeweler. The International Gem Corporation puts out an excellent catalogue with a great deal of useful information, beautiful color plates of gemstones, and a wide selection of shapes, sizes, and kinds of gems. But a trip to a good lapidary is essential. At the lapidary workshop the jeweler can see and handle all kinds of gemstones, polished and rough, and can begin to get an idea of the individual quality of each stone.

16–3 Designing Gemstone Forms   The contemporary jeweler is seldom satisfied to be limited by convention. He will eventually wish to determine gemstone shapes for his own jewelry (Figs. 350, 351). For cabochons, a sketched plan and side view will usually give the lapidary sufficient information to go to work, if the dimensions are indicated in millimeters (Fig. 345). The exploration of faceting for transparent gemstones can be done with Plexiglas. This material, while soft, can be filed and polished to approximate the faceted gemstone. The lapidary will be able to duplicate your Plexiglas pattern in the gem you select. It is best to have him practice on a quartz at first. While careful drawings can be made, the advantage of Plexiglas is that of direct experience of the transparency and the facets.

Fig. 350. Margaret De Patta. Ring. c. 1946. Gold, with faceted crystal and inclusions of tourmaline.

Fig. 351. Margaret De Patta. Pendant. 1961. Crystal, with slabs of amethyst, spinel, Chatham emerald, and white gold. St. Paul Art Center, St. Paul, Minn., Permanent Collection. This piece illustrates De Patta's exploration of transparencies. Note thin slabs of gems overlapped to produce color density. Slabs are locked between shapes of crystal.

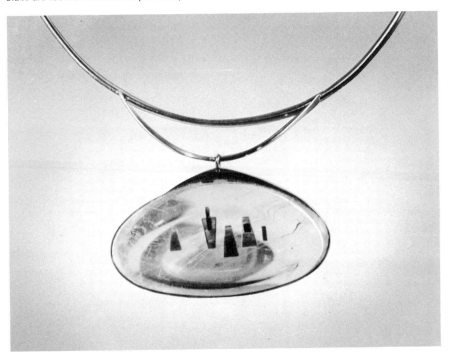

16–4 Designing Jewelry for Stones   The jeweler considers the quality of hardness of stones in choosing them for pieces of jewelry that may be subject to wear. For example, it is unwise to design a ring utilizing any stone softer than No. 5 on Mohs' scale of hardness, which is as follows:

1. talc	6. orthoclase
2. gypsum	7. quartz
3. calcite	8. topaz
4. fluorite	9. corundum
5. apatite	10. diamond

In this scale, talc is the softest and diamond is the hardest. If softer gemstones are used in rings, protective strips or other design features will be required to protect the stone from bumps and abrasions. Most brooches and ear clips are relatively protected from scratching and wear, and for these, softer gemstones may be utilized. The type of setting should also be chosen in relation to the quality of hardness, or vice versa. Whereas the close setting is appropriate for almost any gemstone that is cabochon cut, the paved setting or any special setting which requires the chasing of metal against the stone may not be appropriate for stones that are soft or brittle. A slight blow may crack or shatter them.

From the design standpoint a gemstone is a specially differentiated shape that must be integrated into the composition of the piece of jewelry. It is differentiated from the other shapes by its color, texture, pattern, and unique characteristics as gem material. But it is as *shape* that it must be integrated into the form of the jewelry. Though gems of standard shape and size may be fitted into many designs, the contemporary jeweler will be interested in picking unusual stones as he finds them at his lapidary shop or at one of the many rock shops along the road. These stones may be of unusual shape and call for a different approach. The jewelry piece must actually be designed around the stone, providing the form which will best supplement the characteristics of the gemstone. The stone may be traced on paper and sketch designs made around the tracing, or, if casting is contemplated, a wax pattern may be modeled directly around the stone (Figs. 352, 353).

left: Fig. 352. Gregory P. Bacopulos. Cast ring. 1965. 14-kt. gold, with quartz amethyst. The wax pattern was modeled to fit the stone.
right: Fig. 353. Hazel Olsen Brown. Cast pin. 1967. Gold, with black baroque pearl and blue-white fresh-water pearl. The wax pattern was modeled around the pearls.

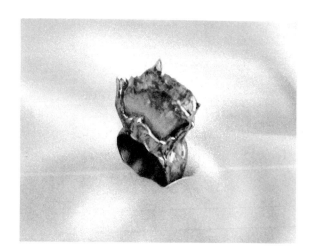

17

STONE SETTING AND SETTINGS

Gemstones and other nonmetallic materials have been an important part of jewelry from the beginning. Here, the technical problems of setting gems are presented, along with a description of some traditional types of settings.

The two requirements for a gem setting are that:

1. The setting must hold the stone securely and permanently.
2. The setting should reveal the gem to the greatest extent possible, rather than cover it up.

17–1 Closed Setting (Bezel Setting) The closed setting (Fig. 354a) is the one most commonly used for cabochons (16–1) and irregularly shaped stones. Success in setting a stone always depends upon the accuracy of the fit of the setting, and nothing less than an exact fit should be acceptable. If the bezel is too large, it cannot be burnished smoothly around the stone, and it becomes bumpy and visually unattractive. Bezels for cabochons should almost always be made of fine silver or fine gold so that they may be burnished more easily over the stone.

The procedure for making a bezel is as follows:

1. Make a strip ring for the stone from 20- to 26-gauge fine silver wide enough to lift the stone to the proper height (Fig. 354b). This bezel ring must be made to fit the stone exactly. It is better to make it a bit too small, since it can be planished to enlarge it, whereas if the ring is too large, it must be cut to smaller size and resoldered.

   After soldering, the ring is planished on a bezel mandrel, with a raw-hide mallet, to make it perfectly round. If the stone is oval or of irregular shape, it is held in the center of the ring and rolled around on a flat surface. The stone presses the ring into the correct shape. If the bezel is too large, it will be difficult to burnish down evenly around the stone.

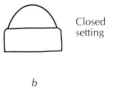

Closed setting

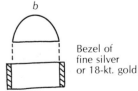

Bezel of fine silver or 18-kt. gold

Fig. 354. a. Closed setting (bezel setting) around a cabochon. b. Strip-ring bezel with stone above.

239

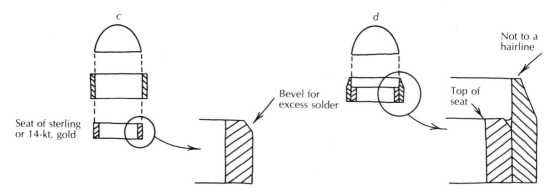

Fig. 354. c. Seat with bevel at top outside edge. d. Bevel filed around outside of bezel.

After shaping, the ring should be filed smooth on the side. Be careful not to rock your file. There should be but one plane running around the strip. Then file the top and bottom edges, being careful to keep them parallel, and, finally, use the emery stick to take out the file marks (Chap. 15).

2. From 18-gauge sterling silver make a strip ring to fit inside the bezel. This is the "seat." The seat must be cut to a width that will support the stone in the bezel and leave just enough metal above the seat to grasp the stone when burnished against it (Fig. 354c). The seat should fit snugly but not too tightly in the bezel. If it is so large that it must be forced into the bezel, there is a danger that the pressure will open the seam of the bezel at later soldering. After soldering the seam of the seat, file the side around and the top and bottom smooth. Be sure that the top and bottom are parallel, so that the stone will sit squarely in the bezel. File a bevel around the top of the seat on the outside. This will allow for excess solder and prevent the seat edge from being filled up.

3. After the seat is soldered into the bezel, try the stone and see if there is enough metal to burnish over the stone. It is always wise to allow extra material. The extra material may now be filed down until there is neither too much nor too little (Fig. 354d).

4. Now take a fine flat file and file a bevel around the outside of the bezel, extending from the top down to the level of the seat inside the bezel. Be careful to avoid filing a feather edge at the top of the bezel. The purpose of this bevel is to remove all excess metal, so that burnishing the bezel over the stone will be easier.

5. The bezel should be finished by emerying and polishing.

The stone is not set until all soldering, coloring, and finishing have been done. Then the stone is placed in the bezel, squarely upon the seat. A pusher, which has a polished flat face, is used to press the bezel firmly and evenly against the stone (Fig. 355). All the small corners that are formed must also be pressed against the stone. Then the burnisher is used to rub the bezel smooth and tight against the stone (Fig. 356).

Many bezels may require something more than burnishing to bring the metal down around the stone. Either the bezel is too heavy, or perhaps a heavy

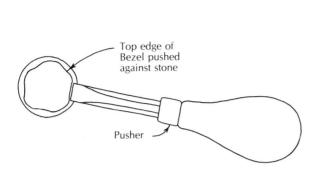

Fig. 355. Plan view of bezel with stone in position,
showing pusher against side of bezel and angular facets made by pusher.

Fig. 356. Philip Morton. Ring. 1968.
14-kt. gold with star ruby, diamond,
and two lapis lazuli spheres.

bezel has been designed. Sometimes claws of a claw setting cannot be pressed down against the stone. In such cases the piece of jewelry is set up in a ring vise and placed in the bench vise, or placed on the ring mandrel and supported. Then the bezel is moved against the stone with careful taps on a chasing tool having an appropriately shaped flat end. The secret of setting the stone by this method is to use a small-ended chasing tool and very light taps of the hammer, so that a small amount of the metal is moved at a time.

17–2 Claw Setting and Flange Setting   The claw setting was much used in earlier times and is still used in the jewelry trade for a great many settings. It is not often used by contemporary jewelers in its traditional forms, because there is much interest in devising forms of claw setting that reflect the form of the design. Both conventional forms and some contemporary solutions will be discussed.

One conventional claw setting is made from a closed setting, as follows:

1. Prepare a bezel setting high enough to provide material for the claws to reach up and over the edge of the stone. The bezel ring should be made of heavier metal than would be usual for a regular closed setting—18- or 16-gauge metal should be used, depending upon the size of the stone.

2. When the closed setting is completed and emeried, mark out around the top edge the location of the center points of the claws and their widths. This can be done on a circle template (**10–3**). Scribe a circle around the outside of the bezel with the dividers to locate the depth of the claws (Fig. 357). If the seat is wide enough, the slots between the claws may run down below the top of the seat.

3. File away the metal between the claws with a needle file, or saw out the slots with the jeweler's saw. Care must be taken to shape each claw exactly. With irregularly shaped stones the claw size and spacing may vary.

4. Emery and finish the edges with emery paper wrapped around a small mandrel or needle file.

5. After the bezel has been soldered in place, the stone is placed in the setting and excess metal on the ends of the claws may be removed and the ends finished.

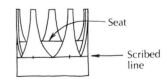

Fig. 357. High bezel with slots filed, showing seat and scribed line around outside.

The stone is set in one of two ways. One is to make the claws in such a way as to bend them over or against the stone (Fig. 358a). In this case the claws must not be too thick, and may be wider. The other way is to make the claws somewhat heavier and to file slots in the inside of each claw to receive the stone. (Fig. 358b).

Another method of making a simple claw setting for a cabochon is to scribe a trace of the stone on the sheet metal. Then lay out radiating lines for the claws (Fig. 358c), from the center, if the stone is round. If the stone is elliptical, the claws must be proportioned around the circumference. Lengths and widths of the claws are laid out according to the size of the stone. However, the outline of the seat for the stone is usually cut back somewhat from the edge of the stone, parallel to the boundary line, so that it is not visible, and the claw outlines are extended beyond the perimeter of the stone to this inner line. The claws are then sawed out along this inner perimeter line and the outline lines.

Now an engraved line is made just to the outside of each scribed line, on the original stone circumference, which will still appear running across each claw. This line must be graved to about two-thirds of the thickness of the sheet metal (Fig. 358d), and placed in such a position that when the claw is bent up, perpendicular to the horizontal surface, the inner face of the claw is on the scribed line of the circumference of the stone (Fig. 358e). If the face of the claw is outside this circumference line, the stone will fit too loosely in the setting. If the face of the claw comes within the circumference line, the setting will be too small for the stone.

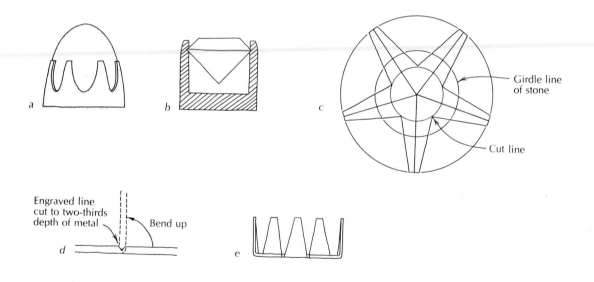

Fig. 358. a. Finished claw setting with claws pushed over against stone.
b. Heavy claw setting with slots filed into claws to hold stone.
c. Layout around round stone, with five radiating center lines, widths and lengths of claws drawn out, and inner cut line.
d. Engraved line cut to two-thirds depth of metal, showing position of prong bent up for soldering by dotted lines.
e. Setting with claws bent up into position.

above left: Fig. 359. Elaine Politas. Ring. 1968.
Cast sterling silver with aquamarine. The two-prong setting
is becoming popular among contemporary jewelers
in America and in Europe.
above right: Fig. 360. Margaret De Patta.
Rings illustrating flange setting.
right: Fig. 361. Friedrich Becker.
Ring with special stone form. 1967.
White gold with light blue topaz.

Using the strip-solder method (8–20), heat the setting and touch the strip solder to each seam at the root of each claw.

The setting may now be file-finished, emeried, polished, and placed in position on the piece. At the time of setting, the length of the claws is adjusted, the ends are finished, and the stone is then set.

More contemporary settings of the claw type and the flange type have been devised by many contemporary jewelers (Figs. 359–361).

17–3 Paved Setting and Gypsy Setting   In a paved setting the stone is set down into a metal cavity cut or drilled to size, and the surrounding metal is chased over the edges of the stone. The process of chasing must be done gently to avoid crushing the stone; and, of course, this type of setting should not be

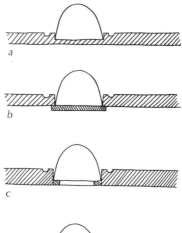

a

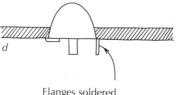

b

c

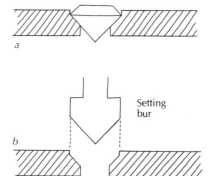

d

Flanges soldered
in place, then bent
up to secure stone

Fig. 362. a. Section view of paved setting, showing groove cut around stone for chasing metal against stone.
b. Alternate method for paved setting, with disk soldered under stone.
c. Small seat soldered into paved-setting hole.
d. Hole tapered from back, with cabochon inserted from back and held by small flanges.

used for a soft stone. The stone should probably have a hardness of about 6 on Mohs' scale. To facilitate the chasing, a groove may be carved or chased around the edge of the hole, leaving a small flange for chasing over against the stone (Fig. 362a).

An alternate method is to drill or saw a hole through the metal, to the exact size of the stone, and then solder a disk under the hole as a landing for the stone (Fig. 362b). A small seat may be soldered in place if the metal sheet is thick enough (Fig. 362c).

If the stone has tapered sides, as on a cabochon or high cabochon, a tapered hole may be drilled or sawed from the back and small flanges soldered in place, to be bent over against the bottom of the stone for setting (Fig. 362d).

In the gypsy setting, which is used to set a faceted stone flush with the surface, a beveled seat is carved or soldered into a hole cut to fit the stone (Fig. 363a). A cabochon may be set in the same way, by drilling a hole with a cone bur (Fig. 364) and then drilling a seat in the metal with a setting bur (Fig. 363b).

Fig. 363. a. Section view of gypsy setting with beveled seat and stone in position.
b. Section view of hole drilled for gypsy setting and grooved channel for stone made by setting bur.

a

Setting bur

b

Fig. 364. Steel burs.

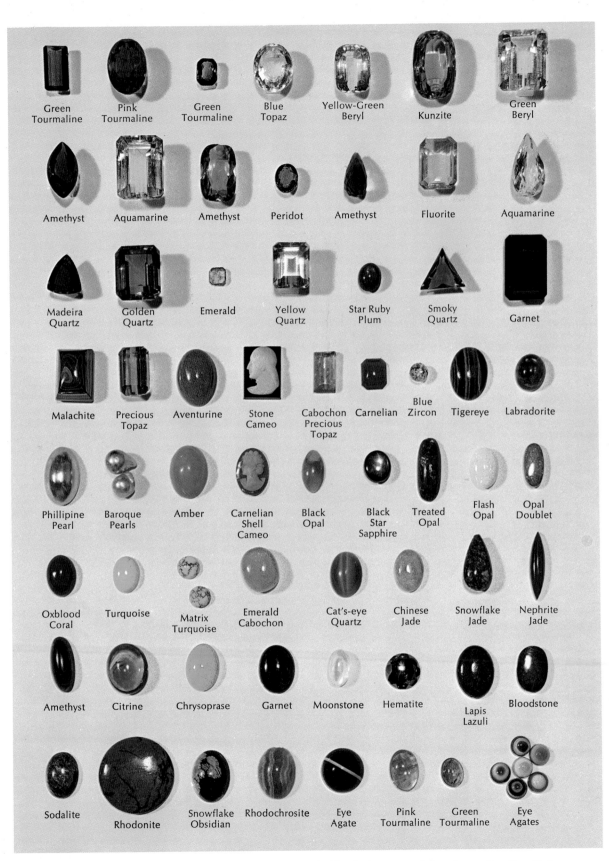

Plate 15. Commonly available gems and semiprecious stones, supplied by the International Gem Corporation, New York.

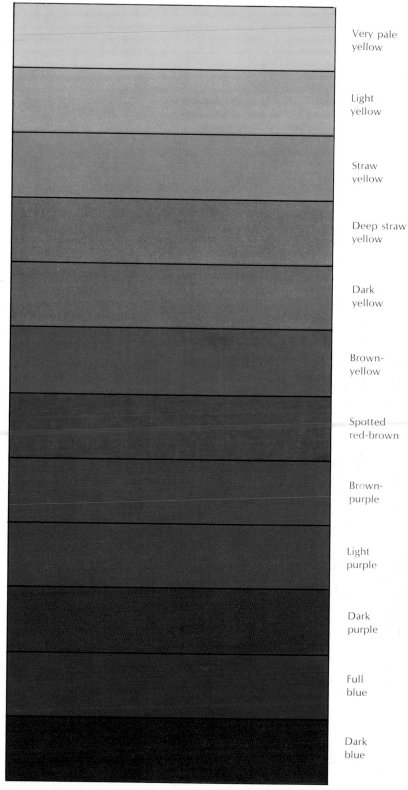

Very pale
yellow

Light
yellow

Straw
yellow

Deep straw
yellow

Dark
yellow

Brown-
yellow

Spotted
red-brown

Brown-
purple

Light
purple

Dark
purple

Full
blue

Dark
blue

Plate 16. Chart of "drawing" stages from pale yellow to dark blue
when tempering carbon steel by the color method.

17–4 Bead Setting   The bead setting is used for transparent gems, ordinarily set at the surface of the metal, rather than in a claw setting. This is done by drilling a tapered hole with a cone bur, and then putting in a seat with a setting bur, so that the girdle of the stone is just below the surface. The location of the beads is then marked out around the stone, and a graver is used to carry a small curl of metal up to the edge of the stone (Fig. 365a). A beading tool is then used to burnish the curl into a bead that rests against the edge of the girdle, holding the stone in place (Fig. 365b). This type of setting is usually used with platinum, palladium, or white or yellow gold manufactured crowns **(17–6)**, and standardized patterns have been developed in the jewelry trade. There is room for experimentation, however, on the part of the contemporary jeweler. Silver may be too soft, unless more massive beads are used.

17–5 Channel Setting   The channel setting is used when rectangular or round-faceted gems are to be set in a solid line. The channel may be made along a surface of a metal sheet or it may be raised above the surface in various ways: arched, straight, curved, or even tapered (Fig. 366).

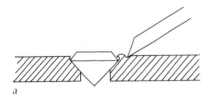

a

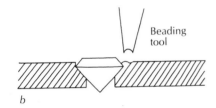

Beading tool

b

Fig. 365. *a.* Section view of faceted stone in shoulder setting, with girdle just below surface and curl of metal rolled up for bead setting. *b.* Section view of bead formed with beading tool.

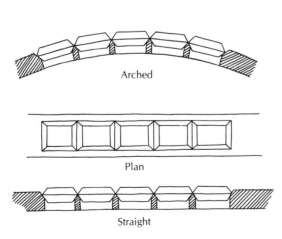

Arched

Plan

Straight

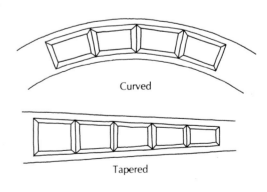

Curved

Tapered

Fig. 366. Channel settings: arched, straight, curved, and tapered.

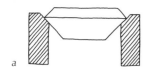

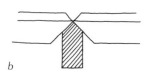

Fig. 367. a. Section sawed out at bevel of stone. b. Beveled metal support between two stones.

The procedure is to saw out the shape of the stone with a bevel that matches the angle of the stone below the girdle, so that the girdle line is slightly below the surface (Fig. 367a). The next adjacent hole is sawed in such a way that the metal between the two holes supports the stone but is not visible (Fig. 367b). The row is continued in this manner to the desired length.

The stones are set by chasing the edge over, as in the paved setting, or by bead setting.

17–6 Crown Setting A wide range of forms and styles of crown settings are manufactured and available from the supply house. As you will see from the illustrations (Figs. 368, 369), the crown is made with claws in which slots are filed to receive the stone, or it is designed for bead setting.

In general, the crown setting is either a variation of the coronet setting, which may also be developed from a truncated cone layout (Fig. 370) or from a box-frame setting (Fig. 371).

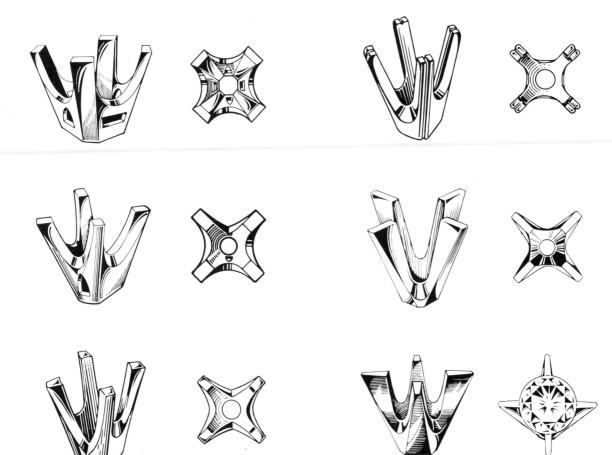

Fig. 368. Four-prong crown settings.

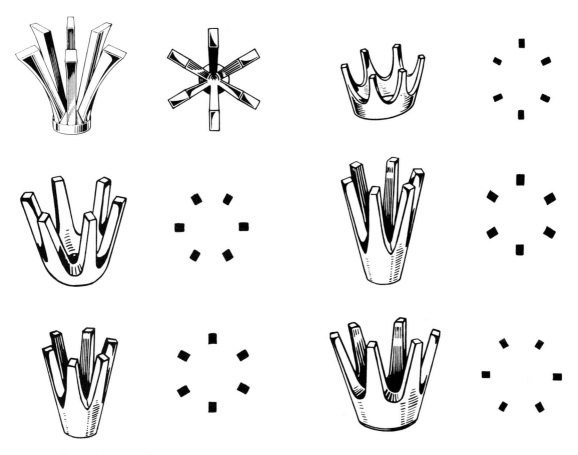

Fig. 369. Six-prong crown settings.

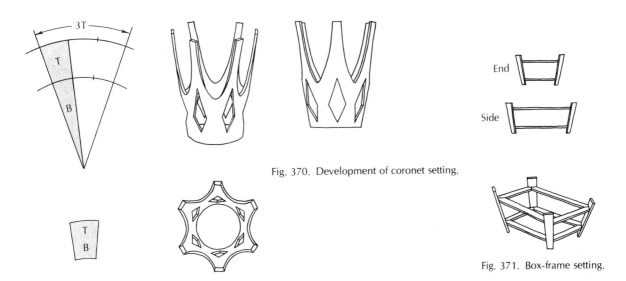

Fig. 370. Development of coronet setting.

Fig. 371. Box-frame setting.

End

Side

Stone Setting and Settings 247

18

TOOLMAKING

The processes of blacksmithing are too extensive to treat adequately here. Nevertheless, the jeweler should be able to make his own punches and small tools.

18–1 Forging Carbon-steel Drill Rod for Punches and Chasing Tools   A blacksmith's forge will probably not be available to you; therefore your metal must be heated with the oxygen torch. Prepare the annealing pan with firebrick or asbestos blocks set up as a shelter against which you can lay the length of tool steel for heating (Fig. 372). This will help to hold the heat and make it easier to bring the steel up to forging heat.

The end of the tool should be heated to a bright red color and laid immediately upon the anvil. Small pieces of metal lose heat rapidly, and you must be prepared to strike several blows immediately with the forging hammer or a heavy ball-peen hammer. Do not continue to hammer the tool after the red color disappears, as the metal is too cold and will tend to crack. When you are forging flat tapers in a piece of drill rod, hold to the same planes and work

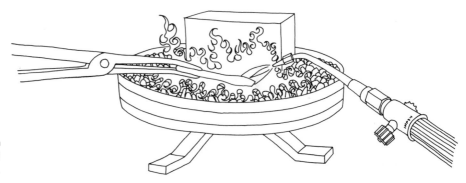

Fig. 372. Annealing pan with firebrick set up, tool steel and torch in place.

alternately from one side to the other, gradually bringing an even taper down symmetrically (Fig. 373). After final tapers have been made, take care to straighten the tool perfectly with light blows in order to eliminate any asymmetrical curves or bows. A tool must be in perfect alignment (Fig. 374); otherwise, when it is struck on the end, it will tend to spring or to bend and weaken the impact of the blow. When forging is completed, bury the tool in a sand box and allow it to cool slowly and naturally so that it will anneal and remain soft.

18–2 Grinding Tool Steel   Grinding wheels are available in a wide range of grades and sizes. If you consult your catalogues, you will see that there are small, lead-centered grinding wheels for use on the tapered mandrel of the buffing lathe. If considerable toolmaking is done, a regular grinder, with standard-size grinding wheels, should be used. Safety goggles or a face mask should always be worn when grinding.

For the buffing lathe, a 3-in.-diameter wheel is a good size. Both a fine and a coarse carborundum wheel are needed.

At the outset it might be well to state that grinding wheels are never used for grinding nonferrous metals, for such metals tend to clog the surface of the wheels.

When grinding tool steel, certain precautions should be taken:

- Do all preliminary shaping on the coarse wheel.
- Avoid heating up the metal on the grinder, as this will destroy the temper. Have a small can of water beside the grinder. Apply the tool to the wheel for an instant; then dip it into the water to cool it. Continue grinding in this way until the shape has been achieved.
- Use the fine wheel to finish surfaces and to sharpen edges. Even more care is required to avoid burning the steel when the fine wheel is used. Cutting edges and thin sections heat up very rapidly, and the tool must not be pressed too heavily against the fine wheel. It should be held very lightly in the fingers, so that, as a given plane is pressed against the wheel, it will not be cut into a new plane.
- Always move the tool across the face of the wheel. If you hold it in one place, you will wear a groove in the wheel. The coarse grinding wheel may be used to determine the quality of a given steel. The sparks from carbon steel fly off and burn in little sizzling stars, very brightly. The sparks

left: Fig. 373. Forged length of drill rod with flat taper.
below: Fig. 374. Completed forged chasing tool.

from wrought iron or mild steel, which cannot be hardened, fly off as little, dull, red, round dots. Always make this test if you are not sure of the quality of steel, since your tools should all be hardened and tempered.

18–3 Tool Steels There are two general types of tool steels, carbon steel and special alloy steel. Of the alloy steels, Ryerson V. D. tool steel is excellent for making small punches and chasing tools, but it must be quenched in oil. Keep a gallon can of crank-case oil in the shop if you plan to use this alloy steel.

A good all-around tool steel for jewelry tools, hammers, punches, and chasing tools is a basic open-hearth, sulphurized carbon steel, such as 1942 SAE No. 1115. Its identification color is black. It hardens at 1425° to 1450° F. and should be water-quenched. Such steel can be purchased in squares and rounds from ¼ to 6 in. in diameter, or in hexagons from ¼ to 2 in. in diameter. Carbon-steel drill rod, either square or round, can be secured in 3-ft. lengths in any diameter up to 2 in. These are fine for making punches and chasing tools. A ³⁄₁₆-in.-diameter round or square steel drill rod makes a good size of chasing tool; it should be cut into 4½-in. lengths.

18–4 Characteristics of Steel It is characteristic of carbon tool steel that, at a certain "critical point" in its temperature, the composition of the steel undergoes changes, both as the temperature increases and as it decreases. At normal temperatures, steel holds its carbon in a form called "pearlite" carbon. As the steel is heated to the critical point, the pearlite carbon becomes martensite, or hardening carbon. If the steel is allowed to cool quite slowly, the martensite changes back to pearlite carbon again. The critical point at which it changes back is somewhat lower in temperature. This latter critical point is called the "recalescence point." The former critical point is called the "decalescence point." These critical points have a direct bearing upon the hardening and drawing of steel.

18–5 Hardening Steel To harden steel, it is necessary to heat it up to a temperature above the decalescence point. Thereupon it is quenched in a bath of water. When steel is heated above this point, it becomes nonmagnetic, and this is a simple test of whether your steel is heated enough before quenching. Visually, the steel should be heated to a bright, white-red; at a cherry red it will still be magnetic.

After the steel has been hardened, it is very brittle and, therefore, not suitable for use, since a sharp blow will crack it apart. It must therefore be "drawn" to a suitable hardness.

18–6 Tempering Carbon Steel by the Color Method Tempering of small tools can be done by holding them in the annealing tongs and applying a small flame to the center of the tool until the desired color is reached, whereupon the tool is thrust into a bucket of water and swished around until it is completely cool. This is a subtle process, and the heat should be applied quite slowly. The hardened steel will be coated with oxides, which must be emeried off until the clean, bare metal is visible. As the steel is heated up from the center, a succession of colors will appear and move one after the other away from the heated portion. These colors are listed in the order of their appearance (Pl. 16).

Very pale yellow	Above this color the steel is completely hard and brittle.
Light yellow	
Pale straw yellow	Draw twist drills and center punches to this color.
Straw yellow	Draw chasing tools and repoussé punches to this color.
Deep straw yellow	Draw chisels to this color or to straw yellow.
Dark yellow	
Brown yellow	
Spotted red-brown	
Brown-purple	
Light purple	
Dark purple	
Full blue	
Dark blue	At this color the steel is again soft.

18–7 Making Repoussé Tools Repoussé work requires tools in a variety of shapes and sizes. Initial work should always be done with large, blunt, rounded tool ends. In general, the size of the tool is determined by the size of the work.

For jewelry work one of the most useful tools is a punch made from 1/2-in. round drill rod, which is ground to the general shape of the thumb, and polished down smooth. This shape may be achieved more quickly by forging it first and then grinding the final form. The tool is used to do the main work of pushing out metal from the back.

Another basic repousse tool is made from 3/8-in. square drill rod, with the working end ground by beveling to about 1/4 in. square. The end is just barely domed, and the corners and edges are rounded. This tool is used to flatten and smooth work. Other tools can be made in sizes and shapes according to need (Fig. 375).

Fig. 375. Repoussé tools of various kinds and sizes, with plan views of end shapes.

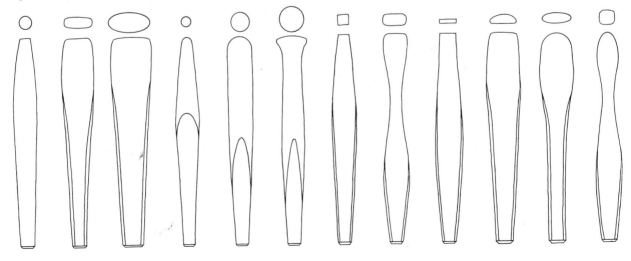

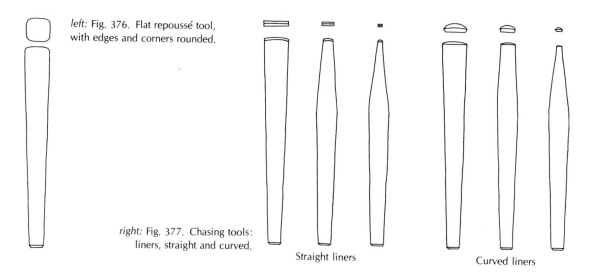

left: Fig. 376. Flat repoussé tool, with edges and corners rounded.

right: Fig. 377. Chasing tools: liners, straight and curved.

Straight liners   Curved liners

Remember that the problem of repoussé is always to push the metal down without cutting into it; therefore, most tools should have rounded corners and edges (Fig. 376). Better-balanced tools and punches can be made if a taper is forged from the back end down about two-thirds of the length, and another taper forged from this point down to the working end. Such tapers must be made carefully and symmetrically around the axis of the tool. If they are forged and ground out of line, they will have a tendency to spring or bend when struck. After being forged, the tapered faces should be ground and finished perfectly, and then the working end shaped and file-finished.

18–8 Making Chasing Tools   Chasing tools should always be tapered as described above. The two basic chasing tools are the straight liner and the curved liner (Fig. 377). Study the illustrations carefully and note that the straight liner is ground perfectly symmetrical at the point of the two intersecting bevels, which are ground about 40° off the axis of the tool (Fig. 378a). The sharp edge is taken off the intersection of the bevels so that it is not a sharp chisel, but this edge should not be rounded off too much. The curved liner is made by grinding one flat 60° bevel on one side. The other side is ground to a curve by holding the tool at an angle of about 60° and rotating it on its axis to grind a symmetrical curve across the face of the side (Fig. 378b). Both of these tools must be made in an assortment of widths; other tools may be made according to special needs: square-ended, ball-point, flat-rounded, and so on.

18–9 Making Punches   The size and proportion of punches vary with their purpose. Your own experience will help you to determine the size and kind of drill rod to be used. For ordinary small punches, 4½ in. is a good length, and ³⁄₁₆ in. is a good diameter for most punches. The square stock will give you a larger end area for special designs.

The first step is to grind the ends flat and square. Then the working end should be filed smooth with a fairly fine file. Never use your silver files for work on steel. Use separate files kept especially for this purpose.

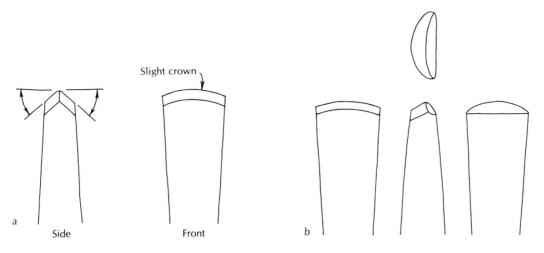

Fig. 378. *a.* Faces on point of straight liner. *b.* Faces on point of curved liner.

Cutting designs and shapes in the end of a punch involves certain limitations. Cuts with files and the jeweler's saw, unless they run completely across the end, must be made into the punch from the sides. These cuts must be made at an angle of about 45° to the axis of the punch (Fig. 379a). The purpose of this angle is to carry the cut back from the end so that, when the punch is driven into the metal to any given depth, the cut will register throughout the depth. Cuts made with the saw or the file, or holes drilled into the end, must be made a little deeper than the impression depth you wish to achieve. In the development of more elaborate designs, special punches must be made, hardened, and tempered to impress special shapes into the end of the main punch.

Punches for more permanent use should be made of slightly heavier stock, and a taper running back about 1 in. should be ground evenly around the working end. The back end of all punches should be given a small bevel grind, perhaps ⅛ in. wide (Fig. 379b). The purpose of this bevel is to eliminate the corners, which, under continual striking, tend to mushroom over. This can be

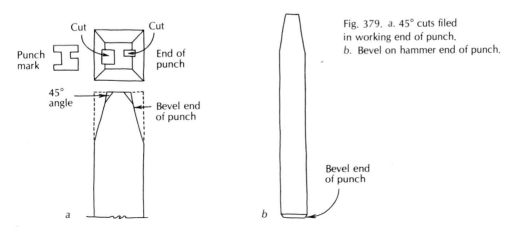

Fig. 379. *a.* 45° cuts filed in working end of punch. *b.* Bevel on hammer end of punch.

dangerous to the eyes, because the edge tends to flake off as it spreads over the sides. Therefore, as this mushroom develops, take time to grind the flange away, so that the back of the punch is always clean and safe.

18–10   Hardening Tools   After the fine grinding of the tools, the sides and ends are always trued up and finished by filing. Strive to achieve perfect, true, and symmetrical finishing. For hardening tools a bucket of cold water and the annealing tongs are needed. Place the tool in the annealing pan and heat its full length to a cherry red. Now bring the working end up to a bright red or even white heat. At this temperature bright white specks will appear on the metal. When this point is reached, have the tongs ready to grasp the back end of the tool and plunge it into the water, swishing it around slowly until all hissing and bubbling have stopped. It may then be taken out and dried.

18–11   Tempering Tools   Polish the end of the tool at least halfway up from the working end, so that the bright, clean metal is visible. Now seize the back end of the tool with the annealing tongs. Hold a soft, small flame at the center of the tool, and from time to time run the flame up to the working end and back. If you heat the tool slowly, you will be able to get a very uniform straw color over the entire lower half. You must be careful not to apply too much heat to the working end, however. When the proper straw color has covered the working end, plunge the tool into the bucket of water. When the hissing stops, the tool may be withdrawn. If you apply too much heat, the color changes will appear too rapidly and move down the tool too rapidly. As a result, you will get a very narrow band of straw yellow. Experience will make this clear to you.

18–12   Final Finishing and Polishing of Tools   After tempering, the final surface is given to the working end of the tool. This should be done by emerying the faces of the tool with coarse and then fine paper. Then the tool is finished on the tripoli wheel. Do not grind away the clean plane intersections of the chasing tools. Their marks should be crisp and clean, not blurred or rounded.

19

MARKETING
AND PRODUCTION

This book has been primarily concerned with the student or craftsman at work in the studio or workshop, struggling with the problems of design and technique and with the development of his own personal mode of expression. The subject of marketing, however, brings the student out of his workshop and face to face with society and the question of his economic relationship to the contemporary world.

Whatever the future may bring for the artist-craftsman, his present status is still marginal, though it has improved considerably over the past twenty years. That is to say that esthetic standards, quality of materials and workmanship, originality of conception, and expressive significance are generally undervalued by the utilitarian society we live in. Only a relatively small percentage of the population will pay for these cultural values. It is problematical whether the arts and crafts can escape the demands and pressures of mass culture. The handcrafts may survive by reason of the peculiar relationship in which the craftsman stands to his work. The craftsman is a person who finds it essential to affirm the human values involved in working with his hands. Not least of these human values are the integrative benefits which result from carrying out a complete process of production from the initial stage of planning and design through the various technical procedures to the final product and its marketing. What other occupation in modern society offers this kind of complete and comprehensive activity?

In a world of partial-function personalities the craftsman and the artist belong to the small minority striving to become whole personalities. Schiller, as early as 1795, discussed in his *Letters on Aesthetic Education* the disastrous effects upon personality produced by specialization of labor:

> When the commonwealth makes the office or function the measure of the man, when of its citizens it does homage only to memory in one, to a tabulating intelligence in another, and to a mechanical capacity in a third; when here,

regardless of character, it urges only towards knowledge, while there it encourages a spirit of order and law-abiding behavior with the profoundest intellectual obscurantism — when, at the same time, it wishes these single accomplishments of the subject to be carried to just as great an intensity as it absolves him of extensity — is it to be wondered at that the remaining faculties of the mind are neglected, in order to bestow every care upon the special one which it honours and rewards?

The craftsman rejects the demands of society that he specialize as a *function* and insists upon preserving himself as a whole personality, combining his creative imagination, his feeling, his thought, and his sensory and physical capacities into a unified agent of being and doing. The integrative effect of art activities has been a major theme of both Viktor Lowenfeld and Herbert Read. Society may yet come to incorporate these insights into its educational and economic institutions. Automation and our emerging electronic culture may accelerate the process. Even now the younger generation is urgently calling for this type of change in the educational program.

It is the demand for wholeness, then, which places the craftsman in a marginal economic position in today's society. At the same time he accepts the responsibility for preserving the values of quality, craftsmanship, and expressive meaning. These three values correspond exactly to the benefits which emerge from functional wholeness — the aspects of performance which integrate feeling, thought, sensation, and intuition.

19-1 Marketing   If the craftsman is to survive, he must realistically meet the market as to price and performance without sacrificing any of his artistic and personal values. This will require both efficiency and industry.

The student jeweler will eventually find himself selling early jewelry pieces to friends and acquaintances, usually at modest prices. This situation is very exciting, of course, because a new source of income suddenly appears. The problem of marketing seems fairly simple, and it may continue to be simple in certain favorable environments. The college community, near the campus or in the college town, offers a fairly good local market for the beginner. After graduation the student might well move from the school workshop into a small shop on the edge of the campus or into his own home workshop and develop a good livelihood. This would be a most natural and satisfactory market solution. Even there, however, competition is likely to offer a challenge to the beginner.

In large population centers the contemporary jeweler may follow one of two marketing routes. The first route is the gradual development of a personal following in a community large enough to support full-time activity. As the jeweler's reputation spreads from customer to customer, private commissions come in. His marketing program can be improved by periodic clearance sales and by small mailing flyers. The beginning jeweler can broaden his audience by giving talks to local groups, by exhibiting in local shows, and by teaching courses in one of the community's education programs. This kind of marketing program can be carried out in the home studio on a personal basis, or it may be extended to a shop in the suburbs, a summer tourist location, or a downtown commercial location, depending upon the temperament of the craftsman.

The second marketing route leads into a retail shop operated by someone else. Such a shop may be in a museum, gallery, department store, or gift shop. From the craftsman's point of view this marketing route is less desirable than the other, because he must produce his work and sell at a wholesale price in order to accommodate a reasonable retail price in the shop. Theoretically the craftsman must work for half the price he can get when he sells out of his own shop. However, the established craftsman finds that it costs as much, or more, to sell out of his own shop as it does to sell through a retail outlet. Interrupting production sequences to wait upon customers is time-consuming and seriously interferes with efficient production. The craftsman may, of course, set up his own retail outlet, but if he does, he must hire a staff to operate the shop, allowing himself not more than one afternoon a week for supervision and for appointments for custom work *at the shop.*

At the point of marketing the craftsman must relate his output to the prevailing market for his product. His jewelry is now competing on the display shelf with other jewelry. If he has truly found his own personal expressive mode, he never competes with other jewelers, for his own work is unique. If he has nothing in particular to offer as personal expression, he might better become a benchworker for a designing jeweler.

The craftsman's work must compete in price with other jewelry on the market. It must also compete as to quality of design and execution. Those who work in sterling will automatically reach a broader but lower-priced market. Those who work in gold and the more precious gemstones will automatically restrict their clientele to buyers in the higher income brackets. Aside from this distinction of competitive price the other dominant factor that will determine sales to a retail shop is reliability. No retail shop will long endure a craftsman who cannot be depended upon to produce consistently for the market that the shop has created.

Pricing a product requires familiarity with the market. First of all, the jeweler must have an accurate idea of how much his work costs to produce. He must also be aware of the price that comparable merchandise commands. In most cases the jeweler should set the retail price, but if he sets it too high, his work may not move off the display shelf.

The retail price is arrived at by doubling the total unit cost of an item, as derived from the average unit cost calculated from the *Production Record* (Fig. 381), the actual wholesale price (see below). There will probably be some variations in labor cost from time to time or from worker to worker, as well as variations in cost of materials. The retail price should be held unless the unit cost begins to get too far out of line with the current retail price. When a price increase is contemplated, the retailer should be given the courtesy of advance notice with an explanation. The loss of an efficient worker or an increase in materials cost is perfectly understandable to a businessman.

Some retailers like to buy at wholesale prices and set their own retail prices. Many such retailers take more than a 100 percent markup on an item that can bring a higher price. It is to everyone's advantage to have the craftsman set the retail price in his invoice and then deduct 50 percent from the total amount to arrive at the wholesale price. By setting the retail price, the craftsman controls his relationship to the competitive market and ensures that all his outlets are on an equal footing. The craftsman must have a clear and frank understanding with each retail outlet on this question to avoid future misunderstandings. Once the craftsman has set a price, he must hold it consistently for all purchasers. He cannot ethically sell the same piece at one price to one shop and at another price to another shop. Nor can he fairly sell a production piece from his studio at a lower price than he sets for his retail outlets.

It is extremely important for the jeweler to establish a reputation for reliability and fairness. It is good policy to stand behind every piece he produces. If any piece is found to be defective or to have come apart, for any reason, it is best in the long run to replace or repair the piece without question. Such problems will not often occur with good work, but when they do, this sales policy is effective and creates good will.

There can be no production without sales. Therefore, the craftsman must appreciate and understand the role of the retailer as the other side of his economic existence. A retail outlet will work hard for a cooperative and appreciative craftsman.

Occasionally the producing or designing jeweler may be asked by a customer or a retail outlet to do a repair job. As a matter of good will he may wish to accommodate the request. As a guide for the beginning jeweler, typical prices for repair work are given in the table below. These prices are, of course, subject to change.

Repairs

Hard-solder (silver or gold)	$ 2.50 up
Soft-solder	2.00 up
Platinum	4.50 up
Solder 2 rings together	3.00 up
Solder in new crown	7.00 up
Change crown	11.50 up

Prongs and Bezel Work

Repair less than 4 prongs (each)	$ 3.00 up
Repair 4 or more prongs (each)	2.00 up
Prongs on man's birthstone ring	12.00 up
Bezel and set stone	14.00 up

Brooches

Replace pin stem (sterling)	$ 2.00
Replace pin stem (10-kt. gold)	4.00
Replace joint or catch (sterling) plus soldering	2.00
Replace joint or catch (10-kt. gold) plus soldering	4.00

Ring Sizing

Woman's (sterling or gold)	$ 2.50 up
Woman's (platinum)	5.00 up
Man's (sterling or gold)	3.00 up
Man's (platinum)	7.00 up

19–2 The Exhibition as a Marketing Aid   The importance of exhibitions as historical records of the artistic status of contemporary jewelry and as a measure of individual craftsmanship is fairly well understood. Up to a certain point the exhibitions and the awards for craftsmanship establish a prestige that is useful for publicity and for a marketing program. As between two craftsmen of equal merit, the one shown in major exhibitions and honored by awards may often have the marketing advantage. However, in submitting his work to exhibitions, the craftsman should beware of losing his essential unity in his effort to produce "exhibition pieces" as a special departure from his "bread-and-butter" items. An overemphasis on the prestige of exhibitions may lead to a deprecating attitude toward the work produced for sale, and thus the sustaining values of craftsmanship can be subtly undermined.

Another side to this particular question is the view of some successful merchandisers of quality crafts that the "exhibition piece" is too far removed from the interests of the man on the street. While this view may reflect the natural bias of a marketing specialist whose concern for sales is greater than for artistic expression, it does, nevertheless, point up the craftsman's problem in relating his esthetic position to the prevailing market.

When approached with a certain caution, and regarded essentially as a record of individual artistic and technical progress in the field, the institution of the exhibition offers the craftsman another method of orienting himself to his market.

The current market position of the craftsman is rather favorable. There seems to be an unusually large demand for craft products of all kinds, due in part to the increased interest in the arts and the crafts that has developed since World War II and in part to the prosperity of the postwar period. On the other hand, the craftsman must be prepared to survive through unfavorable economic periods and must therefore cultivate the most advantageous methods of marketing and production.

19–3 Production Design   Once a design has been projected for possible production, it must be carefully analyzed in terms of multiple or serial processing. For example, suppose a ring calls for a separate ring band to be made up in two sizes: 6 and 9. If a ring enlarger (Fig. 183) is at hand, the craftsman will not waste time making the bands to the exact sizes required. He will cut band lengths to two standardized sizes, each slightly below the required measurement, solder them directly, and then stretch them to the required sizes. This type of sizing is particularly useful if the band is patterned and cannot be cut down or enlarged without interfering with the pattern.

Many repoussé patterns may be preformed in a kick press with appropriate dies and then formed by hand repoussé with a considerable saving of time. Standardized shapes of sheet metal may be cut much more rapidly with cutting dies on the kick press than with the jeweler's saw. However, the cost of such cutting dies must be justified by the volume of sales of the particular design. Initially a new design will probably be produced completely by hand. If it finds an especially good market and orders arrive in larger quantities, the cost of dies will be justified by the saving of labor time.

Many small shapes can be sawed out rapidly if an impression of the shape has been stamped out by means of a die in a drop hammer. More exactness of shape can be gained by this method than by tracing the shape with a template. This is especially true of such small shapes as the claw setting made from sheet metal.

The utilization of basic design units for more than one design is a possibility worth studying. While this idea may be carried too far, it is especially fruitful in the development of matching sets of jewelry. Bracelets, necklaces, and ear clips may all be based on identical design units. Cuff links, tie clips or tie tacks, and buckles may likewise be assembled from identical design units.

The jeweler cannot develop too soon an attitude of production efficiency as a part of the process of design. Simplicity of design involves just this concept. Directness of production arises out of the simple relationship of tools and materials, that is, process.

All beginning jewelers have encountered the design that looked really good but took 42 hours to make. Even at $1.00 per hour it is priced out of the market. It could be sold for $11.50, but the designer is lucky to get his materials back. Today a craftsman can hardly afford to work for less than $5.00 per hour. Therefore, as a first step in increasing production efficiency, designs must be evaluated in terms of marketability. Designs that cannot be produced efficiently must be discarded. This obstacle is not too great if the craftsman is willing to do his design homework, and his resources as a designer will be sharpened by experimentation. A definite search must be made for direct designs in terms of production means. Only those items which lend themselves to efficient multiple production, as well as to favorable market acceptance, should be selected.

In the development of production designs today's jeweler must utilize every kind of production aid. Disk-cutting dies must be used in place of saw-cut disks. Drop hammers, kick presses, forming jigs, and other machines that can reduce production time must be considered in the initial planning.

19–4   The Production Record and Job Card   A *Production Record* is a book in which to keep the records of the designs reproduced for marketing. Each design must have a code number, and there must be a list of the sizes and kinds of materials required and a list of the sequence and types of operations that must be performed, along with the time required for each operation.

Many contemporary jewelers prefer to produce one-of-a-kind designs, and there is certainly a market for custom jewelry, particularly in the more expensive categories. However, the majority of jewelers find themselves working for the most part in a price range that commands a larger market and reproducing designs that, for one reason or another, become popular. Such items are known as "bread-and-butter" designs. The *Job Card* and the *Production Record* are two devices that help the craftsman to organize his production program.

The *Job Card* (Fig. 380) is a simple device for keeping track of materials and labor cost with a minimum of bookkeeping. For every production order the craftsman takes a *Job Card* to his bench. Each card is numbered and dated. The item of jewelry is listed with its code number and retail price. The various materials are itemized with sizes or weights at their unit costs. The hours of labor, labor rates, and total labor costs are recorded. In this manner the direct costs are kept on the production of the jewelry item. To this can be added an overhead percentage to cover such costs as rent, light, and heat. This will usually amount to 10 or 15 percent of direct costs. A factory markup, which is the

Fig. 380. Job Card

389 Number	PHILIP MORTON				Goldsmith Jeweler

Item: Hand-Forged Necklace, 14k Y. Gold				Code: 812 G
Date: 12/1/67 Worker: Staff				Price: 75.00

	Materials	Quantity	Unit Cost	Cost	
1	14k Y. Gold Wire, 14 ga	72" 1 oz 12 dwt	2.00 dwt	63.96	
2					
3					
4					
5					
6					63.96
	Labor	Hours	Rate	Cost	
7	(P.M.) Forging & Planishing	9½	5.00	47.50	
8	(R.S.) Forming & Stamping	3½	4.00	14.00	
9	(J.T.) Finishing, Polishing				
10	& Cleaning	3	3.00	9.00	
11	Packaging & Pricing	½	3.00	1.50	
12					72.00
13				Total Direct	135.96
14	Overhead		10%		13.60
15	Factory Markup		40%		54.38
16	Number Made: 6	Unit Cost: 33.99		Total Cost	203.94

Fig. 380. *Job Card.*

Fig. 381. Page of *Production Record.*

PHILIP MORTON, Goldsmith	PRODUCTION RECORD		Code Number 812 G

DESIGNED BY: P.M.	DATE: 4/15/67	PRICE: 75.00	ITEM Hand-Forged Necklace

Materials Required:
12" 14k Yellow Gold wire, 14 ga

See Photograph # 884

Pattern or Sketch

Date 1967	Job No.	Quantity	Customer	DIRECT COST Labor	Matls.	INDIRECT COST O.H.	Markup	TOTAL COST		UNIT COST	
4/15	291	6	Inventory	85.00	57.80	14.28	57.12	214	20	35	70
4/25	327	6	Marshall, Inc.	87.00	57.80	14.48	57.92	217	20	36	20
5/2	402	6	S. S. Roach	82.50	57.80	14.03	56.12	210	45	35	07
7/15	556	6	Contemporary Gifts	74.00	59.90	13.39	53.56	200	85	33	47
10/10	675	6	Marshall, Inc.	70.05	63.96	13.40	53.60	201	01	33	50
11/15	841	6	Inventory	72.00	63.96	13.60	54.38	203	94	33	99
11/18	860	6	Racing Gifts	73.25	63.96	13.72	54.88	205	81	34	30
12/1	880	6	Inventory	72.00	63.96	13.60	54.38	203	94	33	99

profit margin added to the direct costs and overhead, must also be added. This can be as much as 100 percent of direct and overhead costs. In this way a total cost is arrived at. If a dozen units are produced on the particular *Job Card,* then a unit price can easily be derived and recorded. The name of the craftsman is recorded, so that production time comparison can be made from job to job or from worker to worker. On the back of the card may be made a sketch of the jewelry item, with any detailed notes concerning methods or procedures of production that are time-saving or particularly useful.

The *Job Card* is filed numerically after the information is posted to the *Production Record.* When another job order comes in for the particular jewelry item, the *Job Cards* for that item previously used can be found from the *Production Record* so that evaluations and comparisons of current cost can be made. As labor and materials costs go up, the craftsman is alerted to the necessity for increasing his retail prices.

The *Production Record* (Fig. 381) is a ledger type of record in which the important data for each item of jewelry are recorded. A current page is allowed for each jewelry item, which will have a code number, the current retail price, a sketch or tracing of the design pattern, and the production and cost data that are collected on the *Job Card.*

The code number may be merely a consecutive number, but it is more useful to develop a system such as the one the author follows.

> 100 Wedding band
> 200 Engagement and dinner rings
> 300 Man's ring
> 400 Earring—dangle type
> 500 Earring—button type
> 600 Earring—pierced-ear type
> 700 Bracelet
> 800 Necklace
> 900 Pendant
> 1000 Brooch
> 1100 Cuff link
> 1200 Tie clip
> 1300 Tie tack
> 1400 Barrette
> 1500 Comb
> 1600 Watch band
> 1700 Buckle

The plain number refers to sterling silver. Add "G" to the number to refer to 14-kt. gold. Matching sets such as an ear clip, bracelet, and necklace have the same code number within the appropriate category number:

> 507G Earring—button type
> 707G Bracelet
> 807G Necklace

The craftsman will need to identify his pieces on his invoices and on the purchase orders from retail outlets. If he controls the retail price, as he should, he will attach a price tag on each piece as it is finished and packaged in a small plastic envelope. On one side of the price tag the retail price appears. On the other side the code number is written in ink. The retailer utilizes the price tag for reordering by saving it as each item is sold and then writing out a new purchase order from the tags, periodically, as they accumulate. Thus the craftsman should be sure that he has accurately recorded both the code number and the price.

The *Production Record* also keeps a record of the dimensions and gauge sizes of the pieces of wire and sheet that are required for each particular design. Each new *Job Card* is filled out from the permanent record of this information in the *Production Record*. It shows the number of parts required when, as in the case of a link bracelet, one or more parts must be duplicated. From the total number of pieces and the sizes and weights, the cost of materials can be calculated. This cost and the labor time are recorded in the appropriate place on the *Production Record* from the *Job Card*.

19–5   Production Methods and Problems   One of the first and most obvious methods of improving production is to organize the workshop in some convenient physical space pattern, so that a logical production flow is possible. The question of physical arrangement of equipment is important even in the one-man shop. The single craftsman carries out each of the operations, and special separate space centers should be available for each. Regardless of the size of the shop, there will be a flow of production more or less similar to that shown in Figure 382.

Fig. 382. Flow diagram for jewelry workshop.

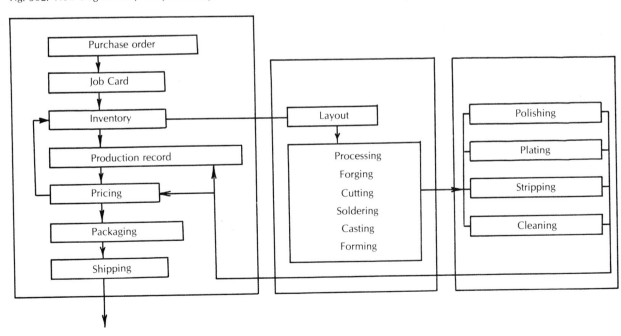

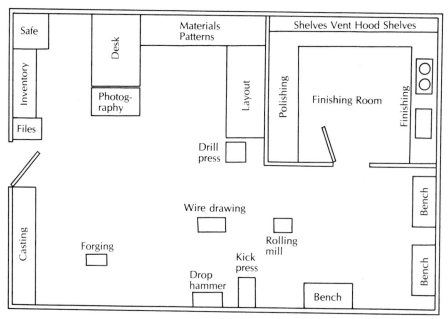

Fig. 383. Simple shop layout.

When a workshop grows beyond the one-room size, finishing operations are usually the first to be segregated (Fig. 383), because of the fumes and dust arising from polishing, stripping, plating, and cleaning. The casting and forging operations are usually the next to be segregated, because of the noise, heat, and fumes.

A sketch or tracing of a particular design may not be sufficient for the rapid reproduction of a sheet-metal shape. If sheet shapes require duplication, it is useful to make accurate templates from 24-gauge brass sheet (Fig. 384). These templates allow quick tracing with a sharp scribe. They are identified by the code number of the design.

Some small shapes can be stamped out with dies, rather than sawed out with the jeweler's saw. A number of dies are on the market, such as the circle-cutting die (Fig. 385). The craftsman can also secure from a tool and die company special cutting and forming dies, which can be operated with a hammer or a kick press.

The *Production Record* should show layout sketches with dimensions for all the separate parts that must be formed or bent. The *Production Record* should also list a sequence of operations for the craftsman to follow. If a design utilizes a number of identical units, such as a link, labor time can be reduced by carrying out processes in sequence. If you have an order for three link brace-lets, you may increase production efficiency by producing at least six, or even twelve, bracelets at one time, putting the excess number in inventory for future orders. A single jewelry item should seldom be reproduced one at a time.

If the item is a bracelet made by shaping and hammering wire, such as the one illustrated in Figure 390, each step of the process should be taken for all the bracelets. For the sake of illustration the procedure for producing a similar bracelet is outlined as follows:

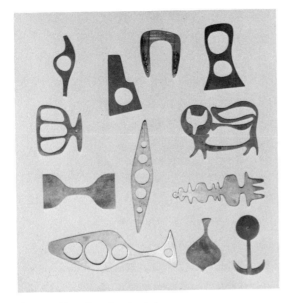

Fig. 384. Templates for sheet shapes.

Fig. 385. Circle-cutting dies.

1. Look up the code number in the *Production Record* and record the information on a *Job Card*. It is found that each bracelet requires 8 pieces of
   14-gauge sterling wire, each 2½ in. long; 8 pieces of 18-gauge sterling
   wire, each ¾ in. long; two 18-gauge jump rings, ³⁄₁₆ in. in diameter; and
   one medium-size sister hook.
2. On a coil of 14-gauge sterling wire measure off one 2½-in. length of wire.
   Then, using this as a unit measure, cut off 47 more lengths for six bracelets.
3. Repeat the process for ¾-in. lengths from a coil of 18-gauge wire.
4. Take each length of 14-gauge wire and hammer each end flat. Twelve
   blows with a planishing hammer give just the right, uniform flatness to
   each end.
5. Flatten each of the 14-gauge wire units between the flattened ends, but in
   a plane perpendicular to them. In carrying out this process a slight curvature should be maintained in the unit (Fig. 386). Do not make the units
   too thin.

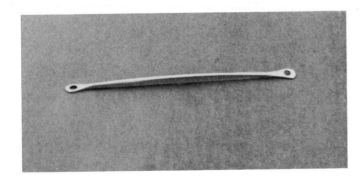

Fig. 386. Hammered unit of wire
for spiral bracelet.

Fig. 387. Ends of wire twisted around roundnose pliers for spiral link.

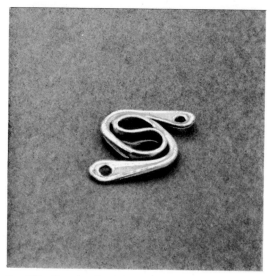
Fig. 388. Completed spiral link.

6. Smooth the hammered ends of the 14-gauge wire with a fine file to remove any roughness. One stroke around each edge of each end will suffice. This is done to all the units.
7. Center-punch each end of each 14-gauge wire unit.
8. Drill a No. 46 hole in each end of the 14-gauge wire unit.
9. Polish each 14-gauge wire unit on each side.
10. Mark the center of each 14-gauge wire unit with a pencil. For standardized production, this can be done by marking on a small board the over-all length of the unit and a center mark. Each unit is centered on this marker and the center mark picked up quickly.
11. Take each link and set it into a pair of roundnose pliers jaws just at the center mark. Then twist the ends of the wire into a spiral around the pliers (Fig. 387).
12. Bend the ends of each unit into position against the spiral and adjust each link to size and shape (Fig. 388).
13. Take each ¾-in. length of 18-gauge wire and fuse a bead on one end. Immediately after fusing the bead, dip the unit into a cup of water to cool, and set it aside.
14. Fasten the spiral units together with the 18-gauge wire units, one at a time, using a bead on the free end. Be careful to keep all spiral links facing the same way (Fig. 389).
15. Attach and solder a ³⁄₁₆-in. 18-gauge jump ring on each end of each bracelet, attaching a sister hook to each bracelet with one of the jump rings.
16. Oxidize each bracelet to a clear but not too heavy black, and polish the face and beads of each link.
17. Boil all the bracelets in soapy water or place them in the Ultrasonic cleaning machine. Rinse them in alcohol and dry (Fig. 390).
18. Price-tag each bracelet with price and code number, and package each in a plastic envelope, stapled closed.

Fig. 389. Links fastened together with fused wires.

From the foregoing discussion it can be seen that the systematization of processes and the carrying of a number of units through each stage of production will establish an efficient rhythm of activity. There is no doubt that this type of production organization leads to what may be viewed as a mechanical repetition of movements. It is just in this kind of process that time is saved and efficiency of movement is increased.

An unfavorable reaction to the mechanical routine involved may be balanced by the consideration of two thoughts. First of all, any given sequence of craft operations or movements carries with it all the implications of the subtlety of hand, eye, and mind that are required for every human bodily manipulation.

Fig. 390. Completed bracelet with sister hook.

What we mean, in part, when we describe these activities as "mechanical" is that the various operations become so well mastered that they drop below the level of consciousness and become habit patterns of activity, leaving the conscious mind free to make careful evaluations and judgments of the work in process. The activities become so integrated into the craftsman's repertory of abilities, through repeated practice, that his dexterity and skill reach new levels of performance.

The second thought worthy of consideration is the realization that perfection of every pattern of movement occurs when it becomes completely unconscious through repetition and leads to objectivity and unity of being. It is quite true that inefficient, erroneous, or sloppy habit patterns may be learned. Perfection of form in movement can emerge only from the constant striving for it and an appreciation of the natural rhythm that leads to it.

One final problem of production may emerge when the jeweler has become established and his business continues to increase. He will be confronted by the problem of expansion. Should he restrict his sales to his own hand production, or should he bring in a benchworker or two to assist in production activities?

This question must be answered according to the individual temperament and personal goals of the jeweler. If he is temperamentally oriented toward expanded production, and there can be great advantages in this direction, the American jeweler is faced by a peculiar historical tendency in American craft education. The postwar period has tended to stress the creative artist-craftsman and to encourage every craftsman to become his own designer. In general this approach seems to be an appropriate and desirable one, even though not every excellent craftsman is an excellent designer.

The question that appears significant to ask is why our craft programs are not also aimed to attract the young student who might be interested in craftsmanship, primarily, rather than design. It is the author's belief that the crafts are losing to other fields a good many young people possessing superior ability in mechanical aptitude, coordination, and dexterity, who might well become skilled benchworkers and find great pleasure in craft work. Such people may now find themselves in other production areas offering less satisfaction. A few trade schools offer such programs in limited areas, but there is a great dearth of competent and well-trained benchworkers in most crafts in America today. Every existing larger shop might well consider instituting an apprenticeship program in lieu of other educational craft programs.

APPENDIXES

APPENDIX A
Lists of Historical Exhibitions of Contemporary Jewelry

The original photographs and pieces of contemporary jewelry from the early exhibitions of the 1940s and 1950s have long since been dispersed to a considerable extent, so that it may be of interest to younger designers in the field to review here the beginnings of the trends in which they take part, even though the quality of photographic reproduction may be uneven after so many years have passed.

Exhibitors in the First National Exhibition of Contemporary Jewelry, Museum of Modern Art, New York, 1946

Expressive Means	Jeweler	Location
	Anni Albers and Alex Reed	Black Mountain College, N. C.
Nonrational Plate shape	Ward Bennett	New York
Nonrational Fused, forged	Harry Bertoia	California
	Madeleine Burrage	Maine
Nonrational Linear wire	Alexander Calder	New York
	Izabel M. Coles	New York
Nonrational Fused	Julio de Diego	New York
Rational Plate shape	Fred Farr	New York
	May G. Gay	Oregon
	Alexander Hammid	New York
	Fannie Hillsmith	New York
Nonrational Plate shape	Hurst & Kingsbury	New York
	Adda Husted-Andersen	New York
	Gertrude Karlan	New York
	Hilda Krauss	New York
	Julien Levy	New York

The pieces in Figs. 391–399 were shown at the Museum of Modern Art, New York, 1946.

Fig. 391. Ward Bennett. Hammered silver pendant.

Expressive Means	Jeweler	Location
Nonrational Cast	Jacques Lipchitz	New York
Rational Plate shape	Paul A. Lobel	New York
Nonrational Plate shape	Richard Pousette-Dart	New York
Nonrational Carved	José de Rivera	New York
	Ellis Simpson	New York

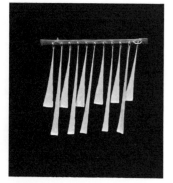

Fig. 392. Harry Bertoia. Hammered wire pin. Sterling silver.

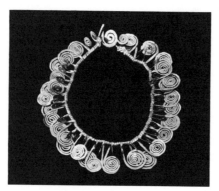

Fig. 393. Alexander Calder. Hammered wire necklace.

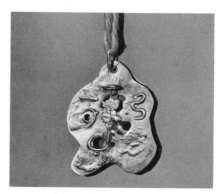

Fig. 394. Julio de Diego. Fused sterling pendant.

Fig. 395. Fred Farr. Sterling wire necklace.

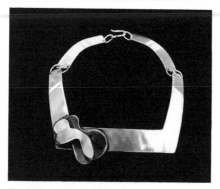

Fig. 396. Hurst and Kingsbury. Assembled plate shapes in sterling.

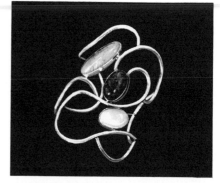

Fig. 397. Adda Husted-Andersen. Wire pin with stones.

right: Fig. 398. Richard Pousette-Dart. Pierced brass pendant.
far right: Fig. 399. José de Rivera. Stainless steel pin.

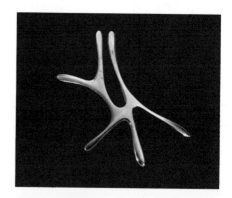

Exhibitors in the Second National Exhibition of Contemporary Jewelry, Walker Art Center, Minneapolis, 1948

Expressive Means	Jeweler	Location
Nonrational Plate shape	David Aaron	Washington, D. C.
Nonrational Enamel	Evelyn Balch	California
Nonrational Plate shape	Ward Bennett	New York
Rational Constructed	Franz Bergmann	California
Nonrational Fused, linear, cast, forged	Harry Bertoia	California
Rational Constructed	William De Hart	New York
Rational Strip plate	Margaret De Patta	California
Nonrational Plate shape	Bess Diamond	Illinois
Rational Linear wire	Claire Falkenstein	California
Rational Plate shape	Fred Farr	New York
Rational Enamel	Doris Hall	Ohio
Nonrational Constructed	Fannie Hillsmith	New York
Nonrational Strip plate	Hurst & Kingsbury	New York
Rational Cast	Adda Husted-Andersen	New York
Nonrational Ceramic	Phyllis W. Jacobs	California
Nonrational Fused, constructed	Sam Kramer	New York
Rational Enamel	Frank Lee	New York
Rational Plate shape	Paul A. Lobel	New York
Nonrational Linear, forged	Louis A. McMillen	Massachusetts

Expressive Means	Jeweler	Location
Nonrational Constructed	Keith Monroe	California
Rational Linear, forged Constructed	Philip Morton	Minnesota
Rational Repoussé	Marianna Pineda	Minnesota
Rational Linear wire	Richard P. Raseman	Michigan
Nonrational Plate shape	Walter Rhodes	New York
Nonrational Cast	Rima	New York
Nonrational Plate shape	Caroline Gleick Rosene	California
Nonrational Plastic	Zahara Schatz	New York
Rational Plate shape	Pearl S. Shecter	New York
Nonrational Linear, constructed	Art Smith	New York
Rational Plastic	Winfield Fine Art in Jewelry	New Jersey
Nonrational Cast	Bob Winston	California

The pieces in Figs. 400–411 were shown at the Walker Art Center, Minneapolis, 1948.

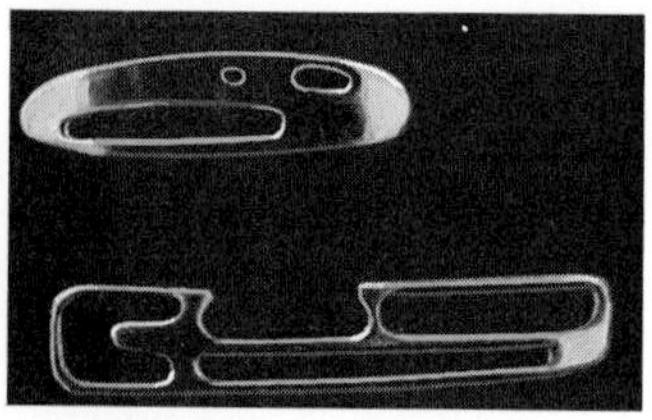

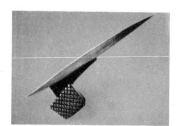

Fig. 400. David Aaron. Brass barrette and aluminum pin.

Fig. 401. Margaret De Patta. Pin. Silver strip-plate construction.

Fig. 402. Doris Hall. Free-form pin and earrings. Enamel on copper. Pin. Enamel on silver.

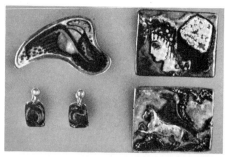

Fig. 403. Sam Kramer. Three silver pins, utilizing seashell, moonstone, glass eye, Indian emerald, amethyst, and two peridots.

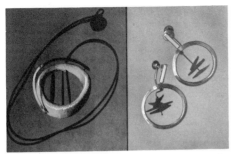

Fig. 404. Keith Monroe. Silver and ebony pendant; brass and ebony earrings.

Fig. 405. Philip Morton. Silver and ebony earrings and pin. Silver wire earrings.

Fig. 406. Marianna Pineda. Sterling repoussé pin with torquoise.

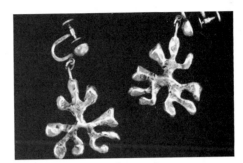

Fig. 407. Rima. Cast-silver earrings.

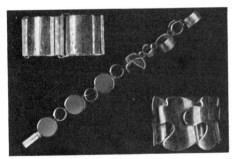

Fig. 408. Caroline Gleick Rosene. Silver and crystal bracelets.

Fig. 409. Zahara Schatz. Bracelet and necklace. Plastic with embedded material.

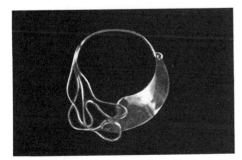

Fig. 410. Art Smith. Brass necklace.

Fig. 411. Bob Winston. Cast silver pendant with three stones.

Exhibitors in the Third National Exhibition of Contemporary Jewelry, Walker Art Center, Minneapolis, 1955

Expressive Means	Jeweler	Location
Nonrational Constructed form	Harold J. Atwater	Clearwater, Fla.
Nonrational Constructed form	Gregory P. Bacopulos	Memphis, Tenn.
Rational Constructed	Mildred Lee Ball	Winston-Salem, N. C.
Rational Constructed	Martha Brennan Barns	Morristown, N. J.
Nonrational Constructed	Jane Beckman	Milwaukee, Wisc.
Nonrational Fused-forged forms	Harry Bertoia	Barto, Penna.
Nonrational Enamel	John and Marsha Best	Arcadia, Calif.
Nonrational Cast	Marsh Bohr	Burlingame, Calif.
Rational Linear Constructed	Frances Holmes Boothby	Weston, Vt.
Nonrational Carved	M. N. Boyer	Honolulu, Hawaii
Rational Strip plate	Michael J. Brandt, Jr.	Sheboygan, Wisc.
Rational Constructed	Howard O. Brown	Rochester, N. Y.
Nonrational Constructed	Juanita F. Brown	Rochester, N. Y.
Rational Constructed	Irena Brynner	San Francisco, Calif.
Nonrational Constructed	Eleanor Caldwell	Hays, Kans.
Nonrational Constructed	O. K. Chatt	Eugene, Ore.
Nonrational Constructed	Maxwell M. Chayat	Clinton, N. J.
Rational Constructed	Betty Cooke	Baltimore, Md.
Rational Constructed	Andrew and Muriel Dey	Deland, Fla.

Expressive Means	Jeweler	Location
Nonrational Constructed	J. DeFeo	San Francisco, Calif.
Rational Strip plate Constructed form	Margaret De Patta	Napa, Calif.
Nonrational Cast	Robert Dhaemers	Oakland, Calif.
Rational Enameled	Virginia Dudley	Rising Faun, Ga.
Nonrational Linear wire Rational Constructed	D. Lee and Mary Dusell	Aurora, Ill.
Rational Plate shape	Roger D. Easton	Cortland, N. Y.
Rational Carved and constructed	Audrey and Robert Engstrom	Sparta, Mich.
Nonrational Enameled	George Faddis	Highland Park, Mich.
Rational Enameled and cast	Lester Fader	New Castle, Penna.
Rational Constructed	Philip Fike	Detroit, Mich.
Rational Constructed Conventional	Robert A. Gabriel	Meadville, Penna.
Rational Constructed	Robert E. Gardner	Pittsburg, Penna.
Nonrational Cast	Jerome E. Gates	Minneapolis, Minn.

The pieces in Figs. 412–417 were shown at the Walker Art Center, Minneapolis, 1955.

left: Fig. 412. Philip Fike. Silver and niello cuff link.
right: Fig. 413. Jerome Gates. Cast-silver ring.

Expressive Means	Jeweler	Location
Rational Constructed	Marilyn Zirkel Goodman	Portland, Ore.
Nonrational Cast	Wiltz Harrison	El Paso, Tex.
Rational Carved and constructed	Lee Haslam	Merion, Penna.
Rational Plate shape	David P. Hatch	Eugene, Ore.
Rational Constructed	Adda Husted-Andersen	New York, N. Y.
Nonrational Fused, cast, and constructed	Sam Kramer	New York, N. Y.
Rational Constructed	Mary Kretsinger	Emporia, Kans.
Rational Constructed	James S. Lanham	Gainesville, Fla.
Rational Constructed	Frederick Lauritzen	Carbondale, Ill.
Rational Linear wire	Bob McCabe	Sacramento, Calif.
Rational Constructed Plate shape	Lawrence McKinin	Columbia, Miss.
Nonrational Cast	Philip Morton	St. Paul, Minn.
Rational Constructed	Earl B. Pardon	Newburyport, Mass.
Nonrational Enameled	Miriam Smith Peck	East Cleveland, Ohio

left: Fig. 414. Mary Kretsinger.
Riveted sterling silver pin.
right: Fig. 415. Lawrence McKinin.
Sterling silver pendant.

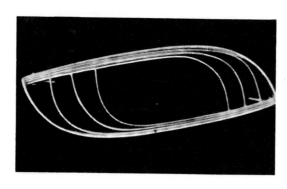

Expressive Means	Jeweler	Location
Rational Linear wire	Coralynn Pence	Seattle, Wash.
Rational Constructed	E. Peter Petersen	New York, N. Y.
Nonrational Linear wire	Nelle and Daniel Peterson	Louisville, Ky.
Nonrational Cast	Angela Petesch	Los Angeles, Calif.
Rational Constructed	Carl O. Podzsus	New York, N. Y.
Nonrational Linear	Dorothy Price	Champaign, Ill.
Rational Forged	F. Jules Reed	Minneapolis, Minn.
Rational Constructed	Maria Regnier	Brentwood, Mo.
Nonrational Enamel	B. M. Reid	San Diego, Calif.
Rational Linear wire	Merry G. Renk	San Francisco, Calif.
Nonrational Strip plate and constructed	Florence Resnikoff	Palo Alto, Calif.
Rational Constructed Plate shape	Ruth Roach	Plainfield, Iowa
Rational Constructed linear	Caroline Gleick Rosene	San Francisco, Calif.
Rational Carved	Hermon Roth	Larchmont, N. Y.
Rational Constructed	Thomas E. Ryder	Villanova, Penna.
Nonrational Forged and carved	George K. Salo	Sutton, N. H.
Nonrational Constructed	Muriel Savin	Richmond, Calif.
Rational Forged linear	Pearl S. Shecter	New York, N. Y.
Nonrational Enamel	Alice H. Schell	Akron, Ohio
Rational Constructed	Christian F. Schmidt	Minneapolis, Minn.

Fig. 416. B. M. Reid.
Enamel and silver pendant.

Fig. 417. George K. Salo.
Silver and rose-quartz pin.

Expressive Means	Jeweler	Location
Nonrational Enamel	Paul John Smith	Attica, N. Y.
Rational Constructed Plate shape	Orville H. Soffa	Oshkosh, Wisc.
Rational Constructed Plate shape	Francis Stephen	Pharr, Tex.
Rational Constructed Plate shape	Annaliese Steppat	New York, N. Y.
Rational Constructed	Jean Sterne	Elkins Park, Penna.
Rational Constructed Plate shape	Bernice A. Stevens	Evansville, Ind.
Rational Constructed linear	Paul R. Suttman	Albuquerque, N. M.
Rational Strip plate	John Szymak	Dallas, Tex.
Nonrational Constructed Plate shape	Ken Thompson	Minneapolis, Minn.
Rational Constructed	Edgar J. Trapp	Indiana, Penna.
Rational Constructed Plate and ·wire	Anne G. Van Kleeck	Columbus, Ohio
Rational Strip plate	Arthur A. Vierthaler	Waunakee, Wisc.
Rational Constructed	Fennell Wallen	San Diego, Calif.
Rational Linear wire	Kay White	Bristol, Conn.
Rational Forged linear wire	Marjorie McIlroy Wildenhain	Rochester, N. Y.
Rational Constructed Carved	Byron Wilson	Oakland, Calif.
Nonrational Cast constructed	Bob Winston	Oakland, Calif.
Rational Strip plate	Alice E. Zimmerman	Evansville, Ind.

**Fourth National Exhibition of Contemporary Jewelry,
Walker Art Center, Minneapolis, 1959**
(Selected listing to show beginnings of tendencies lasting to the present)

The pieces in Figs. 418–428 were shown at the Walker Art Center, Minneapolis, 1959.

Jeweler	Expressive Means	Tendency
Irena Brynner	Nonrational Cast form with stone	Contemporary search for ring forms
Juanita F. Brown	Nonrational Forged form Carved form	Continuation of search for sculptured and forged forms
Margaret De Patta	Rational Constructed form	Creative use of gemstones to exploit transparency
John Dickerhoff	Rational Forged form	Example of forging
Robert Engstrom	Nonrational Cast form	Contemporary search for ring forms beyond conventional forms of stones and settings
Michael Jerry	Rational Cast forms	Characteristic File-Wax forms
Sam Kramer	Nonrational Cast form	Continuation of surrealist direction
Earl Krentzin	Nonrational Cast form	Departure to humorous forms
John Paul Miller	Nonrational Cast and etched forms	Pinpointing a trend away from direct expression to refinement of technique in European tradition
Philip Morton	Nonrational	Simple treatment of found object Opposite side of contemporary tradition from Miller

top: Fig. 418. Irena Brynner.
Ring with black opal
and fresh-water pearl.
center: Fig. 419. Juanita Brown.
Carved bracelet.
above: Fig. 420. John Dickerhoff.
Bracelet forged from heavy-gauge wire.

Fig. 421. Michael Jerry.
Cast-silver pendant with opal.

Fig. 422. John Paul Miller.
Gold and enamel pendant-brooch.

Fig. 423. Philip Morton. Silver
pendant with found quartz pebble.

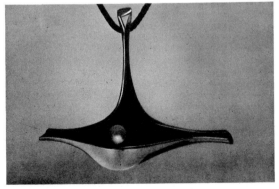

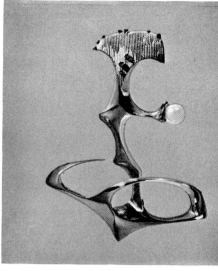

Fig. 424. Ronald Hayes Pearson.
Forged 14-kt. gold necklace.
1958. Commissioned by Charles Hallick.

Fig. 425. Ruth Radakovich.
Cast and forged gold pin
with tourmaline.

Fig. 426. Svetozar Radakovich.
Cast gold pin with pearl.

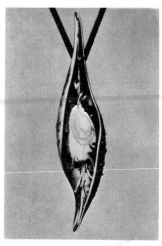

above: Fig. 427. Christian F. Schmidt.
Seed-pod pendant. Fused silver
with cast gold and stone.
below: Fig. 428. Richard G. Thiel.
Cast sterling ring with onyx,
amazonite, and malachite.

Jeweler	Expressive Means	Tendency
Robert von Neumann	Nonrational	Interest in natural forms in style approaching Art Nouveau
Ronald Hayes Pearson	Nonrational Cast forms	Delicate treatment of gold with emphasis on malleability, tensile strength, color, and light reflection
Ruth and Svetozar Radakovich	Nonrational Cast forms	Pure qualities of metal contrasted with stone as focal point
Christian F. Schmidt	Nonrational Fused and cast form	Renewed interest in natural forms reminiscent of Art Nouveau. Emotional richness through torch textures and organic forms of stone and setting
Richard G. Thiel	Nonrational Cast form	Search for contemporary ring forms
Byron Wilson	Rational Constructed form	Exploration of shapes in simple but effective relationships
Bob Winston	Nonrational Assembled forms	Primitive direction influenced by Pre-Columbian art

Jewelers included in Aloi's
"Esempi di Decorazione Moderna di Tutto il Mondo," Hoepli, Milan, 1954

Jeweler	Location
Harry Bertoia	La Jolla, Calif.
Max Bill	Zurich
Burch-Korrodi	Zurich
A. Calderoni	Milan
Margaret De Patta	San Francisco
Ernst Dennler	Zurich
Nanna and Jørgen Ditzel	Copenhagen
Archibald Dumbar	Eefde
Max Fröhlich	Zurich
Thom Hannan	Royal Oak, Mich.
Fannie Hillsmith	New York
Adda Husted-Andersen	New York
Sigrid Keetman	
Tove and Edvard Kindt-Larsen	Copenhagen
Feickert Koch	Hanau
Henning Koppel	Copenhagen
Hilda Krauss	Westport, Conn.
Lucienne Lazon	Rambouillet
Fritz Loosli	Zurich
A. Lucas	London
Lorenzo Martignetti	Milan
Sonja Matare	Buderich
Luigi Mazzetti	Milan
Mellerio dits Meller	Paris
Georges Mendelssohn	Paris
Philip Morton	St. Paul
Genny Mucchi	Milan
Wiwen Nilsson	Lund, Sweden
Orlando Paladino Orlandini	Rome
Sigurd Persson	Stockholm
Mario Pinton	Padua
Gertrud Schick	Aalen
Franco Schreiber	Milan
Martin Seitz	Passau

Jeweler	Location
Pearl S. Shecter	New York
Maud Smit	Eefde
Chris Steenbergen	Eefde
Raymond Templier	Paris
Elisabeth Treskow	Cologne
Wolfgang Tumpel	Hamburg
Ebbe Weiss	Uberlingen Bodensee
Bengt Wettersjo	Stockholm
Walter Zipper	Zurich

Exhibitors of Contemporary Jewelry in the First International Exhibition of Modern Jewelry, London, 1961

Jeweler	Country
Albert, Gilbert	Switzerland
Alemany, Carlos	U.S.A.
Barve, Olov	Sweden
Becker, Friedrich	Germany
Brynner, Irena	U.S.A.
Champagnat, Jean	France
Clen-Murphy, Desmond	Britain
Cooper, John Paul	Britain
Craver, Margaret	U.S.A.
Dahlquist, Inga	Sweden
Ditzel, Nanna	Denmark
Falkenstein, Claire	U.S.A.
Flöckinger, Gerda	Britain
Haendel, William George	U.S.A.
Hartshorn, Esther	U.S.A.
King, Arthur	U.S.A.
Kretsinger, Mary	U.S.A.
Lechtzin, Stanley	U.S.A.
Martinazzi, Bruno	Italy
Morton, Philip	U.S.A.
Pomodoro brothers	Italy
Vierthaler, Arthur A.	U.S.A.

APPENDIX B
Tools, Findings, and Supplies

B–1 List of Tools by Illustration Number and by Section Number The following list names virtually all the tools and equipment discussed in this book in relation to designing and processing. The majority of them are illustrated either separately or in connection with the diagrams and photographs explaining processes and procedures. Some are so familiar in any workshop or studio that they require no illustration, but even for those not illustrated a description of the function and form is given in the sections discussing their use in the jewelry craft. Therefore the reader may find it useful to locate the illustrations or the descriptions from this list.

Annealing booth, Sec. 8–3
Annealing pan, Fig. 372
Annealing tongs, Fig. 372
Anvil, Fig. 164, Step 2
Asbestos block, Sec. 8–26
Beading tool, Fig. 365
Bench pin, Sec. 8–12, Fig. 22
Bismuth block, Sec. 8–26
Blowpipe, mouth, Fig. 211
Brake, sheet-metal, Fig. 244
Buffs, Sec. 15–8
    brush
    cutting
    polishing, Fig. 164, Step 8
    ring
    scratch brush, Fig. 264, Step 13
Bunsen burner, Sec. 14–11
Burnisher, Fig. 239

Butane tank, Sec. 8–4
C-clamp, Sec. 14–7
Casting flask, Fig. 322
Casting-flask tongs, Sec. 14–16
Casting machine, centrifugal, Figs. 313, 329
    pressure, Fig. 336
    vacuum, Fig. 335
Center punch, Sec. 10–2
Charcoal block, Fig. 170
Chasing plate, Fig. 292
Chasing tools, Figs. 262, 377
Chisel, Sec. 11–1
Circle-cutting dies, Fig. 385
Circle-marking template, Fig. 273
Compass, pencil, Sec. 10–1
Cone bur, Fig. 364
Crucible, graphite, Fig. 214
    hand, Figs. 171, 220
Dapping block, Sec. 9–18
Dapping punch, Sec. 8–7
Diemaker's ball, Sec. 11–10
Dividers, Fig. 271
Drawplate, Fig. 236
Drawtongs, Fig. 237
Drop hammer, Sec. 19–3
Drill, bench, Sec. 11–7
    flexible-shaft, Fig. 278
    hand, Fig. 257
Electric waxing tool, Fig. 264, Step 5
Electroplating equipment, Figs. 264, 341
Emery stick, Fig. 339
Engraving block, Fig. 284

Files, Sec. 15–1
    barrette
    half-round
    half-round ring
    hand, Figs. 164, Step 7, 235
    needle
    round
Flux brush, Sec. 8–19
Foot bellows, Fig. 212
Furnace, barrel or bench, Sec. 8–4
    burnout, Sec. 14–16
    gas-air melting, Fig. 215
Gauge plate, B. & S., Fig. 234
Graver, Fig. 285
Graver sharpener, Fig. 286
Grinder, Sec. 18–2
Hammer, ball-peen, Sec. 12–3
    chasing, Fig. 262
    cross-peen, Fig. 238
    forging, Fig. 288
    planishing, Sec. 12–5
    rivet, Fig. 298
    sledge, Fig. 290
Heating frame, Fig. 213
Ingot mold, Sec. 8–12
Jeweler's bench, Fig. 221
Joint tool, Fig. 307
Kick press, Sec. 19–3
Lead block, Sec. 9–17
Mandrel, bezel, Sec. 17–1
    ring, Fig. 248
Mallet, rawhide, Fig. 245
    wooden, Figs. 164, Step 6, 245
Mop, soldering, Fig. 223
Oxygen tank, Sec. 8–4
Pickle crock, Sec. 8–13
Pickle pan, Sec. 8–13
Pitch bowl, Fig. 261
Pliers, cutting, Fig. 164, Step 5
    half-round, Sec. 9–7
    roundnose, Fig. 387
    squarenose, Fig. 243
    snipe-nose, Sec. 9–7
Polishing lathe, Sec. 15–8
Prestone tank, Sec. 8–4
Propane tank, Sec. 8–4
Protractor, Sec. 10–3
Punches, Fig. 379
Pusher, Fig. 355
Regulators, Sec. 8–5
    adjustable
    automatic
    oxygen
Repoussé punches, Figs. 261, 375

Ring bender, Fig. 183
Ring-casting outfit, Sec. 14–7
Ring-size set, Fig. 180
Ring tripod, Sec. 8–26
Ring enlarger, Fig. 183
Ring sticks, Fig. 340
Rivet set, Fig. 302
Rolling mill, Fig. 241
Rubber-mold frame, Fig. 325
Sandbag, Sec. 9–16
Saw, hack, Fig. 334
    jeweler's, Fig. 247
Saw blades, jeweler's, Sec. 11–2
Scorper, Fig. 279
Scraper, Fig. 242
Scribe, Fig. 338
Setting bur, Figs. 363, 364
Shears, bench, Sec. 11–1
    hand, Sec. 8–19
    squaring, Fig. 276
Soldering pick, Sec. 8–21
Sprue base, Sec. 14–14
Stake, T–, Fig. 165
Steel rule, Sec. 10–2
Striker, or sparker, Sec. 8–5
Tin block, Sec. 9–3
Torches, Sec. 8–4
    air-gas
    oxygen-gas
    portable butane or propane
Tweezers, self-locking, Sec. 9–2
    soldering, Figs. 217, 220, 228
Ultrasonic cleaning machine, Fig. 342
Vacuum pump, Fig. 319
V-block, Fig. 277
Vise, bench, Fig. 245
    hand, Sec. 15–3
    pin, Fig. 235
    ring, Sec. 15–3
Vulcanizing frame, Fig. 325
Vulcanizing press, Fig. 326
Wax pressure injector, Fig. 330

B–2   Sources of Tools and Equipment

Allcraft Tool & Supply Co., Inc., 15 W. 45th St. New York, N. Y.	Jewelry tools
American Handicrafts, 20 W. 14th St., New York, N. Y.	Craft tools

Anchor Tool & Supply Co., 12 John St., New York, N. Y.	General tools
Craft Service, 337 University Ave., Rochester, N. Y.	General tools
Denton Precision Casting Co., 665 Eddy St., Providence, R. I.	Casting equipment and supplies
William Dixon, Inc., 32 E. Kinney St., Newark, N. J.	Silversmith and jewelry tools
General Refineries, 292 Oak St., St. Paul, Minn.	Casting equipment and supplies
Paul H. Gesswein & Co., 235 Park Ave. S., New York, N. Y. 10003	Jewelry tools
Grieger's, Inc., 1633 E. Walnut St., Pasadena, Calif.	Jewelry and lapidary equipment and supplies
Kerr Manufacturing Co., 6081 Twelfth St., Detroit, Mich.	Casting equipment and supplies
Linde Air Products Co., 30 Thomson Ave., Long Island City, N. Y.	Torch equipment
C. & E. Marshall Co., Box 7737, Chicago, Ill.	Tools
M. McNamara Stamp & Stencil Works, 40 E. 20th St., New York, N. Y.	Sterling and special stamps
Metal Crafts Supply Co., 10 Thomas St. Providence, R. I.	Lapidary equipment and jewelry tools
Alexander Saunders & Co., Inc., 95 Bedford St., New York, N. Y.	Casting equipment and supplies
Southwest Smelting & Refining Co., Box 2010 Dallas, Tex.	Jewelry and lapidary equipment and supplies
Swartchild & Co., 29 E. Madison St., Chicago, Ill.	Jewelry tools
Torit Manufacturing Co., 1133 Rankin St. St. Paul, Minn.	Casting equipment

Waldree Lapidary Shop, 2267 N. Dearborn St., Indianapolis, Ind.	Lapidary equipment
The Wilkinson Co., 1660 Ninth St., Box 303, Santa Monica, Calif. 90406	Casting equipment

B–3 Jewelry Findings There is such a wide variety of jewelry findings supplied by so many different manufacturers that it is practical for the jeweler to secure his own catalogues and become acquainted with the types, kinds, and prices. Basic types of findings are described and illustrated here.

Ear Backs A large variety of designs of ear back are commercially available from supply houses. These designs vary in size, quality, metal, and type of fastening device. They are available in sterling, 14-kt. gold, and cheaper alloy metals.

The screw back (Fig. 429) is perhaps the most common design, but the clip (Fig. 430) is becoming more popular, because the surface area is greater and holds more firmly with less pinching pressure on the ear lobe. Both these types are made with or without a small open ring to which a dangle may be attached. The type with the open ring usually has a small sphere or hemisphere covering the outer end of the clip. The

Fig. 429. Screw-type ear back.

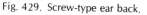

Fig. 430. Clip-type ear back.

type without an open ring usually has a small disk or cup and a small threaded post in its center, to which a bead or pearl may be cemented (Fig. 431). The post is clipped off when the ear back is to be attached to a button type of earring. It is usual for the jeweler to buy the ear back with the small open ring and the cup and post, because the ring may be sawed off if it is not required.

The ear wire for pierced ears (Fig. 431) is made in two styles. One style has a small disk to which a button may be attached. The other style is for use with dangle earrings. For pierced ears there is also a pin-and-clip design, but this is not often used. The ear wire with a post and nut, for pierced ears, is better for button earrings.

There is also an interesting ear back called the wing back, which fits in the ear and has no clip to pinch the ear lobe (Fig. 432). This is unusual in appearance but is extremely comfortable and functional.

Cuff-link Back   The contemporary jeweler often desires to make the cuff-link back a part of the form of his design. For many button-type designs, however, a simple back such as that shown (Fig. 433) will be satisfactory. There is a small cup or depression at the base of this back. One of the harder soft solders should be used to solder it. Care should be taken not to overheat the spring, which is in the swivel part. The best way to solder this back is to clip it to the button with self-locking soldering tweezers, adjust it to the right position with the swivel part up and the button part down, and then apply the small flame directly upward at the underside of the button part. As soon as the solder flows, the cuff link should be quenched in water.

Joint, Safety Catch, and Pin Tong   The illustration (Fig. 434) shows this joint to be spread apart, and this type always comes this way. The flanges should be squeezed parallel, and the resulting rounded bottom should be filed flat before flowing on the silver solder.

The style of safety catch that is the most useful single design has the slot opening at the top and is usable with a short pin tong as well as with a long one. The pin tong comes in a number of lengths from 1 to 3½ in. The short lengths are of smaller-gauge wire and desirable for small pins. The 3-in. length can be cut down to almost any shorter length and is therefore the most useful single size to have on hand.

Sister Hook   This is one of the most practical fasteners for link-type bracelets (Fig. 435). The sister hook will fall open only if the tube rivet becomes too loose. In this case, just burnish the tube.

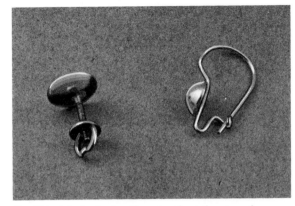

Fig. 431. *left:* Ear back with post and nut, for pierced ears. *right:* Ear wire for pierced ears.

Fig. 432. Wing back.   Fig. 433. Cuff-link back.

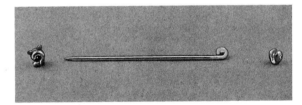

Fig. 434. Safety catch, pin tong, and joint.

Fig. 435. Sister hook.

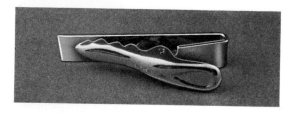

left: Fig. 436. Spring ring.

below: Fig. 437. Tie-clip back.

Fig. 438. Tie tack.

Spring Ring   The spring ring (Fig. 436) is a standard fastener for necklaces and comes in ring sizes ranging from ⅛ to ⅜ in. in diameter.

Tie-clip Back   The all-sterling tie-clip back illustrated (Fig. 437) is one of the best in quality on the market. It should be soft-soldered to the tie clip.

Tie Tack   The tie tack (Fig. 438) is popular for button-type tie clips. The flat disk on the pin is soft-soldered to the button.

B–4   Sources of Jewelry Findings

Allcraft Tool & Supply Co., Inc., 15 W. 45th St., New York, N.Y.	Retail
American Handcrafts Co., Inc., 45 S. Harrison St., East Orange, N. J.	Retail
B. A. Ballou & Co., Inc., Providence, R. I.	Wholesale
W. R. Cobb, 101 Sabin St., Providence, R. I.	Wholesale
Craft Service, 337 University Ave., Rochester, N. Y.	Retail
Findings, Inc., Keene, N. H.	Wholesale
General Findings and Supply Co., Attleboro, Mass.	Retail

Paul H. Gesswein & Co., 235 Park Ave. S., New York, N. Y.	Retail
Grieger's, Inc., 1633 E. Walnut St., Pasadena, Calif.	Retail
J. J. Jewelcraft, 2732 Colorado Blvd., Los Angeles, Calif.	Retail
Karlan & Bleicher, Inc., 136 W. 52d St., New York, N. Y. 10019	Wholesale (ring findings)
Sam Kramer, Inc., 29 W. 8th St., New York, N. Y.	Retail
C. & E. Marshall Co., Box 7737, Chicago, Ill.	Retail
Metal Crafts Supply Co., 10 Thomas St., Providence, R. I.	Retail
Montana Assay, 610 South West 2d Ave., Portland, Ore.	Retail
Southwest Smelting & Refining Co., Box 2010, Dallas, Tex., Box 1298, San Antonio, Tex.	Retail
A. T. Wall, 162 Clifford St., Providence, R. I.	Wholesale
Wildberg Bros. Smelting & Refining, 742 Market St., San Francisco, Calif.	Retail
Wildberg Bros. Smelting & Refining 635 S. Hill St., Los Angeles, Calif.	Retail

B–5   Sources of Gold, Silver, Brass, Copper, Bronze

American Handicrafts Co., Inc., 20 W. 14th St., New York, N. Y.	Silver
T. E. Conklin Brass and Copper Co., Inc., 324 W. 23d St., New York, N.Y.	Brass, copper, alloys
Thomas J. Doe & Co., 55 E. Washington St., Chicago, Ill.	
General Refineries, 292 Oak St., St. Paul, Minn.	Silver and gold
Paul H. Gesswein & Co., 235 Park Ave. S., New York, N. Y.	Silver and gold
Goldsmith Bros. Smelting & Refining Co., 58 E. Washington St., Chicago, Ill.	Silver and gold

Grieger's, Inc., 1633 E. Walnut St.,   Silver
Pasadena, Calif.

Handy & Harmon, 44 W. 46th St.,   Silver and gold
New York, N. Y.

Handy & Harmon,   Silver and gold
3625 Medford St.,
Los Angeles, Calif.

Handy & Harmon,   Silver and gold
1900 W. Kinzie St.,
Chicago, Ill.

J. J. Jewelcraft,   Silver
2732 Colorado Blvd.,
Los Angeles, Calif.

T. B. Hagstoz & Son,   Copper, brass,
709 Sansom St.,   alloys
Philadelphia, Penna.

Hoover and Strong, Inc.,   Silver, gold,
Buffalo, N. Y.   platinum

Southwest Smelting & Refining Co.,   Silver, gold,
Box 2010,   platinum,
Dallas, Tex.   palladium

Wildberg Bros. Smelting &   Gold
Refining, 742 Market St.,
San Francisco, Calif.

Wildberg Bros. Smelting &   Gold
Refining, 635 S. Hill St.,
Los Angeles, Calif.

B–6 Sources of Gems and Semiprecious Stones

E. W. Beissinger, 417 Clark Building, Pittsburgh, Penna.

Eugene Chaput, 210 Post Street, San Francisco, Calif.

Grieger's, Inc., 1633 E. Walnut St., Pasadena, Calif.

Henry F. Harpers, 18 Crawford St., Newark, N. J.

International Gem Corp., 15 Maiden Lane, New York, N. Y.

Sam Kramer, Inc., 29 W. 8th St., New York, N. Y.

William V. Schmidt Co., Inc., 30 Rockefeller Plaza, New York, N. Y. 10020

William Posesse, 21870 Priday Ave., Euclid, Ohio

Vreeland Mfg. Co., 4105 N. E. 68th Ave., Portland, Ore.

The Lapidary Journal, Box 2369, San Diego, Calif.

B–7 List of Supplies and Sources

Material	Section	Supplier (see key)
Barium chloride	15–12	L
Battern's Flux	C–9	—
Beeswax	11–4	L
Borax	8–11	L
Boric acid crystals	C–8	—
Chloride of platinum	15–12	L
Cuprous cyanide	C–7	L
Emery paper	15–6	L
Green copperas	C–15	L
Gum tragacanth	6–23	L
Handy Flux	C–9	J
Hydrochloric acid	15–12	L
Iodine	15–12	L
Lea compound	15–8	J
Liver of sulphur	15–12	L
Mold rubber	14–9	J
Nitric acid	8–14	L
Pitch	9–15	J
Potassium cyanide	C–7	L
Potassium iodide	C–7	—
Powdered pumice	15–11	L
Rouge	15–8,C–5	—
Saltpeter	C–15	L
Shellac chips	11–10	J
Sodium carbonate	C–7	—
Sodium cyanide	C–7	—
Sodium phosphate	C–8	L
Sodium pyrophosphate	C–7	—
Sodium thiosulphate	C–7	—
Soldering salts	8–17	L
Sulphuric acid	8–13	L
Tripoli	15–8	J
Wax, blue	14–13	K
File-Wax	14–12	S
green	14–13	K
red	14–13	DP
Solu-Wax	14–10	S
Yellow ocher	8–14	L
Zinc chloride (soldering salts)	8–17	L

Key	L	Local dealer
	J	Jewelry supply house
	K	Kerr Mfg.
	S	Southwest Smelting & Refining
	DP	Denton Precision Casting Co.

APPENDIX C
Technical Data

C-1   Aqua Regia   This acid, called "royal water," is the most powerful of all acids and will dissolve or etch gold, as well as silver. Add one part nitric acid very slowly to three parts hydrochloric acid. Never keep the bottle tightly stoppered. The fumes are highly corrosive! **Use with care!** Aqua regia should be used outdoors unless there is a ventilated booth with a blower.

C-2   Alloys   An alloy consists of a homogeneous mixture of metals. The composition of some of the nonferrous alloys is given below.

Brass: 66% copper, 33% zinc, .15% lead.
Bronze: 90% copper, .2% zinc, 9.7% tin, .1% lead.
Ormulu (mosaic gold): Equal parts of copper and zinc. Melt the copper at the lowest temperature that will fuse it. Stir well and add the zinc little by little. This alloy first assumes the yellow color of brass, turns to purple, and at last becomes white.
Pewter: 100 parts tin, 17 parts regulus of antimony.
Queen's metal: 4½ lb. tin, ½ lb. bismuth, ½ lb. antimony, ½ lb. lead.
Talmi gold: 86.4% copper, 12.2% zinc, 1.1% tin, .3% iron (may be eliminated).
Tombac: 16 lb. copper, 1 lb. tin, 1 lb. zinc.
Tombac (red): 5½ lb. copper. When melted, add ½ lb. zinc.
German silver: 20 parts copper, 15.8 parts nickel, 12.7 parts zinc.

C-3   Binding-wire Sizes   Use No. 20 for heavy wire, No. 28 for light wire.

C-4   Buffs

Muslin or bristle buffs for cutting compounds.
Flannel buffs for polishing with rouge.
Brass wire wheel (scratch brush) for "satin" finish.
Felt or wood lap for cutting surfaces flat.

C-5   Buffing Compounds

Lea grade C for cutting out deep pits and scratches from silver, brass or copper. (A respirator should be worn when using this compound.)

Tripoli for cutting light scratches and for a "butler finish" for silver. This is the most commonly used finish for silver, copper, brass, and bronze. Tripoli is a cutting compound.

Rouge for high polish on gold and silver. Rouge burnishes, rather than cuts, metal.

C-6   Chaser's Pitch

1 lb. green pitch
2 lb. plaster of Paris
1 oz. tallow

In cold weather the pitch may harden, and additional tallow will be needed. The pitch is melted in an old pan over a gas plate. Heat slowly until it is liquid. Then stir in the plaster little by little and pour the mixture into the pitch bowl. Leave a little to pour in a small pan so that if you need a small amount to fill up the back of a repoussé piece, you will not have to dig it out of the pitch bowl.

C–7 Electroplating Bath Formulas

For copper:

Cuprous cyanide, CuCN	22 grams per liter
Sodium cyanide, NaCN	34 grams per liter
Sodium carbonate, Na$_2$CO$_3$	15 grams per liter
Sodium thiosulphate, Na$_2$S$_2$O$_3$, 5 H$_2$O	2 grams per liter

Operating temperature about 40° C.
Current density is 15 amperes per square foot.

For silver (cyanide):

Fine grain silver	2 oz. troy per gal.
Sodium cyanide	3 oz. Av. per gal.

For silver (noncyanide):

Silver sulphate	30 grams per liter
Ammonia (25%)	75 c.c. per liter
Potassium iodide	600 grams per liter
Sodium pyrophosphate	60 grams per liter

For gold (cyanide solution):

Metallic gold	1 gram per liter
Cyanide KCN (free)	0.1 to 15 grams per liter
Phosphate K$_2$HOP$_4$	15 grams per liter
Ferrocyanide K$_4$Fe(CN)$_6$	10 to 11.5 grams per liter

This is a basic formula for the jewelry plating industry.

C–8 Firecoat Protection

1. Yellow ocher is mixed with a solution of boric-acid crystals dissolved in water to a light, fluffy paste. This is painted over the areas to be protected. When solder seams must be fluxed, do this first and dry the flux by warming the piece. Then the yellow ocher may be painted over the areas and up very close to the seams. If the yellow ocher is painted on first, the flux will tend to draw it into the seam, thereby obstructing the flow of the solder.
2. Boric-acid solution is mixed with alcohol to aid rapid drying.
3. Prip's Flux
   64 grams borax
   64 grams sodium phosphate
   96 grams boric-acid powder
   Make a paste with a little water and then gradually add 1 qt. water. Bring this to a boil. This will give a clear flux that protects against firecoat remarkably and is also an excellent flux for gold and silver.

C–9 Fluxes

Soft-solder Fluxes

For lead, 1 oz. zinc chloride in ½ pt. water
For pewter, 1 part HCl to 18 parts glycerin

Hard-solder Flux

Borax is prepared in sticks for use with a borax slate. A small amount of water is placed in the hollow of the slate, and the borax stick is rubbed in the hollow until a solution of flux is made. This is applied with the flux brush.

Borax powder is available in the grocery store in cartons. This is a convenient form of flux to use in the crucible or in solder powder.

Battern's Self-pickling Flux is a fluoride flux that is very convenient for jewelry work and much used by professional jewelers. It comes in small bottles or pint cans. Since it evaporates, it is best kept in a very small bottle on the workbench. An India ink bottle, well cleaned, makes a good flux bottle, and the flux brush may be put into the rubber stopper.

Prip's Flux is an excellent flux and also prevents firecoat.

Handy Flux is a special preparation that melts at 1100° F., which is just below the melting point of silver solders. It is especially good for soldering copper because copper oxidizes so readily. It is also a good flux for silver soldering steel.

Sal ammoniac is used for soldering iron and steel with lead solder.

C–10 Gauge Sizes

The B. & S. (Brown and Sharpe) gauge is a disk with slots of various sizes cut into the edge. These slots are of standard sizes ranging from 0 to 36. To find the size of a sheet or wire merely find the slot into which the metal fits most neatly and read off the number. A table of dimensions of these sizes is given below:

B. & S. Gauge No.	In.	B. & S. Gauge No.	In.
0	.3249	16	.0508
1	.2893	17	.0453
2	.2576	18	.0403
3	.2294	19	.0359
4	.2043	20	.0320
5	.1819	21	.0285
6	.1620	22	.0253
7	.1443	23	.0226
8	.1285	24	.0201
9	.1144	25	.0179
10	.1019	26	.0159
11	.0907	27	.0142
12	.0808	28	.0126
13	.0720	29	.0113
14	.0641	30	.0100
15	.0571		

C–11 Gold Gold is traditionally produced in a variety of alloy proportions reckoned in karats. Fine gold is equivalent to 24 karats.

18-kt. gold is 18 parts gold, 6 parts alloy metal.
14-kt. gold is 14 parts gold, 10 parts alloy metal.
10-kt. gold is 10 parts gold, 14 parts alloy metal.

These are the standard gold alloys commonly used in the jewelry trade. The three grades exist for good reasons: Fine gold is so soft that it has poor wearing qualities; 18-kt. gold is used in the most expensive jewelry, but it wears rather easily; 14-kt. gold is most commonly used for good jewelry because it has better wearing qualities, while still retaining most of the rich color and quality of pure gold; 10-kt. gold is used in less expensive jewelry and where harder wearing qualities are needed.

The different colors of gold are discussed below.

the mixture is molten, stir slightly with a heated iron rod. Take the button, when cool, and forge or roll it into a thin sheet and cut into paillons or strip.

The jeweler may make his own gold alloys for special purposes; 10-kt. to 12-kt. alloy is excellent for repoussé work in gold.

C–14 Hallmarks Most jewelers and silversmiths buy or make a stamp of identification for their own work (18–9). This mark is stamped near the karat or sterling stamp on the back of the work. In the United States the sterling stamp is required by law to be affixed to any piece of work which is sold as sterling. Likewise, gold work must be stamped according to its karat grade. These stamps may be secured from supply houses (B–2).

C–12 Gold Alloys

	Color	Gold %	Alloy %		Melting Point (approx.)
24-kt.	Yellow	100			1945° F.
22-kt.	Yellow	91.6	4.20 Ag.	4.20 Cu	1860° F.
20-kt.	Yellow	83.3	8.35 Ag.	8.35 Cu	1820° F.
18-kt.	Yellow	75.0	12.5 Ag.	12.5 Cu	1660° F.
14-kt.	Yellow	58.3	20.8 Ag.	20.8 Cu	1565° F.
10-kt.	Yellow	41.6	29.2 Ag.	29.2 Cu	1515° F.
18-kt.	White	75.0	25.0 Palladium		1660° F.
14-kt.	White	58.3	41.7 Palladium		1700° F.
10-kt.	White	41.6	58.4 Palladium		1760° F.
18-kt.	Green	75.0	25.0 Silver		1770° F.
14-kt.	Green	58.3	41.7 Silver		1600° F.
10-kt.	Green	41.6	58.4 Silver		1480° F.
14-kt.	Red	58.3	41.7 Copper		1670° F.

C–13 Gold Solders Gold solders for the various gold alloys are made by increasing the alloy metal enough to lower the melting point sufficiently for soldering. Examine the table of alloys in **C–12**, and note the differences in melting points of the various grades of gold alloys. In yellow gold there is a difference of 50° between 10-kt. and 14-kt. alloy.

To make gold solder for any given gold alloy, take 4 parts of that alloy and add 1 part of fine silver. To make a gold solder for 18-kt. gold, for example, take 4 dwt. of 18-kt. gold and 1 dwt. of fine silver and put them together in a small hole in a charcoal block, add a bit of borax for flux, and melt them together. When

C–15 Removing Lead from Gold or Silver Lead or lead solder will soak into gold or silver if the latter metals are heated to annealing or soldering temperature. The lead that has thus soaked into gold or silver will cause pits and ruin the surface. If the lead cannot be scraped off, the solution given below will dissolve the lead.

Green copperas	2 oz.
Saltpeter	1 oz.
Water	10 oz.

Dissolve the chemicals in the water and boil. When cool, the solution will crystallize.

Dissolve the crystals in hydrochloric acid in the proportion of 8 oz. HCl to 1 oz. of the crystals.

Dilute this in four times its weight of boiling water.

Articles to be cleaned should be boiled in this solution.

C–16 Mathematical Formulas

Inches per centimeter:

1 in. = 2.54 cm.

12 in. = 30.48 cm.

Troy weight (all precious metals are weighed in troy units):

1 lb. av. = 12 oz. troy

1 oz. troy = 20 pennyweight (dwt.)

1 dwt. = 24 grains

Circumference of a circle: 3.14159 times diameter

Circumference of an oval: 6.2 times (a plus b)

where $a = $ ½ major axis

$b = $ ½ minor axis

Area of circle: .7854 times diameter

Area of oval: .7854 times long axis times short axis

C–17 Melting Points of Metals

Aluminum	1218° F.	Lead	621° F.
Brass	1700°–1850° F.	Platinum	3191° F.
Bronze	1675° F.	Silver, fine	1761° F.
Cast iron	2300° F.	Sterling	1641° F.
Copper	1981° F.	Tin	449° F.
Gold, fine	1945° F.	Zinc	787° F.

C–18 Niello

1 oz. fine silver

2 oz. pure copper

3 oz. lead

Melt the silver and copper in a crucible; then add the lead and stir with a piece of charcoal held in the tongs. Clean off the scum caused by the lead. When the mixture is blended, pour it into a pottery jar that has been half filled with powdered sulphur. If you know a potter, have him make a pint bottle with a small neck that is not much larger than 1 in. in diameter. The purpose of the jar is to confine the sulphur fumes. Stopper up the opening with a lump of clay, wrap the pottery bottle in burlap, and shake it vigorously as it cools.

Another formula for niello is:

3 parts fine silver

7 parts copper

5 parts lead

Melt the silver and copper in a crucible in a bench melting furnace; then add the lead. When the melt is thoroughly blended, pour it into a second crucible of the same size, which has been half filled with sulphur. Stir the mixture with an iron rod as it cools. When stirring is no longer possible, remelt the mixture in the furnace and restir in order to mix the components completely and to drive off excess sulphur.

This entire process of stirring the molten metal into the crucible of sulphur must be done under an efficient ventilating hood, because a good amount of sulphur smoke will be generated.

When the mixture is cool, the niello will be in small lumps. Break these up in a mortar and remelt them in a crucible, repeating the process several times.

Crush the niello in grains, rather than to a powder. Place the niello in a glass bottle and wash several times to remove dirt.

For applying niello to three-dimensional work, a torch may be used, provided the flame is not allowed to touch the niello directly.

To apply the niello to engraved work, spread the niello evenly in the lines, about 1/16 in. deep. Place the work on an iron plate and into the kiln. When the niello begins to melt, take an iron rod with a flattened end and spread the niello into all the grooves. Then remove the work and allow it to cool. Then the excess niello must be filed away with a file or a stone.

As a final step, warm the work in the kiln until it is slightly hotter than the hand can bear and then remove it and go over the niello lines with a burnisher dipped in oil. The work may then be polished lightly with tripoli.

C–19 Pickle Solutions

The most commonly used pickle solution for jewelers and silversmiths is one made from sulphuric acid. This solution is usually kept in a half-gallon crock with a lid. The solution is made by adding one part sulphuric acid to from six to twelve parts water. For special purposes a 5 percent or 10 percent nitric pickle solution is also used **(8–13)**.

For jewelry it is most convenient to keep the crock or a Pyrex container filled with only an inch or two of solution, so that only one's fingers need to be dipped in to retrieve the work. Many jewelers prefer to use copper or stainless-steel tongs for removing work from the pickle.

Always add the acid to the water! When acid and water are mixed, considerable heat is generated. Should water be poured into the acid, an explosion will take place. Therefore, be very careful about this procedure. Pour the acid into the water very slowly, pouring close to the near edge of the crock in a small trickle. For a pint of water, you can estimate about 2 tablespoons of acid.

Silversmiths, who usually do large work, often have a special tank made up of $1/8$-in. thick lead to a size 30 in. square and 12 in. deep. A gas burner is placed under the tank so that the pickle can be brought to a moderate heat for more rapid pickling action.

When the jeweler wishes to pickle something quickly, he places his work in a special copper pickle pan with enough pickle to cover the work and brings the solution to a boil over the hot plate. The solution is afterward carefully poured back into the crock, and the pickle pan and the work are rinsed under the water tap. One good substitute for a sulphuric-acid pickle, and less dangerous, is a proprietary product called Sparex.

C-20 Silver and Silver Alloys

Fine silver is used for such special purposes as enameling, because its reflective power under transparent enamels is greater, and because its melting point is higher than that of sterling. Fine silver is used for bezel making in preference to sterling, because it is softer and can be burnished over a gemstone more readily. But for many purposes fine silver is too soft, and it is therefore alloyed with copper.

In continental Europe the standard alloy is 900 parts fine silver to 100 parts copper. American jewelers and silversmiths use the British sterling standard, which is 925 parts fine silver to 75 parts copper.

Silver may be alloyed with gold to produce some very interesting color qualities. Electrum, you will remember, was a natural alloy of gold and silver. Gold and silver in equal proportions, which would be 12-kt. gold, has a beautiful soft color that is quite rich for jewelry.

With silver solders brass is usually used for an alloy metal. Formulas for silver solder are given below.

C-21 Silver Solders

Five standard grades of silver solder may be made as follows:

I.T.,	7 parts fine silver, 1 part fine brass
Hard grade,	5 parts fine silver, 1 part fine brass
Medium grade,	3 parts fine silver, 1 part fine brass
Easy grade,	2 parts fine silver, 1 part fine brass
Easy flow,	2 parts fine silver, $1/2$ part fine brass

C-22 Soft Solders

Common lead solder, 2 parts lead, 1 part tin, (add tin to melted lead)

Soft lead solder, 2 parts tin, 1 part lead
Hard lead solder, 63 percent tin, 37 percent lead (This solder melts at 175°C. and is hardest of all.)
Allstate No. 430 Soft Silver Solder (remains silver-bright)

C-23 Stripping

Stripping refers to the process of boiling silver work in a stripping solution of nitric acid to remove firecoat. Stripping is universally done by silversmiths in the final finishing of work, after all soldering and annealing have been done. The stripping solution is made of 1 part nitric acid, poured slowly into 1 part water. **Always add the acid to the water**.

The solution is placed in a copper pickle pan and brought to a low boil. This must be done either in a ventilated booth that will exhaust the corrosive fumes or outdoors.

The work is boiled for from one to three minutes and inspected. The action of the acid removes the surface layer of the metal. The longer the work is left in the pickle, the more metal is removed. The process should be carefully timed so that the least necessary amount of metal will be removed.

Electrolytic stripping is a far more effective method of removing firecoat, because it leaves a bright, polished surface. It is the standard method in the industry for cleaning gold castings prior to polishing, for it leaves inaccessible and recessed areas bright.

C-24 Testing Gold

The touchstone method of testing gold requires the following equipment:

Stone of slate or basalt, polished smooth
Set of standard gold needles from 4 to 22 kt.
Bottle of nitric acid
Bottle of aqua regia

Gold testing sets may be purchased.

Procedure: Make a streak across the stone with the gold to be tested. Make streaks on each side of the first streak with standard gold needles. Choose two needles at random, estimating the possible karat of your gold.

Across the gold streaks make a streak of nitric acid and observe the reaction at each streak. Watch carefully the color changes and the speed of the reactions. A green color comes from the copper in the alloy. Fine gold gives a yellow color, masked by green. High-karat streaks are not affected by nitric acid, and therefore aqua regia must be tried.

The testing is done by making a comparison of the acid reactions. Identical color reactions on the test gold and on one of the gold needle streaks will establish the quality of the gold being tested.

C–25 Weights of Sheet and Wire Stock

Gauge	Thickness in.	Sterling		14-kt. Gold	
		Wire oz./ft.	Sheet oz./sq. in.	Wire dwt./ft.	Sheet dwt./sq. in.
4	.20431	2.15	1.12	54.2	28.1
6	.16202	1.36	.887	34.1	22.3
8	.12849	.852	.704	21.4	17.7
10	.10189	.536	.558	13.5	14.0
12	.0808	.337	.443	8.47	11.1
14	.06482	.212	.351	5.33	8.82
16	.05082	.133	.278	3.35	7.00
18	.0403	.0838	.221	2.11	5.55
20	.03196	.0527	.175	1.33	4.40
22	.02534	.0331	.139	.833	3.49
24	.0201	.0309	.110	.524	2.77
26	.01594	.0131	.0873	.330	2.19

APPENDIX D
Gemstones
and Other Materials
for Setting

abalone: Mollusk shell of the genus *Haliotis*, greenish or bluish in color, used in small shapes or as pearls; usually small in size and of baroque, or irregularly round, shape.

achrolite: Colorless variety of tourmaline that is rare and expensive if over 5 kt. and perfect.

agate: Variegated form of compact silica, with stripes, bands, or cloudy patterns of various colors; in pure form called chalcedony. Sometimes found with moss or leaf patterns (see moss agate). Widely distributed throughout the world. Hardness 7.

alexandrite: Green variety of chrysoberyl from the Ural Mts., named after Czar Alexander II; under artificial or reflected light, the color appears red. Hardness 8½.

almandine: Hard variety of garnet, rich red, violet, or purple in color, the finest coming from Ceylon and India. Hardness 7½.

amazonite: Pale green variety of feldspar resembling jade, named after the Amazon River but found widely. Hardness 6.

amber: Translucent fossil resin of yellowish to dark brown color, sometimes having insects or plant elements embedded; capable of being polished. Hardness 2–2½.

amethyst: Variety of crystallized quartz ranging from pale violet to dark red-violet in color; named from a Greek word for a remedy for drunkenness and in ancient times so used. Clear stones may be faceted. Hardness 7.

anatase: Metallic or brown stone, also called octahedrite. Hardness 6.

andalusite: Vitreous olive-green to brown stone, sometimes mistaken for tourmaline; named for Andalusia, where it was first found. Hardness 7½.

Apache tears: Popular name for obsidian pebbles.

aquamarine: Transparent member of the beryl family, of cool bluish or sea-green color. Hardness 8.

aventurine: Translucent variety of quartz, pale to dark green in color and spangled with mica and other substances; found in Brazil and India. Hardness 7.

azurite: Compact copper mineral, opaque blue in color and often associated with green malachite. Hardness 4–5.

benitoite: Crystallized sapphire-blue mineral, found only in San Benito County, Calif.; quite rare over 2 kt. Hardness 6¼.

beryl: Transparent silicate of beryllium and aluminum, a mineral family name including aquamarine, emerald, goshenite, heliodor, morganite, as well as cat's-eye varieties in many colors. The term ''beryl'' is sometimes applied to various beryllium stones outside those in the above categories. Hardness 8.

beryllonite: Rare beryllium mineral, transparent and pale. Hardness 5–5½.

bloodstone: Variety of chalcedony, of a dark, opaque green with red oxidized spots like drops of blood, which made it an important talisman in ancient days. Hardness 7.

bonamite: Strong blue-green variety of smithsonite, of limited usefulness in rings, but good for other jewelry. Hardness 5.

brazilianite: Brilliant stone, yellow to yellow-green,

and transparent to translucent, recently discovered in Brazil. Hardness 5½.

cairngorm: Yellow or smoky gold member of the quartz family, available in large sizes. Hardness 7.

cameo: Relief-carved gem of stone, such as agate or onyx, or shell, coral, etc., cut through contrasting layers of color.

carnelian: Variety of chalcedony, reddish to orange-red in color, much used in ancient times. Color may be produced in gray agates by heating. Hardness 7.

cat's-eye: Stone having an "eye," an internal reflection resembling a cat's eye, or chatoyancy. Term used in the gem trade to refer to chrysoberyl and as a prefix to names of other gems having an eye-like reflection.

chalcedony: Translucent variety of quartz. Term refers to blue and gray shades, the red being called carnelian, the green chrysoprase, etc.

Chatham created emerald: Synthetic emerald grown from a natural emerald by a proprietary process. Hardness 8.

chrysoberyl: Brilliant, transparent stone, bright yellow to golden in color; alexandrite and cat's-eye are examples. Hardness 8½.

chrysocolla: Deep blue to bluish-green copper mineral; when translucent and clear, stones are of gem quality. Hardness up to 7.

chrysoprase: Apple-green variety of chalcedony, of gem quality when translucent and pure. Dyed variety called "green onyx."

citrine: Variety of quartz, pale yellow to golden in color, sometimes mistakenly called "topaz." Hardness 7.

coral: Hard skeletal material secreted by colonies of sea organisms; color ranges from white or pale red to deep red (oxblood) and, rarely, to black or blue shades.

cordierite: Two-colored blue stone named for a French geologist; capable, when correctly oriented, of being faceted to produce a gem similar in color to the Ceylon sapphire. Also called iolite. Hardness 7 plus.

corundum: Natural aluminum mineral occurring in various colors. When red, called ruby; when blue, called sapphire. Synthetic corundum can be produced in almost all colors. Hardness 9.

crocidolite: Quartziferous mineral with fibers, often bluish or greenish, producing a chatoyant effect in cabochon cuts. When golden in color, called tigereye. Hardness 7.

crystal: Colorless quartz, faceted for beads, pendants, and other uses; also called rock crystal. Colored varieties called amethyst, for lavender; citrine, for yellow; etc. Hardness 7.

danburite: Transparent to translucent stone similar to topaz, but more yellow than golden; first found in Danbury, Conn., whence the name. Hardness 7.

demantoid: Garnet varying in color from yellow to deep green, and very brilliant; the most expensive of garnets. Hardness 6½–7½.

diamond: Crystallized carbon of high brilliance, in colors from pink, violet, green, and yellow to golden; produces tremendous "fire" when cut correctly. Hardness 10.

dinosaur bone: Textured fossil stone resulting from replacement of bone structure by silica; occurs in a mixture of reds, browns, and tans.

diopside: Transparent pyroxene stone of bright green color, often faceted. The Burmese variety is a cat's-eye. Hardness 5–6.

dioptase: Copper silicate of bright green color, resembling emerald but must be used with caution in jewelry because of its softness. Hardness 5.

dumortierite: Opaque, blue-violet aluminum silicate, named for a French paleontologist. Hardness 7.

emerald: Rare and expensive variety of beryl, green in color. Hardness 8.

epidote: Yellow-green to dark green stone, usually opaque, but sometimes found clear and sometimes mixed with pinkish feldspar. Hardness 6–7.

fibrolite: Aluminum silicate of brown, gray, or greenish color, sometimes mistaken for jade. Hardness 7½.

garnet: Family name for silicates ranging from orange and red to purple and pink, as well as green (see demantoid). Deep red to black garnet is called pyrope. Hardness 6–7 plus.

goshenite: Colorless beryl, named after Goshen, Mass. See beryl.

hematite: Heavy, black, crystalline iron mineral with considerable reflective quality; also called "black diamond." Hardness 5½–6½.

hiddenite: Yellow to yellow-green stone of the spodumene family, named for its discoverer in North Carolina; now also available from Brazil.

ivory: Dense dentine substance from tusks and teeth of elephants, whales, and other large mammals; white, creamy, or brownish in color; readily carved and incised as beads and other jewelry elements but too soft for some purposes. Hardness 2½–3.

jade: Term used for two different minerals. (1) Jadite, a pyroxene, also called "true jade," "Chinese jade"; found mainly in Burma, in a wide range of colors, including white, green, violet, orange, red, and black. Hardness 7. (2) Nephrite, a variety of tremolite or actinolite, ranging from apple-green to green-black and black, found in many parts of the world. The name comes from the Greek word for kidney, and the stone was used as an amulet or remedy in ancient times. Hardness 6½.

jasper: Opaque varieties of quartz, usually found in strong colors of red, yellow, and brown; also, in antiquity, green chalcedony. See bloodstone.

kunzite: Brilliant but rather brittle type of spodumene, lilac or blue-violet in color. Hardness 6 plus.

labradorite: Chatoyant variety of feldspar, first known from Labrador, generally gray with flashes of blue or, occasionally, yellow or orange.

lapis lazuli: Dark blue stone, often spangled with iron pyrites; best varieties come from Russia and Chile. Hardness 6.

malachite: Opaque, lustrous, green copper mineral, capable of a high polish but requiring protection if used in jewelry. Hardness 4.

moonstone: Translucent variety of feldspar with pearly or waxy luster and sometimes with blue chatoyancy. Hardness 6.

morganite: Member of the beryl family, named for J. P. Morgan, obtainable in delicate pink or subtle orange shades, the latter called peach morganite. Hardness 8.

morion: Quartz of smoky black color.

moss agate: Variety of quartz containing fibrous formations of manganese oxide resembling trees or moss. See agate.

nephrite: One of the minerals often called jade. See jade.

obsidian: Volcanic glass in varieties of color and pattern: jet black, snowflake, mahogany, rainbow. Hardness 5.

olivine: Mineral group including peridot. Hardness 6–7.

onyx: Banded agate; also dyed chalcedony known as "black onyx," "green onyx," "blue onyx." "Mexican onyx" is a variety of alabaster.

opal: Form of silica with fiery play of colors, found in many parts of the world, varying from almost black to pale bluish or greenish with flame-colored flashes.

peridot: Member of the olivine family, of clear yellow-green color and high brilliance; expensive when over 10 kt.

pyrope: Deep red, ruby-colored garnet. See garnet, star garnet.

quartz: Crystalline silica occurring in a variety of colors and including many gemstones. See amethyst, citrine, rock crystal, rose quartz, smoky quartz, etc.

rhodolite: Garnet of pale pink or lavender color, transparent and delicate.

rock crystal: Clear, colorless quartz.

rose quartz: Delicate pink quartz, occasionally found clear enough to facet, but more often used *en cabochon.* Hardness 7.

rubellite: Tourmaline of rose-red or pink color, generally more expensive than green tourmaline.

ruby: Red corundum that runs from pink shades to the rich, deep red of "pigeon-blood" gems; one of the most valuable of gemstones. Hardness 9.

rutilated quartz: Clear quartz with slim crystals of rutile embedded in the stone. Hardness 7.

sapphire: Blue corundum ranking next in value to the ruby; also found in colors of white, yellow, green, and pink. Clear varieties are usually faceted.

sard: Carnelian of uniform brown-red color.

sardonyx: Carnelian of dark red-brown color, banded with white or other colors.

siberite: Tourmaline of deep red-violet color.

smithsonite: Translucent stone of apple-green to blue color, named for the donor of the Smithsonian Institution; too soft for rings but beautiful in protective settings. Hardness 5.

smoky quartz: Brilliant but inexpensive stone, also known as cairngorm (see above).

sodalite: Stone somewhat like lapis lazuli, but less expensive. Hardness about 6.

spessarite: Rare stone of brown-red to yellow or orange-brown color, similar to garnet.

sphene: Light-colored titanite with varied color effects, showing green-yellow or red-yellow, depending on the axis on which it is cut.

spinel: Transparent stone of dark color, ranging from orange to red, blue, and purple. Hardness 8.

spodumene: Mineral family of good brilliancy, including kunzite and hiddenite (see above). Hardness 6–7.

star garnet: Garnet with star-shaped crystal reflection in four rays (or multiples of four); usually only in the red pyrope (see above). Hardness 6–7½.

star ruby: Red corundum with six-rayed star reflection. See ruby.

star sapphire: Blue corundum with star reflection; other colors of star sapphire less valued. See sapphire.

Swiss lapis: Dyed agate or jasper, somewhat lighter blue in color than genuine lapis lazuli. Hardness 7.

thomsonite: Decorative stone of pink or red patterns, often in eye shapes; found near Lake Superior. Hardness 5–5½.

tigereye: Chatoyant silicified crocidolite with fibers turned to oxide of iron; generally golden or brown in color but may be turned red by heating the yellow. Hardness 7.

titania: Synthetic stone with fiery play of many colors. Hardness 6 plus.

topaz: Clear, brilliant stone of fine golden yellow color, also occurring in less valued shades of pale to medium blue, pink, and colorless varieties; frequently imitated. Hardness 8.

tourmaline: Group of gemstones occurring in almost every color. Dichromatic. Hardness 7–7¼.

turquoise: Opaque, somewhat porous stone of sky-blue to greenish color, originally known from Turkey. Hardness 6.

zircon: Transparent, lustrous stone occurring in brownish, golden yellow, green, red, and green-blue colors. White stones resembling diamonds in brilliancy and blue stones are made by heating the brownish natural colors. Hardness 6½–7½.

BIBLIOGRAPHY

DESIGN

Ballinger, L. B., *Design: Sources and Resources*, Reinhold Publishing Co., New York, 1965.

Grillo, Paul J., *What Is Design?*, Paul Theobald, Chicago, 1960.

Hambridge, Jay, *The Elements of Dynamic Symmetry*, Brentano, New York, 1926.

Hoffman, Armin, *Graphic Design Manual*, Reinhold Publishing Co., New York, 1965.

Kepes, Gyorgy, *Education of Vision*, George Braziller, New York, 1965.

———, *Language of Vision*, Paul Theobald, Chicago, 1944.

———, *The Man-made Object*, George Braziller, New York, 1966.

———, *Module, Proportion, Symmetry, Rhythm*, George Braziller, New York, 1966.

Klee, Paul, *The Thinking Eye*, George Wittenborn, New York, 1961.

Moholy-Nagy, L., *Vision in Motion*, Paul Theobald, Chicago, 1944.

Mundt, Ernest, *A Primer of Visual Art*, Pellegrini & Cudahy, New York, 1950.

———, *The Nature and Art of Motion*, George Braziller, New York, 1965.

———, *The New Landscape in Art and Science*, Paul Theobald, Chicago, 1956.

Ocvirk, Otto G. et al, *Art Fundamentals*, Willima C. Brown, Dubuque, Iowa, 1960.

Saarinen, Eliel, *Search for Form*, Reinhold Publishing Co., New York, 1948.

Strache, Wolf, *Forms and Patterns in Nature*, Pantheon Books, Inc., New York, 1956.

Sutnar, Ladislav, *Visual Design in Action*, Hastings House, New York, 1961.

Wedd, J., *Patterns and Texture: Sources of Design*, Studio Publications, New York, 1956.

Weyl, Hermann, *Symmetry*, Princeton University Press, Princeton, N. J., 1952.

Whyte, L. L., *Aspects of Form*, Pellegrini & Cudahy, New York, 1951.

MAGAZINES AND PROFESSIONAL JOURNALS

American Jewelry Manufacturer, Chilton Co., Chestnut and 56th St., Philadelphia, 19139.

Craft Horizons, 16 E. 52 St., New York, N. Y.

Form (Swedish crafts), Box 7047, Stockholm, Sweden.

Gold + Silber Uhren + Schmuck, Konradin-Verlage, Robert Kohlhammer, Postfach 625, GmbH, Danneckerstrasse 52, Stuttgart, Germany. (About $14 per year)

Goldschmiede Zeitung (European Jeweler), Ruhle Diebener Verlag KG., 7000 Stuttgart-Degerloch, Postfach 250, Wolfschlugerer Strasse 5a. (About $14 per year)

Kunst + Handwerk (European Handicraft), Arnaldheistrasse 23, 2000 Hamburg 20, W. Germany.

HISTORY OF JEWELRY AND TECHNIQUES

Adair, John, *The Navajo and Pueblo Silversmiths*, University of Oklahoma Press, Norman, Okla., 1944.

Aloi, Roberto, *Esempi di Decorazione Moderna di Tutto Il Mondo,* Hoepli, Milan, 1954.

Baerwald, Marcus, and Tom Mahoney, *Story of Jewelry,* Abelard-Schuman, Ltd., New York, 1960.

Bates, Kenneth F., *Enameling Principles and Practice,* The World Publishing Co., Cleveland and New York, 1951.

Baxter, William T. L., *Jewelry, Gem Cutting, and Metalcraft,* McGraw-Hill Book Co., Inc., New York, 1950.

Murray, *Jewelry Making,* M. Bovin, Forest Hills, N. Y., 1955.

Bradford, Ernle, *Four Centuries of European Jewelry,* Philosophical Library, New York, 1953.

Burlington Fine Arts Club, *Medieval Jewelry,* London, 1930.

Carducci, Carlo, *Gold and Silver of Ancient Italy,* New York Graphic Society, Greenwich, Conn., 1963.

Castellani, Alessandro, *Antique Jewelry,*

Cellini, Benvenuto, *The Life of Benvenuto Cellini,* Phaidon Press Ltd., London, 1949.

Choate, Sharr, *Creative Casting, Jewelry, Silverware, Sculpture,* Crown Publishers, New York, 1966.

Cunynghame, H. H., *Art Enamelling on Metals,* A. Constable and Co., Inc., London, 1901.

Curtis, C. Densmore, *Ancient Granulated Jewelry,* 1917.

Dali, Salvador, *A Study of His Art-in-Jewels,* The Graphic Society, New York, 1959.

Darling, A., *Antique Jewelry,* Century House, Watkins Glen, N. Y., 1953.

Dennison, Walter, and Charles R. Morey, *Studies in East Christian and Roman Art,* Macmillan, New York, 1908.

Deshairs, Léon, *Dessins originaux des maîtres decorateurs,* 1914.

Emerson, A. R., *Hand-made Jewellery,* Dryad Ltd., Leicester, 1955.

Evans, Joan, *A History of Jewellery, 1100–1870,* Pitman Publishing Corp., New York, 1953.

Flower, Margaret, *Victorian Jewellery,* Duell, Sloan, and Pearce, New York, 1951.

Franke, L. E. and W. L. Udell, *Handwrought Jewelry,* McKnight & McKnight Publishing Co., Bloomington, Ill., 1962.

Greek and Etruscan Jewelry, Metropolitan Museum of Art, New York, 1940.

Hald, Arthur, and Sven Erich Skawonius, *Contemporary Swedish Design,* Nordisk Rotogravyr, Stockholm, 1951.

Higgins, Reynold Alleyne, *Greek and Roman Jewelry,* Methuen & Co., Ltd., London, 1961.

Hughes, Graham, *Modern Jewelry, 1890–1964,* Studio Books, London, 1964.

Jessup, Ronald, *Anglo-Saxon Jewellery,* Frederick A. Praeger, Inc., New York, 1953.

Jossic, Yvonne F., *1050 Jewelry Designs,* Alfred Lample, Philadelphia, 1946.

Katalog der Goldschmiede-Arbeiten, Mouseion Benake, Athens, 1938, 2 vols.

Kunz, George Frederick, *Gold Ornaments from United States of Colombia,* 1887.

Kuzel, Vladislav, *A Book of Jewelry,* Allan Wingate, Ltd., London, 1962.

Laurvik, John Nilsen, *French Jewelry, Nineteenth Century, René Lalique,* 1912.

Ludvig, Oswald A., *Metalwork, Technology and Practice,* McKnight & McKnight Publishing Co., Bloomington, Ill., 1947.

Lyon, Peter, *Design in Jewellery,* Peter Owen Ltd., London, 1956.

Martin, Charles J., *How to Make Modern Jewelry,* Museum of Modern Art, New York, 1949.

Neumann, Robert von, *The Design and Creation of Jewelry,* Chilton Co., Philadelphia, 1961.

Otten, Mitzi, and Kathe Berl, *The Art of Enamelling,* published by the authors, New York, 1950.

Pack, Greta, *Jewelry Making for the Beginning Craftsman,* D. Van Nostrand Co., Inc., Princeton, N. J., 1957.

Rosenthal, Rudolph, and Helen Ratzka, *The Story of Modern Applied Art,* Harper & Row, New York, 1948.

Rossi, Filippo, *Italian Jeweled Arts,* Harry N. Abrams, Inc., New York, 1954.

Saville, Marshall H., *Indian Notes and Monographs, The Goldsmith's Art in Ancient Mexico,* Museum of the American Indian, Heye Foundation, New York, 1920.

Shoenfelt, J. F., *Designing and Making Handwrought Jewelry,* McGraw-Hill Book Co., Inc., New York, 1960.

Sinkankas, A., *Gem Cutting, A Lapidary's Manual,* D. Van Nostrand Co., Inc., Princeton, N. J., 1962.

Siviero, R., *Jewelry and Amber of Italy,* McGraw-Hill Book Co., Inc., New York, 1959.

Smith, G. F. H., *Gemstones,* Methuen and Co., Ltd., London, 1940.

Snowman, A. Kenneth, *The Art of Carl Fabergé,* Faber & Faber, Ltd., London, 1962.

Steingräber, Erich, *Antique Jewelry,* Frederick A. Praeger, Inc., New York, 1957.

Thompson, Thomas E., *Enameling on Copper and Other Metals,* Thomas C. Thompson Co., Highland Park, Ill., 1950.

Untracht, Oppi, *Enameling on Metal*, Chilton Co., Philadelphia, 1957.

Viollet-le-Duc, Eugene Emmanuel, *Dictionnaire du mobilier français de l'époque Carlovingien*, 1871–75.

Wiener, Louis, *Handmade Jewelry*, D. Van Nostrand Co., Inc., Princeton, N. J., 1948.

Wilson, Henry, *Silverwork and Jewellery*, Pitman Publishing Corp., London and New York, 1902.

Winlock, H. E., *Egyptian Jewelry, The Treasure of Lahun*, 1884.

Winstein, Michael, *The World of Jewel Stones*, Sheridan House, New York, 1958.

Zarchy, Harry, *Jewelry-Making and Enameling*, Alfred A. Knopf, Inc., New York, 1959.

ESTHETIC AND PHILOSOPHICAL

Barkan, Manuel, *A Foundation for Art Education*, Ronald Press Co., New York, 1955.

Blofeld, John, *The Teaching of Huang Po*, Grove Press, New York, 1959.

Cary, Joyce, *Art and Reality*, Cambridge University Press, Cambridge, England, 1958.

Collier, John, *Indians of the Americas*, Mentor, New American Library, New York, 1947.

Esslin, Martin, *The Theatre of the Absurd*, Eyre & Spottiswoode, London, 1962.

Ghiselin, Brewster, *The Creative Process*, University of California Press, Berkeley, Calif., 1952.

Goodman, Paul, *Growing Up Absurd*, Random House, New York, 1960.

———, *Compulsory Mis-education*, Horizon Press, New York, 1964.

Gordon, W. J. J., *Synectics: The Development of Creative Capacity*, Harper & Row, New York, 1961.

Heisenberg, W., *Physics and Philosophy*, Harper & Row, New York, 1958.

Josephson, E. and M., *Man Alone: Alienation in Modern Society*, Dell Books, New York, n.d.

Jung, C. G., *Psychological Types*, Kegan, Paul, Trench, Trubner and Co., Ltd., London, 1923.

Kohl, Herbert, *The Age of Complexity*, Mentor, New American Library, New York, 1965.

Lippard, Lucy R., *Pop Art*, Frederick A. Praeger, Inc., New York, 1966.

Lowenfeld, Viktor, *Creative and Mental Growth*, Macmillan, New York, 1953.

Mondrian, Piet, *Plastic and Pure Plastic Art*, George Wittenborn, New York, 1947.

Neumann, Erich, *Art and the Creative Unconscious*, Bollingen Press, New York, 1957.

Patka, Frederick, *Existentialist Thinkers and Thought*, Citadel Press, New York, 1962.

Read, Herbert, *The Grass Roots of Culture*, George Wittenborn, New York, 1947.

Rosenberg, Bernard, and David Manning White, eds., *Mass Culture*, Falcon's Wing Press, Glencoe, Ill., 1957.

Royce, Joseph R., *The Encapsulated Man*, D. Van Nostrand Co., Inc., Princeton, N. J., 1964.

Seuphor, M., *Dictionary of Abstract Painting*, Paris Book Center, Inc., New York, 1957.

Watts, Allan W., *Psychotherapy East and West*, Pantheon Books, New York, 1961.

Whyte, L. L., *The Next Development in Man*, New American Library, New York, 1950.

INDEX

Aaron, David, 42, 273
Abalone, 296
Abraham, 40
Abstraction, 4, 7
Achrolite, 296
Agate, 296, Pl. 15
Albers, Anni, 271
Albert, Gilbert, 283
Alemany, Carlos, 283
Alexandrite, 296
Almandine, 296
Amazonite, 296
Amber, 296, Pl. 15
Amethyst, 296, Pl. 15
Alloys, 290
America House, 41
Anatase, 296
Ancient jewelry, 20–21, Figs. 30–35, Pl. 5
Andalusite, 296
Annealing, booth for, 128
    of metal, 127
    pan, 136, 248 Figs. 220, 372
    tongs, 248, Fig. 372
Anvil, 103, Fig. 164 (step 2)
Apache tears, 296
Aquamarine, 296, Pl. 15
Art, kinetic, 80
    minimal, 80
    "op," 9, 80
    "pop," 9, 80
    rococo, 26–27, Fig. 46
Art Nouveau, 24, 28, 34, 38, 52, 54, Figs. 48–
    51, 55, 76, Pl. 6
Asbestos block, 131
Associative values, 11, 13, Fig. 15
Atwater, Harold J., 276
Aventurine, 296, Pl. 15
Azurite, 296

Bacopulos, Gregory P., 276, Fig. 352
Bakken, Haaken, 50, 87, Figs. 69, 142
Balch, Evelyn, 273
Ball, Mildred Lee, 276

Barium chloride, 230, 289
Barns, Martha Brennan, 276
Barrette, 123, Figs. 205, 206
Barve, Olov, 283
Battern's Self-pickling Flux, 289, 291
Bead setting, 245, Fig. 365
Beading tool, 245, Fig. 365
Beardsley, Aubrey, 30, 36, Figs. 49, 55
Becker, Friedrich, 55, 283, Figs. 77–78, 185,
    361, Pl. 2
Beckett, Samuel, 84
Beckman, Jane, 276
Beeswax, 181, 289
Bench pin, Fig. 221
Bending, of metal, 154–163, Figs. 243–260
    of rectangular box, 160–161, Figs. 254–255
    of strip metal, 155–159, Figs. 243, 245–253
    techniques for, 155–156
Benitoite, 296
Bennett, Ward, 37, 42, 271, 273, Fig. 391
Bergmann, Franz, 42, 273
Bertoia, Harry, 37, 42, 53, 271, 273, 276,
    283, Figs. 3, 61, 392
Beryl, 296, Pl. 15
Berylonite, 296
Best, John and Marsha, 276
Bezel, 97
Bezel pusher, 240, Fig. 355
Bezel setting, 239
Bill, Max, 53, 283
Binding wire, 94, 144, 290, Figs. 224–225;
Bismuth block, 143
Bladen, Ronald, 81, Fig. 131
Blake, William, 29, Fig. 48
Bloodstone, 296, Pl. 15
Bohr, Marsh, 276
Bonamite, 296
Boothby, Frances Holmes, 276
Borax, 136, 289, 291
Boric acid crystals, 289, 291
Bosch, Hieronymus, 83, Fig. 135
Botticelli, 24
Boxmaking, 160–161, Figs. 254–255

Boyer, M. N., 276
Bracelet, closed type, 119, Fig. 198
    link type, 118, 119, Figs. 195, 197
    slip-on type, 119, Fig. 196
Brake, 156, Fig. 244
Brandt, Michael J. Jr., 276
Brazilianite, 296
Brooch, 39, 43, 45, 47, 48, 50, 51, 52, 54, 55,
    56, 85, 87, 121, Figs. 56–57, 61, 65,
    67–69, 75–76, 78–81, 87–89, 138,
    141, 203, Pls. 3, 6–8, 11, 13–14
Brown, Hazel Olsen, Fig. 353
Brown, Howard O., 38, 276
Brown, Juanita, 38, 276, 281, Fig. 419
Brynner, Irena, 38, 276, 281, 283, Fig. 418
Buckle, 124, Figs. 208–209
Buffing, compounds, 290
    lathe, 227
    practice, 228
Buffs, 227–228, 290
Bunsen burner, 128
Bur, cone, 244, Fig. 364
    setting, 244, Fig. 363
Burch-Korrodi, 283
Burnisher, 152, Fig. 239
Burnishing, 229
Burrage, Madeleine, 271
Butane tank, 131
Button earring, 118, Fig. 194

C-clamp, 210
Cabochon, forms of, 234, Figs. 343–344,
    Pl. 15
    standard sizes of, 233, 235, Figs. 346–348
Cairngorm, 297
Calder, Alexander, 37, 42, 271, Figs. 52, 66,
    393
Calderoni, A., 283
Cameo, 297, Pl. 15
Capdevila, Joaquin, 55, Fig. 81
    Manuel, 54, Fig. 80
Carbon steel, 250
    drill rod of, 90, 250

Carnelian, 297, Pl. 15
Carpenter, Shirley Lege, 38
Carved form, 100
Carved molds, 106
Carving with scorpers, 183
Cast forms, 39, 48, 50, 105–108, 116, 118, 122, Figs. 57, 68–71, 188, 195, 204, Pls. 13–14
Casting, 38, 105–108, 203–222, Figs. 169–174, 313–336
  centrifugal, 203, 204, 219, Figs. 313, 327, 329
    casting machine for, 204, 217, Figs. 313, 329
  charcoal-mold, 106, 205, Figs. 170–172
  cuttlebone-mold, 205–207, Figs. 317–318
  ingots, 137
  investment-mold, 205, 217, Figs. 327, 333–334
    flask for investment, 218, Figs. 313–314, 327 (step 8), 332
    flask tongs, 220, Fig. 327
  patterns for, 107, 210, Figs. 320, 322-325
  plaster-mold, 205, 207
  pouring, methods for, 203
  pressure, 203, 222, Fig. 336
  principles of, 205, 206, Figs. 313, 332
  rings (flasks) for, Figs. 313, 332
  sand-mold, 205, 209–210, Fig. 175
    flask for sand, 107
  stone-mold (steatite), 205, 206, Fig. 315
  vacuum, 203, 204, 222, Fig. 335
Catches, 199, Figs. 303–304
  for pin tongs, 146, 287, Figs. 228, 434
Cat's-eye, 297
Cellini, Benvenuto, 25
  jewelry in style of, 25, Figs. 43, 44
Cementing, 202
Center punch, 174
Cézanne, Paul, 80
Chain making, 171, Figs. 266-267
Chalcedony, 297
Champagnat, Jean, 283
Channel setting, 245, Fig. 365
Charcoal block, 106–107, 131, 145, Figs. 170–174, 226
Charcoal molds, 106
Chaser's pitch, 290
Chasing, 52, 92, 190–191, Fig. 292
  form for, 190–191, Fig. 292
  plate for, 190, Fig. 292
  tools for, 190, 252, Figs. 377–378
Chatham created emerald, 297
Chatt, O. K., 276
Chayat, Maxwell M., 276
Chisel cutting, 178
Chisels (scorpers), 182
Chloride of platinum, 230, 289
Choker, 119–120, Fig. 199
Chrysoberyl, 297
Chrysocolla, 297
Chrysoprase, 297, Pl. 15
Circle-cutting dies, 265, Fig. 385
Circle-marking template, 175, Figs. 272-273
Citrine, 297, Pl. 15
Classification of means, 82
Cleaning jewelry, 232
Clen-Murphy, Desmond, 283
Claw setting, 241–242, 246–247, Figs. 357–358, 368–370
Clipping, 178
Clips, 195, Fig. 297
Closed setting, 97, 239, Figs. 354, 356

Cocktail ring, 115–116, Figs. 185–188
Code numbers for jewelry, 262
Coles, Izabel M., 271
Coloring metals, 229
Comb 123, Fig. 207
Commemorative values in jewelry, 13
Compass, pencil, 173
Complex jewelry forms, 76
Complex plate-shape forms, 94
Cone bur, 244, Fig. 364
Constructed forms, 100–102, Figs. 161–162
Contemporary architecture, 15
Contemporary civilization, 8, Fig. 11
Contemporary jewelry, abroad, 53–57
  and the past, 15
  as expression, 14
  First National Exhibition in America, 36
  Fourth National Exhibition in America, 39
  history of, 33–47, Figs. 52–88
  in America, 36–48
  pioneers of, 42–48
  recent directions in, 49–53
  Second National Exhibition in America, 37
  Third National Exhibition in America, 37
Cooke, Betty, 276
Cooper, John Paul, 283
Coral, 297, Pl. 15
Cordierite, 297
Corundum, 297
Craft guilds, 23
Craftsman's philosophy, 255–256
Craver, Margaret, 283
Crocidolite, 297
Crown setting, 246–247, Figs. 368–369
Crucible, graphite, 129, Fig. 214
  hand, 136, Fig. 220
Crystal, 297
Cuff links, 122, Fig. 204
  backs for, 287, Fig. 433
Cuprous cyanide, 289, 291
Cutting metal, 178–186, Figs. 276–277

Dadaism, 14, 34
Dahlquist, Inga, 283
Danburite, 297
Dapping, 165
  block for, 166
  punch for, 132
Day, Andrew and Muriel, 276
Day, Russell E., 38
de Diego, Julio, 57, 271, Fig. 394
Defeo, J., 277
De Hart, William, 273
Demantoid, 297
Dennler, Ernst, 283
De Patta, Margaret, 37, 41, 43, 233, 237, 273, 277, 281, 283, 351, 360, Figs. 63, 186, 350, 351, 360
de Rivera, José, 272, Fig. 399
Design, advanced, 79–100
  and contemporary jewelry, 57–78
  and dramatic relationships, 6
  elements of, 57
  and ethics of contemporary jewelry, 33, 53
  field in, 75
  and form, 57
  and formal relationships, 6
  and function, 57
  functional, 4, 111–124, Figs. 4–5
  graphic, 58
  human need for, 4

Design (Cont.)
  ideas for, 58
  and industrial technology, 8
  and jewelry, 4, 11–14, 57–127
  and means of achieving expressive form, 79–110
  principles of, 58
  and production, 259
  relationships in, external, 74
    internal, 74
  and shape 92, Fig. 152
Dhaemers, Robert, 38
Diamond, 297
Diamond, Bess, 273
Dickerhoff, John, 38, 281, Fig. 420
Diemaker's ball, 184
Differentiation of areas with texture, 74, Fig. 116
Dinner ring, 115–116, Figs. 185–188
Dinosaur bone, 297
Diopside, 297
Dioptase, 297
Direct methods of fastening, 193
Ditzel, Nanna and Jorgan, 283
Dividers, 175
Donald, John, 55, Fig. 82
Drawing tubing, 149–152, Figs. 238, 240
Drawing wire, 149–152, Fig. 237
Drawplate 151, Figs. 236–237
Drawtongs 151, Fig. 237
Drill, hand, 163, Fig. 257
  flexible-shaft, 182, Fig. 278
Drilling, 182
Drophammer, 259
Duchamp, Marcel, 80, Fig. 53
Dudley, Virginia, 277
Dumbar, Archibald, 283
Dumortierite, 297
Dusell, D. Lee and Mary, 277

Ear back, clip-type, 116–117, 286, Fig. 430
  pierced-ear type, 287, Fig. 431
  screw-type, 286, Fig. 429
  wing back type, 117, 287, Fig. 432
Earrings, button type, 118, Fig. 194
  dangle type, 116–117, Fig. 193
  pierced-ear type, 27, 118, Fig. 47
Easton, Roger D., 277
Electric waxing tool, 214, Fig. 264 (step 5)
Electroforming, 52, 86, 166–170, Figs. 139–140, 264A, B
Electroforms, 86
Electrolysis, 231
Electroplating, 230
  bath for, 291
  equipment for, 167, 230, 231, Figs. 264A, B, 341
Elipse, development of, 176, Fig. 274
Elvestand, Gudmund Jon, 38
Embossing, 165
Emerald, 297, Pl. 15
Emery paper, grades of, 225, 289
Emery shells, 227, Fig. 340
Emery sticks, 226, Figs. 338–339
Enamel forms, 108–110, Figs. 38, 41, 44, 177
Enantiodromia, 84
Engagement ring, 114–115
Engraving 184–186, Figs. 283–287
  block for, 184, Fig. 284
Engstrom, Robert 38, 277, 281
Epidote, 297
Equilibrium, 75, Fig. 118

Esempi di Decorazione Moderna di Tutto il Mondo, 53, 283
Ethics of contemporary design, 33
European Jeweler, 54
Exhibitions, 259
Existentialism, 14
Expressive form, means of achieving 79–110
objective aspect, 79
subjective aspect, 79
Expressive mode, nonrational, 34
rational, 33

Fabergé, Carl, 28
Faddis, George, 277
Fader, Lester, 277
Falkenstein, Claire, 28, 273, 283
Farr, Fred, 37, 44, 271, Fig. 395
Fastenings, 193–202, Figs. 296–312
Fenster, Fred, 50, Fig. 70
Fibrolite, 297
Field of design, 75, Fig. 118
Fike, Philip, 37, 50, 277, Fig. 412, Pl. 11
File cuts, 224, Fig. 337
Files, 223–224
barrette, 224
half-round, 223
hand, 223
needle, 224
ring, 223
round, 224
File-Wax, 213, 214–217, Figs. 327–328
Filigree, 172, Fig. 269
Filing form, 224–225
Findings, jewelry, 286–288
Finishing metal, 223–232
Finishing tools, 254
Firecoat, 138
protection against, 291
removal of, 138
"First International Exhibition of Modern Jewellery" (1961), 53
First National Exhibition of Contemporary Jewelry (1946), 36–37, 271
Flame, oxidizing, 136
reducing, 136
Flanges, 193, Fig. 296
Flange setting, 241, Fig. 359
Fleming, William, 15
Flexible shaft, 225, Fig. 278
Flöckinger, Gerda, 55, 283, Figs. 83, 181
Flux, Battern's, 131, 291
borax, 136, 291
Handy, 289, 291
Prip's, 139, 291
Flux brush, 141
Fluxing, 139
Focal point, 75–76, 78, 96–97, Figs. 118–120, 128, 155–156
Foot bellows, 128, Fig. 212
Forged forms, 100, 101, 104, Figs. 163, 165–166
Forging, 104, 188, Figs. 165–167, 289
hammer, 188–189, Figs. 288, 290
punches and chasing tools, 248–249, Figs. 373–374
Forming, sandbag, 165
Forming block, 165
Forming metal, 149–172
Fourth National Exhibition of Contemporary Jewelry (1959), 39
Fröhlich, Max, 53, 283
Functional aspects of jewelry, 111–113
Functional needs, 4

Furnace, burnout, 220, Fig. 327 (step 9)
gas-air, barrel, 29, Fig. 215
Fused forms, 82–86, Figs. 133–134, 138
Fusing, 131–132
of beads, 132, Fig. 217
of granules, 132
of wire beads, 132, Fig. 217

Gabriel, Robert A., 277
Gallery wire, 191, Fig. 293
Gardner, Robert E., 277
Garnet, 297, Pl. 15
Gas, low-pressure city gas, 130
Gas plate, 128
Gates, Jerome, 37, 277, Fig. 413
Gauge plate, Brown & Sharp, 149, Fig. 234
Gauge sizes of sheet and wire, 291
Gay, May G., 271
Gems and semiprecious stones, 233–237, 296–299, Pl. 15
designing forms of, 237
faceted forms of, 236, Figs. 349–350
forms of, 234–236, Figs. 343–349
and Moh's scale of hardness, 238
names of, 296–299
sources of, 289
standard sizes of, 235, Figs. 346–348
Geometric forms, 6, Fig. 9
Geometrical layout contructions, 173–178
Gideon, Siegfried, 15
Gold, 292
alloys of, 292
solders of, 292
sources of, 288, 289
testing for, 294
Gold + Silber Uhren + Schmuck, 54
Goodman, Marilyn Zirkel, 278
Goshenite, 297
Graphic design, 58
Graphic studies of texture, 73, Figs. 114–115
Granulation, 20, 52, 133
Gratch-Levy, Hannah Ruth, 55, Fig. 85
Graver, 185, Fig. 287
sharpening of, 185
Green copperas, 292
Grima, Andrew, 5, Fig. 84
Grinder, 249
Grinding tool steel, 249
Gum tragacanth, 102, 289
Gypsy setting, 243

Haendel, William George, 38, 283
Hall, Doris, 45, 273
Hallmark, 292
Hammering, 187–192
Hammers, 188–189
ball-peen, 188
chasing, 109, 190, Figs. 262, 292
cross-peen, 152, Fig. 238
forging, 188, Fig. 238
planishing, 189
rivet, 196, Fig. 298
sledge, 188–189, Fig. 290
Hammid, Alexander, 271
Handy flux, 289, 291
Hannan, Thom, 53, 283
Hardening, steel, 250
tools, 254
wire, 170
Harrison, Wiltz, 38, 278
Hartshorn, Esther, 283
Haslam, Lee, 278
Hatch, David, 38, 278

Heating frame, 128, 129, Fig. 213
Heisenberg, Werner, 83
Hematite, 297, Pl. 15
Hiddenite, 297
Hillsmith, Fannie 37, 45, 53, 273, 283, Figs. 65, 397
Hinge, full, 201, Figs. 309–311
silversmith, 202, Fig. 312
simple, 200, Fig. 305
Historical exhibitions of contemporary jewlery, 271–283
Hydrochloric acid, 230, 289, 290

Ingot mold, 137
Inlay, 183
Institute of Contemporary Arts (Oxford, Eng.), 54
Intuition, 14
Investment burnout, 219, Fig. 327
Iodine, 230, 289
Ionesco, Eugene, 84
Ivory, 297

Jacobs, Phyllis W., 273
Jade, 297, Pl. 15
Jasper, 298
Jauquet, John, Pl. 12
Jerry, Michael, 38, 50, 281, Figs. 168, 201, 421, Pl. 13
Jeweler's bench, 137, Fig. 221
Jeweler's saw, 157, 179–181, Figs. 247, 277
blades for, 179
Jewelry, ancient, 20–21, Pl. 5
Anglo-Saxon, 22
Art Nouveau, 28–30, Figs. 48, 51, Pl. 6
associate values of, 11–13
baroque, 26, Fig. 45
commemorative values in, 13
Celtic, 21–22, Fig. 37
contemporary, 1, 3, 15, 33–56, *passim*
definition of, 11
and design, 11–13, 57–126
Egyptian, 20, Fig. 30
Etruscan, 21, Fig. 35
expressive values in, 14
findings for, 386, 388
French "ribbon" school, 54
functional aspects of, 6, 111
Gothic, 23, Fig. 40
Greek, 21, Fig. 33
historical, 15–30, Figs. 22–35, Pl. 4
magical values in 11–13, Figs. 15–17, Pl. 4
medieval 21–23, Figs. 38–39
Mycenaean, 21
Navajo 19, Fig. 28
Near East, 20, Pl. 5
nineteenth-century, 20
nonrational mode, 34–36
North American Indian, 19
objective aspect of, 14
Pre-Columbian, 18, Figs. 25–27
primitive, 16–17, Figs. 10–23, 27, Pl. 4
processes of, 127–247
rational mode of, 33–34
Renaissance, 24–26, Figs. 41–43
repair cost schedule for, 258
rococo, 26–27, Fig. 45, 47
Roman, 21
and shop layout, 263, 264
subjective aspect of, 141
Sumerian, Pl. 5
symbolic values in, 12, Figs. 17–18
Zuni, 19, Fig. 29

Job card, 260, Fig. 380
Joint, pin tong, 287, Figs. 227, 434
Joint tool, 200, Fig. 307
Joints, interlocking, 198–199, Fig. 303
Jump rings, 147, 162–163

Karlan, Gertrude, 271
Keetman, Sigrid, 283
Kick press, 260
Kienholz, Edward, Fig. 132
Kindt-Larsen, Tove and Edvard, 283
King, Arthur, 283
Kington, Brent, 50, Figs. 71, 191
Koch, Feickert, 283
Koppal, Henning, 53, 55, 283
Kramer, Carol, 46
Kramer, Sam, 36, 37, 46, 53, 271, 273, 278
    281, Figs. 66, 151
Krauss, Hilda, 283
Krentzin, Earl, 50, 281, 283
Kretsinger, Mary, 278, 283, Figs. 134, 414
Kunst+Handwerk, 54
Kunzite, 298, Pl. 15

Labradorite, 298, Pl. 15
Lair, Felt, Figs. 138, 149
Lalique, René, 52, Fig. 76, Pl. 6
Lanham, James S., 278
Lapis lazuli, 298, Pl. 15
Lauritzen, Frederick, 278
Layout, 173–177, Figs. 270–272, 274, 275
    of necklace arrays, 177, Fig. 275
    of ring-band lengths, 177
    rules for, 174
Lazon, Lucienne, 283
Lea compound, 227
Lead block, 165
Lechtzin, Stanley, 50, 87, 134, Figs. 72, 162,
    199, Pl. 9
Lee, Frank, 273
Lein, Malcolm E., 40
Levy, Julien, 271
Line, 58–60, Figs. 91–93
    attributes of, 57
    organic, 61, Fig. 92
    technological, 61, Fig. 93
Line-space relationships, 58
Linear forms, 87–90, Figs. 141–147
Linear organizations, 62, Figs. 95–101
Linear-wire forms, 88
Lipchitz, Jacques, 272
Littledale, H. A. P., 133, 272
Liver of sulphur, 229, 289
Lobel, Paul A., 37, 46, 273, Fig. 67
Loosli, Fritz, 283
Lucas, A., 283

MacCabe, Bob, 278
McKinin, Lawrence, 37, 278, Fig. 415
McMillen, Louis A., 273
Magical values, 11–13, Pl. 4
Magritte, Rene, 5, Fig. 6
Maher, Patrick F., 133
Malachite, 298, Pl. 15
Mallary, Robert, 35, Fig. 154
Man's ring, 116, Figs. 187–189
Mandrel, bezel, 239
    ring, 157–158, Figs. 248, 251, 252
Mallet, rawhide, 156–157, Figs. 245, 250
Marketing, 255, 259
    and the exhibition, 259
Martignetti, Lorenzo, 283
Martinazzi, Bruno, 283

Martare, Sonja, 283
Mathematical formulas, 293
Mazzetti, Luigi, 283
Medieval jewelry, 21–23, Figs. 37–39
Meller, Mellerio dits, 283
Melting metal, 136
Melting points of metal, 293
Mendelssohn, Georges, 283
Mergen, Paul, 50–51, 123, Figs. 73, 207
Metal, structure of, 127, Fig. 210
Michelangelo, 10, Fig. 14
Miller, John Paul, 30, 133, 281, Figs. 56, 422
Millimeter scale, Fig. 345
Mold, rubber, 212, 289
Monroe, Keith, 47, 274, Fig. 404
Moonstone, 298, Pl. 15
Mop, soldering, 143, Fig. 223
Morganite, 298
Morion, 298
Morton, Philip, 37, 38, 53, 87, 89, 91, 92,
    101, 113, 116–118, 122, 123, 241,
    274, 275, 278, 281, 283, Figs. 141,
    145, 150, 161, 182, 189, 192, 194–
    195, 204, 206, 356, 405, 423, Pl. 14
Moss, agate, 298
Mouth blowpipe, 128, Fig. 211
Mucchi, Genny, 283
Mucha, Alphonse Marie, 30, Fig. 50
Museum of Contemporary Craftsmen, 41, 49
Museum of Modern Art, (N.Y.), 36

Natural forms, 6–9, Figs. 7, 10, 12, 13
Necklace, 27, 119–121, Figs. 47, 199, 200,
    201, 202
    layout of, 177, Fig. 275
Nele, E. R., 56, 117, Figs. 86, 193
Nephrite, 298, Pl. 15
Neumann, Robert von, 282
Niello, 293, Fig. 412
Nineteenth-century jewelry, 27, Pl. 6
Nilsson, Wiwen, 283
Nitric acid, 138, 289
Nonrational mode, 34–35, 83, Figs. 53, 54,
    135, 136
North American Indian jewelry, 19, Figs. 28,
    29
Novros, David, 80, Fig. 130

Obsidian, 298, Pl. 15
Olivine, 298
Onyx, 298
Opal, 298, Pl. 15
Organic line movements, 60–61, Fig. 92
Orlandini, Orlando Paladino, 283
Oxygen tank, 129

Pardon, Earl B., 278
Patania, Frank, 50
Patterns, for rubber molds, 108
    for sand casting, 107
Paved setting, 182–183, 243–244, Figs. 280,
    281, 362
Pearson, Ronald Hayes, 38, 47, 133, 282,
    Figs. 57, 68, 163, 424
Peck, Miriam Smith, 278
Pence, Coralynn, 279
Pendant, 16, 39–40, 44–46, 50–51, 82, 93,
    101, 105, 106–107, 120–121, Figs.
    58–60, 63, 66, 71, 73, 83, 85, 133,
    151, 161–162, 167, 169, 173–174,
    202, Pls. 4, 7, 12
Pendant earring, 116, 117, Figs. 190–193
Pennington, Ruth, 38

Peridot, 298, Pl. 15
Persson, Sigurd, 53, 56, 283, Fig. 187
Peterson, E. Peter, 279
Peterson, Nelle and Daniel, 279
Petesch, Angela, 279
Picasso, Pablo, 80, 88, Fig. 143
Pickle, crock for, 128
    solutions for, 138, 293
Pickling, 135, 158
Piercing, 92, 181
Pin tong, 146, 287, Fig. 434
Pin vise, 132, 150, Fig. 235
Pine, Alvin, 50–51, 112, 116, 120, Figs. 74,
    178, 188, 200
Pineda, Marianna, 273, 275, Fig. 406
Pinton, Mario, 56, 119, 171, 183, 283, Figs.
    88, 196, 262, 282
Pioneers of contemporary jewelry, 42–48
Piper, Charles, 41
Pitch, chaser's, 164, Pl. 12
Pitch bowl, 164, Pl. 12
Planishing, 189
Plaster of paris, 144
Plate gauge, Brown & Sharp, 149, Fig. 234
    sizes of, 291
Plate-shape forms, 92–95, Figs. 152–153
Pliers, cutting, 178, Fig. 164 (step 5)
    half-round, 155
    roundnose, 266, Fig. 387
    squarenose, 155, Fig. 243
    snipe-nose, 155
Podzsus, Carl O., 279
Polishing lathe (buffing lathe), 227–228
Politas, Elaine, 243, Fig. 359
Pollock, Jackson, Pl. 1
Potassium cyanide, 230, 231, 291
Pre-Columbian jewelry, 18, Figs. 25–27, Pl. 4
Prestone tank, 131
Primitive jewelry, 16–17, Figs. 19–23
Processes, classification of, 127
Production, code numbering for jewelry, 262
    and design, 259
    flow diagram of, 263, Fig. 382
    methods of, 263
    record of, 89, 260–263, Fig. 381
    sequence of, 265–267, Figs. 386–389
Propane tank, 128
Protractor, 176
Pumice, powdered, 229
Punches, 252, Fig. 379
Punching, 188

Quartz, 298, Pl. 15

Radakovich, Ruth, 38, 282, Fig. 425
    Svetozar, 38, 282, Figs. 58, 169, 426, Pl. 3
Radiolaria, Fig. 13
Raseman, Richard P., 274
Rational expressive mode, 33, Fig. 52
Rawhide mallet, 156–157, Figs. 245, 248, 251
Reducing flame, 128–136
Reed, F. Jules, 279
Regnier, Maria, 279
Regulator, adjustable, 130
    automatic, 130
    oxygen, 130
Reid, B. M., 37, 279, Fig. 416
Reiling, Reinhold, 56, 119, Fig. 198, Pl. 8
Removing lead from silver or gold, 292–293
Renaissance jewelry, 24–25, Figs. 41–44
Renk, Mary G., 279
Repoussé, 104–105, 164–165, Figs. 32, 168,
    261, 262, Pl. 12

Repoussé *(Cont.)*
form for, 104
tools for, 164, 165, 251, 252, Fig. 375–376
Resnikoff, Florence, 279
Reticulation, 134, Figs. 218–219
Rhodolite, 298
Richier, Germaine, 35, 83, Fig. 136
Ries, Victor, 50
Rima, 273, Fig. 407
Ring 117–120, Pls. 2, 9–10
bender for, 114, Fig. 183
casting outfit for, 210
engagement, 114–115, Fig. 184
enlarger for, 114, Fig. 183
interlocking, Pl. 9
mandrel for, 157, Fig. 249
man's, 116, Figs. 187–189, Pl. 10
size set for, 112, Fig. 180
sticks for, 227, Fig. 340
wedding, 113, Figs. 178, 179
Ring tripod, 143
Rivet, 196, Fig. 298
flush, 196–197, Fig. 299
integral, 198, Fig. 301
tube, 197, Fig. 300
pin for pin tong, 146–147, Fig. 232
Rivet set, 198, Fig. 302
Riveting soft materials, 202
Roach, Ruth, 279
Rock crystal, 298
Rolling, of ingots, 154
of metal, 153
of oval rings, 160
of wire, 154
of wire rings, 159–160, 162
Rolling mill, 153, Fig. 241
Rose quartz, 298
Rosene, Caroline G., 48, 274–275, Fig. 408
Roth, Herman, 279
Rouge, 228, 289, 290
Rubber bowl, 219
Rubber mold, 212–213, Fig. 176
vulcanizing frame for, 212, Fig. 325
Ruby, 298, Pl. 15
Rutilated quartz, 298
Ryder, Thomas E., 279

Saarinen, Eero, 3, Fig. 1
Safety goggles, 249
St. Paul Gallery, "Fiber, Clay, and Metal" exhibition 39, 49
Sal ammoniac, 291
Salo, George K., 37, 279, Fig. 417
Saltpeter, 292
Sandbag, 165
Sand casting, 107–108, 205, 209–210, Figs. 174–175, 320–322
patterns for, 107
Sapphire, 298, Pl. 15
Sard, 298
Sardonyx, 298
Savin, Muriel, 279
Saw, hack, 220, Fig. 334
jeweler's, 157, 179–181, Figs. 247, 277
blade sizes of, 179
position for, 180
stringing blade of, 179
use of, 180–181, Fig. 277
Saw frame, stringing blade on, 179
Sawblade sizes, 179
Sawing, 179–181, Fig. 277
Scale, 71–72, Figs. 110–113

Schatz, Zahara, 279, Fig. 409
Schmidt, Christian, 27, 38, 39, 279–282, Figs. 59, 133, 427
Schmutzler, Robert, 28
School for American Craftsmen, 41
Schreiber, Franco, 283
Schrödinger, Erwin, 83
Schwarcz, June, 87
Scorpers (chisels), 183, Figs. 279–280
Scraper, 154, Fig. 242
Scraping, 183
Scribe, 174, 226, Fig. 338
Second National Exhibition of Contemporary Jewelry (1948), 273
Seitz, Martin, 283
Semiprecious stones, 233–237, Pl. 15
Seppa, Heikki, 51, 117, Figs. 75, 190
Setting, bead, 245, Fig. 365
bezel, 239, Fig. 354
box-frame, 247, Fig. 371
bur, 244, Fig. 363
channel, 245, Figs. 366, 367
claw, 241–243, Figs. 357, 358
closed, 239, Fig. 354
coronet, Fig. 370
crown, 246–247, Figs. 368, 369
flange, 241
gypsy, 244, Fig. 363
paved, 182–183, 243–244, Figs. 280, 281, 362
Shaker chair, 45, Fig. 4
Shape, analysis of, 68
area distribution of, 70
attributes of, 68, Figs. 4, 104–105
definition of, 67
graphic study of, 67
integration of, 78
organic, 6, 69, Figs. 7, 107–109
plate, 92–94
relationships of, 77
simple, 67, Fig. 103
sources of, 6
technological, 67, Fig. 102
templates for, Fig. 384
thrust of, 68
types of, 67–71, Fig. 102
Shearing 178–179
Shears, bench, 178
hand, 141, Fig. 222
squaring, 178–179, Fig. 276
Shellac chips, 184, 289
Siberite, 298
Silver, 294
alloys of, 294
lacquer for, 166
solders for, 294
sterling, 294
Simpson, Ellis, 272
Skoogfors, Olaf, 50, 53, Pl. 7
Sledge hammer, 188–189, Fig. 290
Smit, Maud, 283
Smith, Art, 274, 275, Fig. 410
Smith, Paul John, 280
Smithsonite, 298
Smoky quartz, 298
Sodalite, 298, Pl. 15
Sodium carbonate, 291
Sodium cyanide, 291
Sodium phosphate, 291
Sodium pyrophosphate, 291
Sodium thiosulphate, 291
Soft solder, 139, 294
Solder, easy, 139, 294

Solder *(Cont.)*
fifty-fifty, 139
filings used as, 142
hard, 139, 294
hard-grade, 139, 294
medium-grade, 239, 294
of joint for strip shape, 161–162
powder, 142
soft, 139, 294
Soldering, 139, 147
of earback, 140
gas plate, 128
holding for, 143
of joints and catches, 145–146, Figs. 227–232
of jump rings, 147
mop for, 143
paillon method of, 140–141, 144, Figs. 222, 233
pick for, 142
of ring shanks, 148
rules for, 142
salts for, 140
strip method of, 141
sweat method of, 142
tweezers for, 147, Fig. 229
Solu-Wax 213
Sotta, Orville H., 280
Sources of tools and equipment 285–286
Spessarite, 298
Sphene, 298
Spinel, 298
Spodumene, 298
Spring ring, 288, Fig. 436
Sprue base, 218, Fig. 332
Stake, T, 104, Fig. 165
Stamping sheet and gallery wire, 191
Star garnet, 298
Star ruby, 298, Pl. 15
Star sapphire, 298
Steel, characteristics of, 250
hardening of, 250
tempering of by color method, 250–251, Pl. 16.
Steenbergen, Chris, 283
Stephen, Francis, 280
Steppat, Annaliese, 280
Sterne, Jean, 280
Stone setting, 239–247, Figs. 354–371
Striker, 131
Striking, 188
Stringing the saw frame, 179–180
Strip-plate forms, 95–96, 98–100, Figs. 154, 155, 157–160
Stripping firecoat, 138, 294
Structure of metal, 127, Fig. 210
Study of line, 59–60
Sulphuric acid, 138, 289
Surrealism, 34, 83
Suttman, Paul R., 280
Swiss lapis, 298
Symbolic values, 13, Fig. 13
Szymak, John, 280

Tank regulator, 129
Tapering wire, 150
Technical data, 290–295
Technological line movements, 61, Fig. 93
Tempering carbon steel, 250
color chart for, 251, Pl. 16
Templates for shapes, 265, Fig. 384
Templier, Raymond, 283
Texture, 72–74, Figs. 113–116

Texture *(Cont.)*
  torch, 134–135, Figs. 218–219
Texturing, form for, 191
  of metal, 189, Fig. 291
Theatre of the Absurd, 14
Theosophilus, 22
Thiel, Richard G., 282, Fig. 428
Third National Exhibition of Contemporary
  Jewelry (1955), 276, 280
Thompson, Ken, 280
Thompsonite, 298
Tie clip, 122
Tie clip back, 288, Fig. 437
Tie-tack back, 288, Fig. 438
Tigereye, 298, Pl. 15
Tin block, 165
Titania, 299
Tompkins, Donald, 133
Tool steel, 250
  characteristics of, 250
  grinding, 249–250
  hardening, 250, 254
  tempering (drawing), 250, 254
Toolmaking 248–253, Figs. 372–374
Tools, findings, and supplies, 284–289
Tools, source of 285–286
Topaz, 299, Pl. 15
Torch, air-gas, 128, 129
  mouth blowpipe, 128, Fig. 211
  oxygen-gas, 128–130, Fig. 216
  portable butane or propane, 28, 131
  use of, 130–131
Tourmaline, 299, Pl. 15
Trapp, Edgar J., 280

Treskow, Elisabeth, 283
Tripoli, 138
Tube making, 152
Tumpel, Wolfgang, 283
Turquoise, 299, Pl. 15
Tweezers, soldering, 132, 140, 146–147, Figs.
  217, 227–229
Twisting wire, 170, Fig. 265

Ulrich, Klaus, 56, 121, Figs. 87, 202–203,
  Pl. 10
Ultrasonic cleaning machine, 231, Fig. 342

V-block, 180, Fig. 277
Vacuum pump, 219, Fig. 319
Van Berquem, Louis, 233
Vanderbilt-Webb, Mrs., 41
Van Kleeck, Anne G., 280
Vierthaler, Arthur A., 280, 283
Vise, bench, 224
  pin, 132, 150, Fig. 235
  ring, 224
Visual aspects, 4
Visual elements, 4, 57, 58
Vulcanizing frame 212–213, Fig. 325
Vulcanizing press, 212–213, Fig. 326

Walker Art Center (Minneapolis), 37
Wallen, Fennell, 280
Wax, 213
  blue, 218, 289
  File-Wax, 214–215, 217, 289, Figs. 327,
    328
  green, 218, 289

Wax *(Cont.)*
  red, 218, 289
  Solu-Wax 213, 280
Wax patterns, 213, 219
  investing, 217, Fig. 327
  setting up, 217, Fig. 331
Wax pressure injector, 218, Fig. 330
Wedding rings, 112, 113, Figs. 178, 179, 181,
  182, 189
Weights of sheet and wire, 295
Weiss, Ebbe, 53
Wettersjo, Bengt, 283
White, Kay, 280
Wichita Art Association Decorative Arts and
  Ceramics Exhibition (1946), 40
Wildenhain, Marjorie McIlroy, 280
Wilson, Byron, 41, 280, 282
Winfield Fine Art in Jewelry, 274
Winston, Bob, 37, 48, 274, Figs. 280, 282,
  411
Wire Gauge, Brown & Sharp, 149
Woell, J. Fred, 40, Fig. 60
Work hardening, 127
World Crafts Council, 42
Wright, Donald B., 38
Wyss, Gunter, 55, Fig. 79

Yellow ochre, 139

Zaremscy, Zadwiga and Jerzy, 56, Fig. 89
Zimmerman, Alice E., 280
Zinc chloride (soldering salts), 140, 289
Zipper, Walter, 283
Zircon, 299, Pl. 15

PHOTOGRAPHIC SOURCES

References are to figure numbers unless indicated Pl. (plate). Photos of contemporary jewelry generally have been furnished by the artists themselves. Process sequences by jewelers other than the author are credited in the captions.

Alinari—Art Reference Bureau, Inc., Ancram, N.Y. (14); American Museum of Natural History, New York (10, top); Bykert Gallery, New York (130); California Institute of Technology Bookstore, Pasadena, Calif. (12); Dixon, William, Inc., Newark, N.J. (211–215, 278, 284); Dreis & Krump, Chicago (244); Fischbach Gallery, New York (131); Gahr, David, New York (137); Hirmer Fotoarchiv, Munich (9); Holton, George, Photo Researchers, Inc., New York (5); Jelrus Corp., New Hyde Park, N.Y. (329); Karlan & Bleicher, New York (368–369); King, John, New Canaan, Conn. (Pls. 13, 14, 15); Larsen, Lennart, Copenhagen (33); MAS, Barcelona (135); Miller, Charles, Philadelphia (Pl. 5); Moore, Peter, New York (Pl. 4); Museum of Modern Art, New York (6); Ontario Research Foundation, 1968 (210); Peck, Stow & Wilcox Co., Southington, Conn. (276); Richter, E., Rome (10, bottom); Saunders, Alexander, Co., Cold Spring, N.Y. (326); Schmidt, Christian A., Jordan, Minn. (7); Starks, Willard, Kingston, N.J. (49–50); © Ezra Stoller [ESTO], Mamaroneck, N. Y. (1); Stone, Allan, Gallery, New York (54); Southwest Smelting and Refining Co., Dallas (221, 313, 335, 341–342); Wilkinson Co., The, Santa Monica, Calif. (336).